Sir John Tiptoft

Sir John Tiptoft

The Earl of Worcester 1427–1470
'The Butcher of England'

Peter Spring

Pen & Sword
MILITARY

First published in Great Britain in 2018 by
Pen & Sword Military
an imprint of
Pen & Sword Books Ltd
47 Church Street
Barnsley
South Yorkshire
S70 2AS

Copyright © Peter Spring 2018

ISBN 978 1 78346 382 4

Printed and bound in England by TJ International Ltd, Padstow, Cornwall

Pen & Sword Books Limited incorporates the imprints of Atlas, Archaeology,
Aviation, Discovery, Family History, Fiction, History, Maritime, Military,
Military Classics, Politics, Select, Transport, True Crime, Air World, Frontline
Publishing, Leo Cooper, Remember When, Seaforth Publishing, The Praetorian
Press, Wharncliffe Local History, Wharncliffe Transport, Wharncliffe
True Crime and White Owl.

For a complete list of Pen & Sword titles please contact
PEN & SWORD BOOKS LIMITED
47 Church Street, Barnsley, South Yorkshire, S70 2AS, England
E-mail: enquiries@pen-and-sword.co.uk
Website: www.pen-and-sword.co.uk

Contents

List of illustrations

All illustrations are by Emma Spring.

List of plates

EARLY LIFE AND TREASURER – 1427–1455
Plate 1: St Mary's Oxford. (Author)
Plate 2: Cardinal Beaufort's tomb in Winchester Cathedral. (Author)
Plate 3: Westminster Hall. (Author)

PILGRIMAGE – 1458
Plate 4: Palace of the Grand Master of the Knights of Rhodes. (C.C.4, Jorge Láscar)
Plate 5: Signatures on a 1454 warrant of Protector York, Chancellor Salisbury and Treasurer Worcester. (PRO, Author)
Plate 6: Jaffa (c.1900) – still landing by lighter boat. (Photographer unknown)
Plate 7: Holy Sepulchre, Jerusalem. (C.C.4, Jorge Láscar)
Plate 8: Holy Nativity (pre-1900), Bethlehem. (Photographer unknown)

ITALY – 1458–1461
Plate 9: Venice – the Doge's Palace. (Author)
Plate 10: Padua where the Earl of Worcester studied between 1458 and 1461. (Author)
Plate 11: Ferrara, where the Earl of Worcester studied under Guarino da Verona. (Author)
Plate 12: Florence where the Earl of Worcester bought books and almost certainly stayed with the de' Medici. (Author)

DEATH AND BURIAL – 1470
Plate 13: The Tower of London, from Tower Hill. (Author)
Plate 14: Plaque on Tower Hill at the site of the scaffold. (Author)
Plate 15: All Hallows Barking, from Tower Hill. (Author)
Plate 16: Blackfriars. (Author)

HOUSES
Plate 17: Bassingbourn, Cambridgeshire. (Cambridge University Aerial Photographs)
Plate 18: Worcester House. (Agas map detail)
Plate 19: Modern reconstruction of Elsyng Palace in the sixteenth century. (Enfield Council, Forty Hall)

MANUSCRIPT
Plate 20: White vine initial 'G'(rammatica) and wreath enclosing the arms and helm of John Tiptoft, Earl of Worcester. (British Library)

List of maps

Family trees

Family tree – Earl of Worcester's father's Tibetot / Tiptoft line

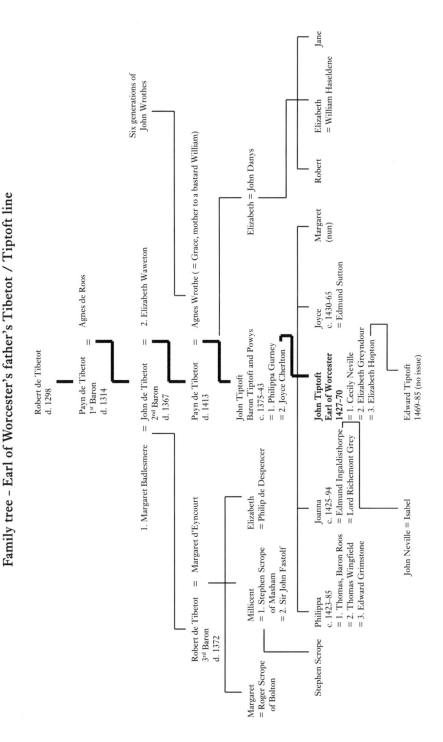

Robert de Tibetot
d. 1298

Payn de Tibetot
1st Baron
d. 1314
= Agnes de Roos

1. Margaret Badlesmere = John de Tibetot
2nd Baron
d. 1367
= 2. Elizabeth Waweton

Payn de Tibetot
d. 1413
= Agnes Wrothe (= Grace, mother to a bastard William)

Six generations of John Wrothes

Elizabeth = John Danys

Robert

Elizabeth
= William Haseldene

Jane

Robert de Tibetot
3rd Baron
d. 1372
= Margaret d'Eyncourt

Margaret
= Roger Scrope
of Bolton

Millicent
= 1. Stephen Scrope
of Masham
= 2. Sir John Fastolf

Elizabeth
= Philip de Despencer

Stephen Scrope

Philippa
c. 1423–85
= 1. Thomas, Baron Roos
= 2. Thomas Wingfield
= 3. Edward Grimstone

Joanna
c. 1425–94
= Edmund Ingaldisthorpe
= Lord Richemont Grey

John Neville = Isabel

John Tiptoft
Baron Tiptoft and Powys
c. 1375–43
= 1. Philippa Gurney
= 2. Joyce Cherlton

**John Tiptoft
Earl of Worcester
1427–70**
= 1. Cecily Neville
= 2. Elizabeth Greyndour
= 3. Elizabeth Hopton

Edward Tiptoft
1469–85 (no issue)

Joyce
c. 1430–65
= Edmund Sutton

Margaret
(nun)

Family tree – Earl of Worcester's mothers Holland/Cherlton lines

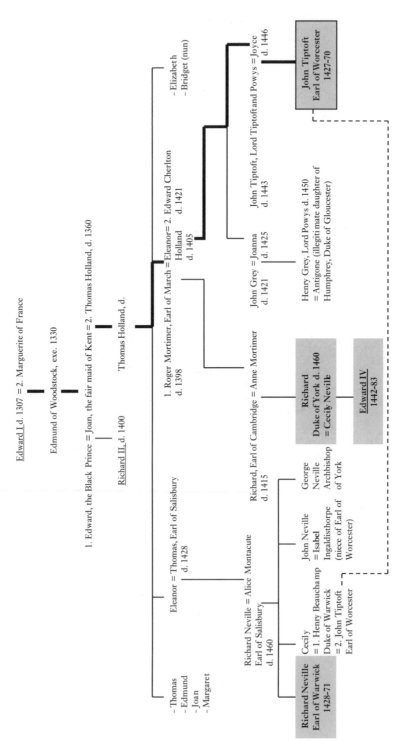

Introduction and acknowledgements

Sir John Tiptoft, the Earl of Worcester (1427–70), is one of the most extraordinary and least understood men of the Middle Ages. His importance—both in his own time and in terms of the course of history—is now barely recognised. At best he is presented as the paradox of the cruel but cultured man: otherwise he is simply sadistic and venal. His political importance in the mid-1450s and 1460s was very considerable and he pioneered many of the patterns of early modern aristocratic life: Oxford, the Grand Tour, and the educated, cultured courtier and soldier serving the state. The contemporary denigration of his character and the blanking out of his achievements reflected a deep antipathy towards the cosmopolitan intellectual that is a recurring trait in the English character—a sentiment which, some might argue, has recently re-emerged with Brexit.

A major hurdle to a deeper understanding of the Earl is that—while there is actually a surprising amount of biographical material—little is in English. However, a careful appraisal of his life, using primary sources across several languages, reveals an individual of great depth and ability who was held in high regard by men of intelligence and education, particularly Italians and Burgundians who frequently understood him much better than the often oafish, little-Englander chroniclers.

Some aspects of Worcester's life are extremely well documented, such as his pilgrimage to Jerusalem in 1458 and the great tournament of 1467 between Anthony Woodville, Lord Scales, and Antoine, the Bastard of Burgundy. In the case of the former there are two accounts by Italians and two by Englishmen (all or part in Latin) which mention the Earl on several occasions. For the latter there are substantial English and Burgundian reports. Parts of these accounts can be found in unpublished theses.

There are two near-contemporary lives, several pages long, and some biographical material in dedications and addresses. The life by the Florentine Vespasiano da Bisticci (1421–98) has been translated from medieval Italian albeit not entirely accurately. That by John Leland (c.1503–52) is full of overlooked material but is available only in centuries-old editions of his particularly idiosyncratic Latin. The only twentieth century biography, Rosamond Joscelyne Mitchell's *John Tiptoft (1427–70)*, was published in 1938 and, while nuanced, is somewhat out of date.

Indeed, the majority of the primary material about the Earl is in medieval Latin, French, Italian, and Irish: much of it is untranslated and some is only available in the original manuscripts. This has tested my Latin and French to the limit, particularly as, when there are published translations, I have tried to check them against the original language where I could access it. I have translated the French and some shorter Latin and Italian material. Such translations may lack polish but, in order to extract the most meaning possible, they err in favour of literality over fluency.

Where contemporary English sources are given in the text these have generally been left with the original spellings. The fifteenth century was not a great time for English letters but the writing is often lively and sardonic and the feeling of the period is diminished by updating the sources. In some places where adjacent quotations mix modern translations with fifteenth century English text, the latter's spelling has been revised as the juxtaposition would otherwise simply be too jarring.

I am very grateful to Kristina Bedford of Ancestral Deeds for translating extremely difficult medieval Latin texts, some of which were available only as photographs of manuscripts and often heavily abbreviated. My nieces, Katherine Blythe and Harriet Spring, have ably tackled passages of Latin and medieval Italian; also, Sarah Harrison, Alys Blakeway and Dr Debby Banham. Dr Ralph Moffat and the Bristol Record Society have generously allowed me to use medieval Latin and French translations and text material. Emily Naish kindly showed me Machon's Register in Salisbury Cathedral library. Enfield Council has given permission to use a reconstruction image of Elsyng Palace. Jorge Láscar has made excellent photographs available under the Creative Commons 4 licence. Dr David Harrison and Barbara Spring have read earlier versions of the text and made helpful comments. Emma Spring has produced some fine illustrations. I am especially grateful to Pen & Sword; and particularly Philip Sidnell, Barnaby Blacker, Matt Jones and Alex Swanston for enabling this project.

Preface

On Tuesday the 18th of October, 1470, Sir John Tiptoft, the Earl of Worcester, made a rather macabre last request on Tower Hill. 'He turned to the villain [executioner] and requested he cut off his head in three blows in reverence of the most Holy Trinity, although it could be cut off in one. This was a sign of the greatest faith and spirit.'[1] This was no ordinary man, having been 'the Grand Constable of England, who had command and control of King Edward's forces'.[2] He had also held 'all the King's treasure in his hands and there were few matters of the Kingdom that did not pass through them'.[3] The seventeenth century antiquarian Thomas Fuller commented: 'The axe did then ... cut off more learning than was in the heads of all the surviving nobility.'[4]

Despite Worcester's great learning and his tenure of the highest offices of the state, English contemporaries had harsh words for him. The chronicler Fabyan wrote that the Earl, 'for his cruelness was called the bochier [butcher] of Englade'.[5] For the Brief Latin Chronicle he was '*Ille trux carnifex et hominum decollatur horridus*', or 'That ruthless butcher and harsh beheader of men'.[6]

The printer William Caxton however, who had learned his trade in Europe, composed a most extraordinary eulogy in the book which he printed in 1481. This contained three translations from Latin, two of which, *The Declamacion of Noblesse* and *De Amicitia*, he attributed to Worcester. 'What grete losse was it of that noble vertuous and wel disposed lord? Whan I remembre and advertyze his lif, his science, and his vertue, me thynketh God not displesyd over grete losse of such a man, considering his estate and connyng.'[7] At the core of both of the texts Worcester selected for translation was the idea that virtue provided the foundation for both true nobility and real friendship. Indeed, without virtue there could be neither. *The Declamacion* argued, 'noblesse is not knytte to blood, but to veray vertu,' and *De Amicitia*, 'ffrendship maybe in no wyse withoute virtue.'

The Declamacion, the Earl's translation of the Florentine Buonaccorso da Montermagno's *De Vera Nobilitate* contained speeches by two suitors competing for the hand of the fair Roman virgin Lucresse. The first was Publius Cornelius of 'worshipful hows and stock'. 'He was noble of byrthe yet therto he was gretely stuffed of Richesse, ... And his grete studye rested in huntyng, hauking, syngyng,

& disporte.' He declaimed: 'Therefore, me semeth, this is the hyest part of noblesse, to come of theyr auncestres of whom they may recounte and reherce the noble dedes many tymes worshipfully achieued.'

The second, Gayus Flamyneus, was 'born of a lower stocke'. He had 'moderate Richesse, … trayning himself alwey to floure in vertue and good maners, but his grete studye was with his diligence and seruyse to helpe his frende and contrey … . In tyme of werre he shewed hymself manly & courageous. And in tyme of peas right besye in his books, so that in tyme of werre he was furnysshed of counseylle.' He pronounced: 'I trowe that noblesse resteth not in the glorye of an other man, or in the flyttynge goodes of fortune, but in a mannes owen vertu and gloyre.'

Buonaccorso provided a discourse, safely transposed back to Ancient Rome, on the nature of true nobility. This lay not in lineage but in personal virtue expressed through service to the state. The Earl of Worcester's recent patriarchal lineage was quite modest. His father had, through a combination of sheer ability and loyal service to the House of Lancaster, been an esquire who rose to the rank of baron and was rewarded with a wife of royal blood. Worcester's cousin on his mother's side was Richard Plantagenet, Duke of York, and on his father's, Elizabeth Daneys, who inherited little more than her father's hope that her uncle, Worcester's father, would find her a good marriage.

The Earl may have chosen *The Declamacion* not just because it was an impressive piece of writing but because it reflected his views and Flamyneus provided a mouthpiece for them. Indeed, in Flamyneus's words might be found a key to understanding the Earl's behaviour: his change of loyalty from the incompetent but incumbent House of Lancaster to the able and energetic York; and his acceptance of Edward IV's marriage to the impoverished but beautiful, intelligent and spirited widow Elizabeth *née* Woodville. (The other dominant peer of the age, Richard Neville, Earl of Warwick, who came from the highest nobility, could not stomach this alliance, having advanced the cause of the noble-by-birth Bona, daughter of the ruler of Savoy.)

Friendship was explored in Worcester's translation of Cicero's *De Amicitia* which examined its nature, foundation, sustenance and breakdown. After the death of Laelius's friend Scipio, two Romans, Fannius and Scaevola, asked him to talk on the subject. True friendship, explained Laelius, lay in mutual agreement, goodwill and affection. Friendship ended when one required of the other unvirtuous behaviour and 'asked unresonably of frendes as that one wille praye the other to be in mynystre of his luste, or an helper of his wronge.' It was no excuse 'whan a man sayth he dyde it by cause of his frende, ffor syth that virtue is the verray knotte of friendship it is harde for friendship to a byde, when men departe from virtue.'

For many years the Earls of Worcester and Warwick, respectively John Tiptoft and Richard Neville ('Warwick the Kingmaker') worked so closely and effectively together in pursuit of common objectives that it is hard to envisage them simply as collaborators and not also as friends. The relationship was reinforced as their families were intimately linked by marriage. Neville's sister Cecily was Tiptoft's first wife and Tiptoft made possible the marriage of his niece Isabel to Richard's brother, John. Worcester and Warwick combined to consolidate the young Edward IV's hold on the throne. Yet in 1469 and 1470, goaded beyond bearing by the King's marriage in 1464 to Elizabeth, Warwick rebelled. The analysis of friendship in *De Amicitia* might provide an insight into the breakdown in their relationship. Both Earls could accuse the other of the loss of virtue, the basis of true friendship: Warwick betrayed his king in 1469 and 1470 while Worcester remained staunchly loyal; and Worcester executed and committed gross acts of degradation on the bodies of Warwick's captured men in April 1470. Both men would soon be dead.

The Earl of Worcester has largely been written out of history as an important figure in his own right. Rather he is recalled as a distasteful curiosity—a butcherly sado-masochist with scholarly pretensions who did Edward IV's dirty work. His true importance should be recognised, as by the mid-fifteenth century the medieval English aristocracy had reached a crossroads, culminating in the mutual destruction frenzy that was the War of the Roses. The Earl's life—with his Oxford education, travels, translations and Italian humanist studies, and his vision of a nobility virtuous through state service—provided the way forward.

The Earl's life was and is remarkable—both in itself and for the light it casts on the challenges of the period and on the timeless questions of the nature of true nobility and real friendship. When recounting that life, John Tiptoft's choice of material to translate, *The Declamacion of Noblesse* and *De Amicitia*, should be recalled for the insights it affords into his character and actions.

Part 1

HOUSE OF LANCASTER

Chapter 1

Family – 1427 to 1440

The education by his parents, was for a long time, in the best care—for instance he was dedicated to good writings and to the virtues.[1]

From the antiquarian John Leland's biography of Tiptoft

The life cut short on Tower Hill in 1470 began on the 8th of May 1427 at the family manor of Great Eversden in the gently undulating country of south-west Cambridgeshire. The building must have been a relatively simple affair.[2] The future Earl of Worcester was not born to great castles like his cousin, Richard Plantagenet, the Duke of York, or his brother-in-law, Richard Neville, the Earl of Warwick. He had an unusually varied ancestry, ranging, on his father's side, from Tiptoft Anglo-Norman knights and Wrothe city worthies, to, on his mother's, Cherlton Marcher lords and Holland elite aristocracy. Reviewing these families and something of the times facilitates understanding the Earl's complex character and independent view of the nobility.

The Tiptofts were an old Anglo-Norman family. The Battle Abbey Roll recorded one Tibtote among William the Conqueror's companions. The village of Tiboutot was about five kilometres south of Fécamp in Normandy. The family fought on both sides during the Hundred Years War. Indeed, between 1415 and 1417 *dominus Thomasyn de Tybutot* was one of seventeen Norman prisoners in the Tower, having been captured at Harfleur.[3] Later the French Tiboutots, compelled by anti-noble revolutionary terror, emigrated to Quebec where numerous descendants remain.[4]

After the Conquest the names of Thiboutot, Toboltot and Tobooutot flit intermittently out of various rolls and records. Clear continuity was not established until Robert de Tibetot, who was the first really to make his mark on history. He was a close companion of Henry III's son, Edward, accompanying him to the Holy Land, via Tunis, on the 9th Crusade (1271–2). He appears to have brought back an African who died a Christian. Sir Robert was the founder of the now destroyed Franciscan friary in Ipswich where many Tibetots were subsequently buried. There a skeleton was excavated in the mid-1990s of a man who—DNA and carbon dating tests revealed—came from North Africa and died between 1190 and 1300.[5] Robert subsequently fought for Edward, once he became king, in Gascony, Scotland and Wales.[6] He became lieutenant of Wales where he brutally put down a revolt provoked by his harsh enforcement of 'English customs'. In 1293, with a fleet of about sixty vessels, Robert attacked some 240 French, Flemish and Genoese ships, decisively defeating them and taking so many captive that all the ports of England were made rich.

Sir Robert died in 1298 and was succeeded by his only son Payn, who was called to Parliament as the 1st Baron Tibetot following the accession of Edward II in 1307. He died splendidly aged 34 in the choicest company. The Lanercost Chronicle describes how at Bannockburn in 1314: 'The great horses of the English charged the pikes of the Scots like into a dense forest. … In the leading division the Earl of Gloucester, Sir John Comyn, Sir Payn Tibetot, Sir Edmund Mauley and many other nobles were killed.'[7] Payn's comparatively early death meant his son John became a ward of Bartholomew, Lord Badlesmere, who married him to his daughter Margaret.

John, 2nd Baron Tibetot, fought with Edward III and the Black Prince in Scotland, France and Gascony and was recorded in the roll of arms of knights present at Dunstable in 1335 in the series of great tournaments in which Edward III sought to harden his knights for his foreign wars.[8] His two marriages had important implications for the Tibetots' fortunes: the first resulted in one son, Robert, the 3rd Baron Tibetot; and the second marriage produced another son, Payn.

Robert, the product of John's first marriage, further enhanced the Tibetots' wealth, so the rumour went, by his discovery of King John's treasure lost in The Wash. Robert's marriage produced three girls, Margaret, Millicent and Elizabeth, who inherited most of his property. Margaret and Millicent were the wards of Richard, 1st Lord Scrope of Bolton, who married them to his sons, Roger and Stephen. The third daughter Elizabeth married Philip, Baron de Despenser.[9]

Payn, the product of John's remarriage, received only two manors and the Tibetot baronage went into abeyance, probably for want of funds. Payn's fortunes rose through service to the Houses of Arundel and Lancaster. In his will of 1392, the Earl of Arundel left his loyal follower, 'Monsr Payn, a cup of silver, and two of my best horses'.[10] Other bequests to followers were for cups only, so the horses reveal that Payn must have been particularly valued. Payn married into a wealthy London family. Although his wife, Agnes Wrothe, brought little property in his lifetime, her male family line subsequently died out, leaving Agnes's line a very substantial inheritance. She was born of six generations of City worthies, all called John, who were also knights and justices of the peace for Middlesex. The second of the six, John Wrothe, was Lord Mayor in 1360–61. Payn's son by Agnes was also called John. And when this John himself begat one son, the future Earl of Worcester, he was, not surprisingly, yet another John. Sir Payn had two other children, Elizabeth and a bastard by the name of William.[11]

Figure 1: The effigy of Sir John Tiptoft, Lord Tiptoft and Powys, the father of the future Earl of Worcester, in Ely cathedral.[12] He wears a collar of SS, the emblem of the House of Lancaster.

The Earl of Worcester's father, John Tiptoft (c.1375–1443), was a man of quite exceptional stature who served three Lancastrian kings both loyally and profitably until his death in 1443. He first appears in history in 1397, when he is recorded as receiving 7½d. daily in the service of Henry Bolingbroke.[13] Being on the right side during the ascent of the House of Lancaster to the throne of England marked the real turning point in the fortunes of the Tibetots, or Tiptofts as the name had become anglicised. When the banished Henry Bolingbroke returned to England in 1399 he was joined by both Sir Payn and John, who was knighted with forty-five others on the eve of Bolingbroke's coronation as Henry IV. As a young man he was an active fighting captain on various borders.

In 1406 Sir John was selected by the Commons as speaker, despite arguing his inadequacy, *'par cause de sa juvente'*, that is due to his youth. He impressed with his able handling of the 1406 Long Parliament.[14] That year he was made Treasurer of the Household and then, in 1407, Chief Butler. The next year he became Treasurer of the Exchequer aged about 33. Before 1408 Tiptoft had been rewarded with marriage to the wealthy Philippa Gournay *née* Talbot who was about ten years older than him and brought a very substantial estate in England and Gascony. Philippa died without issue in 1417. By 1409 'Iohn Tiptost myn Treasuror of Englond' was individually identified in fifth place on the list of those who witnessed Henry IV's will.[15] He was dismissed in 1409 as power swung to the heir, Henry of Monmouth. In 1411 there was the first evidence of an enduring connection between the Tiptofts and Canterbury when, on the 12th of April, Sir John made a pilgrimage there and was received into its association of lay people or confraternity.[16]

Shakespeare's 'vasty fields of France', reopened by the accession in 1413 of Henry V, afforded a new and greater stage for Tiptoft's talents. In 1415 he was made Seneschal of Aquitaine, responsible for keeping the King's southern territory quiet during the invasion of the north of France. In 1416 Sir John began a remarkable new career as an international diplomat, trusted with the most delicate missions. Over the next six years of Henry's reign he negotiated treaties and secret agreements, and resolved disputes involving Castile, Genoa, the Hanseatic League, Aragon, Sicily, Brittany, the Armagnacs, the Emperor Sigismund and the Archbishop of Cologne. In September 1416 he became Steward of Emperor Sigismund's household when it visited London. In December he was ambassador to the Council of Constance. Henry's direct instructions, in 1417, showed how close and trusted he was. 'Tiptoft, I charge you by the Feith that ye owe me, that ye kepe this Matere her after Writen, from al Men secre save from my Brother Th'Emperor owne Persone.'[17]

Henry V died in 1422 in France, leaving a posthumous heir, having made his brothers John and Humphrey, the Dukes of Bedford and Gloucester, swear to expand his French conquests. As he neared 50, John Tiptoft was a man of commanding experience as a soldier, administrator, parliamentarian and diplomat and had executed the most sensitive and secret commissions on behalf of the state.

In 1422 Tiptoft had secured royal permission for his second marriage to Joyce Cherlton because of his 'good service as Seneschal of Aquitaine'. She had been born in 1403 and was the daughter of Edward, Lord Cherlton of Powys, by his first wife Eleanor, daughter of Thomas Holland, Earl of Kent. The marriage again conferred on the Tiptoft family a noble title, that of Baron Tiptoft and Powys.[18] Joyce brought the Tiptofts considerable property as she was the coheir to both the Cherlton and part of the Holland family estates.

Joyce also brought connections to royalty and the upper nobility. She was the great-great-granddaughter of Edward I.[19] Her older half-sister, Anne—by her mother Eleanor's first marriage to Roger Mortimer, Earl of March—had married Richard, Earl of Cambridge, who was beheaded in 1415 after the Southampton plot. Anne had died giving birth to Richard, Duke of York, the future father of

Figure 2: The tomb brass of Joyce Tiptoft, *née* Cherlton, mother of the Earl of Worcester, in St Andrews, Enfield.

Edward IV. Also, Joyce's aunt, Margaret Holland, married John Beaufort, Earl of Somerset, who was father to York's future hated rival Edmund Beaufort, 2nd Duke of Somerset.

Nothing personal is known of Joyce Cherlton other than a short description by the sixteenth century antiquarian, John Leland, calling her a *femina incomparabilis*, or a matchless woman, and what can be gleaned from the image on her beautiful tomb brass, which shows a slightly oversized but notably sweet face.

Joyce's father, Edward, was a Marcher lord, a peer appointed by the king with much independent power to guard the volatile Anglo-Welsh border lands, *ergo* tough, and her mother was a Holland. Edward Cherlton, Lord Powys (1370–1421), was clearly a most striking and forceful youth. The chronicler, Adam of Usk, called him a '*juvenis elegantissimus*', a most elegant young man. While still a teenager he married the widowed Eleanor Mortimer *née* Holland. Adam reconciled Henry IV to Edward and the charismatic young man became a staunch Lancastrian. Edward had his brutal moments. According to Adam, in 1401 some of Usk's burgesses broke into the castle and 'set free one John fitz Pers, late seneschal therein, who, having been accused by evil report of adultery with a certain lady [reputedly the local prioress], had been to all men's wonder, condemned to death by Sir Edward Cherlton, who was her natural brother, and now lay naked undergoing punishment'.[20]

Joyce's mother was a Holland, a name that was a byword for violence, vindictiveness and instability. The constitutional historian Bishop William Stubbs wrote, 'the Hollands were a cruel race'.[21] The 1st Duke of Exeter, John Holland (1352–1400) was the son of Joan, 'The Fair Maid of Kent', by her first marriage to Thomas Holland, 1st Earl of Kent. Joan's second husband was Edward, the Black Prince, making Richard II and the Duke John half-brothers. Holland was Richard II's appointed heir and had a notoriously violent temper. In 1384 he was accused of the cold-blooded murder of a Carmelite friar who had informed Richard of a plot by the Duke of Lancaster to dethrone him. Holland was executed in 1400 for his part in the Epiphany Rising, the objective of which was the assassination of Henry IV and his sons.

John Holland, 2nd Duke of Exeter (1395–1447), was given the chance to redeem his line and fought valiantly at Agincourt in 1415. He recovered his father's dukedom of Exeter in 1439. He had proved an effective but brutal fighter in France, gaining an evil reputation for burning towns and massacres in breach of safe-conducts. The 2nd Duke left a particularly poisonous progeny in the unstable 3rd Duke Henry (1430–75) and three notorious 'Bastards of Exeter', William, Thomas and Robert. Even the rack in the Tower of London was known as 'the Duke of Exeter's daughter' from Henry's time as Constable of the Tower. The younger John Tiptoft shared his Holland blood with another grandson of Cherlton and Eleanor, his cousin Henry Grey (c.1418–50), 2nd Earl of Tankerville and 7th Lord Powys. In 1447 Grey violated a safe conduct to have the old Welsh captain Sir Gruffudd Vychan summarily executed and for this he was called the 'Double Tongued Earl'.

1423 saw the birth of the first child, named Philippa, to John and Joyce. In the following year a second girl was born, named Joanna. The 8th of May 1427 was the date of the birth of the only son John, the future Earl of Worcester. Around 1430 a third daughter was born, named Joyce. There was a fourth daughter, Margaret, about whom nothing is known except that she became a nun.[22] High-born families might give one child to God's service, particularly if there were several daughters.

In the year John Tiptoft was born, 1427, England remained deeply engaged with Europe. Exactly one century later King Henry VIII had determined on his divorce from Queen Katherine leading—in a religious Brexit—to the 1534 Act of Supremacy, which made Henry head of the Church of England. Although England remained closely territorially integrated with Europe in 1427 there were already distinct signs of divergence in military matters, politics, law and learning.

Militarily, in 1427 England was advancing in France—next year the siege of Orleans would begin as English expansion continued along the Loire—but there were omens that the long decades of the dominance of English arms across Europe were numbered. The Battles of Crécy (1346), Poitiers (1356) and Agincourt (1415) are familiar but English leaders, archers and men-at-arms had also played key roles in Spain, notably at the Battle of Nájera (1367), in Portugal at Aljubarrota (1385), in Italy at Castagnaro (1387)—and in France as recently as 1424 the Duke of Bedford had won a great victory at Verneuil. But in 1427, the year of John Tiptoft's birth, his future patron Cardinal Beaufort, as Papal Legate leading the anti-Hussite Crusade, lost the Battle of Tachov in the modern Czech Republic. The Hussites' use of hand gunners and *houfnices* [howitzers] pointed the way forward. In 1429 the French revived under the charismatic Joan of Arc and the English withdrew from Orleans and were badly defeated at the Battle of Patay. At Orleans Thomas Montagu, the 4th Earl of Salisbury, was horribly killed by a French cannon blast. (He left a young widow, Alice *née* Chaucer, who was the granddaughter of the poet Geoffrey and she remarried William de la Pole, the future Duke of Suffolk. She would become an intriguing presence over the next fifty years.) In 1434 Charles VII would take into his service the Bureau brothers, Jean and Gaspard, who made the French siege and field artillery the most advanced in Europe.

Politically, the English were identifying themselves as distinguished from the French by the rule of limited as opposed to absolute monarchy. The lawyer, judge and theorist Sir John Fortescue (c.1394–1479) would write in his *De Laudibus Legum Anglie* or Praise of English Laws,

> The king of England is not able to change the laws of his kingdom at pleasure, for he rules his people with a government not only royal but also political. If he were to rule over them with a power only royal, he could be able to change the laws of the realm, and also impose on them tallages [arbitrary taxes] and other burdens without consulting them; this is the sort of dominion which the civil laws indicate when they state that what pleased the prince has the force of law. But the case is far otherwise with the king ruling his people politically, because he himself is not able to change the laws without the assent of his subjects nor to burden an

unwilling people with strange impositions, so that, ruled by laws that they themselves desire, they freely enjoy their goods, and are despoiled neither by their own king nor any other.[23]

As a result of rule by popular consent England enjoyed wealth and happiness in contrast to the misery in France. Fortescue also praised the English common law with its emphasis on process and proof assessed by juries. By the fifteenth century the English legal system had developed many of the forms that were different to European civil law founded on codes rather than based on precedent. Englishmen were fiercely protective of common law against any encroachment of continental ideas.

Economically, England was a rich country as it was Europe's main supplier of wool and woollen cloth. Tiptoft, however, was born just before the start of the fifteenth century's Great Slump. This gathered pace in the 1430s, which saw harvest failures and livestock disease while trade suffered from bullion shortages. The economy did not recover until the 1480s. Historically, hard times tend not to be happy times and Tiptoft's entire life played out against the backdrop of political and social pressures in part caused by economic weakness.

Overall, as the fifteenth century advanced, Englishmen and women had an increasing sense of their identity, rights and liberties. By continental standards this was a reasonably levelled society. Lords fought on foot with their men and not on horseback above and aloof from them. Parliamentary petitions and legal pleas gave to many the opportunity to protect their rights. Widows, the rich ones at least, had considerable freedom in choosing their second marriages and were also blessed with generous dower rights. Although violent, the English popular revolts of 1381 and 1450 did not have the pent-up inter-class viciousness of the French *Jacquerie* of 1358. A rich wool merchant family like the de la Poles of Hull could rise to a dukedom.

In learning and scholarship, however, England was fast falling behind continental advances based on the reassessment and rediscovery of classical culture. Scholarship had received a huge boost between 1414 and 1418 when the great scholar Poggio Bracciolini—when attending the Council of Constance, like Tiptoft's father, which endeavoured to mend the papal schism—explored the monastic libraries of Switzerland, Swabia and north-eastern France. He rediscovered many lost Latin manuscripts, greatly stimulating humanist studies. Tiptoft would understand the importance of classical study and would seek to close the growing divide between Italian and English scholarship, and be the first to bring Bracciolini's discoveries to England.

In the 1420s Lord Tiptoft and Powys bought two wardships, the purchase of which had important consequences. In 1422 he secured that of Edmund Ingaldisthorpe, who was from a prominent East Anglian family. Edward's mother was a de la Pole and related to the powerful, predatory William, Duke of Suffolk. In 1431 Lord Tiptoft and Powys bought the wardship of Thomas Roos, born to baronial rank. With a wardship came the right to select a marriage partner for the ward. This was particularly valuable as it provided a means to secure spouses for daughters without diminishing the family estate by providing marriage settlements. Joanna and Philippa Tiptoft would be married to Edward and Thomas, respectively.

In 1433 Sir John Daneys, the husband of Lord Tiptoft and Powys' sister Elizabeth, died. He had three children, Robert, Elizabeth and Jane. Daneys' will of 1432 indicated he was reliant on his brother-in-law to help his daughters in finding good marriages: 'To my daughter Elizabeth, a chain of gold, and if the said Elizabeth does not marry through John Typtot nor any dowry be provided for her … then I give her forty pounds.'[24] Only Elizabeth of the three children is known to have married. And indeed she married well, taking as her husband William Haseldene, from a family of prominent landed gentry in Cambridgeshire.

In 1434 the young John Tiptoft reached his 7th year, the age at which gentle-born boys were often moved away from their mother's care. According to Leland, he was educated carefully by his parents. It was becoming increasingly common for great families to employ tutors. The young Tiptoft's long relationship with the priest John Hurley began in the 1430s when he was granted by Lord Tiptoft and Powys the benefice of Hanslope in Buckinghamshire. This priest was to be his tutor and guardian at Oxford in the early 1440s and possibly his companion to the Holy Land and Italy in the later 1450s and early 1460s.[25]

As Steward of the Household, Lord Tiptoft and Powys had been a central member of young King Henry's court. The boy needed to have young companions. In 1425 the Council ordered that crown wards be brought to court so they 'should be near the person of the King, … with one teacher, at the costs of the King'.[26] Fortescue considered the royal court to be the best place for raising young men. 'I cannot but highly commend the magnificence and state of the King's palace, and I look on it as an academy for the young nobility of the Kingdom.'[27]

Lord Tiptoft and Powys' two wards, Thomas Roos and Edmund Ingaldisthorpe, were respectively of baronial and knightly rank. They, and with them the younger John Tiptoft, might have been sent to school at the court and it is possible that the Earl may have recalled his own youth when he translated *The Declamacion*, for he wrote: 'Fforsothe, whan I was right yonge, I was sette to scole.'

In 1430 Lord Tiptoft and Powys spent Christmas with Cardinal Beaufort at Canterbury. In May 1431 he was in France and probably attended, as Steward, the coronation of Henry as King of France in the Cathedral of Notre Dame, Paris. Despite the failure to capture Orleans in 1429, where the siege was broken by

Joan of Arc, the English remained a commanding presence in France, and the captured Joan was burnt in Rouen during the same month as the coronation. The accession of the infant Henry VI had not marked the end of England's fortunes in France. Indeed, the years of his childhood were not associated with irreversible failure there. Yet intelligent observers of character must have become aware that the young Henry did not have his father's firmness or wit. In 1434, Lord Tiptoft and Powys joined councillors who protested to the 12-year-old king that he was susceptible to 'sturinges or motions maad to him apart in thinges of greet weight and substance', and he should not in future lightly gave way to them.[28] Already the pre-teenage king was recognised as easily swayed.

In 1435 the warrior Duke of Bedford died, removing the great war leader of royal blood who was best able to quell faction. He left a young widow, Jacquetta of Luxembourg, who was brought back to England on the King's command by one Sir Richard Woodville, son of the late Duke's chamberlain. During the journey, like Tristan and Iseult of Arthurian legend, the young couple fell in love. Their secret marriage, without royal permission, proved fecund and produced another young woman, Elizabeth, whose second marriage—to King Edward IV—would have momentous consequences.

On the 12th of November 1437 Henry VI came of age and formally reappointed his councillors and officers, including Lord Tiptoft and Powys, thereby asserting the independent authority of the crown. In practice the King had made himself more vulnerable to favourites.

The boy Tiptoft was born into troubled times, with England's status and relationships with the outside world entering a period of flux. He counted a remarkable breadth of ancestry. His paternal Tibetot grandfather inherited two manors and his father increased the number more than tenfold through astute and loyal service to the house of Lancaster. His paternal grandmother's City of London line included a lord mayor. His maternal grandfather was a lordly *juvenis elegantissimus* from the Welsh borderlands who as a teenager had won the older widow Eleanor, born to the 'cruel' Holland race. One cousin was Richard, Duke of York, and another Elizabeth Daneys of Cambridgeshire gentry stock.

Despite the disparity of age and noble rank, John's parents' marriage appears to have brought security and comfort. Five children were born within a decade and none died, an outcome rare before the modern age. His parents provided a stable, prosperous, and possibly a happy childhood home. The younger John Tiptoft's childhood did not give any obvious psychological explanation as to why he died reviled as 'The Butcher'. The breadth, however, of his family background and the remarkable achievements of his father, might have helped shape his ideas about a true nobility that was earned through service and not by blood.

Chapter 2

Oxford – 1440 to 1443

Socrates himself was never more overjoyed, nor gave more plentiful thanks
to the highest creator, than that it should fall his lot to be born not foreign but
Greek. Thus, I was overjoyed and gave thanks that I might have been with
you, for learning and virtue, at Oxford, as if another Athens, and for those
years to devote myself to noble sciences and the finest arts.[1]

> Letter from the Earl of Worcester to Oxford University from
> Italy offering books in 1460

M edieval Oxford might conjure up visions of cloisters, pinnacles and
spires. However, the university that the 13-year-old John Tiptoft went
up to would have seemed a much less ornate and elegant place. Indeed,
the aristocratic Oxford of the glittering spires was largely a later creation, or rather
a pastiche. Also, in the highly hierarchical society of the time it might be expected
that the university was dominated by the aristocratic and the well-connected.
Yet the numbers of secular aristocrats at Oxford in the Middle Ages could be
counted on the fingers of two hands and even nobles destined for the church were
a minority. Since his status as his family's sole male heir precluded a church career,
why, it might well be asked, was the noble young Tiptoft there at all?

One contemporary, the antiquary John Rous, wrote that Tiptoft was 'a man of
vast erudition, whom I knew in my time as a fellow student in the University of
Oxford'.[2] Leland writes that Tiptoft was 'eager for … the clever throng, at Oxford,
in that college for which the name of Balliol is picked out: where noble youths,
drank renewed eloquence from the garland of the celebrated'.[3] This rather met-
aphorically mixed passage has historically been interpreted as meaning Tiptoft
was at Balliol but it might better be read as saying that he aspired to be with an
elite there. In the 1930s evidence of Tiptoft's attendance was found in the bursar's
accounts of the Great Hall of the University, summarised here:[4]

	Autumn	Spring	Summer
Dominus Joh Typtot	1440	1441	1441
Typtot and Hurle	1441	1442	1442
Typtot and Hurle	1442	1443	1443
Typtot[5]	1443		

Thus University College, as it is now named, can claim Worcester as one of its most illustrious alumni. Hurle was certainly the priest John Hurley whose relationship with the Tiptoft household had begun in the 1430s.

The Great Hall of the University, despite its name, was one of the then few colleges, and was founded by one William from Durham who died in 1249. Colleges, self-governing communities of fellows, were comparatively few in number compared to the hundred plus halls, there being also Merton, Oriel, Balliol and New College. Most undergraduates lived in the relatively mundane halls under the supervision of a paid master. The reason for the selection of a college for Tiptoft rather than a hall was probably straightforward: colleges were richer, grander, and more flexible in their accommodation, allowing individual rooms for nobles and tutors.[6]

Colleges were beginning to assume a distinctive architectural form. Merton had the fourteenth-century Mob Quad. New College, dating to the end of that century, set the precedent for the college, cloister, chapel, hall combination that was to become archetypal. Across the high street from University, the construction of All Souls was underway. Not long after Tiptoft left Oxford, work started on Magdalen College between the Cherwell and the City walls, financed substantially by Sir John Fastolf, much of whose estate came from the wife he married in 1409, Millicent *née* Tiptoft.

In Tiptoft's day the Great Hall was very different to the tidy quadrangles of the post-medieval university. The old buildings stood without any 'method' or uniformity. But while Tiptoft was there reconstruction along more regular and rectangular lines was being planned. The founding statutes had provisions for books and the bursar's reports of 1391 described a library on the ground floor.

The decision to send the young Tiptoft to Oxford might be viewed in the context of the times. By the late 1430s it must have been clear that England was under pressure in France, especially when Charles VII entered Paris as king in 1437. Factionalism between King Henry's uncles, the Duke of Gloucester and Cardinal Beaufort, was splitting the government in England. How long France could be held onto would become increasingly dependent on the King, and those around him must have been becoming painfully aware that he was not shaping up well as a leader. Henry VI, while not a scholar or an intellectual, was, however, passionately interested in learning. New ideas about education were emerging at this time, based on a rising awareness of classical history and texts, and, to some more forward thinking minds, these might have appeared to provide answers to England's challenges.

The chief justice Sir John Fortescue wrote in *The Governance of England* that England's decay was due to the King's dependence on private councillors, as was Rome's when the emperor ignored the counsel of the Senate.

> And our Realme is fallen thereby in dekeye and povertie, as was the
> Empire whanne themperoure lafte the counsell of the Senate. But it may
> nat be doubted, that yif oure Kinges be counselled by suche a wise sta-
> blisshed counseile …, and do there after as did the firste emperour that
> gate the monarchic of the worlde, wee shulde firste haue unite and peax
> withinne oure lande, riches and prosperite, and be mightieste and moste
> welthe Realme of the worlde.[7]

Thus the King must be advised by wise councillors, like the Roman senators, if the
country's fortunes were to be restored. And, in England, a Latin-based education
at Oxford might provide a means for training such men.

The developing humanist movement in Italy emphasised the human potential
to attain excellence and advocated a rational and largely secular education based
on the study of the literature, art, and civilization of classical Greece and Rome.[8]
Humanism in England, by contrast, was more associated with the effort to solve
real contemporary political problems—not with a detached love of learning for
its own sake—and the protagonists were initially men in the public sphere, rather
than primarily scholars.

Familial and political circumstance placed the Tiptofts in contact with a number
of circles which had a deep interest in the new learning. The French Wars made
Englishmen aware of continental developments. The Duke of Bedford acquired
Charles V's library of over 800 books from the Louvre. His lieutenant was Sir John
Fastolf who returned from France in 1438. The real Fastolf was a most intriguing
figure and not at all Shakespeare's licentious buffoon. Due to his modest birth, born
of a Norfolk gentleman, and (unfair) allegations of cowardice at the Battle of Patay
(1429), he was given to standing upon his dignity and does not appear an attractive
personality but he is important to understanding the intellectual direction of the
age. Fastolf married Millicent Scrope *née* Tiptoft, the middle daughter of Robert,
the senior John Tiptoft's cousin. He served on several ventures and commissions
with both John Tiptofts, father and son. Fastolf owned a life of Caesar, named the
Serpent of Division, commissioned by Duke Humphrey, which warned of faction's
dangers. His circle was interested in questions of chivalry, nobility, the reasons for
defeat in France, and the proper basis of good governance in England.

Millicent's son was Stephen Scrope. When he came of age in the early 1420s
he joined Gloucester's household.[9] Scrope translated from French the *Dicts and
Sayings of the Philosophers*, which contained excerpts of ancient wisdom. He also
translated Fastolf's manuscript of Christine de Pisan's *Épître d'Othéa*, or the *Boke
of Knyghthode*. Here Othéa, goddess of prudence and wisdom, writes to the young
Hector, giving advice on knightly virtues by setting out the worthy qualities of the
seven planetary gods which knights should emulate.[10]

William of Wyrcester was Fastolf's secretary and a scholar, biographer and annalist.[11] He went to Oxford in 1431 to Great Hart Hall, which was attached to Balliol, and served Fastolf from 1438 until the latter's death in 1459. William composed the *Boke of Noblesse* some time after 1451, in which he identified the reason for the loss of Normandy as 'a failure of the English aristocracy to emulate the self-discipline, organisation, bravery and moral uprightness of the Roman government classes'.[12] The writings of Cicero—perceived as epitomising Roman virtue, good Latin and great oratory—held a particular fascination for Fastolf's circle.

Another scholarly circle was that linked to the King's uncles. Both Cardinal Beaufort and Duke Humphrey employed humanists. Beaufort was served by the great Poggio Bracciolini, who was in England from 1419 to 1423 (and considered the time the least satisfactory of his life). Humphrey patronised scholars and encouraged them to pursue their studies overseas and send books back to his library, particularly those by the great Greek and Latin teacher Guarino da Verona. The young Tiptoft's cousin, Henry Grey, was married to Humphrey's illegitimate daughter Antigone—the very name indicating a classical bent. Gloucester corresponded with leading Italian humanists and commissioned translations of Greek classics into Latin.

After 1436 Humphrey's secretary was Tito Livio de' Frulovisi, who studied under Guarino. In 1433 Tito had written *De Republica*, setting out his views on how the ruler of the state should govern. Here he stressed the importance of rhetoric for effective governance: 'Every form of eloquence is necessary to citizens responsible for government.'[13] Humphrey donated books to Oxford between 1435 and 1444, including Frulovisi's *De Republica*, which were housed in the fourteenth-century Congregation House to the east of the tower of St Mary's church. After 1412 only graduates and students of philosophy for eight years were allowed entry and then only if properly robed and having sworn, before the Chancellor, not to erase, blot or spoil the books. The young Tiptoft, as an undergraduate, was officially barred from Duke Humphrey's collection, so access to books might have been only through his college library. He must have learnt that Oxford's woeful shortage of books hampered study. When Tiptoft offered books to the university in 1460 he was likened, in Oxford's gushing reply, to a second Humphrey.

Did the young Tiptoft go to Oxford for three years at the age of 13 to 16—longer and older than any other secular English aristocrat—merely by chance? Or was it as a result of some grand design to improve the education of young English aristocrats in order to make them fit for the challenges of a changing England and Europe? In addressing this issue certain questions can be asked. First, was Tiptoft sent to university simply because he was a young aristocrat in need of education? Secondly, were there any other options available to him?

Looking at the first question, very few secular medieval lords went to university and those who did tended to be rather young. The other secular aristocrats at university, roughly contemporary to Tiptoft, were: Robert, Lord Hungerford, who was resident at University College, Oxford, for three terms in 1437 but as he was then under 10 years old he cannot be counted as a student; and Henry Holland, later the 3rd Duke of Exeter, who was at King's Hall, Cambridge, between 1439 and 1442 when he was between 9 and 12 years old. Judging by his later record he was not improved by the experience. Tiptoft was notable in going up when he was older than these, and for staying three or more years. He was, therefore, of an age when he could have been integrated into the broader student activities of the university.

As to the second question, there were other options for intelligent young aristocrats. If he were to be sent to a place of education on account of his ability he might have studied law. Fortescue wrote: 'There are not many who learn the laws in the inns except the sons of nobles . . . . Hence it comes about that there is scarcely to be found in the realm a man trained in the laws, who is not noble or sprung from noble lineage.'[14] Fortescue made clear that the inns taught subject matter in English, French and Latin, whereas the universities worked only in the last language. A deliberate decision appears to have been made for Oxford where he would have a Latin-based education.

It seems, then, that a choice was made to send the young Tiptoft to university at an older age than usual for secular aristocrats so that he might engage in the Latin-based curriculum. Who could have made such a decision? The older John, Lord Tiptoft and Powys, was closely linked by office and family to people who were unusually deeply interested in recent developments in Italian learning and who were involved, politically and militarily, in England's relationship with France. Lord Tiptoft and Powys was England's main ambassador under both Henry V and Henry VI. His cousin, Millicent, remarried Sir John Fastolf who patronised a circle with a particular interest in Cicero, and his nephew, Henry Grey, married Antigone, the illegitimate daughter of Humphrey Duke of Gloucester. He worked with both Gloucester and his rival Cardinal Beaufort, both of whom had had Italian humanist secretaries, respectively Bracciolini and Frulovisi. These men were in a unique position to be particularly aware of the vulnerability of England's position in France and of the developments in continental, and especially Italian, learning which offered the nobility a way forward. A Latin-based education at Oxford provided a key to the humanist door and, while it can only be conjectured that it was for these reasons that John was sent there, the decision to send the young Tiptoft was prescient, for he would prove an avid student, to the extent that his public duties permitted.

Tiptoft was at Oxford as a teenager for three years—old enough to have studied as a normal undergraduate. As such he would have started on the grammar, logic, and rhetoric of the *trivium* or three roads. Grammar meant learning the structure of a language and a sound grounding in Latin was essential to learning the other arts. Logic was the mechanics of thought and analysis. Rhetoric was the use of language to instruct and persuade. After two years the student was prepared to study the *quadrivium* of geometry, arithmetic, astronomy and music. Students were expected to discourse in Latin in hall and were fined if they did not. Lectures took place in the mornings and in the afternoon there was revision when students were examined orally on the day's lecture. This type of instruction was complemented by discussion groups and disputations. The texts expounded were usually Aristotle's although the 'Oxford syllabus had begun to admit—alongside the study of Aristotle—a degree of attention to Cicero, Ovid and Virgil'.[15]

Students were generally required to take holy orders before admission and were meant to wear 'decent clerical garb'. Even though the students were largely destined for the church, life was rough, with barbarous initiation ceremonies and feuds with the townspeople. Festivals, often involving the inversion of authority, must have further encouraged disorder. The Great Hall statutes give an insight into the boisterous side of life: 'That all may live honestly, thus it is fitting for clerks, as for saints: no fighting; no speaking scurrilously or basely; no ditties or tall stories of lovers or luxuriousness, inclining to lust; or singing encouraging willingly noise and passion; in order that university students are not inconvenienced.'[16] Rules proscribing such behaviour suggest that it was expected.

Men for whom a higher clerical career beckoned may have gained a taste for sex as students. An inquiry into prostitution in 1443, Tiptoft's last year, revealed that many prostitutes were married and the trade was highly organised.[17] Women, like Chaucer's Oxford carpenter's wife in *The Miller's Tale*, might anyway have found young educated men more attractive than older ignorant husbands. England's great churchmen did not always take chastity too seriously. Cardinal Beaufort (Queen's) supposedly had an affair with Alice FitzAlan, the wife of John, 4th Baron Cherlton. John died childless and his brother, Edward, Tiptoft's grandfather, became the 5th Baron. The Cardinal certainly fathered an illegitimate daughter, Jane Beaufort. Cardinal Wolsey (Magdalen) had a mistress, Joan Larke, and a bastard son and daughter. In Tiptoft's final year John Hurley was not recorded as having a room at University College. Tiptoft was now 16—an age when he might have been open to temptation. The opportunity was most certainly there and he does not appear to have been under the close supervision of an older tutor.

Tiptoft may have had an unfortunate introduction to the Irish at Oxford, who appear to have been particularly unruly. Earlier in the century English students had complained that Irish living together in large numbers sooner or later got noisy, violent and out of control. Exclusively Irish halls were banned.[18]

Generally, mid-fifteenth century Oxford does not sound a very inspiring place, visually or academically. Its last great philosopher was William of Ockham (c.1287–1347) who had spent the second half of his adult life in Avignon and Bavaria, close to the Papal and Imperial courts. The only significant thinker subsequently was John Wycliffe (c.1320s-1384), who was declared a heretic in 1415 at the Council of Constance (and was possibly a source of shame). The young Tiptoft was probably put on his guard against infection by his father, who was one of Lollardy's greatest foes and wrote a lost polemic against its evils. Learning was increasingly unoriginal by north Italian standards. Judging by the statutes and investigations there was, however, much opportunity for singing, swearing, fighting and wenching. Anyway, at this stage the teenage Tiptoft was engaged in, at most, undergraduate studies and entertainments and was probably not unduly concerned by the old-fashioned nature of more advanced studies. He thought well of his time at Oxford as can be seen from a letter he wrote in 1460 from Italy, offering a generous gift of books.

> Even if we have gone, for some time, to and fro openly, in a far distant foreign land, yet, at no time, however, have you, most excellent men, been forgotten by us. Of course, I hold your, or our, most learned University in high esteem. I always have since, as the Greeks say, my little finger nails [youth]—so that I do not know what other course I could possibly have pursued with greater either attention or sense of duty. (The quote is continued at the head of the chapter.)

Oxford replied, presenting Tiptoft's record in the most glowing terms: 'Indeed from your youth we have never remembered other of you than as sufficiently illustrious and having achieved a seemingly divine manner in affairs.'[19] The flattering of rich and powerful alumni who promised valuable gifts has a long history.

The young John spent a longer period of his adolescence at university than did any other secular medieval English nobleman. Medieval Oxford was a distinctly non-noble place. 'Typically, English undergraduates were the sons of lesser gentry, merchants, artisans, government employees…, lawyers, schoolmasters, physicians, and village officials and manorial office-holders.'[20] English university teachers and regents were mostly recruited from the ranks of the graduate students and so were also often of middling to lower social origins.[21] Tiptoft was otherwise unusual in going to a college not a hall; in having, on the basis of the substantial fees paid, at least two rooms when most students shared; in not taking holy orders; and in being accompanied by a personal tutor. He was 13 when he went up, so older than the few secular aristocrats at Oxford or Cambridge but younger than most students who matriculated at about 17. He was at a college, which then would have had few undergraduates, while he was much younger than the fellows.

He may have made friends outside of his class, possibly the Canterbury monk Henry Cranebroke, the antiquary John Rous, and his older tutor John Hurley. In the years when the young Tiptoft would otherwise have been acquiring the military and campaigning arts, perhaps as a page and then a squire to a knight or lord, maybe even in France, he was instead at a seat of academic learning. His different experience may have given him a detached perspective on the English nobility and a broader social view and sense of worth. In *The Declamacion* he compared inherited nobility through lineage unfavourably with that earned by character.

Separation from his own noble caste in an environment that was non-noble may also have meant the young Tiptoft had to learn to be independent and not to need the approbation of the dominant peer group. As the Earl of Worcester he was quite capable of modesty and lacking in pretension.

An Oxford education might be more important for who is met than for what is learned academically. Over his life the Earl was closely involved on many levels with university men and his time at Oxford gave him a point of entry into many circles not easily open to secular English aristocrats. Many alumni from Oxford and some from Cambridge reappear in his life, particularly in Italy and in service to Edward IV. His contemporaries between 1440 and 1443, at the Great Hall of the University, were Robert Flemming and William Orrel—both are seen again in the context of John's time in Italy. Other contemporaries included: the monk Henry Cranebroke (Canterbury College) with whom Tiptoft corresponded; Henry Sharp (Little White Hall), again Italy; John Rous, who explicitly mentioned meeting Tiptoft; and probably John Manyngham, the future Oxford registrar who would dedicate texts to Tiptoft when earl. In 1441 the Catalan chancer Vincent Clement, who reappears during Tiptoft's time in Italy, was awarded a doctorate of divinity by Oxford at the insistence of Henry VI and to the fury of the academic establishment.

Balliol alumni included: the future Archbishop of York, George Neville, and the Bishop of Ely, William Grey; the scholar John Free, to whom the Earl was both patron and friend; and Richard Bole, a king's clerk also appointed to go to the Congress of Mantua in 1459. Duke Humphrey of Gloucester was reputedly at Balliol although there is no evidence. William of Wyrcester, the writer and annalist, was at Great Hart Hall which was linked to Balliol. Other Oxford alumni included: Thomas Bourchier (Nevill's Inn), the future Archbishop of Canterbury and Chancellor; Andrew Holes (New College), Keeper of the Privy Seal under Henry VI; William Wey (Exeter College), a fellow pilgrim; Peter Courtenay, fellow student at Padua and royal servant in England; and John Lee, another appointed to go to Mantua. There were a couple of notable Cambridge alumni: John Gunthorpe, who was a scholar in Italy and a servant of Henry VI and Edward IV; and William Atteclyff who was at Padua and also served both kings. The future Earl of Worcester may have felt comfortable with such people, and they with him, in a way other secular aristocrats did not.

Oxford in the early-fifteenth century was, compared to universities in northern Italy, something of an academic and cultural backwater. But by the end of the fifteenth century it was advancing rapidly in humanist studies and scholarship, associated with the likes of John Colet and the Thomases Linacre and More. Much of the initial impetus to broaden study beyond a restricted scholastic base came from men who were soldiers like Fastolf and judges like Fortescue, who understood the need to re-educate the aristocracy. Fastolf contributed generously to the funding of Magdalen College. Secular nobles, like Duke Humphrey and John Tiptoft, saw and tried to address the necessity for more books.

Humanism in England was not just theory but also *praxis*. The study of Greece and Rome could provide solutions to contemporary political problems. The encouragement of humanist study at Oxford by practitioners of politics, administration, and the law, in turn created demand from the aristocracy to study there— as its members realised a humanist education was the way to advance careers in these areas of state service. 'The introduction of humanist studies goes some way towards explaining the increasing attraction of a university education for the English nobility. Of particular importance here was the humanist ideal, fuelled by the influence of Plato's *Republic*, that only those who were qualified for government, either in terms of specific skills or a broadly based education, were entitled to participate in the exercise of power.'[22] Plato's *Republic* was only available in the west after the fall of Constantinople in 1453 but it was not really until the sixteenth century that young aristocrats went to Oxford and Cambridge in significant numbers. Here Tiptoft, as in many things, would prove ahead of the *zeitgeist*.

The English nobility, in the fifteenth century, were put on notice. 'Unless the nobility embraced higher education as a leading priority, there was a danger that it would be excluded from the business of government and be rendered an emasculated class.'[23] Tiptoft pioneered the academic route that offered the aristocracy a way out of the feudal dead end. 'Humanism brought with it the idea that a meritocracy was a surer and more equitable basis for government and administration than one built upon the outmoded concept of aristocracy by birth.'[24] This last was the message implicit in the future Earl of Worcester's *The Declamacion of Noblesse*.

Chapter 3

Wardship to earldom – 1443 to 1450

We—profoundly reflecting on the vigorous honesty and well considered foresight, and also the pairing of morals & renown of noble birth, of our most dear kinsman John, Baron and Lord Tiptot of Powys, himself our kinsman—with regard to the Earl of Worcester, with the title, style, rank, & seat, and also name & honour to the same owed: we advance, raise, ordain, and create, and also by the encircling of the sword, in fact, grant by investiture to have and to hold the same title, style, rank, and seat, name, and honour, of the Earl of Worcester.[1]

The 1449 patent making John Tiptoft the Earl of Worcester

Medieval wardship was frequently hazardous: the estate might be plundered and the choice of marriage exploited.[2] In 1443 the young Tiptoft's father, Lord Tiptoft and Powys, died and thus the son became a royal ward. The times were particularly dangerous as King Henry was weak and could not control a predatory peerage.

In 1440 Lord Tiptoft and Powys' second daughter Joanna married his ward Edmund Ingaldisthorpe. The marriage may have been delayed until she was about 15 so he was perhaps 19 at the time. The marriage soon produced a single daughter, Isabel. Edmund's mother was a de la Pole—creating a link with the powerful but unscrupulous faction around William de la Pole, Duke of Suffolk, later identified with the King's unpopular marriage to Margaret of Anjou. In 1443, the Lord's oldest daughter was married to his ward Thomas Roos.[3]

Lord Tiptoft and Powys probably died during the last week of January 1443. The last years of his life were disturbed by a bitter dispute in Cambridgeshire with Sir James Butler, scion of the Irish earldom of Ormond and the future Earl of Wiltshire.[4] It is possible that the younger Tiptoft learned early a distaste for magnate conflict and Irish nobles.

There is a much-restored tomb in Ely cathedral with the effigies of one man and two women that is generally ascribed to the son, the future Earl of Worcester. Contemporary chroniclers, however, make it absolutely clear that the Earl was buried in 1470 in Blackfriars church in the City of London. The Ely tomb is almost certainly that of the father. The effigy shows a man wearing a collar of SS, the insignia of Lancaster. While the older Tiptoft died a Lancastrian his son ended his life a staunch Yorkist. The older Tiptoft had close links with Ely and it is highly probable he wished to be buried in the cathedral close to the largest concentration of his manors. Ely's bishop was Thomas Bourchier, whose elevation to the bishopric Lord Tiptoft and Powys had sought in the mid-1430s, although it was not fully secured until 1443. Tiptoft had made provision for the foundation of a chantry for the souls of himself and his wives in the cathedral.[5]

Lord Tiptoft and Powys died at the good age of 68, having risen from a squire to a lord worth well over £1,000 a year and married to royal blood. He left behind a promising son at Oxford and four daughters, two of whom were married, as well as a grandchild. Through his father the young John likely gained a sense of how the inner councils of rulers functioned—both in England and abroad—and discussed how kingship worked under Henry IV and Henry V and how it was increasingly not working under Henry VI.

On a personal basis, the son John was in an exceptional position to observe and learn the arts of deportment and diplomacy. His father had remarkable skills here, having proved able to manage an unruly Parliament as speaker and negotiate with and entertain the Emperor Sigismund and many other European leaders. There was nothing in his record to suggest that he was not a man of reasonable integrity and generally decent and honest in his dealings. In a hard time he was not obviously associated with any extreme act of avarice or cruelty.

The Gournay estates in England, held by the late Lord Tiptoft and Powys, went back to the crown—as determined in 1417 when Henry V bought the reversion. They were passed onto John St Lo on the 16th of October 1443 for seven years. But a year later, on the 4th of October 1444, they were granted to Edmund Beaufort, Earl of Dorset, who lacked the land to support his title. This might be thought a misuse of land in temporary royal possession during a minority, reflecting the King's weakness. However, it is difficult to see why the action was improper—at least in respect of the Tiptoft family—as Lord Tiptoft and Powys had sold the reversionary interest long ago.

The King, ever short of funds, tried to use the income from the Tiptoft estate, to which he was entitled during John's minority, to repay a huge loan of £11,000 to the crown from Cardinal Beaufort. On the 25th of May 1443 Beaufort was granted all the issues of the estate excluding those from the Gournay property.[6] The young John Tiptoft would come of age in 1448. Thus the Tiptoft property would have to produce over £2,000 a year in order to pay Beaufort off. Given the widow Joyce Tiptoft's dower rights it was most unlikely that the £11,000 loan could be paid down from this source—and so, indeed, it proved. The arrangement did, however, possibly ensure that a powerful man, able to look after the older Tiptoft's only son, had secured control when politics were becoming increasingly fractious. After the death of Bedford in 1435, Gloucester and Cardinal Beaufort were the grand old rivals for power. By the 1440s a new generation of the Dukes of York, Somerset and Suffolk were added to the toxic mix of contesting peers.

Yet despite the growing dissent in the kingdom and oppression of the weak there is no evidence of impropriety in the treatment of the late Lord Tiptoft and Powys' children or wards. Indeed, real care appears to have been paid to securing their welfare. On the 16th of May 1443 Lord Roos, married to Philippa *née* Tiptoft, was granted directly the £40 annuity that had been paid to Lord Tiptoft for his upkeep.[7] On the 1st of June 1443 Edmund Ingaldisthorpe inherited his father's lands at the age of 21.[8] Edmund was explicitly identified in the licence as being, through his mother, a de la Pole. This was perhaps no bad time to be onside with the family of the powerful and predatory Suffolk.

It is possible the young John had to leave Oxford to look after his mother and unmarried sisters. The only clue is his letter to Oxford from Italy in 1460 in which he said, 'I have not been able to show clearly enough my loyalty to you in my life thus far, being obstructed by private then public affairs.'[9] An award on the 20th of August 1445 gave his mother Joyce's property, and the keeping and marriage of the young lord, to the Colleges of Eton and King's on her death. It is possible that Joyce's health was failing, necessitating the making of explicit provisions for her son.[10] Henry VI desperately sought funding for his two great projects but no noble ward could have been better personally aligned, through his own education, with the Eton and King's project. The least that can be said is that this appeared a happy combination and it is open to speculation whether this was a sign of favour from the King to the young Tiptoft.

In Gascony there seemed a very different story and, beyond the protection of the late Lord Tiptoft and Powys' friends, the young man really did suffer dispossession. On the 1st of May 1444 the King, almost carelessly, granted to one 'Bidau de Bielle, esquire, at his supplication, because of his good service to Henry V and the current king, particularly [when] Charles VII of France went in Gascony and conquered there several places, the lordships of Maremne, Gosse and Seignanx, any letters patent of grant to [the late] John Tiptoft notwithstanding.'[11] This clearly resulted in a furious response, maybe from the young Tiptoft himself, as the King backed down. On the 20th of June there was an 'Order to Bidau de Bielle ... not to interfere in the lordships of Maremne, Gosse and Seignanx, under pretext of the previous grant by letters patent'.[12]

A year later the King exerted himself to try to protect the young Tiptoft's properties, for on the 14th of July 1445, '[for as] Lord Tiptoft, ... is a minor and is under the King's custody. ... The King orders the King's officers, ministers and bayles of the duchy of Aquitaine to maintain and protect [his estates].'[13] On the 17th of

July 1445 there was a further order, 'that if John Tiptoft, ... has been removed without right, *as he complained to the King*, from his lordships of Gosse, Seignanx, Marensin and Born, to return him these lordships'.[14] That is the last heard of the Tiptoft properties in the Gascon Rolls until 1450 and it seems highly unlikely they were recovered. It does, however, appear that the 18-year-old Tiptoft vigorously asserted his rights personally to the King and, judging by the favour he found from him in England, did it tactfully and persuasively.

At his mother's death in September 1446 control of her portion of the young Tiptoft's estates must have passed definitively to the royal foundations of Eton and King's. Joyce was buried at St Andrew's Enfield in a fine tomb, with an impressive brass, near the site of Elsyng Palace. The brass's text describes Joyce as '*una hered' honorabilissime D'ne Marchie'*, or, an heir of the most honourable Lady March.[15] Joyce's mother's first husband Roger Mortimer, Earl of March, had a good claim to the throne. Only when Edward IV was crowned would it have been safe to advertise Joyce's non-Lancastrian Mortimer connection. Thus the brass was probably commissioned by Worcester following his return from Italy in 1461 when Edward IV was on the throne. Both the Earl and future King were heirs of the most honourable Lady March.

In 1447 Cardinal Beaufort bequeathed 500 marks to John Tiptoft, to cancel a debt Tiptoft owed.[16] This was a very considerable sum of money to lend to a young man still in his teens. Cardinal Beaufort died in April 1447 and by June that year the young Tiptoft had bought out his wardship from Eton and King's aged only 20—before he would normally have fully come of age at 21. Perhaps he persuaded Beaufort to loan him the funds he needed and the generous Cardinal subsequently wrote off the debt.[17]

Beaufort's will also left £1,000 each to Eton and King's, to be deducted from the money the King still owed him and not discharged by monies from the Tiptoft estate. The Beaufort loan was £11,000 and four years of income from the Tiptoft and Wrothe estates cannot have made much of a dent in that figure. Beaufort also left £50 to Tiptoft's old Oxford college, the Great Hall of the University. Thus Beaufort willed funds to the educational establishments which Tiptoft attended or to which he was otherwise attached, possibly indicating some shared interest.

Henry VI has a poor reputation for allowing the plundering of estates of the weak. But in the case of the Tiptoft children and wards, as far as it is possible to see, their treatment was exemplary—at least in England. Also, the selection of Eton and King's as receivers of income from his family properties may well have been in recognition of the younger Tiptoft's academic sensibilities.

Who were the watchful guardians? It is impossible to know for sure but likely possibilities include Cardinal Beaufort and John and Edmund Beaufort, respectively Earl and Duke of Somerset, and possibly the late Lord Tiptoft and Powys' fellow councillors, such as John Sutton, Lord Dudley, and Walter, Lord Hungerford. That the older John Tiptoft could secure his children's protection for several years after his death speaks much for his reputation, the respect he had earned, and maybe the pluckiness and obvious promise of the son.

In 1447 the precocious young John Tiptoft, now himself Lord Tiptoft and Powys, came of age early—perhaps another *juvenis elegantissimus*, like his maternal Marcher grandfather—with the wish to serve about the King's person at his own cost. There then followed a rapid series of startling elevations which, in less than five years, saw him marry a duchess, receive an earldom, be appointed to commissions alongside the highest in the land, and become Lord High Treasurer of England at 24. This might be seen as a series of coincidences but it is just as likely that this was a trajectory for which his upbringing and education had been planned as preparation. Meanwhile, the backdrop to the young Tiptoft's rising star was the collapse of England's fortunes in France.

On the 30th of June 1447, Tiptoft, 'having made satisfaction to [Eton and King's] ..., and desiring to serve about the King's person at his own costs, [was licensed] to enter all the possessions and hereditaments, which came into the King's hands by their [his parents'] death and his minority, without suing livery out of the King's hands.'[18] Thus, before reaching 21, Tiptoft seems to have taken matters into his own hands. He paid off Eton and King's for his wardship. Henry VI waived the normal charge, indicating that the King was cooperating with, indeed encouraging, the arrangement whereby the young man could serve him personally.

In 1447 Tiptoft came to court as a young adult. From the age of 20, and possibly earlier, this educated, intelligent young man was almost certainly much around the King. His father's record of service to three generations of the House of Lancaster and his own education must have attracted him to the young King himself. Older councillors, who knew his father well, like the barons Cromwell, Sutton and Hungerford, were still much in evidence and could have supported and guided him.

The younger Lord Tiptoft and Powys was now in an excellent position to 'network'. The later record showed he had remarkable gifts of eloquence and diplomacy and, while he may have honed these later, they may already have been much in evidence. How else would he marry within two years one of the greatest heiresses of the age, Cecily Beauchamp, *née* Neville, and become an earl—a rank never held by any previous family member—without any known achievement to his credit. Tiptoft may also have been a young man of independence and sagacity for, in a court riven by faction, he was not identified with, or seen as the enemy of, any of the Dukes of Suffolk, Somerset or York. He was, indeed, related to all three:

his cousin was Richard Duke of York; the mother of his brother-in-law, Edmund Ingaldisthorpe, was a de la Pole; and his mother's aunt had married a Beaufort.

The young Lord may have lived a charmed life. However, politics at home were becoming increasingly vicious. Initially, the rivalry between the ducal factions was fought out by proxy. In 1441 charges of witchcraft had been made against Eleanor Cobham, Gloucester's mistress. Eleanor may have been the mother of Antigone, the illegitimate daughter of Gloucester and the wife of the young Lord Tiptoft's cousin, Henry Grey. The result was that one Roger Bolingbroke was hanged, drawn and quartered, and a supposed witch Margery Jourdemayne was burnt. Eleanor was incarcerated until her death in 1452. On the 7th of December 1446, Suffolk brought to council a certain William Catour who accused John Daveys, York's armourer, of calling York the legitimate King of England. Daveys asked for 'the judgement of god' through trial by combat. He was defeated by the younger Catour, in a combat witnessed by the court, then hanged and his body burnt. In 1447 the Duke of Gloucester was himself arrested on treason charges and died soon after. With the death of Cardinal Beaufort in the same year the older noble generation that had lived through the great days of Henry V were mostly gone, with the exception of John Talbot, Earl of Shrewsbury.

Suffolk may, ultimately, have been realistic in pursuing a peace policy with France but this was deeply unpopular and his credibility was anyway undermined by his and his followers' grasping behaviour. In March 1448 England finally ceded Maine, which was due to France under secret provisions of the marriage treaty of Margaret of Anjou to Henry VI, formulated in 1446. This accelerated the destruction of Suffolk's reputation and undermined that of the King and his new queen. In March 1449 Suffolk stupidly broke the truce with France with the capture of Fougères in Brittany, providing an excuse for a ferocious French counter-attack.[19]

Aged 21, the 2nd Lord Tiptoft and Powys made a most remarkable marriage to the widow of a duke. This was no secretive affair as on the 3rd of April 1448 a royal licence was issued to Cecily, Duchess of Warwick, and John Lord Tiptoft and Powys to marry. A papal dispensation in Rome, dated the 13th of May 1448, was granted for the marriage as both were descended from Thomas Holland, 2nd Earl of Kent.

Cecily was born in about 1425, the oldest daughter of Richard, 5th Earl of Salisbury, by Alice Montacute. She was close in age to the oldest son of the same marriage, another Richard, who would become famed as Warwick, the Kingmaker. In 1434, in a joint marriage, Cecily had married Henry Beauchamp (1425–46) and Richard had married Henry's sister Anne. Henry's father was the great Richard Beauchamp, 13th Earl of Warwick, who died in 1439. Henry V's will had made Beauchamp responsible for his son Henry's education, a duty he performed from

1422 until 1437. In June 1446 Henry Beauchamp died leaving a 2-year-old daughter Anne, who became the 15th Countess of Warwick and a great heiress.

There was no obvious dynastic reason why Lord Tiptoft and Powys, of recent baronial rank, and the Duchess Cecily might come together through marriage. Possibly the early death of his friend Henry Beauchamp left Henry VI without a young companion. Henry VI had raised Beauchamp from earl to duke in 1445 and would raise Tiptoft from baron to earl in 1449, so the young Tiptoft might have taken Beauchamp's place as a royal favourite. John Tiptoft and Cecily Beauchamp could also have simply been similarly aged young people at court who shared a mutual interest in education, books and literature. Widows had considerable discretion in the choice of their second husband. Indeed upper-class widows in the fifteenth century appear to have been remarkably independent about second marriages, often marrying men of lower status.[20] (Fifteenth-century examples included Queen Catherine's marriage to Owen Tudor and Millicent Scrope's *née* Tiptoft to Sir John Fastolf.) In Cecily's case her relative youth and importance may have meant her discretion was circumscribed. But that would only tend to confirm that the marriage had royal and familial approval.

Perhaps Cecily liked John, enjoying his company and his learning. Maybe he wooed her as Flamyneus did Lucresse in *The Declamacion*, with books and learning. 'And first I shal shewe you my lyberary, wel stuffed with fayr bookes of Greke and latyn, wher vnto in euery aduersyte is my chief resorte for counseyll and comforte. And ther shal we dyuerse tymes haue commycacyon and comforte of the connynge and doctrine of my lady and maystresse phylosophye.'[21]

It is possible that a bond formed early between John and his father-in-law Richard Neville, Earl of Salisbury, as a result of the marriage. The former was still a very young man without an obvious patron or mentor after the death of Cardinal Beaufort. Within five years York, Salisbury, and Tiptoft would be respectively Protector, Chancellor and Treasurer of England. And Tiptoft would be the principal non-Neville mourner at Salisbury's funeral in 1463. The young Richard Neville, the future 'Kingmaker', and John Tiptoft must have been thrown together as brothers-in-law by the marriage and perhaps recognised as among the most brilliant young men in England. Both would soon become earls. Richard and Cecily had younger brothers who would also be prominent in Tiptoft's life. John would marry Tiptoft's niece Isabel, and George, who would later become Archbishop of York, shared his scholarly interests.

Within two months of Tiptoft's marriage to Cecily, his 6-year-old stepdaughter died at Ewelme in Oxfordshire, the location of the de la Pole palace and the exquisite almshouses built by the family. Anne Beauchamp was Suffolk's ward and he planned to marry her to his son John, born in 1442, the sole child of his marriage to Alice *née* Chaucer. Given her share in the Beauchamp and Despenser estates

Figure 3: Cecily Beauchamp, *née* Neville, the young Earl of Worcester's first wife, from the tomb of Sir Richard Beauchamp, Earl of Warwick. Also, the Earl's seal, quartering Tiptoft and Powys, with his wife's shield superimposed.

she was a very valuable young person and William must have decided to keep her under his wife's control.

When Anne's father Henry died in 1446 his dukedom became extinct and his earldom was inherited by the infant Anne, who became the 15th Countess of Warwick. On the child's death her title reverted to her aunt Anne, the wife of Richard Neville, who became an earl *in iure uxoris*. The younger Anne was buried in the great Benedictine abbey of Reading about a dozen miles from Ewelme. Children died young and frequently but, in retrospect, it was the first in a quick succession of calamities that would strike down the women and children related to Tiptoft by blood or marriage.

Not only did John Tiptoft make a highly advantageous marriage at 21 but on the 16th of July 1449 he was made an earl. Richard Neville, son of the Earl of Salisbury, and John Tiptoft's brother-in-law, was similarly confirmed as Earl of Warwick on the 23rd of July. The somewhat older James Butler had been created Earl of Wiltshire on the 8th of July. He was reportedly the handsomest man in England and favoured by the queen. These elevations reflected the need to bring on younger blood. At the beginning of 1449 the Dukes of Suffolk, Somerset and York were respectively 52, 42, and 38 years old. The Earls of Shrewsbury and Salisbury were just over 60 and under 50. Veteran councillors like Lord Hungerford and Lord Dudley were 60 and 49. The wars in France no longer provided the means for able young men to make their reputations: the House of Lancaster needed to select men who would safeguard its future. Some would prove dubious investments.

The charter recording Tiptoft's creation as Earl stated, in excessively flowery and almost incoherent Latin, 'With regard to making John Tiptoft the Earl of Worcester. …It is agreed that to be a fortunate polity for the future which, to many nobles, he shines brightly in adorning—not only in maturity of council but also in exercising arms—for instance just as the sky is rendered richly adorned by stars and brightness.'[22] This reference to able performance in council and at arms is surprising as there is no surviving record of either. The terminology might be conventional or possibly some of the lost teenage years may have been spent campaigning. The charter continued: 'Thus, not only royal powers but royal crowns shine, by the light of dignitaries, and how much nobler and stronger should he have been, who is exalted by offices of honour, … so more is accomplished from him, to whom more is committed, of conduct, and to the polity.'[23]

As the younger John was only 22 when he was made Earl, the rank may have been awarded due to singular royal favour and the *anticipation* of future great service for which an exalted title would encourage the behaviour expected to merit it. The young earl, now married to a duchess, was expected to match, perhaps exceed, the example of his father. The title of the Earl of Worcester had, however, not so far proved particularly auspicious in terms of survival. There had been three previous creations: Waleran de Beaumont (died 1166); Thomas Percy (executed after the Battle of Shrewsbury 1403); and Richard Beauchamp (died 1422)—and none left male heirs.

After John Tiptoft was made Earl of Worcester, the sons of the sisters *née* Cherlton, Joanna Grey and Joyce Tiptoft, had attained earldoms in England and France respectively. Joanna's son Henry Grey was 2nd Earl of Tankerville in Normandy. But in October 1449 the Duke of Somerset surrendered the castle of Tankerville to the French. Thus ended in practice the Tankerville earldom.

The rising young men, Wiltshire, Worcester and Warwick, were listed among the thirty-one nobles present in the Parliament in Winchester which ran from the 16th of June to the 16th of July 1449, their presence recorded in notes which have, unusually, survived.[24] Parliament then moved to London from Winchester and reconvened at Blackfriars from the 6th of November to the 4th of December, and then to Westminster, from the 4th to the 17th of December. The new Earl of Worcester was appointed a trier of petitions for Gascony and the other lands overseas and for the Channel Islands. Perhaps this was because he had inherited, although probably in practice had little control over, many estates in the region. Considering petitions was a major part of parliamentary business. Since the end of the thirteenth century these were divided between those from England, Ireland and Gascony. They were taken by receivers who, in turn passed them to triers who would determine the response which was also decided by the King. The young Earl seems to have impressed by his diligence and acuity for he soon became much appointed to commissions.

On the 28th of January 1450 the Duke of Suffolk—held responsible for the loss of Anjou and Maine, suspected of treacherous negotiations with the French, and seen as fomenting misrule in England—was arrested, imprisoned in the Tower of London and impeached by the Commons. Worcester was named among those gathered on the 17th of March as witnesses in the King's 'inner chamber' at Westminster'. There the Chancellor, John Kemp Archbishop of York, told the kneeling Duke that it was the King's command that before the 1st of May he absent himself from the King's realm of England for five years.[25] He set sail on the 30th of April but his ship was intercepted *en route* to Calais by the *Nicholas of the Tower*. 'And yn sght of all his men he was drawyn out of the grete shippe yn to the bote; and there was an exe, and a stoke, and oon of the lewdeste of the shippe badde hym ley down his hedde, ... and smote of his hedde withyn halfe a doseyn strokes.'[26]

Parliament sat at Leicester from the 29th of April to the 7th of June, when it was adjourned following news of Cade's rising. This was to prove the biggest popular rebellion since the Peasant's Revolt and started a time of troubles in England that never really ended for the rest of the Earl's life. Worcester was cursed to come of age in interesting times: politically, the inadequacy of Henry VI could no longer be explained away on the basis of youth and inexperience; militarily, England was being ejected from France; and economically, at the end of the 1440s wool exports fell sharply.

During 1450 the Earl's third sister Joyce married Edmund Sutton when she was about 21. His father was John Sutton, 1st Baron Dudley, who had been a long-standing fellow councillor with the older late John Tiptoft. He lived an extraordinarily lengthy life for the period, born in 1400 and not dying until 1487. He may have discussed or even agreed Joyce and Edmund's marriage but then deferred final approval due to doubts over the value of the Tiptoft connection while the only son was an unproven minor. The younger Tiptoft's brilliant marriage to Cecily Beauchamp and early earldom may have assuaged those doubts.

For a brief time all four Tiptoft siblings eligible to marry (the fifth was a nun) had done so: two young women had married into baronial families, the Roos and the Suttons, and another to well connected East Anglian knights, the Ingaldisthorpes. And the young John had married into the peak of the social and political hierarchy, taking a duchess for his wife.

In the second quarter of 1450 the blowback from the rout in France was truly coming home to England. But for the young earl this may have seemed a good time. Both his parents had died but this was not unusual for the period. All his sisters were alive and bearing healthy children. A stepdaughter had died but he may not have known the child very well. He had survived his minority and become a charmed figure around court, rising high in the King's favour yet without antagonising any faction. He was an earl and married to a duchess. He personally might have had much with which to be satisfied, but in politics storm clouds swirled.

Chapter 4

Commissioner – 1450 to 1452

On diverse previous occasions [various traitors] imagined and compassed the death of the King and the destruction of his realm. And they finally agreed that they and other felons, traitors, lollards and heretics, being their accomplices and their association, would depose the King from the government of his kingdom and take the government of the said kingdom upon themselves; and that they would take, kill and finally destroy the lords spiritual and temporal of the realm, especially those opposing them in their plans; and that they would institute 12 peers from among themselves to rule the said kingdom. ... and believing and proposing as lollards and heretics that all things should be held in common: against the sacred law of the church and the laws and customs of the Kingdom used and approved time out of mind, etc.

Taken 30 June 1451 at Tonbridge before Edmund, Duke of Somerset, John, Earl of Shrewsbury, John, Earl of Worcester, Ralph de Cromwell, kt., William Beauchamp de Saint Amand, kt., John Prisot and John Portyngton, justices of oyer and terminer.[1]

An indictment, before a commission of oyer and terminer at Tonbridge of 29 June 1451, of various traitors where the Earl of Worcester was present.

Noble rank in later Medieval England might seem an exalted status, entitling the peer to attend great tournaments, magnificent Masses and fine banquets, to go hunting and hawking, and to engage in the thrills of fighting in exquisite armour while pursuing courtly love. In practice the nobleman was increasingly heavily burdened with administrative, conciliar, judicial and political duties. At 23 Worcester had already attended several sessions of Parliament. Now he was to have his fill of commissions.

Unrest started in Kent, at first peaceful, led by Jack Cade who styled himself John Mortimer. The county men saw themselves as petitioners, not rebels, who wanted corrupt advisers and officials removed, alienated lands resumed to the crown and York to be recalled from Ireland. Parliament, then in Leicester, adjourned on the 6th of June. The men of Kent set up camp at Blackheath five days later. Henry VI sent a force to disperse them on the 15th of June but they refused and gave the King's men their petition.

The petitioners then fell back to Sevenoaks where, on the 18th of June, a pursuing royal army was defeated. The following day other royal troops at Blackheath mutinied and called for the arrest of the Treasurer, Lord Saye and Sele, and John Sutton, Lord Dudley, as well as the late Suffolk's miscreant servants, Thomas Danyell and John Trevelyan. On the 25th of June the King withdrew to Kenilworth. Four days later William Aynscough, Bishop of Salisbury and the King's confessor, was murdered in Edington church in Wiltshire.

On the 2nd of July Cade broke into London and Lord Saye and Sele was murdered. Cardinal Kemp reached an agreement with the rebels that a commission would look into their grievances and they would receive a pardon, which was issued five days later. Cade, however, continued the fight and was pursued and killed. The King returned to London on the 10th of July.

Worcester's location in the disturbances caused by Cade is unrecorded. He may have been caught up in more personal concerns for, on the 29th of July 1450, his first wife Cecily died. Given her recent marriage and young age, this might have been of childbearing complications. She was buried in Tewksbury Abbey with her first husband, Henry Beauchamp.

There are only the most tenuous clues as to the emotional impact of her death. Worcester kept at least two of her books, a fine Book of Hours and John Lydgate's *Fall of Princes*. Otherwise, he would write in April 1452 to his friend the monk Henry Cranebroke referring to 'special remembraunce of her soule whom I loved best and God pardon, and charitable memoyr of me most wretched and sinful creature offending gretely the rather and soner recover mercy and grace by means of your praier offered up for her and me to our Lord Ihesu.'[2] At this date he was married to his second wife Elizabeth but the reference in the letter was to someone who had died. The date indicates the soul was Cecily's. The letter ended by invoking Christ's mercy: 'Whoo of his high bounte Lord Jesu dresse so the paces of your pilgrimage in this miserable and complainabe lif, that ye may enjoye the habitacioun, your laborious viage here finesshed, of perpetual quiete and rest, amen.'[3] The passage may allude to St Augustine's idea of life as a demanding pilgrimage but the sadness was all the Earl's own.[4]

In July 1450 Somerset surrendered Caen and returned to London on the 1st of August, abandoning English soldiers and thereby infuriating York who had been a diligent, and largely unpaid, governor of the territory. Two days later the English were defeated at the Battle of Formigny. This was the first major defeat since Patay in 1429 and was far more strategically significant as a total rout from Normandy ensued, resulting in defeated soldiers trailing back to an England rocked by

Cade's rebellion. England was left only with the possession of Calais, which lay in Burgundian territory.

After the revolt had been put down in mid-1450 there was further plotting of the King's death and the destruction of the realm in Kent that August. Into this volatile mix came Worcester's cousin, the Duke of York, returning from Ireland without royal recall. Lord Dudley, the father-in-law of Worcester's sister Joyce, joined him. York's stated intention was not to usurp the throne but to restore order and remove Somerset, whom he saw as disgraced by the shameful loss of Normandy. York marched into London with his sword, point upwards, held before him.

In order to quell the disturbances in the City, created by open hostility between York and Somerset, a show of strength was determined upon, to be led by Henry VI. In total 10,000 men supposedly traversed the City, a formidable number to push through the narrow streets of medieval London. In the van were the Duke of Norfolk and the Earl of Devon with 3,000 men. 'And then came the King and with him the Duke of York, the Earl of Salisbury, the Earl of Arundel, the Earl of Oxford, the Earl of Wiltshire, the Earl of Worcester and others with four thousand of armed men.'[5] The Duke of Buckingham and the Earl of Warwick brought up the rear with another 3,000 men. Such would prove the ferocity of the times that, within twenty years, of the six who escorted the King, two, York and Salisbury, would be killed at the Battle of Wakefield and three, Oxford, Wiltshire and Worcester, would die on the block. Henry VI would also die, probably on the order of York's son, Edward IV. The chronicler Gregory wryly observed, this 'was a gay and a gloryus syght if hit hadde ben in Fraunce, but not in Ingelonde.'[6]

A petition of the Commons on the 20th of January named twenty-nine people to be removed forever from the presence of the King. First was Somerset, second the redoubtable Alice de la Pole, *née* Chaucer, wife of the late Suffolk, who, despite her husband's death, was still perceived as a malign influence. There may have been careful preparation for the repression of the unrest in Kent as a commission of inquiry was issued on the 13th of January 1451 appointing Warwick, Worcester, Thomas Roos and others, including Sir John Fastolf.[7] Eleven men were to be investigated, described as 'late' of places in Kent.

The first major commission of oyer and terminer to which Worcester was appointed, dealing with unrest in south-east England after the Cade revolt, was that of the 27th of January 1451.[8] Such commissions, which constituted a major element of the Earl's political life, were judicial like those of the peace, of assize and of gaol delivery.[9] But oyer and terminer commissions, unlike these last three which took place in regular cycles, were set up to deal with specific situations, as was the more limited commission of inquiry. The value of the oyer and terminer was that it provided flexible powers to investigate and try specific incidents in determined timeframes.[10]

Several hundred people could be crammed into the great halls where the county courts were usually held, generally the town guildhall or the local castle.[11] There may have been the smell of sweat and fear, with grand juries bullied to produce indictments of people they knew, petty juries belaboured to condemn, and the arraigned often facing a terrible death. The great lords were present at, and controlled, the indictments. They drove the process by providing enforcement power through their authority and their retinues. Their role was certainly efficient rather than decorative. The chair of the session was taken by a magnate if present. The peers' 'greet attendaunce' of retainers and servants could quell any overt attempt to threaten their proceedings.

There is a rather informative and graphic description of the stages in the process at a session held in October 1452 at Stamford. It is an insight into the brutality of justice in Worcester's world:

Indictment:	before James, Earl of Wiltshire, and other justices of *oyer and terminer* … it was presented by the oath of twelve jurors that John Wynawey of Grantham, …, 'yoman' and others on 24 February last at Stamford … conspired the King's death … and supported the Duke of York and the Earl of Devon in their wicked purposes;
Arraignment:	and afterwards on Tuesday … the said John Wynawey was brought to the bar in person …
Plea:	and pleaded guilty,
Sentence:	and so it was considered that he should be drawn from prison through the midst of Grantham to the gallows there and hanged, and thrown to the ground while alive and his vitals removed and burned, and that his head should be cut off and his body divided into four quarters, to be set where the King should will.[12]

Generally, however, the justices of oyer and terminer were not very blood-thirsty.[13] Most cases were terminated by a pardon – although this still meant a fine. Therefore the commissions of 1451 and 1452, which were particularly marked out by their brutality, indicated a serious determination to make examples, reflecting the fear felt by the regime.

Membership of a commission of oyer and terminer involved the mixing of three groups: the men of law, the magnates, and local gentry. Given that these men travelled to sessions around the country, the young Worcester, still only 23, spent much time with dukes, senior earls and barons, as well as senior judges. His intelligence, Latineity, and perhaps his toughness may have impressed the King, lords, judges and clerks alike, for rapid promotion soon followed.

The terms of reference for the commission of oyer and terminer of the 27th of January 1451 were to deal with all those offences committed in Kent since the pardon of the 7th of July 1450. The commission, however, was really 'a punitive show of strength only thinly veiled by the trappings of legal procedure'.[14] Thus the Earl of Worcester's career as a commissioner of oyer and terminer started with an exemplar of particular brutality for which he had been present for much of the groundwork with the earlier commission of inquiry.

On the 28th of January 1451, Henry VI set out on a judicial progress, leading several thousand men, to show Kent men what traitors might expect. This was a high-powered commission, with two dukes, Somerset and Exeter, four earls, Shrewsbury, Arundel, Wiltshire, and Worcester, and six other lords.[15] Shrewsbury—in Shakespeare's Henry VI, 'valiant Lord Talbot, Earl of Shrewsbury, created, for his rare success in arms'—was a vigorous, tough man in his mid-sixties who had held much of France with small forces through his sheer ability and force of will.

A vivid but miserable picture of the commission can be built up from the Chronicles and Patent Rolls. Indeed, it cannot have been a joyous throng that followed the road to Canterbury in the depressing month of February. The King, notorious for repeatedly undermining his own authority with ill-earned pardons, was this time either in no mood for forgiveness or was forced by those senior peers around him to rein in his mercy. The focus of the progress was Canterbury—a doleful time for the Earl perhaps to renew the acquaintance of the monk Henry Cranebroke. On the 8th of February, 'the kynge went in to Kent to Caunterbury and sate and did grete justice upon tho that rose with the capteyne, and ther dyed viij [8] men upon a daye'.[16] The executed were allowed burial complete. 'And the dampnyde [condemned] men were drawe, hanggyde, and quarteryde, but they were pardonnyde to be buryde, bothe hyr quarters of hyr bodys and hyr heddys with alle.'[17] This might not seem too generous to those punished, particularly as they were not in a position to know about it—indeed burial entire may have had more to do with a surfeit of body parts than mercy—but for contemporaries, degradation after death was perceived as part of the punishment.

On the 9th of February men were agitating at Maidstone and Birling, trying to stir up the populace to ride to Canterbury and force the King to grant letters of pardon. It is possible that the retinues of the magnates were then essential in keeping order. In Rochester on the 15th of February, when returning to London, there were further executions. 'Ande at Rochester ix men were be-heddyd ..., and hyr heddys were sende unto London by the kyngys commaundement, and sette uppon London Brygge alle at one tyme'.[18]

At Blackheath, on or before the 23rd of February, the commission was met by the miserable spectacle of unpunished evildoers pleading for mercy: 'divers such rebels, naked to the middle, … prostrated themselves to the ground before the King through public streets, with cords bound round their necks, and prayed for pardon.'[19] This was a brutal episode, intended from the outset to make a powerful example to and of the men of Kent. There was much drawing, hanging, beheading and quartering of modest men driven to rebellion by misrule. The chronicler Gregory wrote, 'men calle hyt in Kente the harvyste of hedys.'[20]

Worcester was not solely involved in commissions intended collectively to repress rebels. On the 6th of April there was a commission to proceed in the indictment of John Trevelyan.[21] He was a Cornishman in an age when several notable ruffians came from that county and a member of the hated group around the late Duke of Suffolk that was attacked in doggerel: 'The Cornysshe Chowgh offt with his trayne hath made oure Eguile blynde.'[22] The chough was the bird emblem of Cornwall: the eagle was, improbably, Henry VI. The commission clearly did not wing the chough, for Trevelyan was a great survivor, living until 1494. One of his sons went on to become chaplain to Henry VIII.

In June Worcester was appointed to a high-powered commission of oyer and terminer to investigate the death of Suffolk.[23] At Tonbridge, on the 27th of June, Richard Lenard, Thomas Smyth and others were indicted for murder, and Lenard, 'oon of the lewdeste of the shippe', was accused of actually beheading Suffolk.[24] However, no one appears to have been punished, perhaps because of fears that investigating too closely would reveal an aristocratic conspiracy.[25] Shrewbury's will, witnessed by Worcester on the 1st of September 1452, showed he had a part interest in Suffolk's death ship, the *Nicholas of the Tower*.

On the 22nd of October there was a commission of oyer and terminer to look into the matter of Thomas Danyell, another of Suffolk's party.[26] After Suffolk's murder in 1450 he switched patrons to Somerset and was pardoned by the King. In 1451 he married Margaret, the sister of John Howard, the future Duke of Norfolk. He lived until around 1482 and caused mayhem in East Anglia for years. Well connected miscreants still thrived.

The repression of January and February in eastern Kent did not stop further unrest in western Kent and Sussex. There was also unfinished business in Wiltshire going back to the murder of the King's confessor, Bishop Ainscough, in June 1450. On the 20th of May Henry VI responded by issuing commissions to go into all the counties south of the Thames: Suffolk, Surrey, Sussex, Kent, Hampshire and Wiltshire.[27] The King again went with the commission to Kent and Sussex. Worcester's presence was confirmed on the indictments. On the 24th of June in Croydon the commission hanged a Henry Bedell from Thornham for his part in the April risings at Eastry and Brenchley.[28]

The commission spent the period from the 26th of June to the 1st of July at Tonbridge in Kent. A couple of indictments provide an extraordinary vision of a radicalised society, close to descending into levelling anarchy, where a dark surreal humour yet reigned (one is shown at the chapter beginning). Political agitation was degenerating into lawlessness. In October 1450 at Penshurst 130 men had carried out a massive poaching raid on the park of the Duke of Buckingham. The indictment of the 29th of June stated it was to be inquired whether 30 named people,

> with others unknown to the number of one hundred men in riotous manner and arrayed for war, viz. with jakkes [jacks], saledes [salets], brygandes [brigandines], breastplates, hauberks, cuirasses, lances, bows and arrows, and covered with long beards and painted on their faces with black charcoal, calling themselves servants of the queen of the fairies, intending that their names should not be known, broke into the park of Humprey, Duke of Buckingham, called 'Redeleff' at Penshurst and chased, killed and took away from the said park 10 bucks, 12 sores and 60 does belonging to the said Duke.[29]

All this riotous activity was 'against the King's peace and the form of the statute of parks and fish-ponds lately issued'.[30]

The session at Tonbridge was the beginning of another judicial progress through the south-east as the King took his justice in person to deal with a particularly rebellious area. The commission then proceeded in Sussex to Lewes (7th and 8th of July) and then Chichester (9th to 13th of July), Winchester (14th of July) and Salisbury (20th of July). The King punished those who had killed and despoiled the possessions of the Bishops Moleyns of Chichester and Aynscough of Salisbury.

Although not as bloody as the 'harvest of heads' this commission was brutal enough, with executions and much humiliating prostration required in exchange for pardons. At Chichester on the 12th of July William Page, who had taken part in the pillaging of Ainscough's valuables in June 1450, begged mercy of the King— successfully for there was later a 'pardon to William Page ... gentilman, who with others submitted to the King ..., stripped to the waist and prostrate to the ground before the King in the public streets'.[31]

This was the one time when Henry was notably harsh and it coincided with the Earl's involvement in the commissions, although Henry's steadfastness was probably connected more to the presence of Shrewsbury, a very hard man. Worcester, however, learnt that severity was required in certain situations. He also appears to have done his career prospects no harm at all by staying close to the King.

Intelligent men would have realised that disorder followed from the inadequacy of the King and his advisers and not from the wickedness of the people. Also, it was modest men who were paying the price. Many of those tried and condemned in 1451 were lower gentry and substantial farmers. Unlike the earlier Peasant's Revolt of 1381, the excuse could not be advanced that the King was inexperienced: indeed the child Richard II's behaviour had then been exemplary whereas now Henry VI was the same age as his father Henry V when the latter had become monarch and nearly three decades had passed since his birth, affording plentiful time to learn the art of kingship. The question thus posed was over Henry VI's very fitness to be the King at all. In addition, by the end of 1451 Worcester was an experienced commissioner. He may have reflected on the commissions to investigate Trevelyan and Danyell and wondered what was their point, given that such men not only survived but thrived? Perhaps there were better, more permanent, ways of dealing with well-connected miscreants than common law commissions?

The Earl of Worcester would die excoriated as 'the Butcher of England'. Very early in his public career he was a commissioner who was involved in, and a witness to, a series of brutal executions. Did this harden him beyond what could usually be expected of a man in his position and did he develop sadistic tendencies that could later be indulged under the cover of public duty? Would this make Worcester like Ser Maurizio da Milano who, in the early sixteenth century, was the Chancellor of the *Otto di Guardia*, the body of eight men responsible for safeguarding Florence's internal security? Ser was also named 'The Butcher' because he took such delight in tormenting men.[32] These questions cannot be fully answered yet but for now the point can be made that death, even if cruelly inflicted, was regarded as justified if the punishment fitted the crime—and the condemned could save their souls by the manner of their dying. The stern judge attracted no opprobrium if the sentence was appropriate. Both the judges and the public, who had suffered from the crimes of the sentenced, were expected to witness the execution of justice.

Men imposed and, with women and children, witnessed cruel sentences done for the communal good. This behaviour in the cause of justice was not, *by the standards of the time*, sadistic. Nothing that is known of the Earl's own behaviour in the next decade showed him as anything other than decent by the standards of the time and any psychological impact deriving from participation in the post-Cade repression must have been deep and suppressed if it existed at all.

Figure 4: Executions were close up and personal—as in this detail, from a later fifteenth century manuscript, showing the hanging of traitors. Witnesses stood near and priests accompanied the condemned men to safeguard their spiritual welfare. Their souls could be redeemed by accepting death in an appropriate state of contrition.[33]

On the 10th of June 1451, Worcester married for a second time. His new wife was a widow six years older than himself, Elizabeth, *née* Greyndour, the second wife and widow of Reginald West, Lord de la Warre, who died on the 27th of August in 1450. The Earl was still young at 24, and a wife, for the purpose of companionship and childbearing, must still have seemed desirable.

The Greyndours were a prosperous knightly family with a record of fighting in Wales. Elizabeth was an only child and her father Robert had died in 1443. She inherited a respectable estate and was financially more attractive because she was awarded a third of de la Warre's properties in dower to hold for her life. She was not, however, from an elite noble family.[34] Given the eligibility of the young earl, his choice revealed either that Elizabeth had considerable charms or that he did not wish to marry again into the top level of society.

It is only possible to speculate how the Earl and Elizabeth might have met. There were a couple of admittedly tenuous links. Firstly, Worcester's brother-in-law,

Sir Edmund Ingaldisthorpe, was the second cousin of Reginald West's first wife Margaret Thorley, as Edmund's and Margaret's mothers were de la Pole first cousins. Secondly, Sir John Barre, Elizabeth's stepfather, was the nephew of the Earl of Shrewsbury, with whom Worcester worked on the commissions in 1451. Another possibility was quite simply that Worcester and Elizabeth met while he was travelling in the vicinity while a commissioner of oyer and terminer in 1451. Reginald West was buried in Broadwater church in Sussex and she may have remained in the locality. Worcester could seem almost impetuous with his remarriages to women of modest noble station; in 1467, *en route* to Ireland, he unexpectedly married a widow with whom he had no known prior connection.

In 1451 the Earl of Worcester was enrolled as a Freeman of the Merchant Taylors, then the Company of Taylors and Linen-Armourers.[35] Linen was used to make the heavily padded garments worn beneath metal armour.[36] The Taylors were city elite. Henry VI, the Dukes of York (1434) and Norfolk (1438) and the Earl of Oxford (1434) were fellow freemen. Nearer in date and closer through ties of family and affinity were the Earl of Warwick (1452) and the Bishop of Ely, Thomas Bourchier (1444).[37] The banqueting space in their New Hall (since at least 1347) in Threadneedle Street could hold two hundred people. The young Earls of Worcester and Warwick and other nobles could attend dinners together and meet with the citizens of London.

Despite marriages and participation in many commissions the Earl of Worcester maintained his scholarly interest in classical studies, making him unique among the higher contemporary secular nobility. A correspondence of three letters survives between Worcester and the Canterbury monk Henry Cranebroke. The selected letters have been neatly transcribed onto a single sheet and must have been part of a larger exchange. The first, in Latin, was from Worcester to Henry Cranebroke, dated the 9th of January 1451.

> Well beloved brother, in your letters, which I received with delight, composed as they are with Ciceronian elegance, not common ermine. Again and again, sound advice, honourable suggestions and fatherly wisdom, flow from the sweet font of love. I fully understand, obliged on account of these, which should raise you to the height of honour, to desire deeply, to want, and to satisfy, and so in being thirsty, satisfied. As far as I have it in me to bring it about, that I should be able to push myself, and so I will show myself true by witness and examiner of the heart. Nevertheless, lest my unpolished pen or rather length of writing inflicts weariness, keep faith. To God and saint Thomas I commend you. Farewell. 9 January 1451.[38]

The letter is a short crescendo of slightly clumsy platitudes, which defy clear translation, written in an error-prone attempt at classical Latin. Perhaps at this time the Earl was trying to translate Cicero's *De Amicitia* from Latin to English. This translation lacks the facility of *The Declamacion of Noblesse* which was likely to have been contemporaneous with or following his studies in Italy. The circle around Fastolf, who was appointed to some of the same commissions as Worcester, had a particular interest in Cicero.

In April 1452 the Earl wrote a personal letter in English to Cranebroke, which is discussed above in the context of the death of his first wife the Duchess Cecily. There is an intriguing reference in this letter to a jewel: 'Right dere and enteerly beloued brother and frend, I haue put me … to cause you … to haue a sight of the Juel wich your corage hath whette so you to see, … exortyng you therefore to be of the liche corage and entent to the report of the manifolde, goodly, holesum and notable virtues'.[39] The context links the jewel to the one the Earl 'loved best' and, given the use of the past tense, this seems more likely to have been the dead Cecily than the still quick Elizabeth.

Remarkably, there is a famous mid-fifteenth century gem associated with the Nevilles and with childbirth—and Cecily was born a Neville and had been of childbearing age. In 1985 the Middleham Jewel, a gold lozenge-shaped pendant box on the top of which is affixed a 10-carat blue sapphire stone, was found on a bridle path near the northern Neville power base Middleham Castle. On the front

Figure 5: The Middleham Jewel associated with the Neville family. Was this, or something similar, the jewel that the Earl of Worcester, whose late wife was Cecily *née* Neville, lent to his correspondent the monk Henry Cranebroke?

and back are respectively images of the death and birth of Jesus. The imagery is generally associated with protection against the dangers of childbirth.

The Middleham Jewel has been connected to Neville women but not Cecily. Worcester certainly kept books of hers after her death, which may have been due to child-bearing complications, and might have retained other possessions as well. She may have owned the jewel, or one similar, for protection against the dangers of pregnancy and it is possible that after her death the Earl initially kept it and showed it to Cranebroke. But following the death in childbirth of his second wife it is plausible he had no use for, or perhaps even faith in, such a jewel and returned it to the Nevilles at Middleham where it was lost. This, of course, is speculation but might cast some light on the type of jewel referred to in the letter.

In 1451 John Manyngham, the Registrar of Oxford University from 1447 to 1451, dedicated to Worcester a manuscript known as Manyngham's 'Miscellany' which survives in Trinity College, Dublin.[40] This contains humanistic texts compiled by Manyngham connected to manuscripts given to Oxford by Humphrey, Duke of Gloucester.[41] Tiptoft's arms are found in one of the initials.[42] The dedication, whatever its precise date, made clear two things: the Earl was noted as interested in scholarship in the early 1450s and he had sufficient status to be worth dedicating material to that took no little effort and cost to produce.

The final surviving letter in the correspondence between Worcester and Henry Cranebroke is dated December 1452. The Earl probably met the monk at the coronation of Archbishop John Stafford that month and chided him for not writing. The monk, who presumably had more time than the Earl, wrote a rather longer letter than the two that survive from the Earl to him, in somewhat better but extremely deferential and wordy Latin. Cranebroke sounded intimidated by his friend's vertiginous elevation and was perhaps surprised the holder of so high an office wished to maintain his relationship with one so lowly. In the letter, much shortened here, the monk lamented:

> I was accused, deservedly, of the error of ingratitude. ... I was not directed [by] your most agreeable power, nevertheless, according to my smallness of greeting. ... law and nature, Christ, likewise all authorities condemn the ungrateful, they are lamented to be born. ... Therefore wherever my lord should be, in what manner you please in body ... situated, I will be present as a servant, ... always ... in monuments of letters, nor will I be absent in the heart's and labour's effect. ... The people's teacher, that most gentle Paul, ... said: 'For ye suffer fools gladly, seeing ye yourselves are wise [Cor. 11:19]'.[43]

Perhaps the most remarkable point was that so high an earl corresponded at all with a junior monk of Canterbury. It might reveal who the Earl really trusted and felt comfortable with—monks and scholars. It is also hard to accuse a man of snobbery who had such friends. Cranebroke may have been immensely proud of his friendship, and of this letter, for it is the only one that he wrote to the Earl which he copied into his note book.

By the second half of 1451 the political pressures caused by the 1450 Cade rebellion, the return of York, the suppression of Cade and of further uprisings seemed resolved. The Earl had remarried and by the end of the year his second wife would be pregnant. But politically and militarily the underlying situation was deteriorating. On the 30th of June 1451 Bordeaux surrendered to the French and three weeks later the loss of Bayonne marked the end of over 250 years of English rule in Gascony where Worcester nominally held the great Gournay estate.

Early in the new year of 1452 simmering tensions at the highest level between the bloodlines of John of Gaunt threatened to fracture the peace. Summoned to the Lancastrian stronghold of Coventry, York demurred, perhaps fearing similar treatment to that which had awaited Gloucester in 1447. On the 9th of February the King called up his nobles and knights, including Worcester, under the guise of preparing to contest a French siege of Calais. In reality he was preparing for a showdown with York who would be confronted with overwhelming force.[44]

The same month saw a rising in Stamford in Lincolnshire where the conspirators were accused of plotting the King's removal in support of York. York and Devon had gathered forces and evaded those of the King but having found the City of London closed they retreated to Dartford in Kent. The King was joined by most of his great nobles, including the Dukes of Exeter, Norfolk and Buckingham and the Earls of Salisbury, Shrewsbury, Wiltshire, Warwick and Worcester. The Duke of York was supported only by the Earl of Devon and Lord Cobham.

By the 2nd of March both Henry and York faced each other at the heads of large armies. A settlement was negotiated between the King and York by the Earls of Salisbury and Warwick, and the Bishops of Winchester and Ely. York was to disband his forces in return for the arrest of Somerset. Arbitrators, including Worcester, were appointed to reach agreement between Somerset and York. York did disband and found himself, with Devon and Cobham, effectively captured. Henry refused the Queen's demand to arrest York but similarly failed to arrest Somerset. In St Paul's Cathedral, York swore 'that he had never rebelled against the King and would not rebel against him in the future'. He retired to his stronghold at Ludlow and could only watch as a trail of repression followed in May from Kent to his Midlands power base.

1451 and 1452 was a time of bitter political turmoil into which Worcester was drawn as a potential combatant, an arbitrator, and a commissioner executing bloody justice, as well as a time of intense personal lows and highs involving marriage and death and hoped-for fatherhood. Political crisis and personal tragedy were coterminous in the Earl's life and perhaps became identified in his mind, resulting, through association, in a deep, possibly subconscious, animosity towards those who fomented disorder—and a determination to deal severely, and, if necessary, pre-emptively, with them.

Chapter 5

Treasurer and councillor – 1452 to 1453

The foresaid very noble and magnificent Lord John of Worcester, the illustrious Earl, great Treasurer of England, explained to the foresaid very reverend father in Christ [Archbishop Kemp], and reverend fathers and other prelates and clergy gathered together there as previously mentioned, in his crystal-clear vernacular, the threatening dangers of the commonwealth of this once very famous and flourishing realm, in a solemn and elegant speech devised and delivered to them with great sharpness of mind.[1]

> The 25-year-old Treasurer, the Earl of Worcester,
> fundraising at Convocation in 1453

The Earl of Worcester was made Treasurer, the most important office usually held by a secular noble, on the 15th of April 1452.[2] At 24, he was the same age as William Pitt when Pitt was appointed in 1783 to the office of prime minister, which had evolved from that of treasurer. Contemporaries were struck by his youth. Reports of his appointment spread as far as Italy for in 1460 the humanist Ludovico Carbone declaimed, in his eulogy for Guarino da Verona, whose school in Ferrara Worcester would attend, that the Earl 'imitated his father's wisdom in the 25th year of his life, that before him it happened that no-one [at that age] had merited to be created great Treasurer of England, which is held out to be the highest honour among the English, second only to the King'.[3] Carbone, as a proficient public speaker, doubtless sought briefings from the Earl's colleagues.

Accepting the appointment certainly meant jumping in at the deep end. The Treasury was one of the oldest, largest and most complex administrative bodies in England; it was also in desperate straits. Due to constant disorder, revenues had collapsed when the young earl took charge. In the financial year ending during the third quarter of 1447 income was £117,504; in 1447–48 it was £67,341; 1448–49, £76,450; 1449–50, £81,090; and 1450–51, £77,466. In the year that Worcester took over revenues had fallen to £37,678.[4]

Given the parlous state of the kingdom's finances, and the need to raise funds for an expensive campaign to recover Normandy and Gascony, which had been completely lost in August 1450 and June 1451 respectively, why was the appointment of this very young man made? Worcester may have showed himself to be exceptionally able and persuasive at court and on commissions. His time at

Oxford, later in age and longer in time than any other secular medieval aristocrat, may have reflected the nascent understanding—by senior nobles and councillors and maybe the King who prized learning—that a more educated aristocracy was required better to fit such roles. The need for new blood was pressing after the territorial losses in France and the breakdown of order in England seen not only in Cade's rebellion and the showdown with York but also magnate feuds that had become openly violent. In September 1451 the Talbots had taken from the Berkeleys their castle, and in Devonshire the Earl of Devon besieged the Bonvilles's Powderham Castle.

Worcester's appointment was possibly agreed by the King, his main councillor, the Duke of Somerset, and the old but still vigorous Earl of Shrewsbury who was about to lead an expedition to recover lost territories in France and who needed to be confident it would be properly resourced. The four men had worked together recently on the commissions of oyer and terminer and the Earl doubtless impressed with his diligence, loyalty and zeal. Worcester would witness Shrewsbury's will on the 1st of September 1452 and the old warrior likely made it a condition of his leading the campaign to recover Gascony that there was a man he could trust at the Treasury. He knew Worcester had a huge vested incentive in the campaign's success, for the new Treasurer hoped to recover very substantial lands there. The loss of the Gascon Gournay estates still rankled. On the 20th of August 1450 there had been a 'grant to the Earl of Worcester, of the lordships … of Gosse, Seignanx, Maremne, Marensin, Born, Mimizan … Brassenx, Saubusse, Pontonx-sur-l'Adour … PouyPouy …. Oeyregave, Saint-Geours-d'Auribat, Sabres, Laharie, Labouheyre, which … are now in the hands of the King's adversaries'.[5] On the 14th of April 1451 it was optimistically determined that the Earl would be allowed to enjoy his estates. 'Order to the … king's officers to permit John Tiptoft, Earl of Worcester, … to have these aforementioned lordships and enjoy them in perpetuity without impediment … *after they will be conquered by the King's force.*'[6]

Generally, new blood was sought to get a grip on finances. In March 1452 John Sutton, Lord Dudley, was made Treasurer of the royal household in place of Lord Stourton. Dudley was the father of Worcester's brother-in-law Edmund. There is one contemporary comment by William of Wyrcester which makes the event sound like a coup. 'John Lord Beauchamp was expelled from the Treasury of England and John Tiptoft Earl of Worcester substituted in his place.'[7] William often added illuminating biographical details relating to the Earl, as he does when reporting the Earl's sudden remarriage in 1467 or Edward's initial displeasure over the execution of the Earl of Desmond in 1468. Therefore his use of the word '*expulsus*' carries weight. That said, Beauchamp had overseen a disastrous fall in revenue, albeit in challenging times. As consolation he received £400 for his services.[8]

The young Worcester was now referred to in the grandest terms, although the sense of exaltedness might be somewhat lost in translation. The Register of Archbishop Kemp called him 'the very noble and magnificent Lord John of Worcester, the illustrious Earl, great Treasurer of England'.[9] Henry Cranebroke, awed by the elevation of his friend, wrote to 'the most remarkable and most dread lord, lord John, Earl of Worcester, the faithful Treasurer, of the English Kingdom, from Henry, the most insignificant of God's flock'.[10]

Worcester was appointed Treasurer three times—in 1452, 1462 and 1470—all times when additional income was required for military operations, so his role merits examination. The Treasury was the most powerful and prestigious of all royal offices, responsible for raising and securing revenue. The Treasurer was its chief officer with a staff of over 100. Treasurers came and went, kings were crowned and deposed but the Treasury, managed by highly experienced civil servants with a lively sense of their own importance, maintained an annual routine split into Easter and Michaelmas terms, roughly corresponding to the second and third quarters and to the fourth and first quarters of the year.

The Treasury was situated in the north-east and north-west wings of Westminster Hall. The former contained the Receipt where money was handed over to be counted and was recorded in writing and on tallies or cleft sticks. The latter held the Audit and the Court of the Exchequer where its barons sat as a law court, and settled financial disputes between the Crown and taxpayers.

The Treasurer, rather like a modern minister, was an external political appointee, usually holding the post for two or three years and generally from the middle but well-connected secular nobility. The Chancellor of the Exchequer was the chief officer under the Treasurer. When, by the eighteenth century, the office of the Treasurer became known as the Prime Minister, the Chancellor was recognised as the head of the Treasury. The Auditor's function was to certify monies received. The Remembrancer compiled the memorandum rolls and thus 'reminded' the Barons of the Exchequer of business pending. The Pipe Rolls were the responsibility of the Clerk of the Treasurer. They were the records of the yearly audits of the accounts and payments presented to the Treasury by the sheriffs and other royal officials. The various sheets or membranes were joined and rolled for storage. The rolls, along with the Domesday Book and other records, were kept in the Treasury for daily reference (the earliest date from the twelfth century and the series would extend to 1833).

In good times a young man of 24, even an aristocrat in a hierarchical society, might face formidable managerial challenges imposing his authority over experienced and tough older officials who had long developed expectations as to job security and promotion. Like in any other venerable but powerful organisation

Figure 6: Court of the Exchequer from a law treatise of the mid-1450s. The court is presided over by the Lord High Treasurer—at this time the Earl of Worcester—and the Barons of the Exchequer.[11]

Plan 1: Westminster Palace – where the Earl of Worcester worked as Treasurer, Councillor and Lord Steward of the Household and where he was condemned to death in 1470.

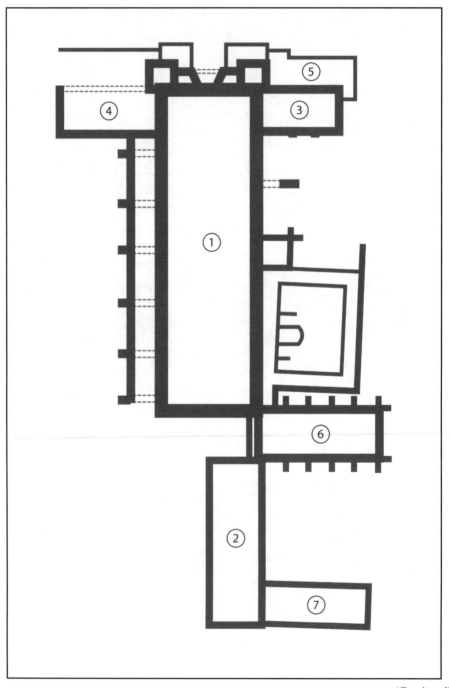

(Continued)

(Continued)

1.	The Great Hall
2.	The Lesser or White Hall – site of the trials of the Earl of Worcester (1470) and Perkin Warbeck (1499), both sentenced to death by the 13th Earl of Oxford
3.	Receipt of the Exchequer – the Earl of Worcester was Treasurer in 1452–55, 1462–3 and 1470
4.	Exchequer Audit and Court
5.	Star Chamber – where the council often met
6.	St Stephen's Chapel
7.	Painted Chamber – where the House of Lords met

inevitably there were office politics, exacerbated at this time by vicious court infighting. A flavour of such fifteenth century politics might be gleaned from piecing together the fallout from the displacement of Thomas Thorpe, who had been the Remembrancer since 1444 and was well-connected to the Beaufort family. His office was in the gift of the Treasurer and on appointment in April 1452 Worcester switched Richard Forde to it from the Office of the Pipe. It says a lot about the remarkable self-confidence of the young Earl that he peremptorily removed someone as experienced, connected and cantankerous as Thorpe to put in his own man. The furious Thorpe complained to Somerset, but Forde could not be dislodged, perhaps due to the Earl's backing, so Thorpe demanded the role of 3rd Baron of the Exchequer. Forde arranged that the incumbent Baron, Sir William Fallan, would resign on receiving from Forde a bond to pay Fallen forty marks yearly for life. On the 2nd of December 1452 Thorpe was duly made 3rd Baron. In 1455 Forde petitioned Parliament that he was impoverished and successfully requested that the requirement to pay the forty marks be voided, so the unfortunate Fallan lost both position and pension.

As Treasurer the young Earl was appointed *ex-officio* to the royal council. At Westminster this met in the Star Chamber which, conveniently, was adjacent to the Receipt of the Exchequer. The council advised the King on administrative and judicial matters. Its range of tasks was huge, and regular members, of which the Earl proved one, gained a deep insight into the functioning or malfunctioning of the realm. The Treasurer had a particularly demanding role as finance lay at the core of most problems. 'Subjects appealed to the council to authorise payments, allow sums in accounts, grant licences or enquire into all manner of grievances; money was often short and arrangements had to be made to borrow, to satisfy creditors and pacify unpaid garrisons; the terms of service of commanders, the sustenance of troops and the details of diplomatic negotiation were discussed.'[12] The core council was, effectively, a professional body and in practice the bulk of the work was done by a small number of experienced men. Worcester rapidly made himself one of these.

The Earl first attended the Council on the 19th of May 1452 and soon established a record of high attendance. Between the 22nd of March 1450 and the 29th of August 1453, Cardinal Kemp, Chancellor, attended on 38 occasions, followed by Worcester, who was appointed late in the period, on 25.[13] The Earl now had a substantial income: the Treasurer's wages were 500 marks and an earl councillor received a further 200 marks (a mark was two-thirds of a pound).

In the month of Worcester's appointment the council oversaw a period of repression that followed on from further unrest. At the end of the first week of May there had been a rising in Kent led by one John Wylkyns. The response was immediate, with a commission of oyer and terminer formed under Shrewsbury, who had led notably tough commissions in 1451. The commission was appointed on the 11th of May and sat at Dartford from the 12th to the 16th. The Earl of Shrewsbury 'rode into Kent, and set up five pair of gallows, and did execution upon John Wylkyns, taken and brought to the town as for captain, and with other mo [sic], of the which eight-and-twenty were hanged and beheaded; the which heads were sent to London. And London said there should no mo heads be set up on there'.[14]

Worcester was appointed to a major commission of oyer and terminer on the 6th of July which was to accompany the King through the southwest from Wiltshire to Devonshire and Cornwall and then on to the west Midlands.[15] It was subsequently extended to include Wales.[16] The commission's purpose was to put down insurrection and to send a message to York and his supporters. This was the largest and longest commission of the reign, consisting of fifteen lords and six justices headed by the Dukes of Buckingham and Somerset and the Earls of Warwick, Worcester and Wiltshire. The circuit took in the Tiverton and Ludlow homes of the Earl of Devon and the Duke of York. This commission met up with the great progress of the King that had started earlier from Eltham on the 23rd of June 1452. Given Worcester's treasury duties his attendance, if he was present at all, was likely to have been curtailed.

Again personal tragedy struck the Earl of Worcester, at a time of commissions. The Earl's second wife Elizabeth must have been heavily pregnant at the time of the royal progress, which returned to Eltham on the 6th of September. The *inquisition* after the death of a tenant-in-chief to establish what lands the deceased had held—reported that Elizabeth died on the 1st of September 1452 and John, Elizabeth and Worcester's son, died on the same day. Her nearest heir was Joanna, her father's sister. It was not, however, until the brief return to the throne, called the Readeption, of Henry VI in 1470–71 that information emerged explaining how Worcester retained, in his lifetime, his second wife's property: 'The said late Earl took the said Elizabeth to wife, and they had issue, one John, who afterwards died without heir of his body, and the said Elizabeth survived him and died so seised [had ownership] without heir of her body, after whose death the said late Earl entered into the premises [held her estates], for term of his life by *the courtesy of England*, and died seised thereof.'[17] Such tenancy was the practice of English law, which gave a husband the holding, in his lifetime, of the lands of his wife from the moment when a child capable of inheriting the land from the wife was 'born and heard to cry within the four walls'. This holding endured even if the child died before the wife or if the husband remarried.

Now, one might wonder if there was not sharp practice suppressed during the life of the Earl that only emerged after he was executed. A child 'capable of inheriting the land' does not sound like one who died the day it was born. The Greyndour family must have been unhappy that the estates would not be returned to it until after the death of a healthy 25-year-old man. There was, however, evidence of a continuing relationship between the Greyndour relatives and the Earl which lasted until his death. In 1455 Elizabeth's mother Joanna Greyndour established a chantry chapel and the souls of the dead prayed for included Elizabeth, sometime Countess of Worcester, and her first husband, Reginald. But there was no mention of the soul of the dead baby.[18] After his return, however, from the Holy Land and Italy Worcester appeared to be much more involved in advancing his late wife's family.[19] Even if he continued to hold the estate until his death it might have been in the Greyndour interest to be associated, in troubled times, with an important earl close to the King.

Within a little over three years Worcester's stepdaughter, his first wife, his second wife and their child had died. His own early life had been singularly free of family tragedy. All his sisters and his father's known wards appear to have survived and they had many children. The Earl had long been spared relatives' untimely death until it rapidly mowed down all of those for whom he was responsible.

When death was viewed as the judgement of God, Worcester may have seen himself as cursed for some sin known, suspected or hidden. He threw himself into work, making the most of being the youngest Treasurer and became the most consistent presence on the council. And then, when political change meant his service was no longer called for or he no longer felt able to provide it, he went on a pilgrimage, perhaps intended earlier and of necessity delayed, to gain redemption. When, in the later 1460s, he remarried his third wife, this seems almost to have been on impulse, before doubts could take hold, and in very different circumstances, *en route* to Ireland where he would make a new start.

The years of Worcester's two short marriages from 1449 to 1452 coincided with revolt and repression. That so eligible a widower with so many attractive qualities—who must have been a hugely desirable catch for any lady of the Court—did not remarry for fifteen years reveals how deep these deaths cut. Unrest and dissent threatened not just the state: they had cruelly detached the Earl from spouses when they needed each other most, therefore conditioning him ruthlessly to repress rebels. Woes betided those who, in future, disturbed good order.

On the 1st of September 1452, the same day as Elizabeth's death, Shrewsbury, who was about to lead an army to recover Gascony, made a will, presciently, it turned out, as he was killed in France the next year. Worcester was the only non-clerical executor who did not belong to Shrewsbury's family, possibly indicating an unexpectedly close link between the 25-year-old Treasurer and the old warrior four decades his senior. [20]

The death of the Archbishop of Canterbury, John Stafford, on the 25th of May 1452 resulted in his replacement by John Kemp, who was in his mid-70s and uncertain to live much longer but with the merit of being no supporter of York. There are two sources for the coronation ceremony: Prior Stone's Chronicle and the Register of Kemp.[21] Both described Worcester's presence at the centre of events. That of Stone recounted: 'And when [Kemp] arrived at the entrance to the church, he was received there by the prior and convent in white copes, with the response *Sint lumbi* [Luke 12:35] … . And with the Archbishop came the Bishop of London, the Earl of Worcester … .'[22]

The (unpublished and untranslated) Register of Archbishop Kemp also noted the prominent presence of the '*domino Johanne Wygorni comite illustri*' or the illustrious John Earl of Worcester.[23] Throughout his life the Earl of Worcester displayed a remarkable ability to be near to the centre of great events, including religious coronations. He was close to the Archbishops of Canterbury at their enthronements in 1452 and 1455. He was also seated at the select high table for the feast at the enthronement of George Neville as Archbishop of York in 1465. He was a man who relished ceremony and instinctively grasped its importance to networking and projecting authority.

Worcester, again a widower, might have spent Christmas with the King and Queen at Greenwich, for the Queen gave rings to his servants.[24] Others whose servants were so recognised included Somerset, the Archbishop of Canterbury, Exeter, York, the Duchess of Suffolk and the Bishop of Winchester. The presence of Alice de la Pole is intriguing for it indicates that the selection was not based purely on political etiquette.[25]

On the 1st of February 1453 Lord Cromwell had recorded an exemplification, witnessed by Worcester, establishing the falsity of supposed accusations of treason made by a priest Robert Colynson. Shortly after the execution of John Wylkyns at Dartford in May 1452 Colynson had accused Cromwell of treason on the basis of statements he said Wylkyns made to him in confession before his death. Cromwell established that Wylkyns had already made his confession to a priest on the boat coming down to Dartford from The Tower. Cromwell also revealed Colynson's disreputable past, his expulsion from Cambridge for an unpriestly life and seditious sermons, his womanising, fraud and general evil living. Cromwell was cleared but the fact he had been forced to defend himself at all before the King and council against charges made by a man so discredited underlined the sad state of the kingdom.[26]

Despite the bad blood between them, Worcester and Thomas Thorpe did a remarkable job fundraising. The latter, both a Treasury Baron and the elected Speaker, worked on the secular Commons, while the former wooed the Convocation of Canterbury, the assembly of the province's bishops, deans, archdeacons, abbots and diocesan proctors. The clergy, as a separate estate of the realm, could not be taxed through Parliament and had to be tickled separately into stumping up the funds. The young Earl led the charm offensive. The Convocation that met in February 1453 is extremely well documented in the Register of Archbishop Kemp. This contains a fascinating and revealing description of the impact of Worcester on an audience. He emerges as a skilled and persuasive speaker. Convocation met at St Paul's on the 7th of February and was addressed by the Treasurer three days later. The delegation was led by the one-time brothers-in-law, the Earls of Worcester and Warwick. Here Worcester was dominant. Indeed, although the two Earls were nearly the same age and it is now Warwick who is the better known, it was Worcester who first made his mark. The Register set the scene:

> When that day and hour arrived, the noble, famous and magnificent lords Richard of Warwick, John of Worcester, illustrious earls, as well as [other named] outstanding and very powerful men … entered the foresaid chapter-house, and having made, at their first entrance, mutual greetings, back and forth, as is the custom of this kind ….[27]

Worcester made a speech in English (described in the quote at the chapter beginning) in which he drew the attention of Convocation to the great threat posed to the realm by its enemies and requested a subsidy for the expedition to France led by Shrewsbury.

> With the lord's consent, begging and imploring the same prelates and clergy, moreover, from his heart, [aid for] the very famous, very powerful and magnificent prince, the illustrious Earl of Shrewsbury, leader of the royal army in parts of Aquitaine, which he had recently seized from the hands of the very hostile and very factious French, and returned successfully to obedience to our most serene Lord the King.[28]

The Archbishop of Canterbury responded positively and the appeal was success-ful. The Canterbury Convocation voted the government tenths, a tax assessed at ten per cent of the value of moveable goods, as did that of York.[29] The clerics, most of whom would have known the Earl's father, were won over by the elegant elo-quence of this patriotic young man.

Apart from raising money from Convocation the Earl dipped heavily into his own pocket. 'The Treasurers of England could not easily escape the unwritten obligation on them to contribute some of their personal wealth to the exchequer when they were seeking to persuade others to lend: ... at the height of the Gascon crisis in 1453, the Earl of Worcester found £2,300.'[30]

The relentless round of commissions of oyer and terminer continued.[31] Already these had covered the whole of the south, southwest and West Midlands. There were a couple of commissions to a single county, Buckinghamshire, and the ever-unstable Kent. Worcester was appointed a member of all these commis-sions, each of which was led by Somerset. It is unlikely, however, that he was much present given his treasury duties, but he was very much identified with the King's party.

On the 8th of January the progress of the commission of oyer and terminer, headed by the King, was extended to cover the East Midlands and East Anglia. On the same day a further commission was appointed, this time led by three dukes and three earls, including Worcester.[32] The royal progress started at Greenwich a month later and proceeded through Essex, Suffolk, Norfolk, and back to Suffolk, stopping at Berkhamstead Castle.

The King arrived at Reading to open Parliament in the refectory of the great abbey on the 6th of March. That day the Commons petitioned Henry to declare his half-brothers Edmund, Earl of Richmond, and Jasper, Earl of Pembroke, to be his legitimate siblings. The King consented in an event to which Worcester was recorded as a witness.[33] Thomas Thorpe was appointed Speaker two days later. Worcester was again appointed a trier of petitions for Gascony and the other lands overseas.

The Earl presented a budget statement at the beginning of this parliament which provided him the first opportunity. A reference in the records of the Privy Council for November 1453 noted the following: 'Remembering also many and divers declarations made in parliament before this time by the Treasurers of England as Lords Cromwell, Sudeley, Saye, the Bishop of Carlisle and the lord Beauchamp and others, and especially by the right noble lord, the Earl of Worcester, current Treasurer of England, in the last parliament of the state of this land.'[34] The disclosure of improving finances influenced the Commons' generosity in taxation grants in the first session of parliament.[35] Worcester could have pointed out a massive recovery in revenues. In November 1452 to March 1453 revenue was £38,675 compared with £18,738 in the previous six months and £18,940 in the half year before that.[36] The Commons, presided over by Thomas Thorpe, authorised the enlistment and payment for six months of 20,000 archers on the 18th of March.[37]

Parliament continued in session until the 28th of March in Reading and was then adjourned and reopened in Westminster between the 25th of April and the 2nd of July. These sessions must have been more confident in spirit as Shrewsbury was recovering ground in Gascony and in England the King was showing greater vigour in enforcing law and order.

In this period much Council time was taken up with organising the trial by combat, before the King, between John Lyalton and Robert Norreys, men otherwise hardly known to history, after the former accused the latter of treason. The Council, with the Treasurer present, recorded that 'It was therefore necessary that the sheriffs of London should be directed to gravel and sand the place, to erect a scaffold for the King, and to make lists and barriers for the battle; and that the serjeant of the King's armoury should be commanded to provide armour and weapons for the combatants.'[38] Later Lyalton, the appellant, petitioned 'for a tent or pavilion for the day of battle, and that Clampard the smith might be commanded to deliver to him such weapons as were necessary'.[39] Both appellant and defendant were assigned an armourer and painter at royal expense.

There is no record of the duel ever being fought so Lyalton and Norreys were possibly reconciled and returned to appropriate obscurity.[40] In 1453 the council had to waste time organising Clampard and others, at royal expense, so a duel could be fought between two comparative nobodies when it was trying to restore control of Gascony in France and law and order in England. Earlier, Cromwell had gone to inordinate effort to clear his name against accusations from a rogue like Colynson. There was something rotten in the state of England under Henry VI and Worcester was an ever-present witness. It is hard not to believe that the Earl must have seen such duels as a ridiculous distraction and come to think that there must be more efficient ways than unfought trials by combat for determining the result of accusations of treason.

In 1215 the Fourth Lateran Council had banned the participation of the clergy in ordeals (which included trial by combat) as mere men must not demand that God arbitrate their affairs. In England ordeal was largely replaced by trial by jury but, increasingly rarely, there were combats. The last certain one in England was that in 1446, described above, between William Catour and York's armourer John Daveys, who had been accused of calling his master the rightful king of England. The unfortunate Daveys lost and was hanged and his body burnt.

Despite the promising start to the Gascon campaign, the defeat and death of the Earl of Shrewsbury at the Battle of Castillon on the 17th of July 1453 finally ended England's pretensions in France. Shrewsbury's death had implications for English politics. He had played a central part in the suppression of the rebellion in Kent in 1451 and 1452 and generally made Henry VI act with some backbone. Although rash he was an exceptionally able and decisive commander and, had he been in control, the outcome of the 1455 campaign that culminated in the House of Lancaster's defeat at St Albans might have been quite different. His death probably emboldened York and contributed to Henry VI's increasing sense of ineffectiveness and despair.

From the 2nd of July to the 12th of November Parliament was adjourned. July and August conciliar warrants (written council orders) showed Worcester was a constant presence providing continuity. The warrants survive for nine days of July, of which the Treasurer was absent for two, and for ten days of August when he was present throughout.[41]

On the 20th of July 1453 a letter was sent from the King, chasing up money which was due but that had not been sent to the Treasurer and was needed for Gascony (news rendering it superfluous, due to defeat at Castillon, would not arrive for some time).[42] On the last day of July the King wrote to the ports of England requesting help to resupply Shrewsbury.[43] Worcester had delivered as Treasurer: unfortunately it was already 'game over' in Gascony. Meanwhile, in the vacuum created by her husband's inadequacy, the Queen, Margaret of Anjou, sought to establish herself as an independent force. On the 21st of July 1453 a major charter of privileges, allowing her autonomous administration of her estate, was granted to the Queen, witnessed by the Earl of Worcester.[44]

The council membership became increasingly compact in July as the ineffectual king first sought to impress his authority and then approached breakdown. The principle attendees were the Treasurer, Worcester, the Chancellor, Kemp, and the Keeper of the Privy Seal, Bishop Waynflete, as well as Somerset, the Prior of St Johns, the Dean of St Severin, Lord Dudley and Thomas Thorpe. 'In the summer of that year, a small body, resembling a modern cabinet, met regularly until the King's collapse and dealt with business both routine and political.'[45] The council now was becoming the only source of authority. By default its regular members potentially had great power.

On the 27th of July the King started on another campaign of law enforcement to try to exert his authority over warring magnates. On his way west to deal with the dispute between Somerset and Warwick, at the royal palace of Clarendon near Salisbury, he experienced a complete mental collapse.

In 1452 two events took place which changed the direction of Worcester's political and personal life. In April he was appointed Treasurer. He had been taken into the heart of government at a time when the King would become totally incapable and a new system had to be developed. Then in September 1452 his second wife and son died. This meant he could become the government servant *par excellence* – always ready and available to serve. The wife of that great royal servant of the next century Thomas Cromwell died in 1528 before he assumed office under Henry VIII and he never remarried.

Despite his youth and lack of experience in office the Earl demonstrated that he could assume the highest responsibility at a time of great political and personal stress. Shrewsbury's campaign did not fail because it was inadequately funded from England. Even if antagonistic to each other, the Treasurer, Worcester, and the Exchequer Baron and Commons speaker, Thomas Thorpe, performed prodigies in extracting funds from Parliament and Convocation. The campaign collapsed as the old but vigorous Shrewsbury had become an anachronism, blasted to pieces by the French field artillery of the Bureau brothers. The achievement of the Earl was, however, not forgotten. In both 1462 and 1470, when Edward IV faced invasion, Worcester was again put in charge of the Treasury.

Chapter 6

'Triumvir' and Sea Keeper – 1453 to 1455

Therle of Woryster moved hit was thowht to hym nessessarye and full expedient to all the Lords that shuld take uppon theme the sayd charge to have knolege of the execyone of theire power and to ffyend meanes how such charges as rest upon the Kinge shuld nowe be borne. Also in which wes the Lords of the counsell shuld nowe be contentyd of theire duety and as for hym selfe he wold be ready to doo such servyse to the Kinge as he could.[1]

Minute of the Great Council of April 1454
considering York's Protectorship

In July 1453 King Henry suffered a complete mental breakdown, rendering him effectively incapable of movement and communication. England had coped with minorities and absent kings—if not always very well—but had no precedent for a completely non-functioning adult monarch. This added a further governance challenge when the system was already hugely stressed due to defeat overseas and magnate feuds at home. One man was consistently at the centre of government as Treasurer and councillor throughout this period: the Earl of Worcester.

The madness of Henry VI is often attributed to his grandfather, the French King Charles VI. But their madnesses were completely different. The French King experienced many bouts of lunacy extending over several decades: that of Henry VI lasted for less than eighteenth months and although subsequently he was often feeble he was not again mad. Also, Charles's madness evinced itself in violence so wild that, on its first occasion, he killed several of his retinue. Later he was convinced he was made of glass or that he was, unpatriotically, St George. He was often highly mobile, rushing through the Hôtel Saint-Pol in Paris, necessitating the bricking up of doors. Henry VI was absolutely none of these things. He sat immobile and passive, unable to recognise his family or courtiers. He would not even understand that his wife had given birth to a child. It is also worth considering that Charles VI's other English descendants through his daughter Catherine showed no sign of madness. Jasper and Edmund, her other sons, were completely sane. The clinical sanity of Edmund's own son, Henry VII, was almost overdone.

Henry VI's condition does not sound like inherited mania but the absolute, indeed almost rational, breakdown of a man who had been king for as long as he could remember, locked in a role for over three decades for which he was quite unsuited but out of which the only escape was abdication, death, or mental collapse. Henry's mind appears to have taken the last option.

Weak, then non-existent, kingship meant the period was troubled by constant disputes between magnates who refused to obey the Council's instructions and to appear before it. There were three conflicts that particularly threatened to rip the realm apart (excluding the chronic hatred between Somerset and York).

The first magnate dispute, between the Neville and Percy families, pushed the former towards the Duke of York. In 1452, William Percy was made Bishop of Carlisle, a position usually held by a Neville. As tensions rose Thomas Percy, Lord Egremont, the younger son of the Earl of Northumberland, armed his retainers. The Earl of Salisbury, Richard Neville, complained to Henry VI about the Percys but the King's summons was ignored three times by Egremont, explained by justifiable fears he would be attacked by Salisbury's aggressive son John Neville. On the 24th of August Egremont attacked the wedding party of another Neville son, Thomas, and Cromwell's heiress, Maud Stanhope, furious that she had brought manors to the Nevilles once owned by the Percys. The resulting skirmish at Heworth Moor proved remarkably free of fatalities but marked the first fighting of the Wars of the Roses.

The second dispute was between Nevilles and Beauforts. On the 21st of July Henry presided over a council at Sheen to deal with the dispute over Despenser lands in Glamorgan where Warwick threatened property that should have gone to Beaufort's wife, Eleanor *née* Beauchamp.

The third was between Holland and Plantagenet. The 2nd Duke of Exeter had distrusted his unstable son, Henry Holland. Before his death he ensured Henry was made a ward of York who, on the 30th of July 1447, had married the 17-year-old to Anne of York, his eldest surviving daughter. The 3rd Duke of Exeter developed a profound dislike for his father-in-law whom he blamed for his unhappy marriage.

These disputes provide a key as to why the Nevilles switched loyalty between Dartford in 1452 and the 1st Battle of St Albans in 1455, changing the balance of power between Lancaster and York. Such shifts would also test Worcester's allegiances. He had been elevated and favoured by the obviously incompetent Lancastrian king but was closely linked by blood and marriage to York and the Nevilles.

These disputes involved the top nobility but, generally, conflicts between regionally powerful nobles were endemic, undermining law and order across the country. For example, there were conflicts in the West Country between the

Courtenay Earls of Devon and the Bonvilles, and between the Berkeleys and the Lisles; and in East Anglia, between the Mowbrays, de la Poles, Cromwells and Pastons. Worcester would have seen the constant flouting by nobles of orders from the King and from the Council. He cannot have enjoyed the impotence of the body of which he was a leading member.

In October 1453 events took place which changed the political dynamic and reversed the positions of Somerset and York. On the 8th of the month a small group of Council members, which did not include Worcester, decided to call a Great Council, having failed to impose their authority on feuding magnates who were ignoring summonses. York was not invited. Five days later Queen Margaret gave birth to a son, Edward, meaning York was no longer heir presumptive and was possibly perceived as not so great a threat to the court party.

On the 23rd of October another Council meeting, with Worcester present, issued an invitation to York to attend the Great Council. There were five bishops and three other secular lords in attendance. Worcester's absence at the meeting on the 8th of October and his presence on the 23rd implies that he had a pivotal role in making sure his cousin York was invited. Sir Thomas Tyrell was told to inform York that the council intended 'to sette rest and union betwixt the lords of this lande. And for asmuch as there hath bee and yit it is supposed is variance betwixt hym [York] and sum other of the lords'.[2] The Council was pre-empting a change in the balance of power: with the King mad and Shrewsbury dead, York might anyway have felt emboldened to move on London in force were he not invited to come in peace. But with hindsight it is possible to see York's summons as a key step on the road to the 1st Battle of St Albans as it forced open the breach between York and Somerset.

At the Great Council on the 21st of November 1453 York swore he was the King's true man, as recorded in an exemplification at his request, 'in the Sterred Chambre, being present the lordes, the Cardinal Archbisshop of Caunterbury … Worcestre, Tresourer of England … The Duc of York reherced unto the seid lordes that he was the Kinges true liegeman and subgit.'[3] At the same meeting Norfolk presented articles of accusation against Somerset who, within two days, was in the Tower. The reversal of the relative positions of York and Somerset was astonishing and the articles must have been seen as compelling.

Remarkably, three minutes survive of the Great Council meetings in November and December 1453 and April 1454 revealing detailed records of the debate and decisions.[4] The first minute was of a very well attended meeting with fifty-two lords on the 30th of November 1453 in the Star Chamber, so it must have been quite a press.[5] The prominent absentees were Somerset, who was now in the Tower, and Exeter who saw himself as the rightful authority, should the King not soon recover, and was busy plotting an alliance with Lord Egremont against the Nevilles. This Council intended to reassert royal authority, noting that it had been repeatedly flouted and that this set a bad example, and stated it would in future act to compel those disobedient to obey such authority.

On the 5th of December twenty-three lords, including Worcester, met in the Star Chamber and tried to resolve the question of who should exert royal authority in the absence of the royal person who was incapacitated by insanity. The Council assumed responsibility for 'the pollytyque rule and gouernance ... of his lands ... in such as of veary neseseyte be entended untill the tymeme there poure be more ample by awtoryty suffycently declared'.[6] Thus the Council would make decisions on issues which could not be deferred. Notwithstanding this rather limited and necessary assumption of authority, only fourteen out of the twenty-three sub-scribed, including York. A majority of those present on the 5th December who had *also* been at the 23rd of October Council meeting which issued the invitation to York to attend to the Great Council, did not subscribe to increasing York's power, and their number included Worcester. Thus they cannot be accused of inviting York because they saw personal advantage in his being made more powerful.

York was not the only person who considered himself the right candidate to rule during the King's madness. The spirited Queen Margaret, now mother of a healthy male heir, threw her hat into the ring and would remain a determined and divisive figure for the next sixteen years. A letter, dated the 19th of January, to John Paston described how she presented a bill of five articles.[7] The second empow-ered her to appoint the three great officers of state, the Chancellor, Treasurer and the Privy Seal, as well as other officers. If implemented the Queen would have become regent and exercised *de facto* royal power. England had never had a female regent. The last French queen to take an active, and bloody, part in English politics—Isabella, wife to Edward II and the She-Wolf of France—was not an auspicious precedent. The same day Exeter and Egremont, both absent from the Great Council despite summonses, made sworn confederation against the Nevilles, Cromwell and their supporters, disputing the ownership of manors earlier purchased by Cromwell.

The Lords were aware of the King's condition but the Commons remained in ignorance. Parliament was due to reconvene at Reading on the 11th of February. Someone had to go there, prorogue and bring it to Westminster. Worcester, who had so ably addressed Convocation and established himself as a diplomatic and compelling orator, was chosen.[8] The Earl addressed the Commons and some lords in the refectory of Reading Abbey, 'with thanks having first been given to both the aforesaid lords and Commons for their labours and attention on behalf of the said lord king, declared how the same lord king was unable to be present on the afore-said day and at the said place on account of certain reasons'.[9] The Earl was able to be diplomatic, tactful and capable of a certain wry humour. The 'certain reasons' were only the madness of King Henry.

Two days later Archbishop Kemp eventually had to ask who, during the King's incapacity, should exercise his power to hold parliament, 'and it was aunswered advised and accorded by the lordes here undre subscribed that the said power sholde be committed to the Duke of Yorke.'[10] Worcester was among the twenty-six signatories, empowering York as the King's Lieutenant to hold and dissolve Parliament.[11] The Earl was also among those who voted in favour of the motion that the Queen's bill for what were effectively regency powers should be considered in Parliament.

The Commons petitioned for the release of their Speaker, Thomas Thorpe, on the basis of parliamentary privilege, after his imprisonment by York, as he, on the King's orders, had confiscated the Duke's property. York's response had been to sue the speaker in the Exchequer Court, securing £1,000 damages and Thorpe's imprisonment in the Fleet. The Commons, angered by the disrespectful treatment of their Speaker, now proved recalcitrant, rejecting requests for £40,000 to defend Calais, and sought an explanation as to the use of funds voted at Reading.

On the 14th of March 1454 Thomas Courtenay, the Earl of Devon, was indicted for treason for his part in York's confrontation in 1452 at Dartford—before the Duke of Buckingham, Humphrey Stafford, acting *pro tempore* as Lord Steward of England. The Earl was rapidly cleared by the Lords. Worcester would have noted that judgement by peers was a hopelessly ineffective way of securing the condemnation of a fellow lord.

The Speaker, responding to a request for taxes, on the 19th of March reminded the lords that the Chancellor had promised at the beginning of the Parliament at Reading to establish a 'sad and wise' council 'of the right discrete lordes and other of this land' to which men might come for justice. Kemp, who had resisted increasing York's authority, died suddenly three days later, creating unexpected opportunities. He had been appointed in a period of Lancastrian assertiveness. Now, with the King mad and Somerset in the Tower, the positions of Archbishop of Canterbury and Chancellor were both vacant. By a succession of unexpected events—first the collapse of the King into catatonic madness, then the death of the man who held the position of both Chancellor and Archbishop—the highest ranking sane man in the realm, in terms of office, was now the 26-year-old Treasurer, Worcester.

Chancery was now without a chancellor and seals, meaning government was incapacitated as well as the King. One further desperate effort had to be made to establish whether the King had any ability at all to indicate his views. Hence a deputation of twelve lords went to Windsor to inform him of the situation and to see if he could advise on the appointments of a new archbishop and chancellor and also on who should constitute the membership of the 'sad and wise' council. The inert king clearly thoroughly impressed the delegation with his utter incapacity for on the 27th of March, York was appointed the Protector and Defender of the Kingdom of England and the King's Chief Councillor.

On the penultimate day of March the Council recommended the promotion of Thomas Bourchier, Bishop of Ely, to the Archbishopric of Canterbury. Bourchier's appointment to Ely in the mid-1430s had been driven by Worcester's father. In Bourchier's place at Ely was appointed William Grey, who was an alumnus of Balliol (Leland wrote that Worcester associated with a brilliant circle of Balliol men). Both Grey and Worcester had shared scholarly interests and studied, at different times, under Guarino da Verona. They would be patrons of the scholar John Free. The fathers of both William Grey and York had been executed for their part in the 1415 Southampton plot.

On the 2nd of April the Earl of Salisbury, Worcester's one-time father-in-law, was made Chancellor. The appointment of a non-cleric was very unusual and might indicate a determination to pack secular lords close to York in all key high offices. The occasion saw a public spectacle of the type much associated with Worcester. 'Richard, Earl of Warwick, John Earl of Worcester, the Treasurer of England and John Viscount Bourchier, brought into the Great Chamber of Parliament at Westminster, ... a wooden chest, locked and sealed, ... containing the King's three great seals, one being of gold and the other two of silver.'[12] The Earl of Salisbury took the Chancellor's oath, and the box was opened and the seals given to the new Chancellor, who returned them to the box which was then taken to the Neville residence in the City of London called *Le Erber*. This ceremony might imply that the Nevilles, Tiptoft and the Bourchiers had taken over, under Richard Plantagenet, Duke of York. Indeed, although opportunistic, what happened had the character of a coup and some peers, particularly the Beauforts, Percys and Hollands, thought things were happening a bit too fast. Conflict with the Percys had pushed the Nevilles into alliance with York. Now York and Salisbury could support each other from positions of power, as respectively Protector and Chancellor, while Worcester, linked to both by blood and marriage, was Treasurer.

On the 3rd of April the lords assembled in the Star Chamber. The Chancellor, Salisbury, stated that York had declared he would not assume the role of Protector unless the lords, named as Continual Councillors, would agree to approve his title and the associated responsibilities. Salisbury then asked these lords in turn for their views. The Great Council minutes are an excruciating and unintentionally hilarious litany of excuses.

The Duke of Norfolk said he would not spare himself from service, except when vexed by infirmity which was often. Similarly, the Duke of Buckingham could not attend daily as he was frequently visited by sickness and could not then endure to ride. The Archbishop of York and the Bishop of Winchester explained they would do such service as they could reasonably do. Similarly, other bishops who were unusually concerned about attendance to their diocesan duties. Warwick said he was 'yonge of age and yonger of discrecyon and wysdome so that he was unable to attend'. Oxford would serve as much as his sickness would let him but he was many times full sore vexed. Shrewsbury was ready to do as other men did—which appeared not a lot. And so on, until the Earl of Worcester spoke saying he was ready to take on the charge and the council should be content to do its duty. (The quote is at the chapter head.)

Viscount Beaumont was at least honest when he remembered that he was with the Queen, from whom he would not depart in taking upon him this charge. The venerable lord Cromwell was also prepared to do service and concurred with the recommendation made by Worcester, and followed by the Prior of St John, that the Commons should be involved. Cromwell, 'advysynge as it was moved before bye therle of Worsyter and the prior of St. Jhonnes that declaracyone shold be made to the Commons'.[13] The Prior of St John also stated, 'hit should be declared in the commene howse the eastate of the land'.[14]

Nearly everybody—with the exception of young Worcester and old Cromwell— declared themselves too old, young, ill, inexperienced or conflicted to serve consistently. The Earl was a man who did not shirk his duty or avoid responsibility even when the road ahead was uncertain and possibly dangerous; was undaunted by standing alone; and he was, further, the first to make a constructive statement about governance; here the prudence of involving the Commons. This suggests that Worcester, despite his youth, was an independent and intelligent presence in Council. His views about the Commons were subsequently taken up by two other older peers. His advice about the Lower House indicated that, unlike later allegations to the contrary, he was in tune with the trend of English constitutional politics and not a proponent of continental absolutism.

The Continual Council now began to resemble the modern cabinet as Henry VI was unable to perform even a 'decorative' function. At its secular core were three men, effectively a 'triumvirate' of Protector, Chancellor and Treasurer— respectively the two Richards, Plantagenet and Neville, and Tiptoft. Worcester was the most experienced major and secular figure to survive from this period into the 1460s when Edward, the son of York, would be king and the Chancellor, Salisbury's son bishop George Neville, would hold his father's office. The seeds of the Yorkist government lay in this solution to the crisis caused by the madness of Henry VI.

The Continual Council made valiant efforts to deal with the country's problems, which included rampant piracy. It made a contract with several leading nobles to keep the seas for three years on the 3rd of April 1454. The core list included the

Chancellor, Lord Salisbury, the Treasurer, Worcester, the Earl of Wiltshire and Lord Stourton.[15]

On the 13th of April 1454 Worcester was commissioned to create Henry's son, Edward, as Prince of Wales and Earl of Chester, 'to invest him therewith by a circlet on the head and a golden ring on the finger and a golden rod'.[16] These accoutrements must have been quite a lot for a baby less than one year old to bear. York was also a commissioner so he explicitly recognised the Lancastrian succession.

The Continual Council tried hard to secure Calais. On the 16th of April a privy seal letter, signed by Worcester, was sent to twenty-four persons of the King's Council, instructing them to assemble on the 6th of May to provide in particular for the defence of Calais. This included the Dukes of York, Norfolk, Buckingham, and the Earls of Warwick, Oxford, Salisbury, Worcester, and Shrewsbury, 'for somoche we have ordened that our Counsaill shall in goodely haste be assembled . . . of the whiche ye be oon.'[17] This identified the formally nominated Continual Council.

There survive thirty conciliar warrants for May issued by the Continual Council.[18] With a few uncertain exceptions Worcester signed them all. The impression is of a hardworking body desperately trying to re-establish the authority of the government with the Earl conspicuous among its members for his commitment. In June 1454 William Grey, recently elevated to the bishopric of Ely, joined the council. There followed a period of intense activity as it tried to exert its authority over feuding magnates who had refused its earlier summons. Also, the council endeavoured to reform the ill-run royal household and tried to finance properly the defence of Calais.

In June York travelled north to restrain his miscreant son-in-law Exeter who was supporting the disruptive activities of the Lord Egremont. In July, after the failure of an attempt to ambush his own father-in-law, Exeter was arrested and confined to Pontefract Castle. Exeter would become a Lancastrian, not so much because he was for Henry VI, but as he was against the Duke of York.

On the 18th of July the Great Council was assembled to deal with the issue of what was to be done about Somerset, who remained in prison, uncharged and untried, contrary to Magna Carta. York got around the question of bailing him by suggesting that the advice of judges and absent lords should be considered. The issue was further delayed by deciding charges should be put off until the 28th of October.

On the 13th of November the Great Council set out to reform the notoriously inefficient royal household. Six days later ordinances for its regulation were issued.[19] Twenty-nine peers were noted as present, including Worcester. In the 1460s the Earl would be Steward of Edward IV's exceptionally well managed household. In 1448 the young John Tiptoft had come of age and asked to serve about the King's person. From that date, and possibly before, he had seen how poorly managed was Henry VI's court and learned lessons to put to use later.

Between the 9th of May and the 30th of December 1454 and the 4th of July and the 16th of December 1455, out of 64 Council meetings of the secular nobles, Salisbury (Chancellor) was present at 59 followed by Worcester (Treasurer) at 42.[20] Despite the burden of government the council found funds to support Greek scholars who had fled the Turks following the capture of Constantinople. The Exchequer accounts for 1455–6 show separate money gifts to four Greeks then residing in England, given at the urging of the council, authorised when Worcester was Treasurer and William Grey, the scholar Bishop of Ely, was a councillor.[21] One Greek, John Argyropoulos, ungratefully complained about the delay in payment and called the English a barbarous nation.

On the 3rd of April Worcester had been appointed a keeper of the sea, thereby starting a nautical association which would be continued during the reign of Edward IV. Piracy was endemic in an era when it was a cliché that nearly every merchant-man could be impressed as a ship of war, but it was equally true that vessels, when trade was unprofitable or targets particularly tempting, could indulge in piracy.

It was hard not be impacted by piracy. Just looking at the family and in-laws of the Earl of Worcester, in 1404 Lord Tiptoft and Powys, having been appointed Seneschal of Les Landes and Constable of Dax, sent a ship, with contents worth over £3,000, to the relief of Bayonne. Pirates from Bilbao took his boat and imprisoned the crew. Henry IV wrote to his nephew, King John of Castile, seeking redress. In 1410 Sir John Greyndour, grandfather of Worcester's second wife Elizabeth, became involved in piracy against Genoese merchants to whom Henry IV had granted liberty to trade with England. Thomas, Lord Berkeley, seized a Genoese carrack and removed its cargo. The king demanded Berkeley make restitution and his affinity, including Sir John, returned part but retained most of the Genoese property. Worcester's own pilgrimage would, when traversing the Mediterranean, be beset by piracy and in the mid-1460s there was a murky incident where one of his own ships appears to have been overcome by the ingrained contemporary piratical instinct.

In the 1440s a poem of unknown authorship, the *Libelle of Englyshe Polycye*, addressed England's naval strategy. The *Libelle* argued that prosperity and tranquillity could only be ensured through control of the English Channel and defence of the Calais Wool Staple. It pronounced, 'cheryshe marchandyse, keep thamyralte [the admiralty], that wee bee maysters of the narrow sea.' The rise and fall of English power on land under the Lancastrians was mirrored at sea. Henry V modernised and expanded the English navy. He harnessed the irrepressible propensity to piracy with the Conservator Statute, under which privateering was regulated through a Conservator of Truces assigned to each port. Like governance in general, the system only worked when the King was strong.

After the loss of Normandy and Gascony under Henry VI the piracy problem became rather more serious as England, for the first time in three centuries, controlled no part of the French coastline. Those indulging in piratical activity could now take refuge on French lands. The Protectorate's strategy was to establish control over commerce in the channel. Access to Calais depended entirely on control of the sea from the English coastline. Efforts to raise further funds in 1454 from the Commons to keep clear the approaches to Calais were rejected in March with the riposte that the King had already been granted for life the necessary customs and subsidies. Thus the Protectorate had to find another way to suppress piracy and in effect it was farmed out as a private business operation.[22]

In April 1454 the Council insisted that no English ship should sail to an enemy port without its express permission, warning that few safe-conducts would be issued henceforth.[23] A Great Council was summoned to meet at Westminster on the 25th of June to co-ordinate the entire defensive strategy for land and sea, including Calais.[24] The navy was paid by transferring tonnage and poundage—the taxes on every cask, or tun, of wine imported and on every pound in weight of merchandise traded—to the Sea Keepers.[25]

Despite all the planning it is uncertain when the fleet actually put to sea and which Sea Keepers went. William of Wyrcester wrote to John Paston on 5 July informing him, 'The Lordys that be appoynted to kepe the see maken hem redye yn all haste; and the Tresourer [Worcester] also, the Lord Wyltshyre for the west coost.'[26] This indicated that in early July the fleet had yet to go to sea but that this was imminent. In mid-July a couple of letters of protection—which secured an individual from prosecution at home while serving overseas—were issued on the 13th of July to 'Thos. Wareyn, of Bristol, in the retinue of the Earl of Worcester'.[27] Four days later another letter went to James de Court.[28] There was a third letter without a date but of the same period to Simon Spert of Sandwich.[29] Bristol and Sandwich possibly marked the beginning and end of the naval sweep. The Treasurer, Worcester, had the central role in raising and disbursing funds. On the 19th of July, 'after indentures made for safe guard of the sea, … they [the Sea Keepers] shall have all the said subsidies in all ports of the realm, that they … shall during that term nominate to the Treasurer … and at their nomination the Treasurer shall cause warrants … to be addressed to the nominees.'[30]

The sea-keeping fleet only went to sea once, probably between mid-July and mid-August. Indeed, the only evidence that it went at all was yet another commission to investigate piracy by the very Sea Keepers intended to stamp it out. On the 22nd of August a commission was issued for the arrest of the *le Barge of Beryk* and its master who, when keeping the sea, 'robbed and spoiled the King's lieges and allies'.[31] Five days later another commission was put out for the arrest of the Calais captain (and later redoubtable Lancastrian fighter) Andrew Trollop for the same offence.[32] It is hard to imagine a more apt, premature end to a venture at this particularly inadequate period of British governmental history than the anti-piracy sweep degenerating itself into piracy. Even the sincerest efforts of York and the Continual Council could end in farce.

Surprisingly, the one explicit reference to some success by the sea-keeping venture comes from Italy. In the 1460 funeral oration for Guarino da Verona, Ludovico Carbone said Worcester (a pupil of Guarino) 'had returned the British Sea to peace with his understanding and expertise in military affairs'.[33] At the very least, Worcester ensured the enterprise got enough money to get to sea once. The sea-keeping did not fail in 1454 because the Treasurer did not provide the necessary funds. In 1462, when the Yorkist regime needed to resume naval operations to stop invasion and protect Calais, the man turned to was once again the Earl of Worcester.

The keeping of the seas may have resulted in Worcester possessing at least one ship and by the 1460s various records establish that he had several. Despite the final loss of Gascony in 1453 trade with the region had duly resumed. On the 28th of September 1454 a licence was granted to 'Arnaut Macanan and Ricart Macanan … that they … can take a certain ship called *la Mangdeleyn*, of London, of which …. John [Tiptoft], Earl of Worcester is owner … as far as the King's city of Bordeaux.'[34] Further protections, which were not obviously linked to keeping the sea, were offered in October 1454 to John Colyns and John Owletawe in the retinue of the Earl of Worcester.[35] This may reflect increasing involvement in trading when, following the disruption caused by the loss of Gascony, such activity was re-established.

It is a sad reflection on Henry VI's kingship that things were better when he was impassively imbecilic. While he was in such a state the political situation had been stabilised and magnate disputes suppressed, there were serious efforts to reform the royal household, clear the seas of pirates, restore trade and resource Calais. Worcester's name is recorded on conciliar warrants dealing with all these issues. His Council attendance was exemplary. There is no evidence that the King's incapacity was egregiously used to advance his personal financial interests.

Having, to some extent, solved the problem of running the realm without a king under the Plantagenet, Neville and Tiptoft 'triumvirate', supported on the clerical benches by the able Bourchier of Canterbury and Grey of Ely, the question again had to be reframed as to what to do when the incompetent king recovered and his understandably vengeance-seeking favourite, Somerset, was freed and the sidelined Queen could influence events. Realistically, no amount of diplomacy could resolve this problem and the outcome could only be determined through an effusion of blood. Only now, with Shrewsbury dead and the proto-Yorkists experienced in power, the balance was very differently weighted than it stood in 1452 at Dartford.

The King had largely regained his sanity by Christmas Day in 1454. On the 27th of December the Queen informed her husband that Archbishop Kemp had died and that he had a son. Given his statement about the baby Edward having been fathered by the Holy Ghost he may have had doubts as to paternity, which many subjects shared.

Meanwhile, on 26th of January 1455, Worcester was again at the centre of ceremony at the delayed enthronement of Bourchier. 'At the Archbishop's table at dinner, the Archbishop sat in the center, with the Bishop of London, the Bishop of Rochester, the Prior of Christ Church Canterbury to the right; the Bishop of Winchester, the Bishop of Ross, the Earl of Worcester, Treasurer of England, to the left.'[36] Worcester was the sole non-cleric honoured at the top table. Perhaps this was in respect of his rank as Treasurer but it may also have reflected his family links to Bourchier, going back to his father's efforts to advance him to Ely in the mid-1430s and, perhaps, the fact that the Earl may have had a role in promoting Bourchier to Archbishop in 1454.

York surrendered his office of Protector early in 1455.[37] On the 5th of February twenty-seven peers, including Worcester, agreed Somerset's release and he was freed on bail.[38] On the 4th of March an arbitration panel was appointed to judge the issue between York and Somerset, both Dukes having entered recognisances of 20,000 marks. Again, as in 1452 after Dartford, Worcester was one of the arbitrators.

Three days later Salisbury was replaced as Chancellor by Archbishop Bourchier. Salisbury may have resigned as he would not agree to release Exeter from Pontefract Castle where he had been incarcerated by his father-in-law, York. Salisbury had his own family reasons for welcoming the incarceration of Exeter who, in league with Egremont, challenged the Nevilles in the north.

On the 19th of March the more compliant Chancellor Bourchier was ordered to release Exeter. On the last day of the month Somerset's bail was discharged after he had been 'Committed to the Towre of London, and there kepte bi the Space of One hole Yere, Ten Weks and more, and as he conceived, without any resonable Ground or lawefull Processe.'[39]

Worcester is generally described as having been replaced as Treasurer on the 15th of March by Wiltshire, who was betrothed to Somerset's daughter Catherine.[40] He may have continued to hold office for all practical purposes. At least some observers did not detect a change, for he was still titled 'Worcestre Tresorer of England' on the discharge of Somerset's bail, dated the 31st of March.[41] Similarly, the Giles Chronicle described him as holding the same office during events which probably took place in April, leading up to the 1st Battle of St Albans. But on the 18th of March Wiltshire contributed over £800 as he was called upon as the new Treasurer to dip into his own pockets, so he must have performed some function in the role.

Worcester was Treasurer from April 1452 to March 1455. In purely financial terms his term of office did, after a weak start, see a significant rise in income.[42] In the first six months of his appointment, April to September 1452, receipts were low at £18,738, depressed by the stand-off at Dartmouth. Subsequently, they recovered sharply, reaching £38,675 between October 1452 and March 1453 and £66,125 between April and September 1453. The financial year to September 1453 saw total revenue of £104,800, which was the first time it had exceeded £100,000 since the year ending September 1447. The big push in the second and third quarter of 1453 was to fund the Gascon campaign. 'This was the last reasonably prosperous term in the whole of Henry VI's unhappy reign.'[43] Subsequently receipts fell and, in the year ending September 1454, they were £71,125. In the last six-month period when Worcester was Treasurer receipts declined to an undistinguished £26,062. In the next six months under Wiltshire, which saw the 1st Battle of St Albans, they collapsed to £13,479.

There had been a huge effort to raise funds, in which Thomas Thorpe played a significant part, but after the Gascon campaign was funded the system nearly broke down again—perhaps understandably because it was almost immediately clear the monies sent to Gascony achieved nothing. There was great reluctance, overcome only partially by the requirement to defend Calais and the mainland, to contribute more. York's imprisonment of Thorpe, an able Treasury official and speaker popular with the Commons, cannot have been helpful. Thorpe resumed his Treasury career when, on the 24th of March 1455, he became Chancellor of the Exchequer. Notwithstanding, while Worcester was Treasurer, funds were raised for two major campaigns: to recover Gascony from the French and to clear the channel of pirates. Neither failed through want of money.

Worcester also performed the role expected of the Treasurer in putting up his own money when he contributed 'loans' of £2,333 6s. 8d. on the 18th of May 1453. Subsequently, on the 5th of December 1454, the Earl provided a further £1,500. In November 1454, in repayment of the £1,500, Worcester was to be allowed direct payment of customs on wool and hides in the ports of London, Boston and Ipswich.[44] In September 1456 he was granted a licence to ship wool abroad in consideration of monies lent to the crown.[45] Under Henry VI—and it would prove so again under Edward IV—Worcester personally lent huge sums to the crown. It is hard to accuse him of venality in taking on the Treasury. Even his detractors would never level against him the charge of exploiting his offices for greed.

In summary how did Worcester respond to the challenge created for governance when the King was incapacitated? There were perhaps two important interventions. Firstly, he was one of a small group of councillors who recalled York in 1453. Secondly, he was the first councillor to declare in April 1454 that he would serve the Duke of York wholeheartedly when all before him, and most others after, made feeble excuses. Another point is that there was one figure who provided continuity in government during the lacuna when the King was dead to the world, his heir was a baby, and the Chancellor, the Archbishop of Canterbury, had died. For a time the senior sane healthy office-holder in the kingdom was the Treasurer.

This was, perhaps, Worcester's finest hour. He alone of the great nobles rose above faction to serve the incapacitated king and, thus, in effect, the country. People may have remembered the young Earl's efforts. He worked closely with York and Salisbury between 1453 and 1455. This was observed by York's son, the future Edward IV, and Salisbury's sons, the Neville trio of Richard, John and George. In the summer of 1461 the King and certain unidentified key nobles recalled Worcester from Italy, a true Flamyneus as in *The Declamacion*, who 'trayning himself alwey to floure in vertue and good maners, but his grete studye was with his diligence and seruyse to helpe his frende and contrey whan eyther of them had need of his helpe.'

Chapter 7

War and retreat – 1455

And on the following Sunday [after the Battle of St Albans] … the King has crossed in procession into the church of St Paul's in London, to be crowned. … And the Earl of Warwick carried the royal lance of honour and state … and the Earl of Worcester bore the royal sword in the procession.[1]

> Procession to St Paul's following the first Battle of St Albans

The Erle of Warwyk ys at Caunterbury with the Archbyship, and the Erle younger brothere maryed to Sir Eadmund Yngylthorp doughther upon Seynt Marks Day. The Erle of Worcestr broght aboute the maryage.[2]

> Paston letter of 25 April 1457

The recovery of the King's sanity and the release of Somerset meant fighting was probably inevitable. Somerset, understandably since he was not charged or tried, wanted revenge for his incarceration—and York could not feel safe without Somerset's elimination from government and, indeed, from the royal presence. Which side would Worcester choose? At Dartmouth he, like the Nevilles, was with the King. But now the Nevilles were siding with York against Somerset and Worcester must have known that government had been better when York, Salisbury and he had held office. An aspect of his personality that emerged over his life was a dislike of divided loyalties. This appeared to result in him either finding a way to withdraw, as in 1458 and 1467 when he went abroad, and then—if making a hard choice was absolutely unavoidable—decisively coming down on one side or the other. How might the Earl deal with the coming showdown in 1455?

After the 15th of April at Westminster a select council called an exceptional council to Leicester for Whitsun. York assumed that this would secure Somerset's controlling position should the King became incapacitated again. He therefore resolved to preempt the council by stopping the King from reaching Leicester. On the 19th of May Chancellor Bourchier was ordered to write to York, Norfolk, Salisbury and Warwick, warning that if they did not disband their retainers they would be seen as traitors.

The Giles Chronicle recorded that the King sent a delegation to York. Clearly the King still regarded the Earl as not just a persuasive diplomatic speaker but also a man of trusted loyalty. 'Since their [York's and the Nevilles'] association proves to be known [to] the King, he in accordance with timely counsel has sent

... the Bishop of Coventry and Lichfield, the Prior of the Hospitallers and the Earl of Worcester ... in order that [the three] might appease their unfair and unjust opinion.'³ It sounded as if the King hoped to make a personal plea to the Yorkists through intermediaries acceptable to them. Giles reported that York and the Nevilles, 'circumspect in danger and in the diligence of their defense, held on to the royal messengers in their retinue, so that continuously every day they might prevail to lead their army close to the forces of the King'.⁴ Conciliatory letters from York came to nothing as these were intercepted by Somerset and Thomas Thorpe.

Worcester was probably not that unwillingly detained by the Yorkists. He had, until very recently, worked closely with York and Salisbury. Also perhaps having seen the determination of York and his allies, and the size of their forces, he might have seen which way any fighting could be expected to go.

On the 21st of May Henry VI left London for Leicester. Henry's forces were led by the Duke of Buckingham, who was appointed Constable. He did not expect an actual assault on the King's men and moved on, unprepared for it, to St Albans. The next day, after fruitless negotiations, Richard Neville, the Earl of Warwick, led a surprise attack through the back streets and gardens. The Duke of Somerset, Sir Henry Percy, the Earl of Northumberland, and Lord Clifford were killed and the King captured at what would be called the 1st Battle of St Albans. There was no report of Worcester's presence so it seems likely he and his two fellow delegates were held or stayed back somewhere *en route*.

The 1st Battle of St Albans was significant in two ways. Firstly, battles on English soil, especially where the King was present, had been rare in the last two centuries. The previous civil war battle was Shrewsbury, on the 21st of July 1403, where likely both the Earl of Worcester's father and grandfather, John and Payn, fought with Henry IV against Henry Percy, known as 'Hotspur'. Prior to Shrewsbury it is necessary to go back to 1264, when Simon de Montfort defeated Henry III. In the decades, however, following St Albans, kings of England would fight, be captured and die on English battlefields on more occasions in a concentrated period than ever before or since. Secondly, the rebel attack was led by Richard Neville, the Earl of Warwick, who now moves to centre stage and increasingly dominates it, just as the Earl of Worcester, who was a key player in the previous three years, retires over the year, leaving public life in England and then the country altogether. The very young Edward Plantagenet, oldest son of the Duke of York and Earl of March, barely a teenager, fought the first of his many battles.

The King returned to London on Friday the 23rd of May with York, Salisbury and Warwick now in control. On Whitsunday Warwick and Worcester, respectively, carried the royal lance and sword in procession to St Paul's with the King in an effort to provide a balanced escort that might be palatable to Henry. So far Worcester appears to have shown a genuine determination to do his duty and not to take sides. On the 26th of May the Earl was summoned to assemble in Parliament at Westminster on the 9th of July.

In June there occurred a peculiar episode involving the Earl of Worcester and the indomitable Duchess Alice de la Pole, Constable of Wallingford Castle. On the 26th of June a council minute recorded that Worcester had been commanded by the King, on the advice of the Council, to go to Wallingford and there take charge of the Duke of Exeter, ever an unstable character who had tried the previous year to ambush his father-in-law, the Duke of York, now the power behind the throne.[5] The Earl had not done this, it was minuted, because Alice had told him he was infringing on her rights as Constable and she alone had power over Exeter. The Earl was discharged from his duty and Alice was instructed to make sure she kept Exeter under proper control 'at her peril'.

There was almost certainly more going on here than initially meets the eye. Following St Albans, the Duchess of Suffolk may have quietly switched allegiance from Lancaster to York and, as Constable of Wallingford Castle, agreed to take charge of Exeter. Worcester's mission might have been to test Alice's loyalty to the regime but in doing so he pushed her too far, presenting her with an impossible choice; given her legitimate powers as Constable, to surrender her prisoner would have destroyed her authority. Perhaps an agreement was brokered between Worcester and Alice, who had been keeper of his stepdaughter, Anne Beauchamp, by his first marriage to Cecily Beauchamp. That stepdaughter had been intended in marriage to Alice's son, John, the future 2nd Duke of Suffolk restored in 1462. Also, the Earl's brother-in-law Edmund Ingaldisthorpe was the son of a de la Pole. Some rapprochement was indeed reached between the ducal families of de la Pole and Plantagenet as, before February 1458, John would marry Elizabeth Plantagenet, the second of York's daughters.

Overall, there is insufficient information to interpret this event. The Duchess defied the crown and the Earl did not fulfil his orders. But both survived and perhaps cooperated to achieve a reconciliation of Plantagenet and de la Pole. There was also the issue of respect for traditional rights. The powers given to Worcester may genuinely have been excessive and inconsistent with Alice's rights as Constable. Worcester might appear weak in not exploiting his powers in this curious incident but he cannot be accused of insensitivity to traditional rights or of being an advocate of autocracy.

Alice, who reappears frequently in this record, was a compelling and intriguing presence throughout the period. She proved full of contradictions. The still functioning school and almshouses at Ewelme, near Wallingford, built by her and the late duke, are among the most exquisite of medieval survivals. Yet before June 1448 she visited Norwich with Sir Thomas Tuddenham, one of the local toughs linked to Suffolk, and two others, all disguised, she as 'an huswyf of the cuntre'. They left as night fell, going in the direction of a hovel called Lakenham Woods, 'to tak the ayr and disport theym self', but got into a fight with one Thomas Aylmer, keeper of the city ditches, who did not recognise them—they were, after all, in disguise—and quite reasonably distrusted their intent. For his pains Aylmer was imprisoned by Tuddenham. Alice, who was reported as 'sore afrayed', and Tuddenham then held a great hatred against the city, resulting in the arrest of Norwich's Mayor and others who displeased them.[6] In 1462 Tuddenham, Alice's partner in possible indelicacy, would come up against a much more decisive and harsher Worcester.

Parliament assembled on the 9th of July 1455 and Worcester was again appointed a trier of petitions for Gascony and other lands overseas. York blamed Thorpe in Parliament for causing the Battle of St Albans and he was dismissed from all offices and forced to pay York the damages awarded against him in 1454.

Five committees were established to consider important issues: the King's household, gold and silver, Calais and Berwick, safe-keeping of the sea, and Wales. At the age of 28, and after six years of parliaments, commissions, and service as Treasurer, Councillor, and Sea Keeper, Worcester was now an elder statesman and sat on the first two committees. The committee to look at the household included three ex-Treasurers. Worcester had been about the King's person since 1447, so had long experience of royal mismanagement. Earlier in 1454 he had sat on the committee then appointed to look at the household. Worcester was also the only lay peer to be included on the committee to consider the shortage of bullion. Trade and business were endemically hampered by the lack of good coinage, which tended to be hoarded. Now this was particularly severe and the paucity of bullion was a major cause of the Great Slump of the decades of the mid-fifteenth century. This was an issue which the Earl would grapple with again when Deputy Lieutenant of Ireland.[7] Worcester, Salisbury, Shrewsbury and the Lord Stourton were discharged at their request from keeping the seas.

On the 24th of July the lords swore to be loyal to the King. Worcester remained constant in attendance as a councillor. The most consistent secular council attenders during York's second period of supremacy were his own supporters and kinsmen—the two Bourchiers, Salisbury, Warwick, Fauconberg and Worcester.[8]

On the 10th of November the Council, including Worcester, decided that York should open Parliament as the King's lieutenant. On the 13th of December the Council, again including the Earl, signed a letter from the King to the garrison of Calais. This was the last time he was obviously associated with an act of government for over six years.

What might be the mental health of a man of 28, who had experienced service on bloody commissions, occupied the position of treasurer, the highest in the land usually held by a secular noble, had been a continual councillor when the King was mad and the only person to hold high office throughout that time, and had seen the total breakdown of royal authority and a brief war. He had also lived through the deaths of two wives, a stepdaughter and a son. He might have been torn because of loyalty to the House of Lancaster, in whose service his family had thrived, and to Henry VI, under whom his own personal advancement had been spectacular. He had seen that decent men had paid a terrible price for the current monarch's manifest inadequacy. Worcester had done a remarkable job as servant of the state while avoiding openly taking sides. His nobility was that of Flamyneus in *The Declamacion*: 'Grete grace and fortune I haue receyued of our goddess to haue so grete benyuolence and frendelyhed of all folks, ffor there is no man in this cyte, ne in all the world, hath cause to hate me, yf he not an enemye to our comyn weal.'

The Earl was mentally and emotionally exhausted, and riven by divided loyalties. He was either counselled, or personally had concluded, that he must seek redemption from those sins for which the people closest to him had paid with their lives, by pilgrimage to the holiest of all places, the Church of the Holy Sepulchre in Jerusalem. The antiquary and illustrator John Rous advised the Earl to go to the Holy Land. He 'urged John Tiptoft to take with him some illustrious man in the art of portraiture to illustrate what he chose and through this on return employ skilled craftsmen to rework the results in the best way'.[9] Rous was an illustrator and possibly had himself in mind.

This was an opportunity to escape an England on the verge of breaking into civil war. The scholar John Free emphasised, in a dedication of 1461 to Worcester, the desire to escape conflict: 'The ancestral gods, under whose divine will is our Britain, have admonished you, so excellent and great a man, that you should prefer peace to war … or you, an upright man, with all factions strengthening, would sully your reputation by embroiling with wicked and factious men.'[10] The antiquary Leland described Worcester's divided loyalties: 'John has felt deeply on both sides the wounded prides of Henry and Edward. Wherefore prudently he has preferred peace in all matters, and, [became] a pilgrim with great dedication to the most holy city.'[11] Fuller said, 'This Earl could not be discourteous to Henry VI who had so much advanced him, nor disloyall to Edward IV in whom the right of the Crown lay. … he resolved … to quit his own and to visit the Holy Land.'[12] The sixteenth century historian John Bale simply wrote that, torn between Henry and Edward, he departed preferring, before all things, tranquillity.[13]

Sailings to the Holy Land took place from Venice in the spring, meaning the pilgrims from England had to be ready to leave for Italy by the new year. In 1456 there was possibly not sufficient time to prepare. Therefore it might be expected that the Earl would remain in England in 1456 and 1457 but set forth for Italy early in 1458.

During 1456 the Queen's party re-established authority over governance, displacing the Yorkists. Worcester appeared, however, to have left government even before the Duke's resignation on the 25th of February 1456, which marked the end of his second Protectorate. Still the Earl did not avoid appointment to commissions. On the 30th of April 1456 there was a very high-powered commission of oyer and terminer under the Dukes of Exeter and Buckingham, and the Earls of Pembroke, Salisbury, Northumberland, and Worcester, to look at treasons in London and the surburbs. These peers had fought on opposite sides at St Albans and the commission's intention, as much as to deal with disorder, may have been to present a show of unity for what remained a fractured regime. On the 6th of June there was another commission, led by six earls, again including Worcester, to look at treasons in the perennial hotbeds of dissent, Kent and Sussex.[14] On the 2nd of March 1457 there was a commission to inquire into trespasses in Kent, led by the Archbishop of Canterbury, Worcester and various local knights.[15] After this the Earl focused on personal and family matters as well as planning for the pilgrimage. He needed to recruit a large, highly skilled choir, willing to undertake an arduous and possibly dangerous journey.

On the 2nd of September Worcester's brother-in-law Edmund Ingaldisthorpe died. He and the Earl's sister Joanna had one child, Isabel, who now needed someone to defend her interests and help find her a husband. His will, dated the 4th of August 1456, indicated a good relationship with Worcester. He gave his wife Joanna several manors for life which would then pass to Isabel, his daughter, and then, if she had no children, to Worcester to be sold to pray for the souls of various Ingaldisthorpes and de la Poles. He was buried in the Burgh chantry of Borough Church in Cambridgeshire. The inscription defined him as the brother-in-law of Worcester: 'He married the sister of the Earl of Worcester. … This man was a knight.'[16] Given the terms of the will perhaps Worcester had a vested interest in not helping Isabel to find a husband.[17]

A mid-eighteenth century source recounted that Joanna, the widow of Sir Edmund Ingaldisthorpe, subsequently 'married Thomas Grey, younger son of John Lord Grey of Ruthyn, and brother to Edmund Grey, the 1st Earl of Kent: this Thomas was created Lord Grey of Richemont in Bedfordshire.'[18] No date was given but, if true, this adds a tragic dimension to the aftermath of Edward's assumption of the throne for, in November 1461, Grey was attainted and then executed the following month. Joanna, who did not remarry a third time, proved very close to her brother, Worcester, eventually willing her body to be buried with his. She called herself Ingaldisthorpe in surviving records from the 1460s to the 1490s, which might have reflected her inclination but was also wise given Grey's execution as a traitor.

April 1457 saw a major court action over whether Isabel Ingaldisthorpe was a royal ward and, thus, the responsibility of Queen Margaret. She was the only child and a tenant-in-chief in her own right. The Queen insisted on payment for her marriage, claiming Isabel was underage and that she, Margaret, had the right to keep Isabel's inheritance. The Nevilles maintained that, at 14 and as a married woman, she was of age to enter her inheritance. Fortescue, the chief justice of the King's Bench, ruled Isabel should be a royal ward.[19] The Nevilles agreed on the 27th of June 1458 to make ten biennial payments of £100 to Margaret pending the resolution of the case.[20] (Salisbury later disputed the settlement. In 1460, when the house of York was dominant, Sir John Neville and Isabel would secure an act in parliament cancelling and securing recompense for monies forfeited to the Queen.)

It was the Earl of Worcester who brokered his niece Isabel's partnership to his former brother-in-law John Neville, son the Earl of Salisbury and brother of the Earl of Warwick. A letter to Sir John Paston reported that Worcester brought about the marriage between John and Isabel.[21]

The row over the marriage is notable on several levels. It provided a reason for the deterioration in the relationship between the Queen, and hence the Lancastrian cause, and the Nevilles. Worcester still appeared an honest broker to the Queen and not a Neville partisan. Bringing about the marriage may show the Earl in an attractive light. By securing his niece's marriage he removed himself from any interest in his brother-in-law Edmund Ingaldisthorpe's inheritance. He must have exercised considerable diplomatic talents, schmoozing the Queen and reconciling her to a marriage between her ward and the Nevilles who had played such a major part in humiliating her husband the King at St Albans.

Isabel, an only child, now stood to inherit a large fortune, provided her uncle Worcester remained single and childless as, through her mother Joanna, she was a coheir to the Tiptoft estate. John Neville, as a younger son, could not expect much although Salisbury settled eight Montagu manors in jointure on him in 1458 and must have valued his wife's expected inheritance.

Worcester's and Warwick's legal affairs and advisers became increasingly intertwined, indicating the close relationship between these men. The former 'appears to be active on Richard Neville's behalf. As a councillor or perhaps feoffee of Barnard Castle in February 1456 he sued by attorney in the Durham palatine court eighteen tenants of Barnard Castle and its constituent manors for detinue [withholding] of rent.'[22] During this period—when the marriage of his niece,

Isabel Ingaldisthorpe, to John Neville was negotiated—Worcester developed close relationships with the lawyers Robert Ingleton and Henry Chevele.[23] They worked respectively for the Neville and Ingaldisthorpe families and would become Worcester's attorneys while he was in Italy.[24]

Robert Ingleton had risen through Neville patronage and in 1456 his public work abated as the Nevilles withdrew from government. In 1457 he received properties from both Worcester and Salisbury's brother, Lord Fauconberg.[25] Some time in or after 1448 the manor of Poynetts in Middlesex was put into the hands of Worcester as trustee. In 1457 Poynetts came into the possession of Ingleton who, in the same year, acquired the manors at Whiston and Woodford in Northamptonshire from Fauconberg. That Chevele was employed by Worcester's brother-in-law Sir Edmund Indgaldisthorpe is known from a letter written by Queen Margaret to him, regarding the behaviour of his 'servant' Henry Chevele at some time before September 1456, when Sir Edmund had died. She complained, 'Chevele … unjustly and ayenst al right lawe and good conscience, holdeth a certein place and lande in the towne of Asshedon … appertenyng of right unto oure welbeloved Thomas Gale and Isabell his wif, … unto greet hindring, prejudice, and derogacion of our said servant and his wyf.'[26] After Ingaldisthorpe's death, if not before, Worcester must have employed Chevele. The significance of the Earl's relationships with Ingleton and Chevele was that the news he received, when abroad in Italy from his attorneys, was filtered through a particularly Neville prism.

By 1457 preparations for Worcester's departure must have been well underway and common knowledge. If he was known to be passing through Italy then his route and oratorical skills must have recommended him for diplomatic duties. The Earl was appointed, with Robert Flemming and Sir Philip Wentworth, to offer the King's obedience to Pope Calixtus III (1455–8).[27] Flemming had been a commoner of the Great Hall of the University, Worcester's college, from 1430 to 1444 and Wentworth's grandmother was born Elizabeth Tiptoft, who was Worcester's father's cousin.

On the 18th of November 1457 Worcester obtained an *obtinet licentiam*—or permission from Rome—to visit the Holy Sepulchre in a party of six. This must have been applied for several weeks, if not months, earlier.[28] The Earl probably departed London early in the New Year. He left the Manyngham 'Miscellany', the gift from Oxford's Registrar, with Henry Cranebroke as the monk copied Bruni's Xenophon into his own note book in 1459—revealing that, *en route*, the Earl stopped off at Canterbury and said goodbye to his old friend and his fellow monks.

The first half of the Earl of Worcester's political life in England—when he was seen as a loyal Lancastrian like his father and grandfather before him—was over.

His political apprenticeship had started early and been profound. Before his 30th birthday he had been Treasurer, Councillor, and Sea Keeper and was much called upon to serve on commissions. He had been at the heart of government when it might have broken down due to the incompetence and then incapacity of the King. When he was recalled—nearly four years later to an England ruled by the Yorkists—deaths in battle or on the block would mean that he would be the most experienced secular peer in matters of governance, finance, fund raising, shipping and law.

Part 2

PILGRIM AND SCHOLAR

Chapter 8

Venice to Jerusalem – 1458

On that same night, Lord John Tupthoff [sic], Earl of Worcester in England, with his retinue, was standing in order to sing the Mass of the Holy Cross on Mount Calvary with polyphonic song.[1]

Eton fellow William Wey in his *Itineraries* describing the night of Sunday the 25th of June 1458

The Earl of Worcester's pilgrimage to Jerusalem had an especially powerful religious focus. The Eton fellow and pilgrim William Wey, in his *Itineraries*, described, '*comes Wyngorie … stabat … in monte Calvarie,*' or, 'the Earl of Worcester was standing … on Mount Calvary.' *Calvariæ* was the Latinised version of the Greek *Kraníou*, which in turn stood in for the Aramaic *Gagultâ*, or the place of the skull, and designated the site of the cross. Wey was perhaps subtly invoking the great medieval Latin hymn, *Stabat mater dolorosa juxta Crucem lacrimosa, dum pendebat Fílius*, literally, 'the sorrowing mother was standing beside the Cross weeping, while the Son was suspended.' It is hard to see what more Worcester could have done to get closer to the passion of the Crucifixion than to stand himself in the same place as Mary, on Mount Calvary, singing the votive Mass of the Holy Cross. To emulate as a pilgrim such an experience—with a large English choir, skilled in part song, or polyphony—took serious planning and great avowed intent.

A pilgrimage to the Holy Land could be no spontaneous act. It was both hazardous and expensive and required the necessary permissions from the papal penitentiary. Lawyers with power of attorney had to be appointed, wills written and executors named. The pilgrimage itself required sailing through seas prone to storms and filled with pirates and hostile Turks. Then, on landing, Palestine was in Saracen or Muslim hands and treatment could be harsh. Much humility was required and this was not a quality with which the European nobility was amply endowed.

Thus the later medieval pilgrimage was a highly organised affair that combined sea cruise and package tour while having a fundamental religious purpose. Frequent stops by galleys, needed to take on fresh water and supplies and to carry out repairs, meant many opportunities for sightseeing along the Balkan coast, and at Corfu, Crete and Rhodes, places familiar to modern cruise ships. Churches to hear Mass and see relics featured highest on the list of places visited but other sites included fortifications and palaces, and there were local dance performances. The pilgrim could anticipate, and hope to look back on, the trip of a lifetime with both thrills and scares—with the added satisfaction of spiritual redemption.

Worcester's pilgrimage is especially fascinating because it became unexpectedly intertwined with a conspiracy to draw the absent Earl's name into a court action against the Genoese of London over a shocking act of piracy. By the end of the fifteenth century it was clear that England's maritime future lay around the Atlantic. But in the mid-century the Mediterranean seemed the greatest area of opportunity. Early in 1457 the Bristol merchant Robert Sturmy received licences for a trading expedition intended to open up the eastern Mediterranean.[2] His 1458 mission was particularly sensitive as he planned to buy alum, essential to the production of England's main export, wool, direct from the north-eastern Mediterranean, thereby cutting out the Genoese who dominated this highly profitable trade. The licences covered three ships, le Katerine which belonged to Sturmy, le Mary Heytone, owned by another merchant John Heytone, and a third unidentified carvel of Lord Stourton who, like Worcester, was a councillor and had been a keeper of the sea.

These three ships were attacked in a savage act of piracy that was extraordinarily vividly described in the record of a trial of the Genoese before the English royal council—a most remarkable transcript of which survives in the Cologne city archives.[3] The Genoese of London were eventually required to pay damages of £6,000 on the 25th of July 1459.[4] The documentation describes the Earl of Worcester, on both his outward and return voyage between Venice and the Holy Land, as being chased by pirates in a manner indicating that his name was misused, while he was far away, in order to heighten hostility to the Genoese. While there was undoubtedly a degree of skulduggery to ensure that the case was taken seriously and the Genoese were forced to pay compensation, it was also remarkable how much genuine effort there was to gather witness evidence for far distant events. The court action documention described a fourth ship belonging to Worcester as being in the Mediterranean. If the Earl's boat was not a fiction then his party, which must have comprised at least thirty people as it was known to include a choir of over twenty, might have travelled by sea to the Mediterranean in his ship.

Several of Worcester's fellow travellers from Venice to the Holy Land can be identified. There survives in the Venetian archives a decree by the Senate, dated the 14th of May, consenting to a petition by the Earl to allow Antonio Loredano to accompany him everywhere in his visits to the holy places as his personal guide.[5]

Antonio owned a galley, fairly new, with three banks of oars. Tiptoft was described as '*quidam dominus Anglicus boni status et reputationis in partibus suis*', or 'a certain English Lord of high importance and reputation in his own land'.[6] As Loredano was to be the Earl's personal companion, the captaincy of the *Loredana* was given to the experienced Baldessare Diedo. He proved an exceptionally skilled sailor who navigated through storms, outran pirates and had the quick wit to deceive them when challenged.

Worcester's fellow pilgrims included Italian men of breeding and lively intelligence—qualities they recognised in the English noble, whom they respected and liked. The Milanese nobleman Roberto da Sanseverino was the 40-year-old son of Leonetto Sanseverino and Elisa Sforza, sister of Francesco Sforza, the Duke of Milan. He was a soldier of wide interests, warm character and somewhat pompous temperament, who wrote a highly readable account of the pilgrimage, *Viaggio in Terra Santa*, which mentions Worcester on several occasions.[7] He took with him two friends, Carlo Bosso and Giovanni Matteo Butigella. He called the Earl, clearly recognising his importance, '*Sig.*[or] *d. Giouanne anglese conte et argentero de ingilterra*', or 'Lord John, the English Earl and the Treasurer of England'.[8]

There were two cousins of the important Paduan family of Capodilista who had served the city and its university for generations. The older was Gabriele, who wrote an *Itinerario in Terra Santa*. The younger was Antonio, already a wealthy and successful man. Gabriele called the Earl, '*Signore Inglese, nominato Conte Giouanni de esseter, grande Signore et parente del Re de Ingilterra,*' or, 'an English Lord, named Earl John of Worcester, a great lord and relative of the King of England'.[9] Clearly, the Italians believed Tiptoft a very superior person.

William Wey was on a second galley that left at roughly the same time but went and returned separately. He recorded his experiences in his *Itineraries*, which described two pilgrimages to the Holy Land and another to Santiago de Compostela. He had been an original fellow of Eton College, which had had Worcester's wardship. Another Englishman, William Denys from Devonshire, gave evidence in the action before the King and council against the Genoese for piracy, that he had voyaged to the Holy Land in the same galley as Worcester.[10] The Earl had a large number of choral clerks and presumably some personal servants. The clergy provided him with the capability to hold substantial sung Masses in the holy places. In total there were 100 pilgrims in the *Loredana* and 97 in the second unnamed companion galley in which sailed William Wey. A pilgrim galley could hold at least 170 pilgrims so it seems that 197 wanting to travel in 1458 were divided nearly equally between the two ships.

The galleys that took the pilgrims to the Holy Land were allowed thirteen days between arrival and departure at Jaffa. Thus the voyage between Venice and Jaffa, which took between one and three months, depending on the weather, pirates and disease, comprised the greater part of a pilgrimage. The voyages were, in themselves, memorable and the diaries describe them at length.

The first report of Worcester was on the 14th of May, when the Venetian Senate agreed to his engaging Loredano as his *patrono* or personal guide and courier.[11] This was the same Sunday as the *Sposalizio del Mare*, or the Marriage of the Sea. A solemn procession of boats, headed by the Doge's *Bucentaur*, had rowed past the Lido into the Adriatic Sea since about the year 1000. In 1177, in return for Venice's services against the Holy Roman Emperor Frederick I, Pope Alexander III gave his ring to the Doge, bidding him cast it into and so wed the sea on Ascension Day, a ceremony that has been repeated annually ever since. The Earl must have witnessed the spectacle and possibly was an honoured guest that day.

Lesser pilgrims could not engage a personal *patrono*. They paid the captain an all-in price of 30 to 60 ducats covering the basics of the voyage and donkeys in the Holy Land. A ducat was equivalent to an English Crown, making four to a pound. The pilgrims then bought mattresses and supplementary provisions, particularly wine and eggs. The mattresses could be resold on return at a discount.

The outward and return voyages took between one and two months, sometimes even longer if stormy or windless weather caused severe delays. Therefore the Earl of Worcester spent a significant period on a Venetian pilgrim galley. A remarkably detailed description of such a ship, called the *Jaffa Galley*, can be found in Canon Pietro Casola's account of his pilgrimage to Jerusalem in 1494.[12] This indicates a specialist type—like the modern cruise ship, albeit rather less comfortable. The hull was over 140 feet long and about 35 wide. There was a platform projecting beyond the hull surrounding the whole ship to which were tied merchandise and barrels. The bottom of the hull was filled with sand and gravel ballast on which the pilgrims' casks of wine and jugs of eggs were stored. Above the ballast was a platform which provided the floor of a hall nearly 90 feet long. The hall's ceiling was the ship's deck. This hall provided the accommodation for the majority of the pilgrims, numbering one hundred and seventy. They slept heads facing seawards and feet to the centre line where their chests were stacked.

Between the mizzen and the rear end of the galley was the area called the poop, which had three vertical divisions. The lowest was reserved for munitions and some more distinguished pilgrims at the discretion of the captain. The middle division contained tables for eating and an altar and at night provided further sleeping locations possibly for nobler women. A veritable armoury of bows, crossbows, swords and other weapons hung from the roof and were not there for show. Above, at deck level, was the castle, which was covered first with canvas and then coloured cloth decorated with the ensign of the Holy Sepulchre. In the castle lived the captain and 'any great persons', which in 1458 must have included the Earl of

Map 2: 1458 – Pilgrimage voyage from Venice to Jaffa.

(Continued)

(Continued)

1.	Venice	17 May	Departure
2.	Ragusa (Dubrovnik)	24–25 May	Overnight rest
3.	great storm	28 May	Waves placated by casting saints' names into sea and promises to say Mass to said saints
4.	Durazzo (Durrës)	2–3 June	Overnight rest and repairs following the storm
5.	Candia (Crete)	7–8 June	Despite plague and a ban on disembarking some pilgrims got ashore
A.	*Malta*	*9–12 June*	*Sturmy's convoy attacked by pirates*
6.	Rhodes	10 June	Worcester's galley chased by pirates
6.	Rhodes	10–13 June	Stays as guests of the Grand Master of the Order of St John, invitation to execution of Turks
7.	Cyprus	17 June	Deaths due to disease
8.	Jaffa	20 June	Arrival – disembark next day
7.	Rhodes	22–24 July	On return journey see results of execution of 250 Turks, 18 were impaled, many hanged by the feet. William Denys says Genoese pirates coming from Malta to capture Worcester
5.	Candia	unknown	Denys reports Worcester dismissed the pilgrim's galley to evade capture by Genoese pirates

Worcester, Roberto da Sanseverino with his two companions, and the Capodilistas. With them was the navigating compass. Behind the castle were the rudder handling area, two terracotta water vessels and the latrines.

Ahead of the rear or mizzen mast were two compartments on either side of the ship. To starboard was the captain's canteen, which held water, many different wines, cheese, sausages of meat and of fish. To port was the galley, which contained large and small cauldrons, frying pans, cooking pots and roasting spits, indicating food was reasonably varied. Past the galley were two storeys of cages for live animals, which were killed when fresh meat could not be obtained on land. About the main mast was a forum where pilgrims could gather. Along both sides the oarsmen worked and slept near their chests.

The pilgrims included men, women, friars, priests and hermits from Italy as well as *ultramontanes*, or those from across the Alps. Conditions must have been barely imaginable compared to modern cruise liners, particularly as nearly everyone unused to the sea was sick, and barriers between the sexes, the secular and the religious, the rich and the not-so-rich, and the noble and the base, were tested to

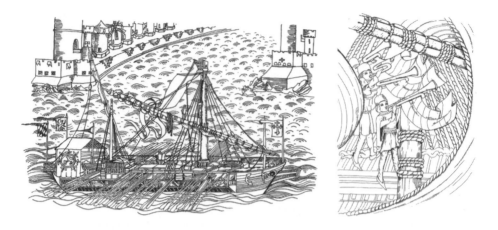

Figure 7: The fifteenth century Venetian pilgrim galley. The second image shows trumpeters behind the mast.

the limit. Yet the surviving accounts, despite the frequent trials, are characterised by a remarkable fortitude, optimism and cheerfulness—the true pilgrim spirit.

All crew members had containers holding a vast amount of merchandise, 'more than three thousand pieces of cloth alone', which they took ashore to establish trade fairs. These were not sullen galley slaves but free, highly experienced, seamen—respected for their obedience and willing—who were largely Sclavenians (south Slavs) and Albanians, alongside a few Lombards, that is Italians. There were several good trumpeters to ensure everything went with a blast.

The Jerusalem pilgrimage was a swansong of a unified medieval Europe: the pilgrim galley was a floating box buffeted on the high seas containing men and women from Ireland to Albania with a Catholic faith intent on the common purpose of reaching the Holy Sepulchre. Within less than a hundred years England was split from Europe and such a voyage—in which the English Earl of Worcester was the leading noble—would be inconceivable.

Adverse winds meant it was not until the 17th of May that the *Loredana* left Venice. The next day the pilgrims saw the coast of Istria and could identify its cities. Making easy progress, the first stop a week later was at Ragusa, modern Dubrovnik, where the pilgrims stayed on the 26th of May. There was much civic ceremony, feasting and sightseeing. The pilgrims explored the fortifications and were given a great meal.

The next stage was much harder, first involving no wind, then a contrary wind and finally a tempest on the 30th of May that 'was such that in the master's and in some of the sailors' opinion it would have been exceptional even in January, and no one of them had seen such a storm ever in that season'.[13] Loredano placed saints' names written down on slips of paper into his hat and select pilgrims drew them out and vowed to say a Mass to that saint if they arrived safe on shore. Then the slips were cast into the sea and the tempest miraculously abated. Roberto drew the name of *Santa Maria di Monte Artone* whose shrine was close to Padua and he did indeed visit it on the14th of January 1459.[14] On the 2nd of June the *Loredana* put in at Durazzo, the modern Albanian city of Durrës, for repairs after the great storm. The pilgrims took the opportunity to visit the walls.

They left two days later and set sail past Corfu, arriving at Candia, modern Heraklion, in Crete on the 7th of June. Due to the plague Loredano forebade leaving the ship but Roberto had already gone onshore and, by the time he had been recalled, Gabriele and Antonio Capodilista had also left the galley. While the brothers stayed two nights with a patrician friend Tadeo Querini, Loredano put a guard on the ship anchored outside the harbour. The pilgrim galley left plague-stricken Candia on the 8th of June.

The evidence given against the Genoese in London later that year said the English convoy landed at Candia towards the end of May after trading in the eastern Mediterranean: 'So [they] accomplisshed theyr seid viage in sauftee thurght Goddes grace unto the porte salve of Candye aforesaid, at which porte the seid 3 shippes [*Katerine*, *Mary Heytone* and Stourton's unnamed carvel] and also another shippe called a kervelle were fully frect [freighted] and charged … with many dyvers merchaundes.'[15] The insinuation was that the fourth 'kervelle' belonged to the Earl of Worcester.

Three English ships now sailed west towards Malta. Heyton's petition, dated the 21st of August 1458, gave a true pirates' tale of deceit, false flags, ship-taking, the bloody slaughter of sailors and the marooning of survivors, revealing the drama to be found at sea in Worcester's time. The vivid description underlined the reality of piracy's peril for those on the sea. On the 9th of June the Genoese put out a small boat whose occupant demanded to know who were in the three ships.

They thene aunsweryng that they were merchauntez of Bristow under the obeissaunces of you, sovereyne lord kyng of England, coming frome Candye laded with merchaundises homeward. The same mane thene aunsweryng in this wyse in the language of Jeane, "*Thane be we all goode frendes and good love betwene us, for all we mene of Jeane*". And all this meane tyme the seid carrake bare a baner of Seynt George …. And assone as ever the seid man retorned frome youre seid besechers unto the seid carrake, they pulled downe the seid baner of Seynt George and sette uppe a baner of the Frenssh kynges of flourdelices and forthewith assautyd your seid besechers in the most horrible and cruell wyse of were, that is to sey with the wylde fyre, brynnyng oyle, unslekked lyme, caltrappes [caltrops or four pronged spikes] and gonnshotte a 1000 of a day and slew of theyr folks your trew subgettes and liegemene to the nombre of 128 (and the remebaunt sore hurte and wounded) and toke and destroyed all theyr seid shippes, merchaundises and goodes and kept theyme prisoners withyne the seid carake by the space of 6 dayes and thene set theyme one lande alle bare without succour or releefe in the Isle of Malta aforeseid .[16]

Several depositions show that the battle lasted three days. The merchants suffered sorely, including Robert Sturmy, who was killed. The two named ships of Sturmy and Heyton were taken. Stourton's carvel escaped.

Meanwhile, further east on the 10th of June, the *Loredana* experienced its own travails and Worcester was also pursued by pirates. Just as the Island of Rhodes was sighted there was an alarm: 'An armed ship with men of Genoa, which was near Rhodes in the shoreline of the sea, made fast, leaving another ship in the said shoreline, and started to follow the galley of pilgrims in which were the said Signor Roberto and his companions, and she [the armed ship] followed it around 6 hours.'[17] When the pirates closed on the *Loredana*, its captain, Baldessare Diedo, shouted that the ship was Catalan with plague aboard. The pirates were uncertain whether to believe him but stood off to confer and then sailed away in search of better prey.

Two sources tell conflicting tales of the pursuing ship. Roberto recorded, 'it was a ship infected with the plague, which lived by stealing, when it could not find a home in any place.'[18] He added the captain of the pursuing ship presented the excuse later that he thought the *Loredana* was a Castilian ship (presumably chasing a Castilian galley was fair game but not chasing a Venetian one, perhaps because it might carry pilgrims). William Denys, the Devonshire pilgrim on the *Loredana*, gave, however, an intriguing twist in his deposition in the action against the Genoese of London. This corroborated the presence of two ships, of which only one gave chase. But he added a new reason for the pursuit. 'When he was in the pilgrim's galley with the Earl of Worcester and others last June twenty miles or so off Rhodes, there appeared two Genoese ships of which the smaller one raised sail and pursued the said galley to Rhodes with the intention of capturing the said Earl of Worcester and the other Englishmen.'[19]

Denys's report has to be treated with suspicion. The pirate assault on the English convoy at Malta, which started on the 9th of June, lasted for three days. Therefore it was not over until after the *Loredana* and the Earl had landed at Rhodes the next day, so the same pirates could not have been involved. The legal action in London against the Genoese, however, needed to name names to be compelling to the King and council: Worcester's was a very familiar name—and that of a man who had fortuitously been close to the pirate action but was conveniently distant from London in the Mediterranean. This resulted in an effort to conflate the Genoese attack on the convoy off Malta with the galleon chase off Rhodes in order to further blacken the reputation of the Genoese.

The pilgrim's galley, having escaped the pirates, landed at Rhodes on the 10th of June. The Earl may have stayed with the castellan of Rhodes castle, who happened to be English.[20] Rhodes was dominated by the Order of the Knights of St John who had left the Holy Land for Cyprus in 1291 and then captured Rhodes in 1309. The Order was ruled by the Grand Master and was composed of seven *lingua* or tongues, Provence, Auvergne, France, Italy, Aragon, Germany and England. The leader of the English tongue was the *grand turcopolier* who commanded the *turcopoli* or light cavalry. Each tongue had an inn where its members gathered and they could offer hospitality to important guests such as the Earl of Worcester.

On the morning of the 11th of June Sanseverino and his party had audiences with the papal legate to the Knights, the Patriarch of Aquilea, and with the Grand Master of the Order of St John, then James de Milly, who was sick in bed with gout. Then, 'having dined … they returned to their lodgings, where … they found a group of important people … [including] the English castellan [possibly the *grand turcopolier*] at Rhodes, who had come to invite them to spend the following day at his garden called *mal passo*, around two miles from Rhodes.'[21] Later Roberto's party were invited to a private citizen's dancing party, to which they went 'for the opportunity it would give [them] of seeing the customs and the manners followed by the Greeks in their festivities'.[22]

The pilgrims also received an invitation to the execution of Turkish prisoners, which had been scheduled for the next day. Roberto recorded that 250 Turks were to be 'cut into pieces or placed on poles … by the knights of Rhodes'.[23] This was justified, as 'they [the Turks] do the same and even worse to them [Christians], when they take them.'[24] The spectacle was delayed as some of the doomed Turks 'had escaped on an incredibly worked boat made of wicker and ox skin,' requiring a delay to recapture them.[25]

Roberto next described the memorable day at *mal passo*:

> Monday 12th of June, having said mass …, around 10 o'clock the horses were taken to the said Signor Roberto and his companions, to go to the said garden; and they went accompanied by the said castellan and many knights. And on having arrived there they went to see the said garden, which is incredibly beautiful and abundant in orange, cedar and laurel

trees, gentle fruits, ornamental fountains, with many fish; ... they went to lie underneath a few beautiful trees, well adorned with tapestries, flowers, and sweet smells, that each in themselves were a great delight: and they stayed there with enough pleasure. Together with them there was an Englishman, called Earl John of Worcester, a great lord and relative of the King of England, and who was himself a pilgrim on the said galley. The abundance, order, and beautiful things were so much, that they would have been a great ornament to a king's court.[26]

It is a sobering thought that, had the galley bringing those captured to Rhodes not been delayed, then the civilised lunch would have been followed by witnessing the tearing to pieces of hundreds of Turks.

After siesta the party was shown by the Knights the hospital and the arsenal of war engines and some very important holy relics, including the relics of Saints Antonio and Caterina and a twig from Christ's crown of thorns that flourished yearly. They then said their farewells to the sophisticated and bloodthirsty Rhodians. The pilgrims left the island on the 13th of June.

Roberto wrote: 'A bird of most beautiful different colours about the size of a starling, exhausted by flying, finding itself far from land, rested in the rigging, where without any resistance or movement it let itself be held.'[27] The bird proved a good omen for, afterwards, the wind increased and they sailed with it all night. The *Loredana*'s pilgrims first saw Cyprus on the 15th of June but landed two days later, delayed by winds, at Limassol where the Capodilistas visited the sugar production business of the banished Venetian Andrea Cornaro. The bloody flux struck those who went ashore due to the unhealthy climate and there were some deaths.

On the 19th of June Mount Carmel, which juts out into the sea from the coast of Palestine, became visible. The pilgrims arrived off Jaffa the next day at 7pm. 'After dropping the sails completely, every man bowed in reverence towards the Holy Land. After this gesture many priests of the galley sang *Te deum laudamus* with such a fervour that there is no heart that would not be moved to the greatest height of devotion, so as to resolve to emend one's life and complete this holy voyage.'[28] The Earl had a large choir and these probably led the singing. The pilgrims, despite pirates, storms and disease had made it to the Holy Land in exceptional time, but the landing would prove a protracted and unpleasant business.

The harbour at Jaffa was long in ruins and galleys were required to wait offshore. 'The galley remained ... that whole night, about half a mile off Jaffa. This happens because of a wicked regulation imposed by the Moors on the pilgrims, who are forbidden to land without a safe-conduct from the officials in Ramleh or in Jerusalem. Anyone landing (without this permit) would be taken into slavery and kept for ransom.'[29]

The next day, expecting the arrival of the notary with the safe-conducts of the Superior of the Convent of Mount Syon of Jerusalem and of the officials from Ramleh, every pilgrim was up at daybreak. They dressed down suitably for travelling in Saracen lands. Roberto gave a revealing analysis on the nature of nobility, from his patrician viewpoint:

> They all dressed in the strangest garments they could, so as not to be recognizable ..., but in the case of some among them nature could not loose its power. In fact, although they were vilely and strangely garbed, nevertheless a man with good powers of observation would have noticed who they were, because of their bearing. This kind of perspicacity is lacking in the Saracens, although in almost all other things they are malicious and rascally. The reason for this change of garments stems from the ill treatment meted out by the Saracens to Christian lords and gentlemen if they recognize them for who they are. For instance, besides inflicting upon them all kinds of tribulations, they search and look for every possible means available to them that would create delays and the opportunity of exacting tributes.[30]

Perhaps his experience as a student had accustomed the Earl of Worcester to wearing the sober garb of a pilgrim. Petty bureaucracy and insolence would prove repeated trials for the pilgrims. These tested their patience while perhaps strengthening their faith.

'Saracen' was the catch-all term used in medieval Europe to describe Muslims. At this time the Holy Land was ruled by the Egyptian Mamluks, who were originally slave soldiers. They had ejected the Mongols from the region in the 1260s and ruled it until 1517 when Jerusalem fell to the Ottoman Turks. In the Mamluk period Palestine was, in practice, unusually tolerant—with Muslims, Christians and Jews all travelling to the Holy City—despite endless pilgrim complaints about the oppressions, mostly petty and bureaucratic, of the Saracens. Pope Nicholas IV (1288–92) had reached agreement with the Mamluks for Latin clergy to hold services in the church of the Holy Sepulchre. In 1300 Robert of Sicily requested that the Franciscans have their church on Mount Syon which lay immediately to the south-west of Jerusalem, where the friars made their base, as well as the Mary Chapel in the Holy Sepulchre, and the Cave of the Nativity in Bethlehem. For two centuries Jerusalem itself was a quiet, indeed decaying, backwater but it was relatively peaceful and the annual arrival of pilgrims must have provided a useful injection into the flaccid economy.

The Saracens did indeed exercise tight control over pilgrims, who were not permitted to wander. The only guides allowed were the Mount Syon Franciscans. In William Wey's accounts the hostility of the Saracens was ever present. Gabriele Capodilista recorded that the pilgrims felt the insults and beatings of the Arabs, another generic term for Muslims, and that the pilgrims were counted and recounted several times as animals and subjected to tolls. The holy places appeared in ruins as only those controlled by the Franciscans could be maintained.

The dislike of the Saracens was possibly coloured by class and religious resentment at having to be subservient to non-noble, non-Christian foreigners. The humble townswoman pilgrim, Margery Kempe, who went to Jerusalem in 1413, described the Saracens very differently. Kempe was disowned by her fellow English pilgrims who, infuriated by her incessent weeping, would not let her accompany them to Mount Quarentyne. She wrote, in the third person, in her autobiography: 'And anon, happed a Saracen, a well-favoured man, to come by her, and she put a groat in his hand, making him a sign to bring her on to the Mount. And quickly the Saracen took her under his arm and led her up on the high Mount, where Our Lord fasted for forty days.'[31] She later recorded: 'The Saracens made much of her, and conveyed her, and led her about the country wherever she would go; and she found all people good to her and gentle, save her own countrymen.'[32] It must be observed—before too flatteringly comparing the Saracens to the English—that the former, unlike the latter, could not understand what she said and were probably spared her lamentations.

The Earl of Worcester had seen great fortifications, observed Greek dances, viewed a bird of exceptional beauty, stayed with serving soldiers, feasted *al fresco*, and seen fellow travellers escape their guide. All this might be par for the course for a more adventurous modern Mediterranean cruise. More in tune with his times and pilgrim's advowed intent, and less familiar to the modern tourist, he had survived a dreadful storm and nearby plague, supposedly been personally the target of pirates, heard accounts of planned impalings which he had only just missed witnessing, viewed great redeeming relics and heard many Masses. Now, with the hazardous outward journey over, began the spiritual stage of the Earl's pilgrimage, when he might gain redemption through a punishing schedule of midnight Masses in the most holy of places.

The Saracens allowed thirteen days between arrival and departure of the pilgrim galleys which was not long given the delays caused by bureaucracy on arrival and the two days needed to travel each way to and from the Holy City. Thus an English pilgrim could expect to take the best part of a year between leaving and returning home—if, of course, he or she survived the experience—for little more than a week in and about Jerusalem. This meant an exhausting schedule, particularly if many nightly vigils were involved and there were visits to the sites outside the Holy City, which included Bethlehem, the river Jordan, Jericho, the Dead Sea and the mountain of Jesus's Temptation. Pilgrims had to follow set itineraries under strict supervision. Many places like Temple Mount were out of bounds.

On the 21st of June the pilgrims were landed in small boats. William Wey explained that from first entry into the Holy Land at Jaffa those who had confessed received remission for all their sins.[33] This was perhaps not unreasonable as the risk of death was not insignificant. He described later how a French priest died and was buried by the roadside near Jericho. At this point, therefore, Worcester—who had gained all the required papal penitentiary paperwork—may have been relieved of the burdens he had carried perhaps since the deaths of his wives and son. Full remission in a spiritual sense, however, was unlikely before the catharsis of vigil in the church of the Holy Sepulchre. Once landed the pilgrims were counted, and then incarcerated for the night in caves which were generally described as foul. At both dusk and dawn an armed man extorted money from each pilgrim.

The next day donkeys were brought by Saracens from Ramleh, about ten miles away. The number of beasts generally exceeded that of the pilgrims which could result in farcical and probably alarming scenes where the Saracens, keen for custom, physically dragged pilgrims to their particular donkeys. They then rode across the coastal plain to Ramleh where they slept in a hospice organised by the Franciscan friars of Mount Syon. Whenever they approached a place of habitation they had to dismount, as Christians could not be seen riding in Muslim controlled areas.

On the 23rd of June the warden of the Franciscans arrived before daybreak and asked all the pilgrims if they had the correct permissions from the papal penitentiary. Those who did not have the requisite papers were rebuked but the warden had the power to absolve them. He then said the first Mass in the Holy Land. Some pilgrims stayed at Ramleh where food was for sale and there were marble baths. Others went the short distance to Lydda where St George, the patron saint of the English, was martyred.

The pilgrims rose at three in the morning and heard Mass. They then went to the place where the Saracens had the donkeys, in order to mount and go on their way, but so many were the insults that the sun was high before they could leave Ramleh, recounted the haughty Sanseverino.[34] The party climbed up from the coastal plain into a mountainous region where pilgrims could be injured by falling stones. A Saracen militia made a show of hostility but did not attack. *En route* to Jerusalem there were a number of halts, including at Emmaus, where the resurrected Jesus had supper with the disciples, and at Arimathea. The last would have been particularly evocative to the English

Map 3: 1458 – Travels in the Holy Land.

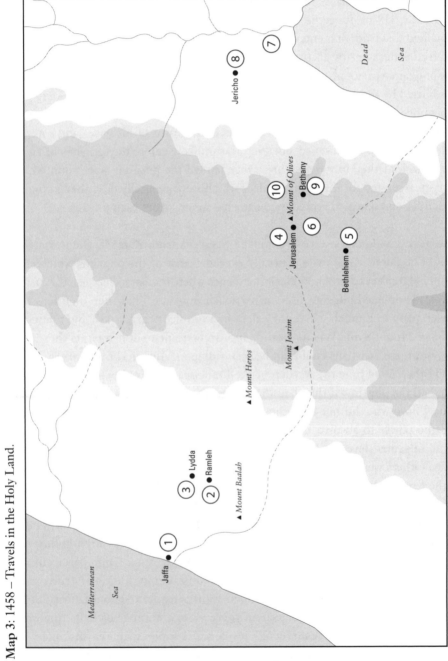

(Continued)

(Continued)

1.	Jaffa	21–22 June	Disembark, spend one night in caves, allocated donkeys
2.	Ramleh	22–24 June	Two nights, friar of Mount Syon preaches sermon with advice on behaviour
3.	Lydda	23 June	Day excursion to Lydda, see shrine marking martyrdom of St George
4.	Jerusalem	24 June	Arrive late evening after halt at Emmaus and Arimathea (locations uncertain), see Jerusalem from Mount Joy
4.	Jerusalem	25–26 June	Worcester and retinue stand on Mount Calvary in the church of Holy Sepulchre to sing Mass
5.	Bethlehem	26–27 June	Bethlehem overnight stay – Worcester hears Mass of our Lord's nativity in the Church of the Nativity
6.	Bethlehem to Jerusalem	27 June	Worcester and others inquire of site where angels announced to shepherds birth of Christ
4.	Jerusalem	27–28 June	Worcester dubs Butigella and Bosso knights of the Holy Sepulchre, holds Mass
7.	Jordan	28–29 June	William Wey and group spends night near to the Jordan river (location of Worcester not specified)
8.	Jericho	29–30 June	William Wey and group spends night at Jericho (location of Worcester not specified)
4.	Jerusalem	1 June – July	Worcester holds Mass
9.	Bethany	1 July	English pilgrims go to Bethany (location of Worcester not specified)
4.	Jerusalem	1–2 July	Pilgrims pass last night at Mount Syon, the place of the Last Supper
2.	Ramleh	2 July	Ride to Ramleh
1.	Jaffa	3 July	Ride to Jaffa, set sail

pilgrims for—according to a history by John of Glastonbury, written around 1350—Joseph of Arimathea had come to England bringing with him vessels containing the blood and sweat of Christ. In later stories these would become the Grail. John further claimed Britain's King Arthur, through his mother, Igraine was descended from Joseph.

After climbing through the mountainous district the pilgrims saw Jerusalem from the hill appropriately named Mount Joy. They arrived late in Jerusalem and went straight to the church of the Holy Sepulchre but they found it closed and were told they would not be admitted until the next day.

The Holy Sepulchre was built over the site both of Golgotha, or Mount Calvary, where Jesus was crucified, and the tomb where he was buried and from which he was resurrected. In the fourth century Helena, the mother of the Emperor Constantine, had found the True Cross near to Calvary and the site was included in a subterranean extension to the east of the main body of the church. Here better than anywhere, like all pilgrims, Worcester might obtain real remission for his sins. Catholic doctrine taught that pardon for sins ultimately came from Christ's finished work on Calvary. Most Christians could not be expected to be physically present on that once green hill far away but they might receive pardon through the rite of the Mass. Hearing Mass on Calvary itself could not but amplify the experience.

All the references, except two, to Worcester in the Holy Land—in the diaries of Wey, Capodilista and Sanseverino—refer to events that took place in the church of the Holy Sepulchre. Maybe part of his programme of atonement and redemption was to say nightly Masses in the most holy places.

During the first night most of the pilgrims stayed at the now destroyed Hospital of St John near to the Holy Sepulchre but Roberto and the Milanese lived more exclusively with the Franciscan Brothers of Mount Syon outside the city walls. It is not clear where Worcester lodged but given that he had a large choir with him, who must have stayed in the Hospital, it is probable he was not at Syon. He may have been found special lodgings by his expert guide Antonio Loredano. On Sunday the 25th of June the pilgrims visited the sites in and around Jerusalem. The itineraries and locations were tightly controlled and, therefore, the order and subject matter of various accounts and diaries read surprisingly similarly. Also, guides over generations developed stories and anecdotes that must have become formulaic. The differences tend to reflect the critical faculties and personalities of the writers. The English chaplain William Wey, rather credulously to the modern mind, did not describe a place in its own right but as the location of an incident from the bible. The sophisticated Italians were more detached, commenting on the ruinous and untended state of the sites and the impositions of the Saracens. Thus, while Wey would simply recount that near the Holy Sepulchre was the house of the rich man who denied crumbs, the aristocratic Milanese Sanseverino found the Garden of Gethsemane 'uncultivated' and generally the urbane Paduan Capodilista commented on how the holy places appeared to be in ruins.

The route taken in the fifteenth century was the reverse of that later followed by the Stations of the Cross. This is now westward from the place of Christ's condemnation at Pilate's House along the Via Dolorosa to Calvary within the Holy Sepulchre. As access to Jerusalem became harder, illustrations of these Stations were placed around local churches and processions could follow the same route between them in imitation of Christ. It was William Wey who first coined the term 'stations' after his second pilgrimage in 1462.

Plan 4: 1458 – Jerusalem – Church of the Holy Sepulchre.

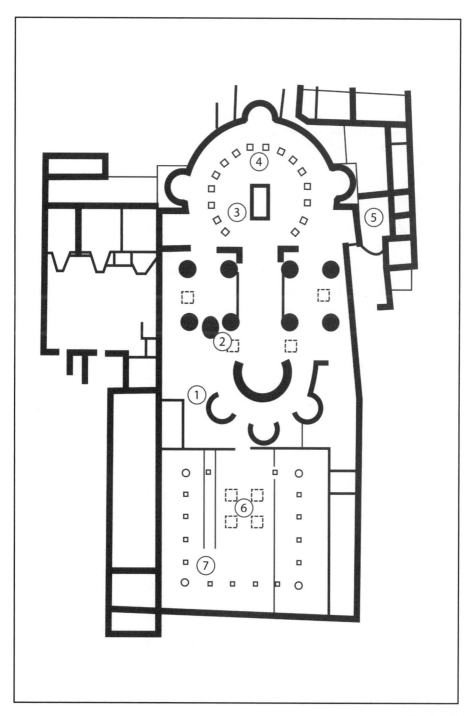

(Continued)

(Continued)

1.	Rock of Calvary
2.	Stone of the appointing
3.	Tomb of Jesus
4.	Chapel of the angel
5.	Chapel of the Apparition
6.	Chapel of St Helena
7.	Chapel of the finding of the cross, underground, location of entrance

Locations where Wey wrote that Worcester held Mass

25–26 June – Mount Calvary, Holy Sepulchre, Jerusalem (1)

26–27 June – Altar of Our Lord's Nativity, church of Nativity, Bethlehem

27–28 June – Mount Calvary, Holy Sepulchre, Jerusalem (1)

28–29 June – Unknown

29–30 June – Unknown

30 June–1 July – Chapel of the Apparition, Holy Sepulchre, Jerusalem (5)

After starting at the Holy Sepulchre the pilgrims moved eastward along the Via Dolorosa, leaving Jerusalem and entering the Valley of Jehoshophat—where the first Christian martyr Stephen was stoned—which runs after the east side of the Old City. They saw a chapel dedicated to Mary as well as her tomb. Having passed across the Valley the pilgrims climbed Mount Olive, on whose western slope was the Garden of Gethsemane. They redescended westwards into the Valley, passing the tree where Judas hanged himself.

The party continued southwards from the Valley of Jehoshophat over the bridge of Syloe and into the Valley and to the Pool of that name at the south-east corner of Jerusalem. Then they came to Mount Syon at the south-west corner of the old city. There they visited the monastery of the Franciscans, which was located on the site of the Last Supper, the tomb of King David and the house of Caiaphas.

That evening those staying in the Hospice near the Holy Sepulchre returned and remained guarded by Saracens until collected by the Franciscans from Mount Syon and taken to the church. Here the Saracens counted them, recorded their names and shut them in for the night with their supper and sleeping necessities.

The first church of the Holy Sepulchre on the site had been built by Constantine the Great in the 320s. After various vicissitudes in 1009, the caliph Al-Hakim bi-Amr Allah ordered its complete destruction, leaving few remains. It was partially rebuilt by the time Jerusalem was retaken by the First Crusade on the 15th of July 1099. The crusaders completed the reconstruction but it was lost again in 1187 when Saladin retook the City, although the treaty established after the Third Crusade of 1189–92 allowed pilgrims to visit the site.

Sanseverino said the pilgrims processed around the church and then sat on the floor to eat and sleep on mats, carpets or the bare ground. Wey described

Map 5: 1458 – Jerusalem and environs – abbreviated list of sites described by William Wey.

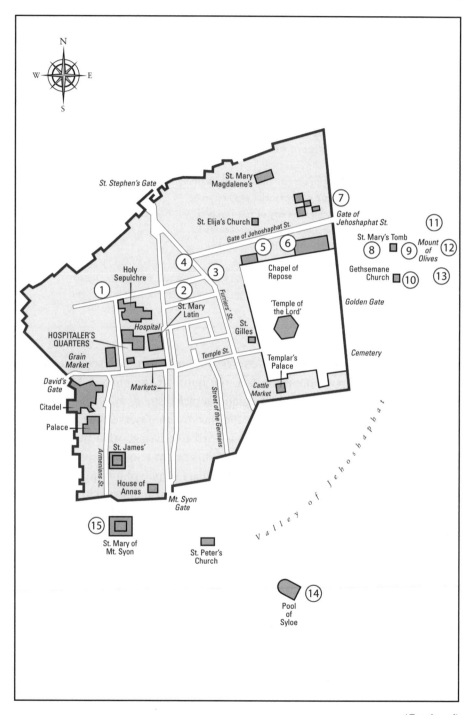

(Continued)

	Path followed in 1468 (now Via Dolorosa, modern route in opposite direction)
1.	Jesus addressed the daughters of Jerusalem
2.	Veronica wiped face of Jesus
3.	Simon of Cyrene took up the cross
4.	Mary fainted seeing Jesus
5.	Jesus flogged, crowned and condemned
6.	Jesus mocked in Herod's house
	Valley of Jehoshaphat and Mount of Olives
7.	Gate through which Stephen was led to be stoned
8.	Cedron stream
9.	Tomb of Mary, Christ prayed on night of last supper
10.	Garden of Gethsemene where Christ was arrested
11.	Jesus appeared to disciples on day of resurrection
12.	Jesus's footprint left behind as he rose to heaven
13.	Tree where Judas hanged himself
14.	Pool of Syloe – blind man's sight restored
	Mount Syon (site of houses of Annas and Caiaphas where Peter denied Jesus)
15.	Monastery of the Franciscans containing the *Cenacle* (site of Last Supper and the Pentecost)

how at midnight the pilgrims said confession and heard Masses and the Earl with his choir sang polyphonically (see the quote at the chapter beginning).[35] Thus one of the greatest peers of England actually stood and sang on the very site of the cross on which Christ died. He was not an observer but a participant in the ritual of the Mass on Cavalry. It is hard to envisage what more could be done in the quest for the remission of sins. This might also indicate that the Earl was an accomplished singer able to hold his part in polyphony and read music. (Charles the Bold, Duke of Burgundy 1467–77, was also unusual in singing with his choirs. This was noted because it was not something usually done by secular nobles—in the Duke's case some thought it was not done too well.) It says something of the essential lack of *noblesse oblige* that the Earl was a participant, not an observer. His student life may have accustomed him to dealing with choral clerks and churchmen as equals.

Wey described which Mass was sung: that, not entirely surprisingly, of the Holy Cross. This was a votive Mass, which honoured a particular mystery of the faith and was not tied to a specific day.[36] Later Wey wrote, on the occasion of another Mass, that the Earl's choir had twenty-seven members. In the fifteenth century England had become rather backward in the visual arts, although its embroidery, *opus anglicorum*, remained much admired. But since John Dunstable (1390–1453), England was the leading nation in music, and the Council of Constance—which the Earl of Worcester's father attended—spread the reputation of the *contenance angloise*, with its pioneering use of thirds, as the most advanced and beautiful in Europe. Wey was no common observer but a bursar of Eton College, which had an extremely skilled choir whose members were required to 'possess the skills of reading, chanting, and singing *cantus organicus*' (it may not be a coincidence that the young John Tiptoft had been a ward of Eton College).[37]

There followed a lively discussion involving the galley masters, the Superior of Mount Syon, interpreters and locals about how best to visit Bethlehem. At about 3pm, presumably to allow for some rest after the previous night's vigil and miss the heat of midday, a party of over forty pilgrims rode their donkeys to Bethlehem. Roberto did not go as he intended to spend more time in the Holy Land. The journey was about five miles and passed many sites, including where Elijah hid from the pursuing Queen Jezebel and the place where Mary dismounted from her donkey and rested.

In Bethlehem they went to the church of the Most Blessed Virgin and left their possessions where they would later rest in the cloister. They saw the tomb of St Jerome, who translated the bible into Latin, now empty as his body had been moved to Rome, and the grave of many of the slaughtered innocents. The altar marked the spot below which was a chapel in the place Jesus was born. Wey reported that 'There at the altar of the Lord's birth the aforesaid Earl of Worcester had the Mass of the Lord's birth with polyphonic song. The morning after the Mass we went out from the holy city of Bethlehem riding donkeys.'[38] The Mass of Our Lord's Nativity, another votive Mass, was sung in the very place of Jesus's birth. Thus Worcester had personally, on consecutive nights, celebrated Mass with his own choir where Jesus's life ended and began.

Wey recounted going to the mountains of Judea, about four miles north-west of Jerusalem, and visiting a church located where the pregnant Mary met Elizabeth. The pilgrims, like her, sang the psalm, 'My soul doth magnify the Lord'.[39] There was no specific mention of the Earl's choir so, given that this would have been an excellent opportunity for it to sing this beautiful psalm in an appropriate location, perhaps this was evidence that neither the choir nor Worcester accompanied this expedition.

In the late afternoon the party, returning to Jerusalem, sought out the place where the shepherds had watched their flocks and the angel announced the birth of Jesus. Capodilista reported a rather charming story of the search for the site of the Holy Mount: 'For the consolation of the reader I will hereby describe a miracle which appeared on the afore mentioned shepherds' hill and it was this that, being the above written Gabriele Capodilista, in a group went to Bethlehem near the church where our Lord was born, and where the said mound was seen.'[40] At Bethlehem the pilgrims had asked:

a monk for information on which mountain it was where the angels announced to the shepherds, and he having showed it with diligence, because the said little mountain is around a mile away from Bethlehem, situated low down in a valley next to which there are a few other little mountains. And having got to the top, with around forty pilgrims amongst whom there was Lord Signor John the Englishman and many other knights; and the said Signor Gabriele called them, with liveliness, wanting to show them the said shepherd's little mountain for his consolation, and all of them came together with great devotion to see it, and he, with great diligence, showed it to them. And another pilgrim, who had already seen it, told him that he was not showing it to them right but that it was another one near there, but Gabriele said the opposite. And while standing bickering, when the sun was above the earth, in presence of everyone, a golden ball left the sky, of the size of a barber's bowl, and it came down perpendicularly with great elegance and fell directly to the top of the little mountain that was being shown by the aforementioned signor Gabriele, and then immediately vanished. At this everyone was left amazed and yet happy, and consoled that the eternal God had been so worthy in his mercifulness for having shown the truth to those pilgrims, and for this everyman left pleased.[41]

Given the unimpeachable source, the aristocratic Italian lawyer, it might be improper to question whether the Earl of Worcester personally witnessed a miracle in the Holy Land.

Worcester and Carlo Bosso rejoined Roberto da Sanseverino and Giovanni Matteo Butigella in Jerusalem and they went together to the Holy Sepulchre at about 9pm. Here Bosso and Butigella were inducted into the military Order of the Knights of the Holy Sepulchre, a chivalrous institution presided over by the King of Aragon. The Father Guardian of Mount Syon, where Roberto and his friends were staying, had the authority to admit pilgrims eligible through their noble birth and military distinction. Knighthood itself was conferred by one of the brothers, himself a noble, but now Sanseverino and Tiptoft were given the honour of presiding over inductions. Throughout his life Worcester was prominent as a master of ceremonies and orator and must have relished this role.

And having done their 'creche' in the said church, the said signor Roberto, according to the order he had taken together with the above mentioned Lord Giovanni, the English Earl and Treasurer of England, called forth Matteo and Carlo, in the place of burial of lord Jesus Christ himself, invoking devotedly his name, and to his praise and glory, put the two Golden spurs on the feet of the said Giovanni Matteo and Carlo, and the said lord Earl gave the golden sword and made them a knight, having given the sacrament and with the ceremonies that were a similar part; and they devotedly for the praise of our lord Jesus accepted the said worthy things, thanking him for having made them worthy of such honours and in such a devoted, and precious and sacred place.[42]

Wey returned from the mountains of Judea to stay overnight at the church of the Holy Sepulchre. 'We entered the church, awaiting there all through the night, the lord Earl of Worcester had mass sung in polyphonic voice above Mount Calvary.'[43] On the 28th of June William Wey and other pilgrims took donkeys to ride to the Desert of the Forty Days. The Earl was not mentioned during this excursion and he may have stayed in Jerusalem. The pilgrims visited the mountain of Temptation where they celebrated Mass. Wey stayed the night, sleeping outside about five miles from the Jordan. A French priest died there and was buried by the roadside. On the 30th of June Wey returned to Jerusalem via Bethany where there was a fine tomb of St Lazarus.

On the night of the 30th of June to the morning of the 1st of July Wey revisited the church of the Holy Sepulchre. 'And then we entered into the church, and there we had the sermon by a priest of England and of the Royal College of Eton of the blessed Mary, of which the text was, "You are a pilgrim in Jerusalem [Luke 24:18]". And there were there twenty-seven Englishmen with the aforesaid lord Earl, who in the morning had sung mass with polyphonic song in the Chapel of the Most Blessed Mary.'[44] Wey was himself 'an English priest from Eton' so he was almost certainly describing himself as giving the sermon. The Chapel of the Most Blessed Mary is on the north side of the church of the Holy Sepulchre. It marks the spot where Jesus appeared to Mary after his resurrection and is now generally known as the Chapel of the Apparition. Wey specifically described the Mass as having been sung in the morning, presumably timed to match the hour Mary met the resurrected Jesus. Thus Worcester is known to have held Masses at night in the place of Jesus's death, and birth, and at daybreak at the resurrection. It is possible there were further Masses in the church of the Holy Sepulchre on the two unaccounted for nights but his position is known only through the words of others and when they say nothing the Earl vanishes from the record.

Wey reported that the day of the 1st of July was spent preparing for the return journey. He stayed the night of the 1st/2nd of July at Mount Syon, the place of the Last Supper. Thus the pilgrims' own final evening meal in Jerusalem was spent at the site of Jesus's and the apostles' Last Supper. On the 2nd of July the pilgrims said goodbye to Roberto and Matteo, who were to stay longer in the Holy Land. After Mass they rode to Ramleh and stayed overnight. The next day the pilgrims rode back to Jaffa.

After a short, spiritually intense, sojourn in the Holy Land the return journey for redeemed pilgrims might seem an anti-climax. The Capodilistas' and William Wey's dates for landing at ports on the return voyage match, so the Paduan nobles may have switched galley now that the Milanese party was mostly remaining in the Holy Land. Worcester—who was not mentioned on the return by the Paduans as he was on the way out—might have gone back on the same galley with William Denys, who described the Earl's involvement in more piratical drama.

Wey arrived at Rhodes on the 22nd of July, having stopped earlier at Cyprus. He remained for two days and described the missed spectacle of the executions to which the pilgrims had been invited on the outward voyage.

> There we heard, before our arrival by water, that two hundred and fifty Turks were brought to Rhodes to whom the following was done. When they entered the city, Christian boys captured by the Turks, in white, went before, carrying white crosses in their hands, dragging the deniers [of the faith] perforated through the noses and others by hands tied behind the back; among whom 18 had stakes placed in the fundament, going out through the backs and chests; and ten were drawn naked through a timber full of spikes of iron. Also, two were beheaded after their baptism; one flayed, another cast from the Tower, and hung by the groin: the remainder were hanged, some by the feet, some by the neck, on both sides of the city in order to be open [to sight] by all passing.[45]

This exhibition, revolting to modern sensibilities, likely made a powerful impression on the Earl, who must have heard accounts of the executions and seen physical remains. The 'stakes placed in the fundament' and the hanging 'by the feet' may have become lodged in his mind. It matches the pattern for the degradation of the bodies of prisoners ordered by the Earl in Southampton in 1470, where the corpses were hanged upside down with a stake forced into the anus on which the victims' heads were spiked.

William Denys later gave evidence in London that, on the return journey, the same Genoese pirates who attacked Sturmy's expedition were planning to capture the Earl: 'Again, he said that having completed their pilgrimage to Jerusalem, they returned to the Island of Rhodes [in late July] where they learned that the Genoese ships which had robbed Robert Sturmy were on their way to capture the same Earl of Worcester and the English who were with

Figure 8: A detail from Guillaume Caoursin's late fifteenth *Gestorum Rhodie obsidionis commentarii* which illustrates episodes from the conflict between the Knights and the Turks on Rhodes.[46] The image shows an engagement between the Knights of St John and the Turks and in the background the execution of captive Turks. Such events almost certainly provided the model for the degradation by Worcester of the bodies of Warwick's men executed at Southampton in 1470.

him.'[47] But these pirate Genoese certainly did *not* chase the Earl of Worcester on the voyage out and, given their need to deal with the *matériel* taken from robbing Sturmy's convoy, it was unlikely that it was these same Genoese who pursued the Earl on the return journey. Indeed, the story that the Genoese pursued the Earl on the return trip looks fabricated to add weight to the accusation in the London court action against them.[48] The memorandum presented to the Council, which repeated Denys's deposition, pushed Worcester to centre stage: 'The seid carrack and vesselles of the Jeanne after the taking of the seid Robert Sturmy and his feleshippe chased and folowed under sayle the erle of Worcestre to have takyne hyme.'[49]

The memorandum said the Earl went from Rhodes to Candia (Heraklion) on Crete, presumably still on the pilgrim galley, stating, 'but, as God wold, he [the Earl of Worcester] escaped from theyme [the Genoese] into the havene of Candie.'[50] Denys now added an entirely new twist for he deposed that Worcester—in order to evade the Genoese pirates who had previously attacked Sturmy's convoy—'for his safety' changed from the pilgrim galley to a light galley, which was presumably faster. 'Again, in Candia – indeed on Corfu – he [Denys] heard that – having been pressed to do so – the *same Earl dismissed the pilgrim's galley and arranged transport with a light galley for his safety* in order to evade ambush by the said Genoese ships, which he [the Earl] had learned were lying off Argos and had a ship called the *Katerina* with them which the Genoese had captured.'[51]

If it was true that Worcester changed ships, was his motive entirely honourable? Was he ignobly pulling rank to get out of danger? Or was he nobly making the other pilgrims safer by leaving them, as it was he who was the target of piratical interest? One thing does seem clear: those bringing the Earl into the court action confirmed that his very name remained sufficiently important to command the attention of the King, the council and the courts of law. Also, he must have still been seen by contemporaries in 1458 and 1459 as a loyal subject of the King since, were his loyalty suspect, the value of invoking his name to gain the support of courts, council and monarch would have been diminished.

Whether this was all an ingenious fabrication—based on the assumption the Earl was literally one thousand miles away and in no position to deny the story—is still hard to disentangle. All that can be said with certainty is that Worcester made it safely back to Venice. But while there can be no doubt that Sturmy's convoy was horribly mauled, almost certainly by Genoese, and that anger in London was huge, it does seem that the Earl's obviously great name and distant location were exploited to create supporting evidence of the piratical duplicity of the Genoese that, at best, stretched imagination and, at worst, was downright dishonest.

Having, however, returned safely to Venice, uncaptured by real or fictitious pirates, the Earl faced a choice: return to cold, wet, divided, backward England; or remain in Italy, at the peak of its *quattrocento* brilliance, of powerful and wealthy patrons like the de' Medici, the d'Este, and the Gonzaga; of the art and architecture of Mantegna and Brunelleschi; and of scholars like Bracciolini and Argyropoulos, who had been to England and found it boorish and barbarous, and Guarino who was so admired by Duke Humphrey. Nor was there a lack of fellow Englishmen. This was an Italy where he could meet many fellow university men, including Robert Flemming, Peter Courtenay, Henry Sharp, John Lee, Richard Bole, Vincent Clement, and John Gunthorpe.

Pilgrims to the Holy Land travelled further when going to the places where Jesus himself had lived and died than did those who made pilgrimages to Canterbury, Santiago de Compostela in Galicia, or Rome. The distances and dangers were far greater than those involved in reaching these other destinations. A man or woman who had been to Jerusalem had put their life on the line. The Earl had joined this select band and appeared to have been unique in this respect among secular living English noblemen from the time of his pilgrimage to his death. Worcester's pilgrimage was particularly religious in its focus. He had gained remission from his sins on arrival at the Holy Land. The long nightly Masses may have strengthened his sense of liberation. He could now face life with renewed confidence—perhaps even overconfidence.

Chapter 9

Italy I – scholarship, 1458 to 1461

On returning from Jerusalem the Earl of Worcester, captivated by the Muses, has remained three years in Italy, and now resides in Padua, for the sake of study, and detained by the refined culture of the Venetians, who being exceedingly fond of books, has plundered, if I may so speak, our Italian libraries to enrich England.[1]

Funeral oration for Guarino da Verona by Ludovico Carbone in 1460

*I*nglese italianato è un diavolo incarnate, or, 'an Italianate Englishman is a devil incarnate': thus, supposedly, the Italians spoke of the English who stayed among them. Also, 'you remain men in shape and fashion but become devils in life and condition.' So wrote Roger Ascham, the Princess Elizabeth Tudor's scholar tutor, in *The Scholemaster*, published posthumously in 1570. Before the Earl of Worcester left England in 1458 there is little evidence that his behaviour was anything other than exemplary. In service of his country he had remained above faction, striving to maintain governance before, through and after King Henry VI's madness, despite cruel personal losses of wives and children. Now he had been to the Holy Land and earned remission for his sins. But, rather than return immediately to England, he would remain in Italy for three years.

Italy, unlike England, was no unified nation but a hotchpotch of duchies and papal states. It had numerous cities exceeding London as *foci* of governance, culture and scholarship. Thus the traveller could, in many locations, such as Venice, Ferrara and Florence, combine both study and observation of varied political and courtly models. And then there was Rome, from where the Vatican City ruled the Holy Catholic Church, which extended from the Iberian Peninsula to Poland, and from Scandinavia to Rhodes. Here gathered pilgrims, petitioners, prelates and proctors from across Europe in a rich cosmopolitan brew.

The university-educated Worcester, who may have retained in his household some of the choir that accompanied him to the Holy Land, had an *entrée* into a substantial expatriate community working in the service of the universal church in Rome, studying at the universities of Bologna and Padua, or employed as composers and musicians. While England had fallen behind Italy in the visual arts and scholarship, its music was the most advanced in Europe. Indeed, due to the destruction wreaked during the English Reformation, medieval English music has survived mainly in northern Italy and southern Germany. The Earl of Worcester, after his years at Oxford, with his scholarly and musical interests, could easily integrate into such English groups—and share the experience of learning in Italy and news from England—while his wealth and status would make him attractive as a patron.

In the early autumn of 1458 the Earl of Worcester returned to Venice. As the humanist Ludovico Carbone charmingly put it—in his eulogy to the great scholar-teacher Guarino da Verona which described his pupil Worcester—apart from the ethereal muses there was the culture, perhaps in the broader sense, of the Venetians to enjoy.[2] The Earl might have been above such things but over ten per cent of the 100,000 plus population of Venice were courtesans and prostitutes. Leland made clear hints at the delights of Venice. 'He visited the City of Venice and, a graceful guest, remained there for some time. Good fortune promoted the choice and … the Venetians were embraced with easy outstretched arms.'

The Earl soon met up with the Capodilistas. For nearly seven centuries their family had stood high in the life of Padua. The Capodilista line traced itself back to Charlemagne's invasion of Italy in the late eighth century, when the Transalgardo brothers took the enemy Lombard commander prisoner and one, Carlotto, became the *capo di lista* or company head. The Capodilistas had a country house halfway along the road from Padua to Abano Terme, six miles away, where nobles and prelates took the curative waters. Here, and in the pleasant Euganean Hills which provide relief to the flat Lombard plain, the great and good of Padua built villas. They entertained visitors and supported able young students. Few families can have been as well placed as Worcester's Capodilista companions to integrate him into the life of Italy's second oldest university city.

Given the tensions in England, which looked increasingly as though they could only be resolved through violence, there was scant reason or inclination for Worcester to resist if invited to stay with the Capodilistas. Both Gabriele Capodilista and his brother Francesco taught law at the University of Padua and could provide introductions.

The Florentine book producer Vespasiano da Bisticci commented, 'he … journeyed to Padua, where he was at the University, to work on Latin, even though he already had full acquaintance in the subject.'[3]

Leland emphasised the scholarly allure of Padua:

> Now he [Worcester] has always held those of refined letters most familiar in mind from tender years and Padua, the neighbouring university, has long sought, with the most vehement ardour, to bring forth the most trained in each of the noble disciplines. Such that, everlasting God, have there ever been to be met so many extraordinarily learned men within one place?[4]

Map 6: 1458–61 – Italy.

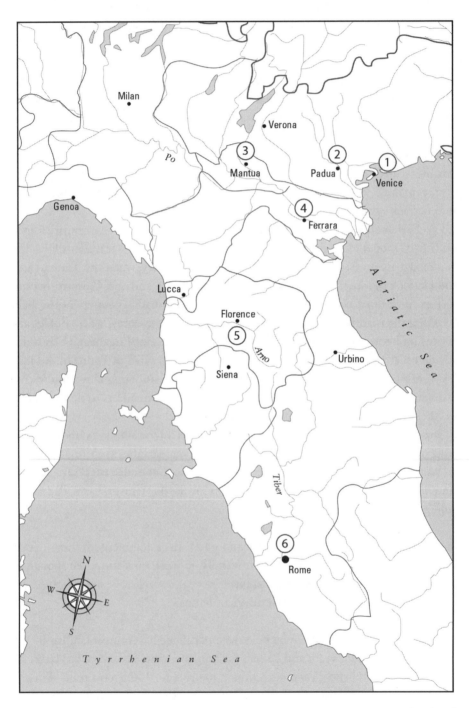

(Continued)

(Continued)

1.	Venice	1458, September	Return from Holy Land
2.	Padua	1458–61	University and book purchasing
3.	Mantua	1459–60	Papal Congress, Worcester's attendance uncertain
4.	Ferrara	1459/60	Attended school of Guerino da Verona
5.	Florence	1459/60	Bought books, visited de' Medici
	Florence	1461	En route to Rome, ordered more books, attended lecture by Argyropoulos, visited de' Medici
6.	Rome	1461	Early summer possible occasion of address to Pope, met cardinals
5.	Florence	1461	En route returning from Rome, collected ordered books
2.	Padua	1461, July/August	Left Italy

Padua's university was already old in 1458. In 1221 a group of professors and students had left Europe's first University at Bologna for Padua, which started as a school of law but expanded to teach a range of arts subjects. In 1399 Padua divided into two, with a *Universitas Iuristarum* teaching civil and canon law and a *Universitas Artistarum* teaching astronomy, dialectic, philosophy, grammar, medicine, and rhetoric. A *Universitas Theologum* was also established in 1373. Padua had come under Venetian control in 1405 but the University maintained special privileges. The student body was divided into *cismontanes* and *ultramontanes* – that is those from this side of and from across the Alps. In the fifteenth century about twenty Englishmen are known to have studied at Padua.[5]

Whether the Earl studied law or the arts, or if he took any formal examination, is unknown as the records for the relevant period are lost.[6] In Ferrara Worcester studied under Guarino, who was not a teacher of law but Latin and Greek, indicating that his interest in Padua lay with the *Universitas Artistarum*, although on his return to England he would be excoriated for his supposed attempted imposition of Paduan Law. Thus he may have attended some lectures at the *Universitas Iuristarum*. There is evidence that the Earl did genuinely study. Between 1459 and 1461 a copy of Silius Italicus's *Punica* and an incomplete text of Valerius Flaccus's *Argonauticon* was made at Padua for Worcester, who annotated its text in a way which suggested he was following lectures.[7]

The noble pilgrims had a brief and joyful reunion. The Milanese Roberto da Sanseverino and Giovanni Matteo Butigella returned rather later from the Holy Land. Roberto had been delayed trying to find guides to go to St Catherine's monastery on Mount Sinai. Giovanni Matteo fell ill and remained in Jerusalem. Even after Roberto's return from a trip that included Cairo, their departure was held back by Giovanni's continued illness and they had a terrible voyage.

On their return to Italy the Milanese stayed at the Capodilista villa and sought out Worcester in Padua early in 1459. Something of the genuine warmth of the Italians towards the Earl was conveyed in Roberto's diary. These Italians saw nothing of the devil incarnate in the English lord in Italy. Roberto and Giovanni 'went to visit the above written lord count Giovanni the Englishman, because they had established that he had been there at Padua to study ... As soon as he saw them he welcomed them joyously and with great good will and wished to do for them everything that he could. And having been together ... after many caresses, hugs and tenderness, they returned together to rest at the house of the said lord Gabriele.'[8]

The Earl of Worcester's wealth meant he could be a patron. This entailed the encouragement and financial support of scholars by those richer, who received in return dedications of great works, reflective of and enhancing their worth and glory. The antiquary John Leland described the close relationship between the great Earl of Worcester and the humble John Free, who was the first English scholar to take up humanist studies as a career.

> The Englishman John Free especially shines forth ... not only due to great distinction of eloquence but also Caesarian [Roman] laws, philosophies, and of medicines ... Earl John has chosen this man in friendship and familiar acquaintance, ... neglecting no untried line of benevolence. ... Free ... indeed ... has admired ... and has cultivated his patron's nobility of character, erudition and authority, and to him, remarkably increasing renown, he has dedicated a small book *In praise of baldness*, translated from Greek into the best Latin. ... He ... has dedicated to the same man a song of Bacchus's epostulation to the goat about his gnawed vine, a marvel always to the discriminating.[9]

Free was a Balliol alumnus who received an MA in 1454. So inspired was he by reports of Italy that he made his way there and somehow gained financial support from Worcester's fellow council member and scholar, the Bishop of Ely, William Grey, also of Balliol. He arrived in Ferrara in 1456 and in 1457 began to study Greek under the master Guarino da Verona at Ferrara. In 1458 he went to Padua to study medicine. Some time the following year Free switched from Grey's to Worcester's patronage.

This relationship between the Earl and the scholar seems to have gone beyond the usual nexus of patron and scholar, implying the Earl actively sought the friendship of a man far lower in social station and rank who was a very promising but still minor scholar. Free, in turn, genuinely admired the Earl and dedicated to him not only an early translation from Greek to Latin of Synesius's *In praise of baldness*, putting him at the frontline of scholarship, but also what sounds to be a humorous poem involving a goat and a gnawed vine, maybe intended to be sung. The *Synesius* survives but sadly not the verse. It was very likely that Free helped Worcester with his Latin letters and speeches and advised him on his book purchases so that his collections contained recent discoveries and translations from Greek into Latin. The joint annotations of texts show them to have been equals sharing the love of the pursuit of learning.

Italians to whom the Earl provided patronage included Francesco Aretino and Ognibene Bonisoli. Aretino's father had been executed for treason in Florence and he was brought up in exile. In the later 1440s he had gone to Rome and studied under Lorenzo Valla and began to translate from Greek into Latin. He served Popes Calixtus III (1455–58) and Pius II (1458–64). On the 22nd of March 1461 Aretino fulfilled a promise to Worcester, which he said he had made eighteen months earlier, by delivering to him his translation of *De Calumnia*.[10] Aretino wrote to Francesco Pellato of Padua calling the Earl of Worcester *'liberalissimus'*.[11] Ognibene Bonisoli was expert in Latin and Greek and taught grammar in Vicenza. In his dedication of Xenophon's *De Venatione*, or, *On Hunting*, he wrote,

> For there is nothing you lack for the accumulation of praise and glory, whom others see endowed with virtues, each man usually having but one virtue—faith Fabricius, piety Regulus, temperance Cato, justice Camillus, magnificence Lucullus, humanity Marcellus. But you we see adorned equally with every good which nature can assign to men or hard work procure. Accordingly, I decided to make this Latin book and dedicate to your name, illustrious prince, a work that I think not displeasing to you since you delight in this exercise, surely you will enjoy reading.[12]

There was a hint in these dedications that Worcester enjoyed the chase, wine and song and was perhaps going bald.

On the 26th of January 1460 the Earl wrote a letter, possibly with the aid of Free, to Oxford University, offering to present a collection of select classical writings upon which students would be able to model their style.

> Still, if the higher powers see fit that I should revisit my homeland and if ever it befell me [that England would be] in a secure state, I will not doubt that [Oxford] will be renowned and distinguished by the greatness

and abundance of services I will have done for you. I want these books, a
list of which I send to you, to remain always with you as a testament and
token of our love. Of which surely you should expend work in continuously reading so you will restore the worth of the lost Latin language,
whereof our ancestors, the ancient Britons, have flourished. ... You will
easily become those whom our most serene and dread king appoints as
orators; of what kind who will not seem uneloquent when they are sent to
the Italians, the leaders of all eloquence.[13]

(The message reflected the *De Republica* by the Ferraran Frulovisi, a pupil of
Guarino and secretary to Duke Humphrey, who 'held eloquence basic for all members of the city government, including the prince'.[14] Humphrey gave a copy of
Frulovisi's work to Oxford in 1443.) In a letter dated the 1st of April 1460 a grateful
university replied, thanking the Earl for the offer and informing him that they
had decided to establish him as successor to the late Duke of Gloucester in their
affections.

The elegance of your Latineity, the uprightness of your character, your
singular eloquence, and above all, your recent generosity to us make
it difficult for us to write in reply. ... [Y]our reputation of excellence
has become widespread, not only among the Italians, the masters of all
eloquence. ... Then, most noble earl, we hold no one more justly and
well-deserving of Humfrey's name and dignity.[15]

Worcester was identified among the English pupils of Guarino da Verona in
Ludovico Carbone's eulogy to the great scholar after his death at the end of 1460.
Therefore the Earl must have attended his school in Ferrara in either 1459 or
1460, or perhaps both. Ferrara lies to the south of Padua on the river Po. Under
the house of d'Este it flourished in the fifteenth century as a centre of art, courtly
culture and learning, first under Niccolò d'Este III (1384–1441). His successors
were Leonello (1407–50) and Borso (1413–71), who ruled when Worcester was in
Italy. Ercole (1431–1505), the younger bastard brother of these two, was one of the
most significant patrons of the arts in Italy. Ludovico Carbone—who fulsomely
described Worcester in his eulogy on Guarino da Verona and wrote him a charming Latin poem sadly turning down service in England—was the d'Estes' in-house
humanist scholar, speech writer and versifier and may have provided the Earl a
bridge into the d'Este court.

Humanist colleges or *contubernia* were established by Guarino, first in Verona in
1420 and then Ferrara in 1436 when Guarino moved there. These institutions were

aristocratic but characterised both by the broad-minded discipline to which pupils were subject and by *curricula* imbued with the importance of rhetoric, direct access to classical texts, and the study of Greek. Guarino had lived in Constantinople and travelled throughout Greece. It is perhaps easy to see how Worcester, a mature student highly experienced in the ways of the world, would have fitted into such an institution. In 1442 Ferrara's university opened and Guarino gave the inaugural oration praising humanistic subjects.

The d'Estes were patrons of Guarino to whom England had paid special attention surprisingly early. Duke Humphrey had instructed his agents to seek out Guarino's works in Italy. Guarino attracted a circle of English students, who were praised in Carbone's funeral oration, which included William Grey, and John Free (both Balliol), Robert Flemming and the Earl of Worcester (both Great Hall of the University), and John Gunthorpe of Cambridge. Possibly the Earl studied with Free and Gunthorpe. Guarino used to request his pupils to write Latin exercises in the form of letters to him that he then corrected and discussed with them. One of the letters in the lost correspondence of the Earl that was in the library of Lincoln Cathedral was from Guarino.[16]

In 1459 and 1460 several important English composers and musicians were resident in Ferrara. Worcester's large choir and personal involvement in choral Masses when in the Holy Land indicate a keen interest in music. Edward IV's court was later noted for the exceptional quality of its singing and it is possible that the Earl learnt from the d'Este court of Ferrara in which city English musicians were prominent. One important English composer was John Hothby who claimed to have travelled in Britain, Germany, France, Spain and Italy before he went to Ferrara. Hothby composed a setting for Lorenzo de' Medici's *Amor ch'ai visto*. Three other Englishmen in Ferrara in the same period were Johannes Bedyngham, Galfridus de Anglia, and Robertus de Anglia. The last was made singing master of the cathedral in 1460. In Ferrara there was the clearest evidence of Anglo-Italian cultural interchange, with English composers setting Italian words to music.[17]

There is surprising evidence that Worcester made a start on importing Italian landscape architecture ideas into England. He appears to have at least begun to build a country retreat at his manor of Bassingbourn in Cambridgeshire—not far from Eversden where he was born—inspired by his time in Italy. Old maps and crop marks show a squared platform surrounded by complex walls approached by a long drive facing south over a great vista (see Plates). Inspiration would have come from the Earl's time in Ferrara and Florence where radical post-medieval ideas about gardens were being developed in the fifteenth century.[18] Leon Battista Alberti (1404–72), in *De Re Aedificatoria*, advised hillside sites with long views, enhanced by platforms.

In Ferrara, the garden, a symbol of nature at peace, was a place where command over natural elements might be achieved. Since the second half of the fourteenth century the d'Este family had established country residences called *delizie*. These were homes built for weekend and entertainment use. While they might be somewhat rudimentary they were well finished and offered comforts to the members of the court and their guests. Their presence civilised nature and marked d'Este control over it and their territory.

Another inspiration for Bassingbourn could have been the villas of the de' Medici where the Earl may have stayed when he visited Florence. The Villa Medici at Careggi was the first such villa situated in the hills near Florence. It was the site of the Platonic academy founded by Cosimo, who died at the villa in 1464. Worcester, who had probably already translated Cicero's *De Amicitia*, was a natural candidate to have been an honoured guest. The Medici villa at Fiesole with its terraces and panoramic vistas was built for the cultivated and scholarly Giovanni de' Medici (1421 – 63). In early 1461 Giovanni sent the Earl a letter, the contents of which are unknown, and the Earl subsequently visited Florence twice that year.

At the beginning of 1460 Worcester had committed himself to providing Oxford with a long list of books and now he had to make good. Sometime before September 1460 he is known to have visited Florence, as he then gave a manuscript of Sallust on Catilene and Jurgurtha to fellow Englishman Peter Courtenay in Padua, which Worcester had ordered from Vespasiano da Bisticci. Courtenay recorded the present on the 19th of September 1460.[19] He was a fellow Oxford man who, in the academic year 1460–61, was Rector of the Jurist University of Padua. He was a cadet branch cousin of Thomas Courtenay, Earl of Devon, who was charged with, and acquitted of, treason in 1454.[20] Worcester bought books on such a scale that before the end of 1460 Ludovico Carbone described him as despoiling Italy.

The funeral oration of Guarino da Verona was given on the 4th of December 1460 by Ludovico Carbone, who described the master's most distinguished students, including five Englishmen, 'men by nature barbarous', whom Guarino had freed from their savage speech and taught to express themselves in the Latin tongue. The Earl was singled out for special notice.

> Even the most illustrious prince John the Englishman, no rather angelic, Earl of Worcester, yearned to listen to Guarino. He himself, being also drawn from the ancient stock of the Kings of England, imitating his father's wisdom, in the twenty-fifth year of his age, a thing which before him happened to no one, merited being created the highest Treasurer of England, which is held the highest rank among the English, second to the King.

In his wisdom and expertise in military matters, he had restored peace to the British sea.[21] (The text is continued at the beginning of chapter 10.)

On the 17th of December 1460 one Ambrosio di Taverna wrote a letter to Giovanni de' Medici on behalf of Worcester, thanking Giovanni for his hospitality, including some *canzone*, offering more foreign songs in future, then asking for a reply so he could assure the Earl of their safe arrival and Giovanni's good opinion of them.[22] A *canzone* was a composition in Italian or Latin, simple and songlike. It is likely that the music was English. In Ferrara there were several English composers and there was experimentation by English composers with putting non-English texts to music. The letter raises questions about the relationship between Worcester and the de' Medicis. Was the gift of music simply a way of giving thanks for earlier hospitality, or was it part of some greater diplomatic game? This will be considered in the next chapter.

In early 1461 men known to Worcester were prominent in examinations and awards in Padua. In March Worcester's friend and client John Free underwent the *publicum examinem,* or public examination, at Padua, witnessed by Courtenay.[23] Also that month, John Free was present at the *doctoratus,* or doctorate award, in Canon Law of John Lee who had been appointed a member of the delegation to Mantua in 1459.[24]

In about May 1461 Worcester left Padua on a journey that would wrap up his time in Italy. It encompassed book buying, library visits and lecture attendance. Bisticci wrote: 'He went from Padua to Florence with the purpose of going onto Rome, taking with him great store of books.' [25] There the Earl continued his book buying spree, 'and in Florence he bought others which he happened upon, and collected a vast number'.[26] Worcester was described exploring Florence incognito.

> While certain books which his lordship desired were being transcribed, he remained in Florence several days, and wanted to see the whole city, and not wanting to be known going about it in his way, and so he went through the whole city, without attendants, alone and he would turn to the left hand, and next to the right hand, and next again to the left, and in this way he saw the whole place. Now having heard of the fame of Messer Giovanni Argiropolo, he went one morning to the University to hear one of his lectures. His presence was unknown to anyone, and the teaching of Messer Giovanni gave him much satisfaction.[27]

This passage gives an intriguing insight into the Earl's character. He was busy buying books. He explored alone without a retinue. He sought out a famous Greek

scholar who had visited his own country—and had been rather rude about it, calling the English a 'barbarous nation'.[28] Perhaps, waiting for books to be copied,
exploring and attending lectures alone in the glorious centre of culture and learning that was *quattrocento* Florence, the Earl was truly happy.

Bisticci reported that when the Earl had seen all there was to see in Florence, he
quitted it and went to Rome, where he saw the whole city and visited the Pope and
cardinals and many prelates there.[29] It seems likely this was when the meeting took
place with the Pope in which Free described the brilliance of Worcester's oration.
Pius did not mention the Earl in his *Commentaries* but the Italian Bisticci confirmed they met so the sources are not just Englishmen. Free's is the only record
of the Pope's reaction. Pius exclaimed, 'you alone of all the princes of our time we
may compare in virtue and in eloquence with the most famous emperors of Greece
and Latin.'[30] Free may have helped the Earl with the text of his speech and, thus,
might well have been paying himself a compliment.

Caxton wrote simply, 'what worship had he [Worcester] at Rome in the presence of our holy fader the Pope.'[31] Leland reported that the Earl visited the Vatican
library at Rome. 'Once the mistress of events, likewise the parent of Latin eloquence and antiquity, as is evident in the Vatican library … , which [he] was to visit.
Through several generations of the nobility no distinguished visitor to the city was
more pleasing than Tipetot [sic]; whose courtesy, kindness, likewise brilliance, and
Ciceronian eloquence captured the eyes, then the minds of all Romans.'[32]

The Earl returned via Florence to Padua in order to prepare to leave for England.
At some point, according to Leland, he gave a (lost) speech to the people of Padua.
Worcester may have talked in the medieval hall, the *Palazzo della Regio*, which had
the greatest unsupported roof area in Europe, exceeding Westminster Hall, where
Worcester had worked as Treasurer. The Earl must have been a truly accomplished
orator to be able to hold his own before the cultured Pope and the learned people
of Padua.

Some generous words to the Earl on his coming departure survive from those
to whom he had provided patronage. Even allowing for the requisite politeness
owed to a rich patron, they do convey a genuine feeling of sadness at his leaving.
On the 22nd of March 1461 Francesco Aretino, delivering his translation of *De
Calumnia*, wrote: 'But if God assents to my wish perhaps something worthier of
your name by me will follow to Britain your humane person … our second Virgil.
For you, greatly preoccupied with affairs, it will bring to mind your most dedicated
Francis.'[33]

In his 1460 eulogy to Guarino, Carbone had called the Earl *dulcissime princeps*
and made a threat: 'I can and I must call him my most gentle lord. For he would be

willing, moved by some good opinion of my ability, to take me with him to England, and I will certainly be willing to serve him, if now the Ferrarans are ungrateful towards me.'[34] In the summer of 1461 Ludovico Carbone addressed to the Earl a graceful elegy declining his offer of employment in England but lamenting that he felt obliged by loyalty to continue serving his master, Borso d'Este, at Ferrara. Yet Carbone yearned to be with the supremely gifted Earl: 'How I wish to live with you, famed companion, as I see you pursue the Palladian arts, when divine Minerva directs your talents.'[35] He concluded: 'England was dear to me because of you ... but my friend, the most agreeable Gunthorpe, told me the King has expressly called you home. So farewell, never mindless of our happiness and you may wish to rely on your Carbone.'[36] John Gunthorpe was an English scholar who studied under Guarino and after papal service would work for English kings.

John Free referred, in his preface to Synesius's *In praise of baldness*, to the Earl's imminent departure: 'But since there have been enough celebrations of you, the happiest guest from a foreign nation, now the very homeland where you were born and educated begs you to return and be happy by work in its service. But to hasten your departure to your homeland I give you this book due to my incredible devotion to you, and likewise may it bear witness, and be a lasting proof, of your countless favours to me.'[37] The relationship with Free was one of genuine friendship and scholarly collaboration. It was a pity that it was cut short by the Earl's recall to England in 1461 and Free's premature death in 1465 in Italy, before he could take up his appointment to the see of Bath and Wells.

Worcester was the first secular English aristocrat after Duke Humphrey to take up the baton of advancing the new learning being defined as humanism. Unlike Humphrey, the Earl spent several years in Italy. The early sixteenth-century scholar Leland wrote on 'The Restoration of Sound Literary Learning' in England which had followed from study in Italy:

> Lo, there flourishes the splendour of learning reborn ... ! The Greek treasures passes into Italy and proclaims that it will restore the liberal arts. .... Fosterer of the talented, our Britain also has borne Free, Tiptoft, and Flemming; then Grocyn followed these lights of learning, and Celling, Linacre, Widow, and pious Latimer, Tunstall the Phoenix, Stokesley and Colet, Lyly and Pace—a festal crown of men! All had sought Italy under a lucky star, and the English Muse shone in Roman Schools. All, become skilled in discourse, returned to their own country and brought their treasures with them, even written copies of the ancient Greek authors, which deserve eternal preservation. Hail to the happy industry of the learned, through which clear light, restored, shines and shadows are driven away.[38]

Leland, who had an exceptionally clear understanding of early English humanism, saw Tiptoft as in the first rank in terms of importance, and central to this was time spent in Italy. Worcester was a pioneer of the tradition that English scholars, serious about their studies, and aristocrats, widening their experiences, should respectively learn from and tour in Italy. The Earl recognised the necessity of getting more books to England as indicated by correspondence with Oxford. The Italians Carbone and Bisticci both confirmed that Worcester purchased and travelled with very significant numbers of books.

Chapter 10

Italy II – politics, 1458 to 1461

I [John Free] speak in words used about you by the great Pius II, who wept for joy when he heard your oration: 'You alone, of all the princes of our time we may compare in virtue and in eloquence with the most famous emperors of Greece and Rome. Even if I should pass over the others in silence—you do not concede yourself not to be a better man, in natural talent or study of the finest arts, than Alexander the Great, foremost of the Greeks, or Lucullus, greatest leader of the Romans'.[1]

John Free's dedication of *Synesius's On Baldness* to the Earl of Worcester describing his patron's impact on Pius II, possibly when delivering the new Yorkist King Edward IV's obedience to the Pope

What else might the Earl have been doing during his three years in Italy, alongside his studying, book buying and enjoying of cultural pleasures? He left England in 1458 so high in King Henry VI's confidence that in the preceding and following years he had been and would be appointed to lead papal delegations. Yet he was recalled in 1461 by Edward IV completely trusted as a committed Yorkist. The Earl's three years in Italy might be examined not only to descry his own possible political activities but also to consider the broader diplomatic context.

Communications between London and Venice were good but with an inevitable time lapse of at least three weeks and usually more. Given the rollercoaster changes of fortune after key battles between 1459 and 1461, it would have been very difficult to be certain who was still on top in England by the time a communication was received in Italy. But in the autumn of 1458 the Earl must have ascertained rapidly that the political situation in England was yet more fragile than when he had left. The Loveday of the 24th of March 1458—intended to reconcile the surviving combatants of the 1st Battle of St Albans—had produced no true love.

The Earl appears soon to have made administrative arrangements for a long stay in Italy. On the 29th of January 1459 letters were issued in England appointing attorneys to represent Worcester while in Italy.[2] These were Robert Ingleton and Henry Chevelle, who had close links to the Nevilles.

Worcester may have hoped that by remaining far away in north-eastern Italy he could stay out of English politics. Although reports of the Earl emphasised his scholarly activities in Italy between 1458 and 1461, he had ended up astonishingly close to the focal point of papal efforts in 1459 to mobilise a pan-European crusade in which the Pope had hoped the belligerent English would play a major role. Try as he might it would be difficult for the Earl not to be sucked into English affairs at a time when the violent showdown between Lancaster and York could no longer be averted.

Aeneas Piccolomini, crowned Pope Pius II on the 3rd of September 1458, was determined to win back Constantinople. The new Pope called on the 26th of September for a new crusade against the Ottomans. He proposed a great congress in Mantua, to which he summoned all the princes of Europe, to meet on the 1st of June 1459. Mantua is only 75 kilometres from Padua and 60 kilometres from Ferrara, and the Earl studied in both places.

In January 1459 Pope Pius II had sent Bishop Francesco Coppini of Terni to England as a papal legate to seek Henry VI's assistance in the crusade. Coppini's secondary mission, given to him by his patron Francesco Sforza, the Duke of Milan, was to encourage England to invade France. Coppini was an indefatigable and ambitious interferer who frequently overstepped his powers. His reporting may have unduly influenced Pius towards a pro-Yorkist position, although the shrewd Pope had no illusions about the inadequacy of Henry VI, and eventually about Coppini.

Coppini saw reward in currying favour with whoever would deliver English participation in the crusade, thereby hoping to ingratiate himself with the Pope. If the Yorkists looked a better bet, then Coppini would promote their cause over that of the anointed king, both at the Vatican in Italy and in England. The Earl of Warwick, particularly, grasped the opportunity to be had in cultivating this ambitious schemer.

Coppini's arrival may have prompted Henry VI to issue a summons on the 20th of February 1459 to a Great Council to meet on the 2nd of April with the purpose of appointing delegates to go to Mantua. There is, however, no record that this council met. In late May or early June Pope Pius arrived in Mantua via Florence. On the 16th of May Henry VI issued a commission to a delegation to present his obedience to the new Pope. Worcester, in recognition of his rank, oratorical powers and his conveniently proximate location, was appointed leader. The other members were 'king's clerks', that is members of the King's secretariat, and fellow Oxford men, Robert Flemming, Henry Sharp, and Richard Bole.[3] Of these, Robert Flemming and Henry Sharp were already in papal service in Italy. Bole had been in Rome in the late 1440s.

In mid-1459 Abbot Wheathamstead of St Albans named the envoys to Mantua appointed by Henry VI as the Bishop of Worcester, the Abbot of Peterborough, the Earl of Worcester, Lord Dudley, Richard Kautone, John

Sprevier, Sir Gervase Clifton, and Sir Philip Wentworth.[4] Only Worcester, and possibly Kautone, were in Italy. The last had been in Rome in the 1440s with Vincent Clement seeking papal licences for Eton and King's Colleges, which then had Worcester's wardship.

There is no record that the Earl did go to Mantua representing England but there is circumstantial evidence that he might have been there even if he kept a low profile. On the 30th of May a papal indult was issued from Mantua to Worcester allowing him, with his 'household', to cause Masses to be celebrated where convenient. The Earl must have petitioned the Pope for this and have expected to be on the move.[5] It does sound like Worcester at least planned to travel with a party of some size and the obvious place, given the context, was Mantua.

The Pope was accompanied by the humanist scholar Franscesco Aretino. Worcester and Francesco may have met at Mantua as, in his dedication of 1461 to the Earl of Lucian's *De Calumnia*, Aretino said he was fulfilling a promise made to Worcester eighteen months earlier when he was translating John Chrysostom's work on St John the Evangelist for Cosimo de' Medici of Florence. The Pope had stayed in Florence *en route* to Mantua.

An indult was issued in Mantua on the 8th of June 1459 to John Hurley, Tiptoft's Oxford tutor, at his and the Earl's petition, for him to leave his benefice in England.[6] The indult said Hurley was Worcester's chaplain and may be 'studying letters at a university'. Thus he too might have been or planned to be a student at Padua. But the indult said Hurley also might be engaged in the service of Henry, King of England, or of Richard, Duke of York. It was understandable that Hurley would be engaged in the services of Worcester and even the King but the inclusion of York is intriguing. This indicates another possible avenue of communication between Worcester and the Yorkists.

Now, bizarrely, the issue of payment to the Earl of Worcester's delegation to Mantua became mixed up with the consequences of the Genoese piracy in the Mediterranean of the previous year—where the Earl was supposedly a target of the pirates. On the 25th of July Henry VI issued a warrant to the Treasurer for the payment of the delegates' expenses. The Council approved advance payments costing the crown £1,780 in cash.[7] The daily allowance totalled £12 13s. 4d.—of which 5 marks, or £3 13s. 4d., went to Worcester.

The usually impecunious Henry VI had the funds for the delegates due to a payment of £2,000 from the petitioners who were the victims of piracy and demanding that the Genoese of London be forced to make recompense for taking of ships in the Mediterranean the previous year. Those petitioning had, rather dubiously, insinuated that a ship belonging to Worcester had been involved—because it had been recorded as present at Candia in Crete at the same time as the three ships attacked by the Genoese pirates—although it was not one of these ships subsequently subject to the piratical assault.

'There can be no doubt that Stourton and the others had attracted the attention of the council by advancing a loan of £2,000 and used that to promote their own ends.'[8] Subsequently, Stourton, whose ship had escaped, and other Bristol merchants, were empowered to receive £6,000—which the Treasury had demanded from the Genoese—by authority of the sentence of the Council.

There is, however, no record of any delegation leaving England or anyone, including Worcester, being paid as members. Whatever the Earl eventually heard of the episode it was not likely to have impressed the ex-Treasurer as to the competence of the Lancastrian regime, which could not even manage to send a delegation to Italy.

September and October 1459 saw the outbreak of open fighting between Lancaster and York. On the 9th of September the Earl of Salisbury defeated the Lancastrians at the Battle of Blore Heath. Lord Dudley was among those captured, finally putting paid to any, admittedly unlikely, hope he might go to Mantua. On the 12th of October in turn the Yorkists were beaten at the Battle of Ludford Bridge. York fled to Ireland and the Earls of Warwick and March, York's son and the future Edward IV, to Calais.

In July 1459 Pius had reiterated to Coppini that it was essential for England to send delegates to Mantua. Coppini bemoaned that all his good work only produced a delegation which was recalled, when almost on its journey, by the machinations of factious people, presumably contending Yorkists and Lancastrians. There was a Milanese report on the 29th of October that the English would come: 'They also say that those of the King of England and the Duke of Brittany should be here about the same time, so that we shall soon have many stately embassies.'[9] But the English did not come. Pius wrote in his *Commentaries* that the embassy members had 'all disregarded the command of their weak and cowardly king'.[10] Presumably this included Worcester who was physically only a small distance away and had papal permission to say Mass wherever he chose to travel. Even if the Earl had been at Mantua he might have been reluctant to appear as a publicly recognised but impotent figurehead for a delegation that could not, realistically, commit anything to a crusade. That said, this does not sound like the behaviour of a man now keen to be identified as a Lancastrian.

In January 1460 the Congress of Mantua was disbanded, having manifestly failed to organise a crusade. Failure made Pius contemptuous of the English King Henry and willing to listen to the Yorkists. Worcester must have sensed the direction the papal wind was blowing and been more open to communication from the Plantagenets and the Nevilles with whom he had governed England during Henry VI's madness.

In the spring of 1460 Coppini thought it advisable to leave England for a time to escape Queen Margaret's ire and return to the Curia to seek further advice. His mission for his patron Francesco Sforza, the Duke of Milan, had been to encourage King Henry to invade France and Margaret of Anjou naturally cannot have favoured such a venture. On the continent, he made contact with the Yorkist Earls Salisbury, Warwick and March, holed up in Calais after defeat at Ludford Bridge. They assured him a Yorkist government would offer its obedience to the Pope and meet his aims.

In March 1460, William Orell, rector of Elington in the diocese of Coventry and Lichfield, was granted, at Worcester's petition, an indult to enjoy the fruits of benefices while engaged in the study of letters in a university, residing in the Roman court, or engaged in the service of any bishop.[11] Orell was another Oxford connection as he had been a proctor from 1439 to 1440 and possibly overlapped with Worcester there. There must have been communication between the Earl and England over this matter and some, possibly political, purpose for having him in Rome.

By April the Pope was expressing Yorkist sympathies in his *Commentaries*. Coppini entered into a pact with Warwick to raise the standard of Rome in England. The Pope appeared to accept Warwick's assertion, through Coppini, that Henry VI was incapable of ruling. In June Warwick drew up a set of *Articles* for Coppini, stating that the Yorkist objective was to reform government and contribute substantially to the crusade. On the 26th of June Warwick left Calais for England and Coppini requested that he be allowed to accompany him. Thus the Papacy appeared to back the Yorkist invasion of England. The significance of such support was unlikely to have been lost on the English in Italy.

On his arrival in London no later than the 2nd of July, Coppini preached to the English bishops in York's support and wrote two days later to Henry VI supporting negotiations with the Yorkists. He also wrote to the Pope, sending the Yorkist *Articles* promising reform and support for the crusade. The Lancastrians refused negotiations and Coppini appeared to side openly with the Yorkists before the Battle of Northampton on the 10th of July, where the Lancastrians were defeated and Henry VI was captured.

There is one extremely detailed letter to the Earl in Italy which reveals quite how close to the heart of events was the source of Worcester's news of England. Worcester must have sent a letter from Venice to England on the 1st of August as the author of the undated response—written after the 13th of October, for it describes events which happened before this date—referred to this earlier letter. He appeared to assume the Earl was already up to date with the consequences of July's Battle of Northampton, which put the Yorkists back in the driving seat, as these were not outlined. This surviving letter gave a detailed account of events in England from the position of a Neville insider, possibly Worcester's attorney Robert Ingleton. Clearly the Earl wanted to be kept in touch very closely with political events at home. The letter set the scene: 'Most ... bountefulle good lorde youre most comfortable letters fro Venys of the last of August I resseived here the xiij of octobre ... whan ther was like to have ben atte Westmestre a mervelous werk.'[12]

In October Parliament, meeting in Westminster, rescinded previous Acts declaring York, Warwick and Salisbury enemies of the throne. York, however, wanted to go much further. The well-informed Pius knew the arguments over who had the right to the throne but believed Warwick opposed York's claim. Warwick's resistance was information which was conveyed to Worcester in Italy in the continuation of the letter.

> Ther cam my lorde of york with viij hundred horse and men harneysed atte x of the clok, and entered the paleis with his swerde born uppe right by for him thorowe the halle and parleament chambre. And ther under the cloth of estate stondyng he gave them knowlich[e] that he purposed nat to ley daune his swerde but to challenge his right and so t[o]ke his lodgyng in the qwenys chambre .... The lordes ... departed from thens and kept ther counsaille atte the blak Freris and sum tyme sent and som tyme wrote to my lorde of York tille atte the last yt was agreed to take such direction as they wolde avise him.[13]

The lords did not acclaim the usurper Duke of York, for all his eight hundred men and sword borne before him. Indeed they retreated to Blackfriars and prevaricated, agreeing to inform him of their decision at such time as they might make it. Warwick then told York of his fellow lords' non-decision. A Concorde was agreed giving York the throne after the death of Henry VI who thus disinherited his own son Edward—an action hardly likely to find favour with the boy's mother Queen Margaret. The disagreement of York and Warwick was unknown by the English chroniclers but was known in Italy. Worcester and the Pope in Italy were receiving similar information from inside Yorkist sources.

On the 16th of October 1460 a papal safe conduct was issued for Worcester and his retinue.[14] The Earl had not needed such a safe conduct earlier for his book-buying forays in Florence and sojourns in Ferarra. This might indicate some recognised change in his purpose in Italy—which had become less related to learning and more to diplomacy—where he needed a substantial retinue, both to impress and to protect, while travelling.

In November 1460, when the Yorkists were in control, the Catalan Vincent Clement was appointed the King's proctor, or resident envoy, in the papal court.[15] The mid-fifteenth century produced a pair of ever-scheming southern European clerics, Coppini and Clement, who made distant wet England the field for their ambitions. In less bitter times their ceaseless, ingenious and often counter-productive machinations would have added greatly to the gaiety of nations. But this was a bleak period and it is possible only to wonder if the game was worth the candle. Clement had been awarded an MA before 1433 by Oxford University. In 1441 he had been the cause of a scandal at Oxford when he was granted an undeserved degree, due to royal pressure, of *Sacrosanctae Theologie Professor*. He was employed by Henry VI at Rome to urge the Pope to grant indulgences for his foundation at Eton.

In November 1454 Clement was papal proctor when the Duke of York was Protector. He was already well known to Warwick, who had thought him a man worth cultivating. He presented Clement to the living of Newport Pagnall on the 21st of January 1458. In that year he was a member of a delegation to the Duke of Burgundy which was led by Warwick. In the cache of lost letters to and from Worcester, which had been in Lincoln Cathedral, there was one from the Earl to Clement. Its content is unknown but the letters probably date collectively to the early 1460s, so Clement might be another ingredient in the conspiratorial Yorkist brew in Italy to which Worcester was linked. On the 9th of December, while the Yorkists were dominant post the Battle of Northampton, a licence was issued in Henry VI's name granting Coppini the right to accept an English bishopric when one fell vacant. Clearly they felt grateful for his services.

In December the Pope appointed Matthew Dewe a papal chaplain after Worcester had petitioned on his behalf, 'alleging Matthew to be his well-beloved'.[16] Dewe had been perpetual chaplain at the altar of St Stephen in the church of St Sepulchre without Newgate in the City of London. This added another contact between Worcester and the papacy.

A letter, dated the 3rd of January 1461, to Giovanni de' Medici from his representa-tive in Venice, Allesandro Martelli, said the latter had delivered all the former's let-ters including one to '*il conte Giovanni inglese*' who can only have been Worcester. The de' Medici representative added that the English Earl was waiting for better news and he seemed inclined to stay on in Italy rather than commit himself to either party by arriving home while civil war was raging.[17] Giovanni's lost letter to Worcester must have contained more than thanks for the music sent by the Earl to Giovanni—referred to in the previous chapter—for Worcester visited Florence twice subsequently in 1461 on his way to and from Rome—possibly in order to discuss financial and political issues.

Worcester may have, at the turn of 1460 and 1461, adjusted to the idea of return-ing, when the time came, to an England run by the Yorkists under the titular King Henry VI as was the situation in 1453–54. He now found his expectations pro-foundly shaken. By late January or early February the news, potentially shattering for the Yorkist cause, of the Battle of Wakefield on the 30th of December must have reached Venice.

Unexpectedly, Lancastrian forces had converged on Sandal, where the Duke of York and the Earl of Salisbury had celebrated Christmas. York unwisely attacked, having hopelessly underestimated his enemies' numbers. He died leading his men, and his second son, the teenage Earl of Rutland, was later killed by Lord Clifford, who thereby avenged the death of his father at the hand of Rutland's father, York, at the 1st Battle of St Albans. Salisbury was captured and executed the next day. Salisbury's second son, Thomas, was also killed. Thomas, Lord Roos, Worcester's brother-in-law, had led the victorious Lancastrian cavalry.

The news of the defeat at Wakefield and the deaths of York and Salisbury, as well as of their sons, must have deeply shaken Worcester both politically and personally. York, Salisbury, and Worcester had been, respectively, Protector, Chancellor and Treasurer in 1454. Apart from their joint roles in government, York was Worcester's cousin and Salisbury had been his father-in-law. Now only Worcester survived and he was in Italy. Neither Salisbury's son, Richard, the Earl of Warwick, nor York's son Edward, Earl of March, had much experience of administration and the latter was still a teenager.

Wakefield certainly disrupted Coppini's plans and on the 9th of January, through one Friar Lorenzo of Florence, he tried to rebuild his relationship with Queen Margaret.[18] Meanwhile, two days later, Warwick—now the senior Yorkist leader with his uncle William Neville, Lord Fauconburg—called on the Pope to promote Coppini, if the Pope wanted to aid the just Yorkist cause. Despite Wakefield the Yorkists intended to fight on and saw the Pope as supportive.[19]

On the 2nd of February 1461 Edward, Earl of March, won the Battle of Mortimer's Cross, putting the Yorkists back into contention. Despite his mani-fest ability Edward was very young and must have sought experienced advisors whom he could trust. The surviving trio of Neville brothers, Richard, John and George, with their uncle William, might ultimately have been expected to look after their own family interests. Edward's own surviving brothers, George and Richard, were very young. Therefore Edward must have sought more indepen-dent and knowledgeable advisers. Men like William Hastings, John Howard, and William Herbert were close and had participated in the fighting of 1459 to 1461. None, however, had Worcester's range of experience in government, or his kin-ship relationship.

On the 10th of February Coppini arrived at Brill [Brielle in the modern Netherlands] from England. Ten days later he wrote to Richard Kautone, a clerk of the Apostolic Chamber, the ministry of home affairs for the papal state. Kautone had been one of the delegates selected at St Albans in mid-1459 to go to the Congress of Mantua in the delegation in which Worcester was the leading secular peer. In the 1440s Kautone and Vincent Clement had worked together in Rome on the foundation of Eton College.[20] By this time there were several men who had been, or were, about the Pope who had some connection with Worcester. These were Robert Flemming, Richard Kautone, Vincent Clement, Henry Sharp and Matthew Dewe.

On the 17th of February, the 2nd Battle of St Albans resulted in a Lancastrian victory over Warwick and the recapture of Henry VI. On the 10th of March Pius II wrote to Warwick consoling him on the death of his kinsmen at Wakefield and assuring him the papacy was on his side against Margaret. On the 29th of March the issue of York or Lancaster was decided by the huge bloody Battle of Towton. The combined forces of Edward, Warwick and Fauconburg, defeated those of Henry VI in the greatest fight on English soil, where possibly more Englishmen were killed than on the first day of the Somme in 1916. Edward was proclaimed King. Forty-one Lancastrians were subsequently executed, including the Earls of Wiltshire and Devon. By early May Pius II had received news of Towton. Carreto, the Milanese ambassador to Rome, wrote, 'his Holiness was very pleased at the news of England'.[21] In June Coppini heard from Sforza of 'the Pope's excellent disposition towards Coppini and toward the new dynasty'.

Some time in the second quarter of 1461, Edward wrote to Worcester recalling him back to England. It seems unlikely that he would have done so if he had not already known that the Earl was supportive of the Yorkist cause. Worcester may also have received instructions to present the obedience of the Yorkists to the Pope. The Earl was possibly also called home by the Nevilles, as Bisticci referred to noblemen who asked him to return, as well as the King.[22]

In June Bishop Booth of Durham repelled a raid led by the Lords Roos, Richemont Grey and Dacre who brought King Henry VI over the border to try to raise a rebellion in the north of England. Edward and the Nevilles must indeed have been confident of Worcester's loyalty to the new regime if the Earl's two brothers-in-law, Roos and Richemont Grey remained obdurate. Edmund Sutton, the Earl's other brother-in-law, with his father Lord Sutton of Dudley, had joined the Yorkist cause. Edward IV of York was crowned King of England on the 28th of June.

Possibly in May the Earl had left Padua for Florence where he bought books and attended lectures but he likely had other motives. The scholarly aspects of his travels in mid-1461 are covered in the previous chapter. In January he had received a letter from Giovanni de' Medici which probably included an invitation to visit Florence. The de' Medici would prove an invaluable source of funds to Edward IV. The Burgundian courtier and chronicler Commynes wrote in his *Memoires* that the Medici agent Gerard Canigiani 'was nearly the means to sustain King Edward IV in his estate, being in great war in his kingdom; and lent at times the said king more than six-score thousand crowns, where he had little gain for his master, though in the end he got his money back'.[23] This rather begs the question of how a young king, threatened by civil war, managed to borrow so much from the de' Medici (the credit rating of English kings was after all not good in Italy as the previous King Edward—the third of that name—had bankrupted the Florentine Bardis and Peruzzis). It is reasonable to suppose that it would have required someone experienced in finance, with rhetorical skills, who had actually been in Florence, and who had the backing of the Pope, to persuade sceptical bankers to facilitate such loans. Only one person fitted the bill: Worcester. In 1462, the year the Earl again became Treasurer of England, a branch of the de' Medici bank was established in London.

After leaving Florence the Earl continued to Rome.[24] Englishmen there connected to Worcester included Oxford alumni Robert Flemming, a contemporary at his college the Great Hall of the University, Vincent Clement, the Yorkist proctor, and possibly Henry Sharpe. There was also his 'well beloved' Matthew Dewe, a papal clerk. It is likely this was when the meeting took place with the Pope at which time the Earl may have presented the new Yorkist King's obedience.

The Earl also worked his diplomatic skills on the papal curia to obtain a plenary indulgence for Christchurch Priory Canterbury.[25] The Earl's chaplain, Master Richard, contacted Prior Goldstone of Canterbury to inform him of the award. The Prior wrote to Worcester to thank him for his negotiations regarding indulgences for the feast of the passion of St Thomas, approving indulgences for the Saint's fifty-year jubilee, similar to that of Santiago de Compostela. The Earl was promised £200 for his expenses.

Worcester returned to Padua via Florence, according to da Bisticci, and probably collected books ordered earlier. He may have completed financial transactions, gaining funds for the new Yorkist regime and using the authority of the Pope, as the de' Medici were the papal bankers.

On the 8th of July a letter written by Ognibene Bonisoli in Vicenza, who had dedicated Xenophon's *De Venatione* to Worcester, mentioned that the Earl was preparing to return to England, so he was likely to have returned to Padua by that date.[26] There is no record of how he travelled but when he did it was to a much changed country now ruled by the young Edward IV. While in Italy between 1458 and 1461 the Earl had completely changed allegiance. Had he remained in England he might have remained publicly locked in loyalty to Lancaster. In Italy he could make the transition imperceptibly until a *fait accompli* regime change meant he could return as a supporter of the new King.

Worcester's father had performed special missions for Henry V who, in 1417, charged him, 'kepe this Matere her after Writen, from al Men secre'.[27] There are good reasons to think the son too worked secretly in Italy. There were many possible connections. His attorneys were Robert Ingleton and Henry Chevele. The former was closely connected to the Nevilles and the latter to the Ingaldisthorpes and the Earl had brought about the marriage of Isabel Ingaldisthorpe to John Neville. His Oxford tutor and companion, John Hurley, was engaged in service to, among others, Worcester and to Richard Duke of York in Italy in 1459. His chaplain Matthew Dewe went into papal service in 1460. Worcester's lost correspondence included letters to Vincent Clement, who had been cultivated by Warwick and represented the Yorkist cause in Rome after 1460, and William Atteclyff, who became Edward IV's secretary. Men whom the Earl knew in Italy included John Gunthorpe, Peter Courtenay, and Robert Flemming; all returned to serve Edward IV, as would have Free if he had not died in 1465. The Earl sent letters to and received letters from the de' Medici, gave them gifts and visited them. Later the de' Medici would make substantial loans to Edward IV. Worcester's travels took him to Rome at the right time for the new Yorkist regime to present its obediences. On his return to England he would be immediately accepted as a leading member of the Yorkist regime without having to prove his loyalty. This was despite having two brothers-in-law who were traitors. Thus it is hard not to conclude that the Earl had already amply demonstrated his loyalty to the Yorkists by his communications from, and his services in, Italy.

Worcester was the perfect discreet intermediary: a secular English noble of proven oratorical and financial skills who could speak and read Latin, and presumably now Italian as well, and who shared the common humanist culture that increasingly bonded the elite of the courts of Pius II, the de' Medici and the d'Este. If his mission were secret then the fact of its execution would not be explicit in the record. In March 1462 Warwick wrote to Coppini: 'They have decided to send ambassadors at Easter next to the supreme pontiff. ... Some say that the Earl of Worcester will go .... I think it will be so if matters keep well.'[28] The Earl would be a man expected by the new Yorkist regime in 1462 to be able to deal with Pius II—perhaps because he had already done so the previous year.

The Earl of Worcester brought back ideas about how a great prince should run his court so as to project his authority. He had seen magnificent courts at work first-hand in Ferrara and Florence. The court of Edward IV was notably more glamorous and efficient than that of Henry VI. The singing was said to be the best in Europe. Chivalry was repackaged for royal service. Great tournaments were held regularly in Florence and Milan, the home of Worcester's friend Roberto da Sanseverino. The Earl would model his ordinances for the great tournament of 1467 at Smithfield on those of Milan.

The Earl would also be accused of coming back with unpopular Italian legal innovations, lampooned as the Laws of Padua, for which he eventually paid with his life. His Italian biographer Bisticci wrote that, as Worcester walked to his execution, 'the people ... rejoiced greatly, and shouted he must die ... because he had brought back from Italy the laws which are called the Laws of Padua ... where he was at the University.'

Worcester remained nearly three years in Italy and thus qualified as an *Inglese italianato*. Judging by his subsequent reputation as the Butcher of England, is there any evidence of his transforming there into *un diavolo incarnate?* Ascham, who coined the phrase, made clear it was the Italians in Italy—not the English in England—who named the Italianate English who stayed among them as devils incarnate. But the Italians had the highest regard for the Lord Giovanni Inglese and were charmed by his patronage, learning and oratory. Pope Pius II, according to John Free, said the Earl alone, 'of all the princes of our time we may compare in virtue and in eloquence with the most famous emperors of Greece and Latin'.[29] The Italians were fulsome in their dedications of translations to the Earl. Ognibene Bonisoli likened him to Fabricius, Regulus, Cato, Camillus, Lucullus and Marcellus, respectively in faith, piety, temperance, justice, magnificence, and humanity.[30] Francesco Aretino called the Earl of Worcester 'our second Vergil'.[31] He wrote to Francesco Pellato of Padua calling the Earl *liberalissimus* or most generous. Ludovico Carbone described the Earl as *dulcissime princeps*, when regretfully turning down the offer to return to England and referred to how 'divine Minerva directs your talents'.[32] Even allowing for the inevitable hyperbole, scholarly Italians genuinely admired and liked the Earl. The seventeenth century antiquary Fuller said, 'he converted the Italians into a better opinion than they formerly had of Englishmen's learning; insomuch that his Holiness wept at the elegancy of the oration.'[33]

Perhaps, however, it is best not to try too hard to over-interpret history and instead simply be relieved that, in a life marked by political strife and personal tragedy, the Earl had an interval of several years to enjoy the *quattrocento* at its freshest. He was in Padua when Mantegna was completing the frescos of the Eremetani chapel and in Florence as the scaffolding was coming off Brunelleschi's dome. He heard lectures by Guarino in Ferrara and Argyropolous in Florence.

Something, moreover, of Worcester's lighter, kinder side may have come out in Italy—away from the endless political and personal crises in England. John Free dedicated to him a song of Bacchus's epostulation to the goat about his gnawed vine and Ognibene Bonisoli, Xenophon's *De Venatione*—perhaps because he enjoyed wine and the chase. The Earl sent *canzone*, or light songs, to Giovanni de' Medici. He was a warm host, for when Roberto da Sanseverino went to Padua in 1459, 'as soon as he [the Earl] saw them he welcomed them joyously and with great good will and wished to do for them everything that he could.' He did not stand at all on his dignity as a great lord. Bisticci described him exploring Florence alone and attending the lecture of Argyropoulos *incognito*. He read and annotated texts with John Free. He appeared a genuine friend of impoverished scholars and men of lowly origin. In 1461 he was called back to England, destined never to return to Italy, and would immediately make a darker mark—perhaps frustrated by the antics of those whose discord forced his return from a cosmopolitan, cultured, continent far more convivial to him.

Part 3

HOUSE OF YORK

Chapter 11

Constable of the Tower – 1461 to 1464

On his return to England, when he arrived he was much honoured, and was one of the principal men of the government, for being learned and a man of the greatest wisdom.

Bisticci's biography of the Earl of Worcester[1]

There come up from the lower house a notable number ... ; and in the parliament chamber without bar had communication with my lords, the Chancellor, Archbishops of Canterbury and York, the Earls of Warwick and Worcester ... .

Fane Fragment recording the Parliament of 1461[2]

In September 1461 the Earl of Worcester returned to England, summoned by the teenage king and important nobles. Despite nearly four years absence he immediately became one of the leading men in the new Yorkist regime whose immediate challenge was how to secure regime change. Worcester came back to a very different world. Most of the secular big beasts of the previous decade had been killed. The Dukes of Suffolk, Somerset, Buckingham and York, and the Earls of Shrewsbury, Salisbury, Northumberland, Devon and Wiltshire were all dead. John Mowbray, Duke of Norfolk, and William Neville, Earl of Kent, would die, in November 1461 and in 1463. Many other lords and knights had gone too. Thus there was a dearth of senior secular noble governmental and administrative experience. The only biggish beasts to survive, alive and unattainted, not of the older generation, were the Earls of Worcester and Warwick, and the latter's experiences had been as a rebel and pirate. The most cohesive power was the Neville trio of brothers, Richard, John and George, respectively experienced militarily at sea, and on land, and in the church and administration. Worcester alone had been a councillor, commissioner, and Treasurer. He was 34 and a very different man from the 30-year-old who had left England in 1458. Before that date, although a man in powerful positions, he appeared a conciliator and team player. After 1461, he was more independent and increasingly severe.

Edward IV had to find the means to exert authority throughout the kingdom. In the 1450s magnate disputes had become endemic. Now trusted noblemen were charged with keeping order in the regions while the King and council ruled from the centre. Edward would take a close interest in the judicial process—even sitting himself in courts of law. He travelled widely to enforce order and extensive use was made of commissions of oyer and terminer to deal with non-aristocratic threats to order. Worcester was an experienced veteran of such commissions. Also, the Earl was essentially a man of London, which was shown on papal documents as his diocese, and without immediate family. Therefore he was without a regional base to distract him and well placed to be constantly about the King when in London or travelling.

Edward IV is generally reported as being closest personally to William Hastings. But Hastings survived the entire reign from 1461 to 1483 so there was a longer period to imprint himself on the historical record. In the early period, before Edward's marriage in 1464, the man much mentioned about the King and living in closest proximity to him was Worcester. In documents Edward usually titles the Earl as his kinsman—Worcester was the cousin of the King's father. Edward was a very young man and might be expected to look for people to provide not just political but also emotional support. In correspondence the King addressed him as 'oure right trusty and entierly biloued Cousin, Therl of Worcestre'.[3] The language might be conventional but the human dimension was important. Edward had recently lost his father and his closest brother. Also, Worcester was a man without a partner or son.

The Chronicle of Canterbury's Prior, John Stone, gives a 'fix' on the date and location of the Earl of Worcester immediately on his return to England. 'On the first day of September the lord John Earl of Worcester came to Canterbury from the Holy Land and from other parts of various kingdoms and was received by the Prior of Canterbury at Saint Martins outside Canterbury and was led to the doors of the church, in the year of the Lord 1461, still in his habit.'[4] Worcester might have been accompanied by carts laden with the books he had, in the words of Carbone, despoiled from Italy. Perhaps he embraced his special friend and correspondent the Canterbury monk Henry Cranebroke. His welcome must have been particularly warm given the jubilee indulgences he had negotiated in Rome.

The Earl paid his respects to the tomb of his mother in St Andrew's Church, Enfield. The magnificent brass must have been commissioned after regime change for its revealing inscription acknowledged her hitherto politically poisonous Mortimer connection.

There were rewards for service to the new King. Like his ancestor Robert, the Earl was made Constable of Portchester Castle, on the 28th of August.[5] The office was of greater importance than the simple name might suggest as, before the development of Portsmouth as a naval base, the navy was based in the waters off the castle.

It is possible the Earl had specially created commissions of oyer and terminer to give him the power to sort out evil-doing in the regions where he was sensitive to challenges to his authority. On the 18th of October he had been appointed to lead a commission to inquire into extortions and oppressions practised by Simon White, bailiff of Litlyngton, Cambridgeshire, and Richard Beeston, bailiff of Stonedon, Hertfordshire.[6] One of his fellow commissioners was William Haseldene who was the husband of the Earl's cousin Elizabeth Daneys. Haseldene must have made a favourable impression for on the 20th of October 1461 the Lincoln's Inn Black Book recorded, 'William Haseldene was admitted to repasts as long as and as often as the Earl of Worcester should be in London.'[7]

On the 1st of November Worcester rejoined the Council with a salary of two hundred marks.[8] Most of the councillors were 'new' men who had served the Yorkists in the fighting between 1459 and 1461.[9] He was made Justiciar for North Wales on the 27th of November. This region proved a thorn in the flesh of Edward IV's regime as Harlech Castle established itself as a Lancastrian hold-out.[10] The next day there followed a grant of the office of keeper of the King's forests of Wabrigge and Sapley, Huntingdonshire.[11]

The Earl was given the important office of the Constable of the Tower on the 2nd of December.[12] The office was responsible for administration and maintenance, securing its prisoners, and keeping the Royal menagerie. The role of the Constable was not simply a profitable sinecure and reward for service to the young King Edward. In the early part of his reign, both for security and to maintain a hold over the City, Edward preferred the Tower to Westminster. Thus, as its Constable, the Earl effectively managed the King's main residence.

The Earl was made a Garter Knight in 1461. Early in his reign Edward IV created thirteen such knights—the most ever in such a limited period. The loss of records makes some dates uncertain but the general order is clear. Worcester was in the first group and was clearly among the King's closest, most honoured circle.[13] Three new members of knightly rank, Sir William Chamberlaine, Sir John Asteley and Sir William Harcourt, had long records as warriors—underlining membership was won not by lineage but by service. Although now largely an anachronism in purely military terms, knighthood and chivalry would be enrolled to project Yorkist authority—and to create a new Camelot composed of men noble through service to the regime. A central role in evolving such a strategy was probably played by the recently returned pilgrim, Worcester, who had been made a Knight of the Order of the Holy Sepulchre in 1458, and between 1459 and 1461 had visited the great ducal houses of Italy.

On the 4th of November Parliament met. The Earl re-established his record of formidable attendance seen in the surviving council records between 1452 and

1455. The Fane Fragment, an unusually surviving journal of the Lords, showed he was the only one of the six earls to attend every day, that is the 28th and the 30th of November and the 1st and 2nd, and 8th and 11th of December.[14] The journal is lacking for the 3rd to the 7th of December. The Earl was also appointed a trier of petitions for England, Ireland, Wales and Scotland.

The Commons set out in a petition Edward's claim to the throne as heir of John of Gaunt's son, Lionel of Clarence, and called the Lancastrian kings usurpers. Worcester joined two committees. The lords appointed one to report to the King which included the Earls of Worcester and Essex, and Lord Audley—past, current and future Treasurers—and Piers Arden, Chief Baron of the Exchequer. Another nine-member committee was appointed to have 'communication with the Merchants of the Staple' about an unknown matter. Securing the finances of the new regime was probably the reason for these committees on which served men of finance while the Wool Staple was England's main source of income.

Parliament passed a statute attainting 113 aristocrats and 96 knights and men of lesser station for their fighting since 1459. Some were already dead in battle like Henry Percy, Earl of Northumberland, killed at Towton, or executed soon after like Thomas Courtenay, Earl of Devon. Those attainted included the King's brother-in-law Henry Holland, Duke of Exeter, married to Edward's sister Anne, and the Earl of Worcester's brother-in-laws, Thomas, Lord Roos, and Lord Richemont Grey, respectively married to his sisters, Philippa and Joanna. Also attainted was Henry Beaufort, Duke of Somerset.

On the 3rd of December Warwick was made Lord Steward of England to pass judgement on those attainted by parliament in November. Among those executed subsequently was Lord Richemont Grey. The epithet, 'a man of no special distinction' was somehow attached to him. Maybe he was not much mourned or missed. The marriage to Joanna, if it happened, hardly registered. She would be known as Lady Ingaldisthorpe. There were advantages in being the mother of Isabel Neville, née Ingaldisthorpe, and not the wife of a man executed for resisting the new regime.

Over the 1460s there is much evidence that in difficult times the Earl of Worcester intervened to look after his sisters and their children. On the 9th of December 1461 a large estate that had belonged to the Earl's attainted brother-in-law Thomas, Lord Roos, was granted to Worcester, Lord Audley, and the clerk Alexander Pruet, 'to hold during the life of Philippa … for her use and profit and the sustenance of herself and her children and servants'.[15] The Earl was also similarly involved in looking after the King's sister, Anne of York, who was unhappily married to Henry Holland, Duke of Exeter, now in exile. On the 22nd of July 1462 there was a similar grant to George Neville, Bishop of Exeter, and Worcester, 'of all goods and debts lately belonging to Henry, late Duke of Exeter, husband of the King's sister Anne, for her use'.[16]

The Earl of Worcester, despite being absent from England for over three years and from politics for six, re-established himself at the heart of government with extraordinary speed—underlining the strength of his reputation and record. The Burgundian chronicler Jehan de Waurin wrote those governing were *'les contes de Warewic [Richard Neville], d'Euxestre [John Tiptoft], et de Fauquemberge [Richard's uncle William]'*, or the Earls of Warwick, Worcester and Fauconberg.[17] The last, Warwick's uncle and an able commander, was made the Earl of Kent in November 1461 and would die in 1463.

The Earl of Warwick's vast estate, worth £7,000 a year, won partly by disinheriting weaker relatives, made him a man able to command recognition on the continental stage and to negotiate directly with the King of France and the Duke of Burgundy—and any who made him lose face before these he would hate indeed. Despite his bold intervention at the 1st Battle of St Albans (won 1455) his battlefield record was mixed: Ludford Bridge (lost 1459), Northampton (won 1460), 2nd Battle of St Albans (lost 1460), Ferrybridge (indecisive 1461), Towton (won 1461), and, in the future, Barnet (lost and killed 1470). At sea he proved a masterly pirate and, based between 1459 and 1460 at Calais, he won plaudits for unscrupulously harassing foreign shipping while at the same time he undermined the Lancastrian regime. He had an instinctive mastery of what is now called public relations. He was careful to cultivate popular favour and, surreptitiously or overtly, to spread his message through manifestos explaining his cause.

Edward IV is an underrated king whose male line was destroyed, after his premature death in his early forties, by his vicious brother Richard III. A man of commanding presence who towered six foot seven in armour, he was a brilliant battlefield leader; a titular and then actual commander at the victories at the 1st Battle of St Albans (1455), Northampton (1460), Mortimer's Cross and Towton (1461), Losecoat Field (1470), and Barnet and Tewksbury (1471). He won the throne as a teenager—and a youth as handsome and attractive as he might be expected to want to enjoy the pleasures, sexual and leisurely, that his victories opened to him. Yet he had early a keen understanding of the importance of the law as an instrument to impose order and of the need for a magnificent yet properly financed household.

Now these three men's challenge was to secure regime change in England, a four-part process consisting of: eliminating the elite internal opposition; defending against external attack; enforcing law and order; and, at the same time, enabling the new regime to project an aura of effective and authoritative government from a well managed royal court and household. The first challenge, quelling internal conspiracy, would not be long in coming. Soon the Earl began the journey from *dulcissime princeps* to *ille trux carnifex*, from the sweetest prince to that cruel executioner.

Chapter 12

Constable of England – 1462

Thei [Oxford plot conspirators] were brought before the Erle of Worscetre, and juged by lawe padowe [Paduan law] that thei schuld be hade to the Toure Hylle, where was made a scaffolde of viij. fote hygt, and ther was there hedes smyten of, that alle menne myght see; whereof the moste peple were sory.[1]

The Chronicler Warkworth on the condemnation of the Oxford plot conspirators in 1462

The Earl of Worcester was appointed Lord High Constable of England on the 7th of February 1462.[2] Now he and Warwick held the highest positions from which to judge peers accused of treason, the former by civil law in the Court of the Constable, and the latter by common law in the Lord Steward's court. These two men were the most powerful men about the King. Worcester's appointment indicated the regime was preparing to face an extremely serious threat where exemplary justice was deemed necessary.

Worcester and the King might have taken in two lessons from history: firstly, Henry IV and Henry V ruthlessly executed rebel peers and established the Lancastrian regime; secondly, Henry VI did not execute such peers and was beset by revolts and magnate disputes. Indeed Henry VI had proved notably weak and inconsistent in dealing with treason. In 1446 York's armourer John Daveys had been hanged after losing a trial by combat against a younger but not necessarily more honest accuser. In 1453, when struggling to restore royal finances, money and council time had to be found to organise a duel between two near nobodies, John Lyalton and Robert Norreys, which probably never even took place. Commissions into the wrongdoings of well-connected miscreants, like Trevelyan and Danyell associated with the late Duke of Suffolk, achieved no result. On the 14th of March 1454 the Earl of Devon, Thomas Courtenay, was indicted of treason before the Duke of Buckingham, acting as Steward of England, and was acquitted by his fellow peers. What was required in 1462 was a system that produced a guaranteed result and brought finality—death—even for nobles of ancient lineage.

Given his appointment as Constable of England, and subsequent role in the arrest and trial of the conspirators, it seems likely that Worcester was involved from the beginning in thwarting Lancastrian plans for an invasion of England in 1462. A letter from Warwick to Coppini described how, in early February 1462, a messenger came to Edward IV revealing he carried letters from conspirators—of whom the most prominent was John de Vere, 12th Earl of Oxford—addressed to Henry VI and the Queen of Scotland.[3]

Many contemporary sources identified the conspirators as Oxford, his son and heir Aubrey, Thomas Tuddenham, William Tyrell, John Montgomery and John Clopton. Tuddenham had been a supporter of William de la Pole, Duke of Suffolk, much involved in local East Anglian disputes, and mixed up in the curious affair in 1448 when he, Alice, and two others were apprehended in disguise leaving Norwich to take the 'ayr and disport theym self'.

The intercepted letters described a plot in which the conspirators, with two thousand horsemen, would follow the King north and kill him and his retinue. Also Henry Beaufort, Duke of Somerset, would invade from Bruges, the deposed King Henry from Scotland, and Jasper Tudor, the Earl of Pembroke, from Brittany. The *Brief Latin Chronicle* added that the conspirators were in Essex in order to meet Somerset's army.[4] According to Warwick's letter to Coppini the messenger had reached York when he resolved to betray the plot.[5]

Edward IV could not but have taken the conspiracy most seriously. The treasonous correspondence was copied and resealed and then carried on by the same messenger. The *Brief Notes* recorded, 'a certain captain rose who with four thousand or more soldiers in Sherwood.'[6] The correspondence with Coppini described clerical support, as imprisoned priests had written notices on church doors stating that the Pope 'gave plenary absolution to all those who would be with King Henry and excommunicated those who were with our king.'[7]

There were omens that mercy might be in short supply. On the 8th of February, the day after Worcester's appointment as Constable, one John Lenche of Droitwich was *tractus suspensus decapitatus et quarterizatus* or drawn, hanged, beheaded and quartered at Tyburn.[8] Lenche had been on the post-Towton attainder list and his sentence would have been determined by the Lord Steward, probably Warwick.

The arrests were made on the 12th of February by Worcester, with Lords Ferrers and Herbert.[9] They took place, according to the chronicles of Benet and Gregory, in Essex which indicated that the conspirators may have already been *en route* to join Somerset's forces. Four de Veres—the Earl, and his oldest and two younger sons—were secured in the Tower, under Worcester's constableship.

There were three separate trials at Westminster. First, Oxford's heir Aubrey de Vere was tried and executed. Perhaps the letters showed he was most deeply implicated in the conspiracy with the King's enemies and, therefore, a guilty verdict without mitigation was most easily sustained without eliciting popular sympathy. Second, the remaining non-peers were tried and condemned, with the exception of Clopton who was acquitted. Finally, the Earl of Oxford was tried. There might have been much unhappiness at the execution of a peer of such an ancient lineage and so far an unpartisan record, so his trial may have been reserved to last after having established a precedent for executions and a sense of inevitability with the earlier trials.

Several chroniclers made it clear that Oxford was tried by the Constable's Court and according to civil law. William of Wyrcester wrote, '*per curiam constabilariae convicti*' or 'convicted by the Constable's Court'.[10] Benet specifically described only the Earl of Oxford as condemned by Civil Law, '*per Jus Civile*', although it was probable that the other conspirators were as well.[11] Warkworth said that high treason was laid to them and then 'aftyrwarde thei were brought before the Erle of Worscetre, and juged by lawe padowe'.[12] The reference to law learned at the University of Padua implied that Worcester used legal practice that was not properly English. Also, Warkworth commented that 'moste people were sory' about the executions – and thus by implication, the means of condemnation.

There are differences in the reported manner and dates of the executions. The Chronicle of London reported: 'And vpon the xxth day of the said moneth the said lord Awbrey was *drawen* from Westynster to The Tower hill, and there beheded. And the xxiij day of the said moneth of ffebruary sir Thomas Todenham, William Tyrell, and John Monomery were beheded at the said Tower hill. And vpon the ffriday next folowyng, which was the xxvj day of the ffebruary, therle of Oxenford was led *vpon foot* from Westmynster vnto The Tower hill, and there beheded.'[13]

This clearly described three different days of executions but with beheading common to each. The difference was that Aubrey was drawn to his execution but Oxford walked. Aubrey's degradation in this respect might have been because his actions had in some way been egregious, either as provocateur or betrayer. The *Brief Notes* is the only source to indicate a crueller death, for him. This says he was *suspensus* and *tractus*, or hanged and disembowelled.[14] The Burgundian chronicler Jean de Waurin, who was first known to have gone to England in 1467, produced a more lurid account.[15] The Earl was disembowelled without prior hanging, emasculated, and then cast, bound, into the fire that consumed his bowels. This is not supported by the English chroniclers who said the Earl was allowed the dignity of walking to the scaffold and was beheaded; had Oxford been so cruelly treated it is unlikely they would have overlooked the opportunity of adding this to the charge sheet of butchery against Worcester.

No record survives of the Oxford Plot trials and the specific charges. In 1463, however, the Earl as Constable would try, and acquit, Sir William Plumpton who had been denounced for the crime of *lèse majesté*, that is violating the King's majesty through encroaching on his powers to treat with foreign powers.[16] Although the powers of the Constable were not specifically defined in 1462, they were in

1467, when the office was granted to Earl Rivers. These were stated to be the same as Worcester's in 1462 and specifically included the power to 'proceed with ... the crime of *lèse majesté*, ... that have been decided in the Court of the Constable of England of old'.[17] The Oxford plotters, who conspired with Queen Margaret, were probably charged with *lèse majesté*.

The trial and judgement by the Constable's Court clearly caused much concern, resulting in the charge that Worcester deliberately sought to replace English common with foreign civil law. The nineteenth-century constitutional historian William Stubbs objected, 'Another abuse ... was the extension of the jurisdiction of the High Constable of England to cases of high treason, thus depriving the accused of the benefit of trial by jury and placing their acquittal or condemnation in the hands of a political official.'[18] Richard II's Statute of 1379–80 defined the jurisdiction of the Court. 'To the Constable it pertaineth to have cognisance of ... things that touched arms and war within the realm that cannot be determined or discussed by common law.'[19] Thus, *within* England the Constable only had jurisdiction in such matters when the issue could *not* be resolved under common law, even in times of war. Much depended on whether a clear state of war existed and no reasonable common law alternative was available. Such a state of war existed in the field when banners were unfurled and at sieges when cannons were fired. In the case of the Oxford plot there was no evidence of this state at all. Also, the plotters were held in London where determination of the issue by common law was eminently possible.

By the fifteenth century the English legal system had developed many of the forms that distinguished it from that of Europe's civil law, which was based on codes rather than precedent. Englishmen involved in law and politics were fiercely protective of common law against any encroachment of continental ideas. Common law was English and it had built into it protections which meant in practice justice might be tempered with mercy: juries were local citizens and unwilling to hang their own fellow men if they were otherwise integrated people of the community; and it placed a very high importance on correct process, making it possible to have cases thrown out on the basis of nitpicking errors in documentation.

While there seems to be no question that the Oxford plot was treasonous, it does appear that the Constable's Court did not have proper jurisdiction because no formal state of war existed and there was a common law alternative in the form of trial by peers in London. The Earl of Warwick was Steward of England and while he would condemn without compunction nobles of more modest or recent noble rank he might have baulked at executing the 12th Earl of Oxford and his heir. It is also probable that their lordships could not, collectively, be trusted to condemn an Earl of previous good record and such an ancient lineage as de Vere. In the Constable's Court, however, Worcester had no qualms about severely punishing nobles with long bloodlines who had strayed from virtue which, as *The Declamacion* demonstrated, was the basis of true nobility.

Whatever the harshness of this decision and the abuse of the law involved in its making, the lesson was made that King and Constable would act together—boldly, decisively and ruthlessly—in order to suppress rebellion and without sparing rank. This was the first of several examples of the King's and the Earl's cooperation to enforce order at all levels of society in times of peace and war. But trial by the Constable's Court or by Worcester was not an automatic one-way ticket to the scaffold. Clopton was not found guilty. Also, with the possible exception of Aubrey, the punishment was not cruel by the standards of the day. The charge, however, that Worcester in this instance misused the powers of the Constable's Court, as there was no declared state of war, appears to be justified.

The simple but brutal question is, did the suppression, and particularly the harsh use of the Constable's Court, work? A clear message got through to the upper nobility that if they conspired against the King, then he, acting through the Constable and without appeal to other peers, would kill quickly. Until the treason of Clarence and the Nevilles in 1469, there were no serious court, or even England-based, revolts, with the exception of the distant north where there was French and Scottish involvement—and nor were there any conspiracies.

Edward, working with Worcester, might appear a proto-Machiavellian Prince: 'It is essential to understand this: that a prince—and especially a "new" prince—cannot always follow those practices by which men are regarded as good, for in order to maintain the state he is often obliged to act against his promises, against charity, against humanity and against religion.'[20] The King and the Earl, however, did not necessarily act against promises, charity, humanity and religion, given the seriousness of the treason. What they did do, it seems, was stretch the civil law.

Suppressing elite opposition came at a price. It may have been effective but Worcester had now begun to make enemies. The London lawyers, and indeed ordinary Englishmen, may have been shocked by his replacement of the common law of England with civil law, lampooned as the Law of Padua. Also, the execution of the de Veres, *pére et fils*, in London may have upset people. Most executions during the Wars of the Roses took place well away from London and followed battles. These, by contrast, had been on Tower Hill, inside the walls of London, following not fighting but a plot unknown to the people. It was also the first execution of an earl there since 1397, when Richard FitzAlan, Earl of Arundel, was executed by the tyrannous Richard II, long before living memory. Worcester—who up to now had miraculously ridden above faction, and been the friends of all from kings to monks—had begun the journey that made him perhaps the most hated man in the British Isles.

Chapter 13

Treasurer and captain 'by water' – 1462 to 1463

Thenn the Kynge Edwarde the iiij purposyd to make an arme into Schotlonde by londe and by water, that the grete rebellyous Harry ande the Quene Margarete shulde not passe a way by water. And the kyng made the Erle of Worseter captayne by water. And thenn there was ordaynyd a grete navy and a grete armye bothe by watyr and by lond. And alle was loste and in vayne, and cam too noo purposse, neyther by water ne by londe.[1]

> Gregory's Chronicle describing the failed effort to block
> Margaret's flight to France in 1465

N ow the new regime had to neutralise threats initiated abroad and involving foreign support, both on land and sea, from Scotland and France. There was no standing navy so one needed to be created, which would cost a great deal of money and involve huge disruption of normal trading as warships were largely adapted merchantmen. The last Treasurer to fund the keeping of the seas and a land campaign against foreigners was Worcester in 1452 to 1454.

The Earl of Worcester was now also involved in diplomacy. On the 8th of February 1462, while dealing with the Oxford plot, he was commissioned as an ambassador to treat with John de Ile, Earl of Ross and Lord of the Isles.[2] Scotland was still very much the *auld enemy*, doubly a threat now that the regent queen mother of Scotland, Mary of Guelders, gave harbour, during the minority of her son, James III, to Henry VI and his rather more dangerous Queen Margaret. The articles of the treaty negotiated between England and the Isles were agreed and sealed on the 13th of February at the Palace of Westminster. Following the conquest of Scotland by England, the Lords of the Isles would hold, as vassals from England, the area north of the Firth of Forth, and the Earl of Douglas the areas to the south.

Worcester was seen as the man who knew how to deal with the papacy. The same letter describing the Oxford Plot, from Warwick to Coppini on the 25th of March, had said, 'they have decided to send ambassadors at Easter next to the supreme pontiff. ... Some say that the Earl of Worcester will go .... I think it will be so if matters keep well.'[3] The purpose of such a mission can only be speculated at but it may have been to do with financing. The Oxford Plot may have made it clear that Edward was not secure on the throne and there could be heavy campaigning costs.

In April there was gossip—dutifully reported to John Paston by his retainer John Russe—that Worcester would be made Treasurer for the second time: 'It is seyd here that my lord Worcestre is lyk to be Tresorer, with whom I truste ye stonde right wel in conseit.'[4] The incumbent was Henry Bourchier, the Archbishop of Canterbury's brother, but perhaps a firmer hand was needed. On the 14th of April the Earl of Worcester was duly appointed.[5] Thus the Plantagenet-Neville-Tiptoft 'Triumvirate' of 1454 was reconstructed in 1462: Edward IV was King where his father, Richard Plantagenet, Duke of York had been Protector; George Neville, Bishop of Exeter, replaced his father, the Earl of Salisbury, as Chancellor; and John Tiptoft, Earl of Worcester, was again Treasurer.

The disruptive threat now came from abroad, requiring the reconstruction of the navy which demanded both money and ships. Worcester acted vigorously, causing much discord and disruption. The impact of the fundraising was confirmed by a rather revealing letter of the 3rd of July 1462 to John Paston from his retainer John Daubeney, who recounted how he had met one Thomas Edmonds and the Debenhams, father and son, who feuded with the Pastons, in a tavern where the situation got heated. Daubeney wrote: 'Lord Tresorer [Worcester] had put hym [Thomas Edmonds] to a gret charge for the vetelyng [victualling] of *Mary Talbot*.'[6] Edmonds offered to buy a hundred bullocks from old Debenham for the *Mary Talbot* which had been arrested for the King's fleet. Overhearing this, young Debenham asked his father if he also could have some bullocks to victual the *Barge of Yarmouth*. Daubeny reported Edmonds then told young Debenham that the towns of Norwich and Yarmouth had already said they would victual the *Barge*. Also, 'that my Lord Tresorer [Worcester] and all the Lords that be at London thynk they [Norwich and Yarmouth] do ryght well her devyer [duty], and be worthey moche thanke of the Kyng'.[7]

Young Debenham took umbrage, assuming Norwich and Yarmouth were trying to take credit for something he had been instructed to do, and he told Edmonds he blamed John Paston for setting up this situation. Edmonds, however, denied Paston was to blame. Daubeney concluded by reporting that subsequently the two towns, knowing of young Debenham's bombastic demands and manner, had let him bear the cost if he was so determined.

The letter is interesting not only for revealing a quite believable row in a tavern, perhaps fuelled by generous quantities of wine, but also for its demonstration of the active way Worcester had motivated, perhaps building on local rivalries, the provisioning of ships for the fleet and the tempers such activity could inflame. The Earl was making his presence felt throughout the merchant community of southern England and not all might be best pleased.[8]

In 1454 Worcester, as Treasurer, had been much involved in funding the defence of Calais which in August 1462 was again in danger. On the 6th to 8th of August

Stone's Chronicle revealed King Edward, the Chancellor George Neville, and the Treasurer and Constable Worcester visited Canterbury where there was the usual ceremonial reception by the Prior.[9] The purpose of the visit was to inspect the preparations at Sandwich and review the navy there.[10]

The records of Convocation and the City of London show the Earl now set out on a campaign of direct fundraising, facing increasingly resentful and suspicious audiences. On the 21st of August 1462 Worcester and other members of the King's council went before the Common Council of London, where the Earl stated that Margaret and the French King were plotting against Calais and asked for a loan of £3,400.[11] The King was promised only £1,000 at this time but he had already appealed for money earlier in the month. The two appeals together brought him something over £2,000.[12] In the following October the City provided a further loan of 2,000 marks (£1,333).[13]

A further Paston letter said, 'There were arrested by the Treasurer forty sails lying in the Thames…; and it is said it is to carry men to Calais in all haste for fear of the King of France for a siege, … . Many men be greatly afraid of this matter, and so the Treasurer hath much to do for this cause.'[14] Arresting 'forty sails', however necessary, must have been very disruptive, whether or not they actually went to sea, and the popularity of the Treasurer, Worcester, must have taken a further buffet.

In October 1462 the Earl became involved in actual campaigning on land, for the first time known of, at the comparatively advanced age of 35. On the 25th of October Margaret landed on the Northumberland coast, having sailed to Scotland to collect Henry and the Duke of Somerset. She established herself at Bamborough Castle and it, along with Dunstanburgh and Alnwick Castles, became the bases for Lancastrian resistance.

On the 2nd of November 1462 funds were requested from Convocation. As in 1453 Warwick and Worcester were the leading members. Other members included the King's brothers, the Dukes of Clarence and Gloucester, the Duke of Norfolk, John Neville and Lord William Hastings.[15] In 1453 Worcester had addressed a receptive audience when seeking funds for the Earl of Shrewsbury's Gascon campaign. Now the arrest of forty ships in the Thames and further rounds with the funding bowl were doing little to enhance Worcester's popularity with the people of London and with the church.

In November Worcester was part of a great retinue that went north in the company of the King.[16] In the following months three northern castles were besieged by Edward's force under the overall command of Warwick. Two sources show that Worcester was at least titular head of one of the sieges. Both agree that he was at the siege of Dunstanburgh but with different nobles or knights. The *Brief*

Notes reported: 'At the seege of Hem [Dunstanburgh] are *comes de Wyceter comes de Arundel dominus de Ogyl et dominus de Muntegew*', or the Earls of Worcester and Arundel and Lords Ogle and Montagu.[17] The Paston correspondence recounted, 'at Dunstanborough castle lieth the Earl of Worcester and Sir Ralph Grey.'[18]

Bamborough and Dunstanburgh had soon had enough and on Christmas Eve they offered to surrender. The Duke of Somerset, Henry Beaufort, then changed sides and joined Warwick at Alnwick. The young King Edward would try to forge a friendship with Beaufort—possibly seeking companionship with a noble close in age and making a genuine effort at reconciliation after the hostility between their fathers which destroyed them both. It ended in betrayal and Beaufort was executed by John Neville, Lord Montagu, in 1464. Probably the only aristocrats whom Edward could really trust at the highest level were Worcester and Hastings.

The Earl of Pembroke, Jasper Tudor, and Lord Roos could not gain from Edward a promise of the return of their estates and accepted the offer of a safe conduct to Scotland. Roos was Worcester's brother-in-law and following his attainder in 1461 his estates were held by the Earl in the interest of Roos's wife, Philippa *née* Tiptoft. Worcester probably preferred to see Roos's request rejected on the basis that the Earl would rather his sister receive, through his control, the income from his brother-in-law's estates.

According to William of Wyrcester's Annals the leading English noblemen could have been destroyed by an invading Scots army in January 1463. 'The Earl of Warwick, the Duke of Somerset, the Earl of Worcester, and many other lords, … when they saw themselves inferior in number [to the Scots], they set up in a certain field between the castle and the marsh; and in this manner the Scots passed by without a loss [to the English]. But if the Scots were bold and clever they could have destroyed the whole nobility of Lords in England.'[19] Wyrcester, an Oxford man, wrote the *Boke of Noblesse* after England's ejection from France, which he blamed on the English aristocracy's failure to emulate Rome's governing classes—a theme that the Earl of Worcester, the translator of *The Declamacion of Noblesse,* would have approved. His Annals contain several accounts involving Worcester which are somewhat amusing, albeit not particularly flattering, that might have been reported wryly by the Earl against himself to the annalist.

Unfortunately, Henry, Margaret and their heir Edward remained at liberty. The Scots and the Lancastrians continued to foment trouble in the north and Edward IV was determined to suppress all rebellion completely by means of a combined land and sea campaign. The next time Margaret tried to invade was the summer of 1463. Ralph Grey, Constable of Alnwick Castle, turned traitor and let Margaret land. Grey had been appointed with Worcester to lead the siege of Dunstanburgh

Castle in December 1461 but felt he had been insufficiently rewarded. On the 3rd of June Warwick went north to assist his brother Montagu.

Responding to Warwick's call for support against Margaret and the Scots, Edward decided to follow Warwick and also made plans to raise a fleet and put it under the command of Worcester.[20] In 1454 the Earl had been appointed one of the keepers of the sea. In 1462 he cajoled and bullied the merchant class to provide and victual the fleet. Now he was to be the naval commander.

In late June or early July in 1463 Worcester was replaced as Treasurer by Lord Grey of Ruthyn—probably so the Earl could devote himself to naval affairs and the role of Lord Steward of the Household, to which he was appointed around this time.[21] Worcester was again a loyal source of funds. On the 22nd of June 1463 the Treasurer, and others of his staff, were repaid a loan of £200 which they had made four weeks earlier.[22] On the last day of June Worcester was granted two-thirds of the tonnage and poundage in London, Southampton and Sandwich until he was repaid £1,948 12s. 3d.[23] On the 6th of July Edward ordered that Worcester should have £4,680 for the keeping of the sea and then set out for Northumberland.[24]

Although the Earl had ceased to be Treasurer the burden of fronting fund-raising would still largely fall on him and with it the associated opprobrium. In 1453 Worcester had addressed a receptive audience when seeking funds for the Earl of Shrewsbury's Gascon campaign. On the 11th of July 1463 the King's representatives were received by Convocation. They included the Earls of Worcester and Essex, and Grey, the new Treasurer. Even though he was no longer Treasurer it fell to Worcester to make the speech. He spoke eloquently of the great dangers threatening the country and requested a subsidy. But the ecclesiastical lords' patience and pockets were overburdened.[25] Between the 11th and 15th of July the grant was discussed without result, Convocation being thoroughly sceptical on the matter, and on the last day the deputation came back, including Worcester and George Neville, the Chancellor. Various letters from the King and Warwick were produced to prove the danger from Scotland and the King's need for money.[26]

Eventually Convocation granted the King a tenth of clerical income, 'at which, many were aggrieved and complained, both because they were poor and because moneys so extorted from the clergy rarely or never lead to any good result, but rather to the confusion and disgrace of those who use them'.[27] Despite no longer being the Treasurer Worcester did not shirk the difficult task. In 1453 the Register of the Archbishop of Canterbury revealed the ecclesiastical lords were charmed by the brilliant young Treasurer; a decade later in 1463 they seemed thoroughly fed up. But this was, however, to prove a very successful fundraising.[28] In the Michaelmas term (September 1462–March 1463) Treasury receipts of £9,501 16s. 7½d. were recorded. But in the Easter term (March 1463–September 1463) the sum increased to £70,414 16s. 11d. Maybe the wholesale arrests of ships in 1462, in order to assemble the fleet, had caused too much upset, as new methods were now used. Instead of creating commissions to obtain ships, Edward IV had purchased five new vessels and hired others (three such ships were owned by Worcester).[29]

On the 7th of August Worcester received a special injunction to prevent Queen Margaret from escaping to France after her failure in the north.[30] The Earl was still at the Tower of London on the 18th of August as John Howard was recorded on that date as receiving bows and arrows and gunpowder from the armoury of the Tower, delivered to him by its Constable.[31] The Earl reviewed his fleet at Sandwich, and bought a new carvel-built ship for the sum of £133 6s. 8d. at the King's expense.[32]

It is not clear when Worcester's fleet sailed to stop Queen Margaret. Mid-August seems most likely. He failed to intercept the Queen and the chroniclers were not flattering about the Earl's naval prowess (Gregory's comment is given at the start of the chapter).[33] A *Brief Latin Chronicle*, whose perspective was the clergy, complained: 'For after the feast of the Nativity of the Blessed Virgin Mary King Edward mustered a great army and prepared to subdue his adversaries by land and sea. I know not, however, what good he did in that expedition. And the Earl of Worcester with his ship and sailors, lurking as it were by the shores and havens of the sea and consuming their provisions, returned empty without doing anything. O unhappy result, shame and confusion! (*O infelix successus opprobrium et confusio!*)'[34]

On the 22nd of August Worcester's fleet escorted ambassadors to St Omer for which Worcester was paid £100.[35] At the end of September the conference moved to Hesdin. There, on the 8th of October, England and France agreed to abstain from fighting each other for a year, neutralising, to a degree, the danger posed by Henry and Margaret.

By mid-1463 it was clear that the Lancastrian and Scottish threat had not been eliminated and further expensive campaigns would be necessary. But Parliament, Convocation and the City were much less willing to provide further funds to a regime that still had not securely established itself. Although Worcester ceased to be Treasurer in June 1463 he appears to have had to lead fundraising endeavours which were increasingly resented. His general popularity, something he never appeared worried about cultivating, suffered further damage following the suppression of the Oxford plot and earlier ship seizures and attempts at fundraising. It was unfortunate that the Lancastrian forces had scattered before the Yorkist army and fleet could engage them. The money so hard-won by Worcester had pre-empted battle, but there was then no proof, through victory on land or sea, that the money had been well spent.

The Yorkist regime was now proving expensive and unable to contain the threat of rebellion. The Earl had added to his growing list of detractors; already there had been Lancastrians and lawyers and he was now adding the City of London merchants and clerics to those who were disinclined to look favourably upon him. There is no indication that he ever flinched from carrying out his duties, however unpopular it made him.

Chapter 14

Lord Steward of the Household – 1463

Michaelmas Term [after November 1462]. Richard Walwyn was admitted to repasts [at Lincoln's Inn] as long as he should remain on the business of John, Earl of Worcester, at London, or at the Tower of London, or near London.[1]

This note in the Lincoln Inn Black Book is the only record of Worcester's residences. Richard Walwyn was the heir of the Earl of Worcester's second wife Elizabeth *née* Greyndour.

S uccessful regime change required not only eliminating, or at least neutral-ising, the elite opposition and foreign foes but the new regime also needed to establish an aura of efficiency and authority. The court of Henry VI was wretchedly managed, both financially and organisationally, resulting in investigating committees in 1454 and 1455, when York was in control, of which the Earl of Worcester was a leading member. The household of Edward IV proved more efficient, economical and stylish. The Earl was the man most in control of the King's main residences as both Constable of the Tower (Edward's preferred residence in the early 1460s) and Lord Steward of the Household. The Tower was also one of the Earl's residences—as the quote at the beginning of the chapter shows—meaning he frequently lived close to the King. His other usual residences were possibly Worcester House in the parish of St James Garlickhythe ('at home') and Elsyng Palace at Enfield ('near London').

Sometime in the first half of 1463 Worcester was appointed Lord Steward of the Household. The great officers running the royal household were its Steward and the Chamberlain, positions held by Worcester and Lord Hastings, respectively responsible for activities below and above the stairs. Thus Hastings controlled access to the King while Worcester was responsible for the administration of the court. This role tends to be overlooked in discussions of the Earl, in which the tendency has been to focus on his scholarly, political and butcherly business. As both Steward and Constable of the Tower the Earl was in a uniquely powerful position to determine the character of the court.

Under Edward IV the royal household was particularly important, providing the core of his regime. On the 5th of February 1463, John, Earl of Worcester, William

Hastynges, knight, king's chamberlain, John Fogge, knight, Treasurer, John Scot, knight, controller of the household, and Thomas Colt were granted the custody of all property and marriage rights of minors in the King's hands as well as clerical temporalities.[2] This is possibly a snapshot of Edward IV's inner circle of Worcester, Hastings, Fogge, Scot and Colt, along with the rewards for their labours. None of them were great hereditary magnates. The avuncular and assured Hastings was probably more about the King's person in London and Westminster, while the experienced, versatile and uncompromisingly loyal Worcester was trusted with complex tasks that involved travel and independent action.

Someone must have been the guiding hand in the improvement of Edward IV's court when compared to that of Henry VI. The obvious candidate is the Lord Steward, the Earl of Worcester, who had come to the mismanaged court of Henry VI aged 20 to serve about the King's person and had been involved in two inquiries into its structure and expenditure in 1454 and 1455. He had also seen the de' Medici and d'Este courts at first hand and probably others in Italy. Edward's court was both magnificently and efficiently run and had a fascination with chivalry. It was also noted for the exceptional quality of its music, an area of keen interest to Worcester, who had taken a substantial choir to the Holy Land.

The Constable of the Tower had charge of its prisoners. Some could be young, long-term charges who required nurturing. Three were of particular note: Henry Percy was the son of the Earl of Northumberland, killed at Towton in 1461; there were also two younger sons of John de Vere the Earl of Oxford, executed in 1462 by Worcester as Constable.

On the 9th of May 1463 Worcester received £87 11s. 6d. for expenses for looking after Percy and the two younger de Veres.[3] Judging by the amount and the provision of gentlemen servants they were well looked after. The documentation gives the name of only one de Vere son, the fourth, Thomas. The other name is illegible but was almost certainly the third, George.[4] On the 18th of January 1464 John de Vere, who was married to another sister of the three Neville brothers Margaret Neville, was licenced to enter his father's estates and titles and the two younger brothers were probably then released. Percy remained under the benign charge of Worcester, and then William Herbert, the Earl of Pembroke, and became a committed Yorkist. This episode had consequences which reverberated for years and cast light on some subsequent, rather confusing, events involving the shifts in loyalty in 1470 in the Percy and Neville families.

Between 1461 and 1464 the King's household must, however, have appeared incomplete and much hit by deaths: Edward IV had lost his father and closest brother; Worcester, earlier, two wives, a stepdaughter and a baby son; and Henry Percy's father had been killed at Towton fighting against Edward. The King's oldest sister Anne was separated from her unruly husband, the exiled Duke of Exeter. It was not perhaps surprising that Edward IV would be attracted to the young and vibrant Woodvilles who provided an instant beautiful and intelligent, if problematical, family. The Woodvilles lived under a double cloud at the manor of Grafton Regis in Northamptonshire. Richard Woodville had married above his station, Jacquetta of Luxembourg, widow of the Duke of Bedford who died in 1435. The family had also been Lancastrians and Richard's oldest daughter, Elizabeth, was the widow of Sir John Grey, killed at the 2nd Battle of St Albans in 1461.

Another prisoner in the Tower in the charge of its Constable was Sir William Plumpton. An interesting perspective was cast on the character of the Earl of Worcester by the Plumpton archive, which shows him in an unbutcherly light. The Plumptons were a northern family whose correspondence of about 250 letters between 1461 and 1552 survives. The early letters record the travails of the rather hapless Sir William who fought on the wrong side at Towton. Plumpton subsequently agreed to pay £2,000 as a bond for good behaviour. Unable to raise the sum, he surrendered himself in July 1462 to confinement in the Tower where he possibly developed a friendly relationship with Worcester, its Constable and gaoler, and the Earl's twice-widowed sister Joanna, who later appears several times in the Plumpton correspondence. Sir William probably owed his life to the Tiptoft connection.

A letter, dated the 14th of October 1462, to Plumpton from Bryan Rocliff, 3rd Baron of the Exchequer, revealed his 'maister the Chief Baron [Richard Illingworth, made Chief Baron of the Exchequer on the 10th of September 1462] comuned to my lord Treasorer [Worcester] of certaine matters, and soe my lord opened that Thomas Beckwith was his Awnte [aunt's] son, and he would make him eschetour [escheator]; saying, that *he loved you right well* and would fayne an end [to ill-will] were taken betwixt you and Beckwith.'[5] Thomas Beckwith's son William was married to Plumpton's daughter Elizabeth and there had been a falling out between the Beckwiths and the Plumptons over the delivery of the marriage settlement.

In December 1463 the Earl was involved in the acquittal of Plumpton on treason charges.[6] In September 1463 Sir William had been released from his unpaid bond of £2,000 provided he remained in London.[7] In the autumn of 1463 Plumpton was denounced for treason by one David Routh for receiving in Hounslow 'false, damnable, deffamatory and slaunderous writing, traitorously by pen and other forged and ymagined, against the King and secretly aiding, divers persons coming out of Scotland fro the King's adversaries'.[8] These were very dangerous charges of *lèse-majesté* that sounded not unlike those which proved fatal to the Oxford plotters.

Plumpton was tried before Worcester at Hounslow, shortly before Christmas, and aquitted. He obtained a record from the Constable on the 20th of January 1464 and carefully retained this document, for obvious reasons, and a copy survives in the Plumpton Coucher Book.

> John, Earl of Worcester, Lord Tiptot, & of Powis, high Constable of England ... we make known ... in the examining process of the inquisition against ...... William Plompton, knight, ... on occasion of the denunciation of a certain David Routh, ... [of] the crime of *lèsé-majesté* ... by authority of our Lord King, by the oaths of 24 good & faithful men of our Lord King taken at Houslow; whereas by the statements & depositions of these witnesses, sworn and diligently examined, we find & manifestly that the said David in false manner & unjustly has denounced the said lord William Plumpton ... we announce, decree, & declare, the said lord William on the occasion of this denunciation, [free] from farther disturbance, vexation, & molestation. [9]

It is difficult to determine quite what legal system was used here. 'Process of inquisition' implied civil law. But under such law the judges determined the facts of the case without a jury and here twenty-four men played a key part in deciding the issue. This sounds like a common law process that became obsolete after the late Middle Ages, involving a writ of attaint. This was issued—by the crown in criminal cases—to inquire whether an earlier jury had given a false verdict in a trial. The correctness of the first verdict was decided by a grand jury of attaint which had twenty-four members, the same number involved in the Plumpton case. Precisely what system was used here may be unclear but Worcester was protecting a man who 'he loved right well'. Plumpton sought confirmation of his pardon from the King which was renewed by a signet letter dated the 20th of January 1464.[10] He was declared a true and faithful subject and allowed to return north in January 1464.

A letter to Plumpton of the 14th of February 1464 from Godfrey Grene, of a family intermarried with the Plumptons, reported that 'Mr. Rocliff hath labored effectually this tearme for your matter of Stamford, and for my lady Inglestrop for your sake ... ; and also he [Rocliff] dined with my lady [Ingaldisthorpe] and thanked her hertely for your sake. I trust by his labour your matter of Stamford shall take a good end.'[11] Rocliff's labour with 'Lady Inglestrop' was possibly to obtain a place in the household of Joanna for Isabel Marley, Plumpton's niece. On the 21st of June 1464 Grene wrote to Plumpton: 'I was with my lady Ingolshop, whose ladyship is well recovered of the great sicknes that she hath endured my day past, at which time my mistris Isabell Marley was in good hele, thankid be God, and lett me witt how she likes right wele and greatly is bounden to my lady.'[12]

At some similar time to Joanna's great sickness, Joyce, the sister she shared with Worcester, died—the date is unknown. Her husband Edmund Sutton soon remarried Matilda, daughter of Thomas Lord Clifford. The Suttons, however, remained close to Worcester and the late Joyce's husband Edmund joined him in Ireland.

One of the key questions of the 1460s is how did the Earls of Worcester and Warwick, who were the major figures of the decade, end up on opposite sides by 1470. For much of their lives the two Earls were extremely close. On the 15th of January 1463 the remains of Richard, Earl of Salisbury, and his son Sir Thomas Neville, killed at the Battle of Wakefield on the 30th of December 1460, were reburied at the Neville abbey of Bisham. The main non-Neville participant was the Earl of Worcester. Salisbury and Worcester may have built up a rapport. The latter was briefly the former's son-in-law. Certainly, they worked together when Salisbury was Chancellor and Worcester was Treasurer during the first York Protectorate. Worcester brokered his niece Isabel's marriage to Salisbury's son John. Isabel also was recorded individually as present at the funeral.

A full description survives of the funeral, preserved to show how an earl should be buried, titled, 'The Enterment of the Erle of Salisbery at Busheme'.[13] The day before the funeral the body of the Earl was conveyed to Bisham Abbey. The Lords who followed were 'The duk of Clarans, the Kyng's brodere, the Duke of Suffolke, the erle of Warwike, the erle of Worcesture, the lord Montague, the lord Hastings, the lord Fitzhughe'.

The following morning at solemn Mass the heralds attended with the deceased's armour and trappings. There was a scene of high drama when a mounted man in full armour, with an axe in his right hand, appeared at the main west door of the abbey church. Then the great nobles offered the deceased's funeral achievements, that is the arms and trappings of the Earl. Examples of these survive from the tombs of Edward, the Black Prince, in Canterbury Cathedral and Henry V in Westminster Abbey. Worcester was first and offered the coat-of-arms to a bishop (possibly George Neville, Bishop of Exeter, the deceased's son) who passed it to the herald king of arms.

There followed the shield borne by the Lord Montagu, the sword by Lord Hastings, and the helm by Lord Fitzhughe. The exercise of giving the achievements was repeated with coins appropriate to rank. Here the offering was led by the King's brother, the Duke of Clarence, the Duchess of Suffolk and her son the Duke, the Earl of Warwick, the Earl of Worcester and so on.

This burial showed how close Worcester and the Nevilles were. There had been further evidence when at the end of 1462 Warwick inherited his mother's estates, bringing fully together his vast property worth over £7,000 a year. He made a new will and the trustees were his brother, Bishop George Neville, the Chief Justices

Sir Robert Danby and Sir John Markham, three prominent retainers, four senior administrators and, finally, Worcester.[14]

The fundamental reason for the breakdown of Warwick and Worcester's relationship will be sought in Edward IV's marriage choice. There is, however, another related question that is important, which is why Warwick's brother John Neville, Lord Montagu, also broke with Edward and therefore, even if unintentionally, with Worcester. Warwick had no male children but through him passed the bulk of the Neville estates. The Neville family name would survive to the next generation through John and Isabel's 2-year-old son George, who carried Tiptoft blood. George's mother Isabel, a single child, would inherit a third of the Tiptoft estate if Worcester did not remarry—as his grandmother Joanna, *née* Tiptoft, was one of three coheir sisters. If, however, Worcester, who then appeared a confirmed bachelor, were to get a wife and beget heirs, then that would have disturbing consequences for the Neville hopes for George's inheritance.

Chapter 15

Keeper of the King's peace – 1464

[The King at Coventry] assigned the Erle of Worcestre, Constable of Inglond and Styward of his howse, and the ij Chyeff Juges, Markeham & Danby, to here the seyd matier.[1]

Edward IV orders the investigation of the Cheylesmore
Park jurisdiction affair

T he challenge in securing regime change—as well as neutralising the old regime elite, fighting off external threats, and establishing a court that projected authority from a well-run household—included ensuring general law and order. In 1464 Edward was particularly active, travelling around the country, meting out justice, and repressing riots and local disturbances.[2] Unlike Henry VI, 'Edward IV realized from the outset that an active peripatetic monarch continually showing himself to the people and ensuring the hearing of their complaints was essential for the restoration of law and order.'[3] The main instrument for dealing with popular as opposed to noble unrest was the commission of oyer and terminer, with which Worcester had great experience as a commissioner going back to 1451.

By 1464, while internal aristocratic opposition had been intimidated by the harsh executions of the Oxford plotters, law and order remained generally problematical. As Henry VI and Margaret were to some degree neutralised by the Hesdin accord, more attention could be paid to keeping the peace. In the first part of 1464 the King travelled widely over a belt of central England extending from Gloucester to Cambridge, suppressing riots and local disturbances.[4] His peregrinations had near their epicentre Grafton Regis, the home of the Woodville family.

The commission of oyer and terminer was grounded in common law. The King and Worcester saw this as sufficient to deal with non-aristocratic dissent. The Cheylesmore jurisdiction matter revealed their respect for ancient rights. This revolved around the question of whether the King or the city of Coventry, had a superior jurisdiction in the park of the royal manor of Cheylesmore. It was described at length in the Coventry Leet Book which recorded the City authority's activities.

Ric Hykman, a dyer, had been arrested in Cheylesmore Park by officers of Coventry corporation. Hykman insisted he had right of sanctuary there and, at the instance of the officials of the royal manor, Edward IV questioned why the city's officers had made arrests in the territory of the manor. On the 16th of January Edward IV wrote from Northampton to Coventry requiring the city to explain its actions. 'Be advise of the Chaunceler of Inglond [George Neville], the Erle of Warrewyk, the Erle of Worcestre and mony other lordes theere then beyng, hit was commaunded the seid Recordowr and his felowes to attende on the kyng.'[5] The City appointed the recorder, William Stafford, to ride to Northampton. He insisted on city officers' historic right to make arrests in Cheylesmore Park.

The King declared he would come in person to Coventry and hear the matter but stipulated that Hykman be released. The recorder resisted, because if he was let free then the city officers would be liable for the money that Hykman was evading paying. The King asked the chief justice, Danby, if this were the case and the judge said the recorder was right. The King backed down, hardly the act of an autocratic ruler. The King went to Coventry and commanded Worcester and the chief justices, Markham and Danby, to hear the matter. The decision was deferred until the records of the Duchy of Lancaster could be searched. On the 1st of April 1464 the matter was debated in London before the King—he then being at the Tower of London. The steward of Cheylesmore had been unable to find any record denying the city of Coventry jurisdiction over the estate. The Coventry recorder beseeched the King that the City could keep and enjoy its liberties. There is nothing in this story which shows the King, Worcester and the chief justices as being anything other than meticulous in observing the privileges and freedoms of English cities and men.

Even if Edward IV and Worcester were respectful of English liberties they also proved themselves harsh at this time in suppressing general lawlessness. On the 25th of January 1464 a powerful commission was appointed to deal with unrest in Gloucester, the West Country and the West Midlands, and its membership included both Warwick and Worcester.[6] After considering the Cheylesmore Park matter, Edward rode from Coventry to Worcester, covering the distance within twenty-four hours.[7]

After two days in Worcester, Edward went to Tewkesbury and from the 4th to the 11th of February he was at Gloucester to deal with rioting in a feud between the countrymen of the shire and the people of its county town, the former favouring the current prior of Llanthony and the latter the ex-prior in a bitter monastic quarrel.[8] The shiremen had extracted a bailiff, John Dodyng, from the priory and murdered him on Gloucester's town cross. Later they reentered the town and killed more citizens. Warwick came first on the scene, 'and with beautiful words petitioned consent of them that quietly they return to their homes'.[9] The King and his lords, almost certainly including Worcester, who was recorded as being constantly with the King, were having none of this. 'Later, however, … King Edward came with many noble and armed men and he ordered to be hanged many of the people of the country, and others he ordered to be beheaded and he ordered the heads to be placed above the gates of Gloucester. And there was made a great calm (*Et facta est tranquillitas magna* [Matthew 8:12])'.[10]

In what seems a separate incident, one Robert Llewelyn and others joined together in a conspiracy. A commission of oyer and terminer was appointed on the 5th of February, led by the Earls of Warwick, Arundel and Worcester and including Richard Woodville.[11] An indictment three days later recorded pleas held at Gloucester before these men that 'Robert Llewelyn, and other … felons … [on various days in the county of Gloucester] … armed in the manner of war came together and conspired against the King's allegiance to raise war against the said king … in felonious and treasonable manner, contrary to their allegiance'.[12] Llewelyn and eight others were sentenced to be drawn, hanged, disembowelled, beheaded and quartered.[13]

The descriptions of the issues in Gloucester are difficult to disentangle. There may have been two different events: one was a very nasty attack on the townspeople of Gloucester, however provoked, by countrymen—as described by the Gloucester annalist; and the other was a treasonous uprising, attempted by Robert Llewelyn, set out in the oyer and terminer indictment. Both were quelled by executions. Differences, however, in policy, or possibly self-interest, may already have been developing between Warwick on the one hand, and Edward IV, supported by Worcester and the chief justices, on the other. Warwick had offered soothing words but the King and Worcester brought harsh punishment.

Edward and Worcester's travels meting out justice in early 1464 brought the King both into the company of the Woodvilles and into proximity of their manor at Grafton Regis. The commission of oyer and terminer to Gloucestershire had included Richard Woodville of Rivers and William Hastings. Woodville was husband of Jacquetta, widow of the Duke of Bedford, and father of a large number of fair children who could expect very modest inheritances. That of Elizabeth was threatened and she was being forced into negotiations for a rather one-sided deal with Hastings. The covenants signed on the 13th of April 1464 indicated that still at this date she had no sound expectation of a royal marriage.

In mid-February the King, Worcester and other commissioners were travelling between Gloucester and Cambridge. Richard Woodville was named on both the Gloucester and Cambridge commissions and his son Anthony on the latter one. A stop at the Woodville manor *en route* would have served to pick up the younger man. This could also have provided the opportunity for a *rendezvous* between the unmarried, handsome young king and the slightly older, beautiful, fecund, widowed daughter in desperate need of a powerful protector.

In Cambridge the quarter sessions had been postponed following their disruption by armed assemblies of malefactors.[14] 'It was only in February when the King himself rode into Cambridge, with his councillor and commissioner, John Earl of Worcester, and two other judges in order to add backbone to the justices that proceedings got under way.'[15] When Parliament reassembled in York on the 20th of February, Edward was still in Cambridgeshire. On the 27th of March there was a further commission of oyer and terminer, including Worcester, in unruly Kent.[16] In late March or early April the King finally went north to join Parliament at Leicester and with him were Worcester and Woodville.

While the King was pursuing issues of law and order—and possibly premarital affairs—John Neville was defeating the main Lancastrian remnants in the northeast. Unexpectedly, renegade forces led by Henry Beaufort, Duke of Somerset, Lords Hungerford and Thomas Roos, and Sir Ralph Percy attacked Neville when escorting a Scottish embassy to York. On 25th April Neville defeated them at Hedgeley Moor, killing Percy. Then, on the 15th of May, he beat the Lancastrians again at Hexham, where its leadership were largely captured and immediately executed, including Beaufort.

Two days later John Neville executed Roos, the husband of Worcester's sister Philippa, as well as Hungerford and three others at Newcastle. The executions lacked a clear legal basis and perhaps demonstrated the independence of the Nevilles from royal authority and their indifference to the law. It was, however, unlikely that much objection was made and it certainly spared Worcester some unpleasant judgements. In the presence of the King at York, Worcester, in his role as Constable, completed the executions of those captured at Hexham on the 26th of May. Although the number of nobility decapitated, fourteen, was the most he ever condemned on a single occasion, this action was not added to the charge sheet against him—presumably as it was seen as both legal and proper.

The next day John Neville, Lord Montagu, was made the Earl of Northumberland, rewarding his recent victories, and in July he received the lands of the previous earl. At this time, Henry Percy, Northumberland's son, was a minor in Worcester's custody in the Tower. The Percy family had been the Earls of Northumberland since 1377 and a great power in the north for much longer. There would be problems when the young Percy came of age in 1470 as neither he nor his great northern affinity would easily accept the loss of the earldom. But John Neville, a second son, now stood high in the ranks of English nobles. He was the Earl of Northumberland and his wife Isabel was a coheir to a third of the widower

Earl of Worcester's estate. Unlike his older brother, Warwick, he had a son, the young George Neville.

In midsummer of 1464 there took place an event that has come to be seen as epitomising for posterity Worcester's arrogance. The London chronicler Gregory described an appalling *faux pas* involving precedence by the Earl at the annual feast celebrating the appointment of new sergeants of the coif, who were important lawyers, recognised by their distinctive headdresses. Gregory placed the outrage during the mayoralty of Matthew Philipp which covered the summer of 1464. That year the ceremony was held in Ely Palace, the London home of the eponymous bishop. Gregory, no friend of the Earl, wrote: 'Thys yere, a-bute Mydsomyr, a the feste of the Sargantys of the Coyfe, the Mayre of London was desyryde to be at that feste. And at denyr tyme he come to the feste with his officers, a-greyng and a-cordyng unto hys degre. For with yn London he ys next unto the kyng in alle maner thynge.'[17]

Gregory contrasted the insensitivity of Worcester to the dignity of the Mayor: 'And in tyme of waschynge the Erle of Worseter was take before the mayre and sette downe in the myddys of the hy tabylle. And the mayre seynge that hys place was occupyd … went home a gayne with owt mete or drynke or any thonke.' The mayor took with him the aldermen and provided them with nourishment of the highest quality. The ashamed officiating officers sent the mayor gifts of food and drink but these were no better than those he had already set out in his own home.

There is no question on the issue of precedence within the City—the mayor had pride of place over all but the King. The story of Worcester's arrogance, on consideration, however, does not ring true. Another description of the affair in the Chronicle of London from 1083 to 1485 does not identify the offender. 'The maire of London shuld have dyned there; and bicause the chief place was not kepte for him while the kyng was not there nor of his blode, he came awey with alle his compeigny of this cite.'[18] Later sources said the offender was Lord Grey of Ruthyn, who was the correct Treasurer for the year. The sixteenth century historian Stowe wrote: 'In the year 1464, the 4th of Edward IV, … Matthew Phillip, Mayor of London, with the aldermen, sheriffs, and Commons, of divers crafts, being invited, did repair; but when the Mayor looked to keep the state in the hall, … the Lord Grey of Ruthyn, then lord Treasurer of England, unwitting the serjeants, and against their wills (as they said), was first placed ; whereupon the Mayor, aldermen, and Commons, departed home.'[19] Hollinshed also made it clear that the Mayor 'found a certain nobleman—Grey of Ruthyn, then Lord Treasurer of England—preferred before him, and sitting in the seat of state'.[20]

Worcester was the master of etiquette and precedence, and wrote ordinances on the latter. He had a great love of ceremony and always played his part faultlessly.

His maternal grandmother Agnes Wrothe was descended from a line of six generations of city worthies, which included a Mayor. He had also been a freeman of the Taylors' company for nearly fifteen years and would have known the city codes.

Gregory was no fan of Worcester and had mocked him for his naval record in 1463. Lord Grey of Ruthyn sounds much the more likely offender against the Mayor's dignity. He was a treacherous fellow whose betrayal cost the Lancastrians the Battle of Northampton. Whatever is the ultimate judgement of the Earl's character with respect to cruelty, it is very hard to make the charge of bad manners stick.

Part of the background to this peculiar affair may have been a legal turf war. Englishmen were increasingly protective of their distinct common law system but it was slow. Lawyers in the Court of Common Pleas, which dealt with cases where there was no royal interest, were seeing work going to other speedier courts. Thus common law lawyers, especially the important serjeants of the coif who had a monopoly on Common Pleas cases, were becoming particularly fearful of the encroachment of other judicial systems, particularly civil law.

The real story, however, was that the Earl's service to the King was making him thoroughly unpopular with the commentariat who represented the city lawyers, merchants and ship owners—and Worcester was becoming a lightning rod for hostility to the Yorkist regime. But maybe there was something deeper. Before he stayed in Italy he displayed an astonishing ability to stay above faction. On his return the cosmopolitan Worcester might have been seen to have scholarly affectations and foreign legal ideas, lampooned as 'the Law of Padua'. Perhaps he was increasingly disliked by the conservative insular English as he could speak Italian with the likes of Venetian merchants, wrote in a clear humanist hand and could use classical Latin with the verbs at sentence ends, so it was hard to understand, and not decent messy medieval Latin with English word order. He had not been married for a dozen years, had lived near the fleshpots of Venice, and executed warriors without it seems ever having been in combat himself. But he was also the grandson of a city matron, Agnes Wrothe, and a fourteenth-century ancestor had been a Mayor of London.

Warwick was a genuine snob who despised the King's low born councillors but he was careful to foster popular support. By contrast Worcester made no effort to curry common favour but believed true nobility was earned, not bred. Basically, anti-Yorkist, and later pro-Readeption, propaganda might have presented the Earl as a dubious clever dick and a toff who had risen above himself—and his fellow Londoners. The little Englander hostility to the Europeanised, cosmopolitan intellectual and expert (someone who does things properly) has deep roots.

In July 1464 Worcester was given the task of conciliating King James of Scotland's brother, Alexander, the Duke of Albany, and the Bishop of Aberdeen, whose safe conduct had been violated. Earlier in the year a ship called the *Katerine Duras* had captured a Scottish carvel and with it Albany who was returning to Scotland. Albany had been granted a safe conduct by Edward IV and the King of Scotland was furious and threatened war. Edward ordered the duke and bishop be freed and on the 1st of June agreed a truce in the chapter house at York with the Scots that was to last for fifteen years. Resolving the settlement between the duke and the bishop and their captors proved harder. On the 8th of July Worcester and others were appointed to investigate the issue.[21] It is surprising that the captors should have felt able to oppose the King, which might imply they were to some degree independent. The *Katerine Duras* might have been linked to Worcester's fellow Garter knight, Galeard de Durefort, *Seigneur de Duras*, who, as a Gascon, could resist royal authority when it suited.

Worcester was also caught up in diplomatic activity involving Brittany, which was then ruled by the able and attractive Duke François II (1458–88), who was determined to maintain independence from the inveterate intriguer King Louis XI of France. François accused the French King of plotting with the English and confiscating the goods of Bretons. Louis counter-accused the Duke of refusing to do homage and treating directly with the papacy. In a habit-and-dagger episode in early August, there appeared in England two brothers of the Dominican order who had come over from Brittany on certain secret matters. These pretend friars were Jean de Rouville, Francois II's vice-chancellor, and Jean de Launay, François' confessor.[22] On the 12th of August Edward empowered Worcester and others to treat with them. A year's truce between England and Brittany, to begin on the first day of October 1464, was agreed. Later, on the 8th of March 1465, Warwick and Worcester, William Hastings and John Wenlock would be appointed conservators of the truce between the King and Francois, Duke of Brittany.[23]

Worcester had by now negotiated with the Burgundians, the Lords of the Isles, the Scots and the Bretons. He had been slated to negotiate with the Pope in 1462 but did not go. His father had been a great diplomat entrusted with Henry V's most sensitive and secret missions to emperors, kings and archbishops when England's power was advancing across France. Worcester shared his father's skills but he played on a much smaller stage and his tasks involved damage limitation and defence.

In December 1461 Worcester and Sir Ralph Grey had, according to Paston, led the siege of Dunstanburgh Castle. Now they were reunited in rather less auspicious circumstances. Grey had been captured when Bamborough Castle fell in June 1464 and in early July he was brought before the Constable for judgement.

A detailed description of the capture and subsequent trial survives (indeed, this is so detailed that there is a temptation to believe that it was intended to set the record straight regarding the proper operation of the Constable's Court, as presided over by Worcester, after the accusations of applying the alien Law of Padua in 1462). The account said the besieged were offered the King's grace if they surrendered but if it was necessary to damage the castle by cannon shot it would cost the 'chieftain's head'. The record made it abundantly clear that a formal state of war existed and, therefore, that the Court of Chivalry had proper jurisdiction: 'Alle the Kinges greet gonnes that where charged at oons to shute unto the said Castelle, Newe-Castel the Kinges greet gonne, and London the second gonne of irne; the whiche betyde the place, that stones of the walles flewe unto the see.' [24]

The words of Worcester were measured and in the context almost generous. Two points were made clear. First, the evidence was so obvious that it did not need to be tested. 'Sir Rauf Grey, ... thees maters shewith so evidently agayn the, that they nedithe not to examyn the of them.' Second, a state of war clearly existed with 'strookes of the great gunnes'. There now followed some true medieval theatre: 'The *Kyng had ordenned* that thou shuldest have hadd thy sporys striken of by hard heles, with the hand of the maister cooke, that whiche is here redy to doo, as was promysed at the tyme he tooke thy spurres.' Indeed when a man was made a knight of the Order of the Bath the King's master cook really did stand by the door of the chapel when the new knight prayed and warned him that 'if thou do anything contrary to the order, ... I shall hack the spurs from your heels'.[25]

The King's sentence followed: 'Item, Sir Rauff Grey, the *Kyng has ordenned* here, thou maist see, the Kynge of armes and heroudes, and thine own propre cote of armes, that whiche they shuld teere of thy body, and so thou shuldist be wel disgraded of thy worshipp, noblesse, and armes.' The King, however, spared such degradation before beheading due to the service of his grandfather, Sir Thomas Grey, who was executed in 1415 for his part in the Southampton plot (the King's grandfather, the Earl of Cambridge, was also executed then). By the standards of the day it is hard to say that Grey was treated badly and he could certainly have died a much more degrading and painful death than beheading.

Earlier in 1464, even before the Woodville marriage, Warwick appears to have pursued a different approach to unrest at Gloucester than the King and Worcester. On the 14th of July Edward IV had written from Doncaster to Coventry regarding one William Huet who had vexed Will Bedon with unfitting and insubordinate language.[26] The King arranged for arbitration with the award to be given by Michaelmas and, if the arbitrators disagreed, for the mayor to act as umpire. As the arbitrators could not agree, the mayor decided that Huet must ask Bedon's forgiveness, and pay him 40s. for damages. Huet refused and was imprisoned. On the 4th of October the King wrote to give thanks to the mayor for punishing a 'refractory' person. He approved of the mayor's decision. 'We no we been enfowrmed

... by oure right trusty and entierly biloued Cousin, Therl of Worcestre.' Huet then obtained the support of Warwick. The mayor, despite the approval of the King, was now forced to back down for 'he laid sourness aside', and allowed mercy, merely binding Huet over and granting 10 marks damages, even though that did not meet the other party's costs. Damages, however, were further reduced from 10 to 5 marks at Warwick's insistence. Huet, who had initially been determined the injured party, now found himself bound over to keep the peace against Bedon.

The incident showed how Edward IV felt at this time that it was necessary to micro-manage issues that threatened dissent. Coventry was a 'hot spot', being a powerful walled city near to Warwick's Midlands power base. It also again showed that the King and Warwick were diverging even before the Woodville marriage was known to the Nevilles. It further demonstrated how Worcester was Edward's 'eyes and ears'.

The last four chapters have looked at the issue of securing regime change. The general challenge was, in practice, composed of multiple elements across the whole range of areas government had to manage. These involved dealing with internal elite opposition, external threats, and popular disorder. Also, power and authority needed to be projected from an efficient and stylish court. Worcester was prepared to play key roles in all aspects of these challenges—often at considerable cost to his personal popularity.

Chapter 16

Integrating the Woodvilles – 1464 to 1465

Also, the King invited my lord and all his noble attendants to the table where he usually dined with his courtiers. And one of the King's greatest earls sat at the King's table, upon the king's stool, in the place of the king; and my lord sat at the same table, only two steps below him. Then all the honors which were due to the King had to be paid to the Earl who sat in his place, and also to my lord, and it is incredible what ceremonies we observed there.[1]

> Tetzel, in the entourage of the Lord of Rožmitál, described Edward IV's court; the most obvious candidate for the single mighty earl, sitting in the King's place, was the widower Worcester, both Lord Steward of the Household and Constable of the Tower.

While Worcester was imposing law and order and using diplomacy to smooth foreign affairs Warwick was being flattered into complicity with Louis XI's machinations. In April 1464 Jehan, Lord of Lannoy, Louis' special envoy, had been in London. The sophisticated seigneur beguiled Warwick with intimations of Louis' particular regard and hints of a French title and territory. Warwick's task, set by Louis, was to secure both Edward's marriage to Bona of Savoy, the sister of the French Queen, and England's secret alliance with France against Burgundy. Edward soon proved to have rather different ideas about marriage.

In mid-September 1464, Edward IV revealed his secret marriage to Elizabeth Grey *née* Woodville to a stunned council. The dynamics of Yorkist politics now lurched in a new direction. For three years Edward IV's grip on the throne had been supported by Warwick, whose main sphere was the land war and continental diplomacy, while Worcester dealt with the navy, finance, household administration, and law and order. The Plantagenet-Neville-Tiptoft alliance had been at the core of government during two periods in the previous decade—that is, 1454 to 1455 and 1461 to 1464. Now the arrival of a new force, the beautiful, brave, but grasping Woodvilles, would split the Plantagenets and the Nevilles against each other, and would also divide brother against brother. The Nevilles and Tiptoft would ultimately be pitted against each other. The game would take seven years to play out, but with the Woodville marriage the die was cast.

How might a situation arise where a great king could marry without the apparent knowledge of those close to him? It can only be speculated as to when the meetings between Elizabeth and Edward took place. One story goes that Elizabeth sought out Edward when hunting in Whittlewood Forest, Northamptonshire, in order to plead for property lost when her husband was killed in 1461 at the 2nd Battle of St Albans. If this, or something similar, occurred it must have been sometime before mid-April when Elizabeth reached a one-sided accord with Hastings to protect her son's inheritance. On the 1st of May tradition has it that Edward secretly married (on the 14th of September Edward told the council at Reading he married four months earlier and this would put the marriage around mid-May, broadly in line with the traditional date).

Warwick's choice for the King's consort was Bona of Savoy. Apart from Bona being the sister of the French queen and his wish to ingratiate himself with the French king it is not actually clear why she was deemed such a dazzling catch for Edward. She was one of nineteen children of Louis, Duke of Savoy, and Anne de Lusignan, Princess of Cyprus, and was hardly going to bring a great dowry.

Several images of Bona survive and show her, in her youth, as attractive if with a rather stolid jawline. There are two thought to be of her in the National Gallery. One, damaged, shows Bona rather statuesquely in profile. Another, by the great Renaissance painter Antonio del Pollaiolo, depicts her and her eventual husband Galeazzo, the Duke of Milan, as Apollo and Daphne. He chases and she, seeking escape, is being transformed into a laurel tree—her outstretched arms rather alarmingly already branches. Galeazzo Sforza earned an unpleasant reputation as a sadist and a womaniser and was murdered, leaving Bona as regent during the minority of her sons from 1476 to 1481. Like Elizabeth Woodville, she then made a clandestine marriage, but baser rather than higher, to Antonio Tassino, the Ferrarese family meat-carver, and was removed from office in 1479.

It seems inconceivable that absolutely no-one about the King knew what was going on. The more realistic question might be who among Edward's companions and advisors were aware and who were unaware? Also, when did they know? Before the wedding or between the wedding and mid-September, when the King told the Council?

Worcester was the King's constant companion in his travels on commissions, often in the vicinity of Stony Stratford, during the period before the marriage. Might the young King have asked the author of *The Declamacion of Noblesse* whether he should marry a foreign princess of old blood or a poor but beautiful English widow of undoubted intelligence and vivacity, not to mention the proven ability to bear healthy sons. Given his preference for nobility based on personal qualities rather than on lineage, as expressed in *The Declamacion*, Worcester was the one person who could not argue against marriage to the fair Elizabeth on the basis of the absence of noble blood equivalent to Edward's—at least on her father's side. On her mother's side Elizabeth had such blood in buckets. Jacquetta's father was Peter of Luxembourg, Count of Saint-Pol. The Luxembourgs claimed to be descended from the water deity *Melusine* through their ancestor Siegfried of Luxembourg (922–98). None of the English nobility could match such a splendidly long line going back to a twin-tailed goddess.

The Earl's second marriage to Elizabeth Greyndour was, and his third to Elizabeth Hopton would be, to women of a similar rank to Elizabeth's father. Also Worcester's grandfather had inherited two manors and risen through service, first to the house of Arundel and then Lancaster. No man in England was more likely both to have known of the impending marriage yet not to have been in a position, even if so disposed, to argue against it.

It would seem extraordinary anyway that none of the King's household knew of the King's marriage to Elizabeth after the event and before its announcement at the council meeting in mid-September. Had there been no conjugal relations between May and September? Or even meetings? And if there were, could there have been no witnesses among Edward's household? Did the King's Steward of his Household and Constable of the Tower, Worcester, the Chamberlain, William Hastings, the Treasurer of his Household, John Fogge, and the Controller of the Household, John Scot, really not know anything?

When King Edward told the council in mid-September that he could not marry Bona of Savoy—as he happened to be married to Elizabeth Grey—he would have expected shock. He might have timed it so that the person most shocked was not there. Warwick had been negotiating the King's marriage to the Queen of France's sister. Indeed, it is hard to envisage a more exquisitely humiliating choice of wife and timing of announcement for the great Kingmaker.

The upstart Woodvilles stood for all Warwick looked down on, his worst nightmare made true. A letter of 1460 from William Paston to his brother John had described the abuse of Elizabeth's father and brother by the Earls of Salisbury, Warwick and March (the future King Edward IV) in Calais.

> My Lord of Salesbury reheted [berated] hym, calling hym knaves son, that he schuld be so rude to calle hym and these other Lords traytors, or they schall be found the Kyngs treue liege men, whan he shuld be found a traytour, &c. And my Lord of Warrewyk rehetyd him, and seyd that his fader was but squyer, and broute up with Kyng Herry the Vte, and sethen [made] himself by maryage, and also made Lord, and that it was not his parte to have swyche language of Lords, being of the Kyngs blood. And my Lord of March reheted hym in lyke wyse. And Sir Antony was reheted for his langage of all iij. Lords in lyke wyse.[2]

St Mary's Oxford—Duke Humphrey's library was housed in the fourteenth century Congregation House to the east of the tower of St. Mary's church in John Tiptoft's time at the university in 1440 to 1443. (Author)

Cardinal Beaufort's tomb in Winchester Cathedral. The Cardinal was granted the issues of the Tiptoft estate from 1443 to 1447 and wrote off a very large loan to John Tiptoft in his will. (Author)

Westminster Hall – the Treasury was housed in the wings on the north end (left image). The Earl of Worcester was Treasurer in 1452-5, 1462-3 and 1470. (Author)

Palace of the Grand Master of the Knights of Rhodes. The Earl of Worcester was on Rhodes from June and July 1458. (C.C.4, Jorge Láscar)

Signatures on a 1454 warrant of Protector York, Chancellor Salisbury and Treasurer Worcester—the 'Triumvirate' who ran England during Henry VI's madness. (PRO, Author)

Jaffa (c.1900) – still landing by lighter boat – the Earl of Worcester arrived here on 20 June 1458. The Earl's choir sang as the sails dropped. (Photographer unknown)

Holy Sepulchre, Jerusalem – the Earl was recorded on nightly vigils here on the 25, 27 and 30 June 1458. His choir sang here each night. (C.C.4, Jorge Láscar)

Holy Nativity (pre-1900), Bethlehem – the Earl was here on the night of 26 June 1458 and his choir sang. (Photographer unknown)

Venice – the Doge's Palace – in the Earl's time non-noble executions were carried out between the twin columns. (Author)

Padua where the Earl of Worcester studied between 1458 and 1461 – the *Palazzo della Ragione* had the greatest floor area of any medieval hall. (Author)

Ferrara where the Earl of Worcester studied under Guarino da Verona - Cathedral plaza, the Castello Estense (Este castle) is in the background left. (Author)

Florence where the Earl of Worcester bought books and almost certainly stayed with the de' Medici – Brunelleschi's dome was completed at the time the Earl was in Italy in 1458-61. (Author)

(*Above*) The Tower of London – from Tower Hill – the Earl of Worcester was Constable between 1461 and 1470. (Author)

Simon of Sudbury, Archbishop of Canterbury	1381
Sir Robert Hales	1381
Sir Simon de Burley, K.G.	1388
Richard Fitzalan, 3rd Earl of Arundel	1397
Rev. Richard Wyche, Vicar of Deptford	1440
John de Vere, 12th Earl of Oxford	1462
John Tiptoft, Earl of Worcester	1470

(*Left*) Plaque on Tower Hill at the site of the scaffold. (Author)

All Hallows Barking – from Tower Hill – the Earl of Worcester was warden of the confraternity between 1465 and 1470. (Author)

Blackfriars – the tree and bench mark the axis of the south side nave columns; the Earl of Worcester was buried further west along this axis in 1470. The friary of Blackfriars was dissolved in 1538. (Author)

Bassingbourn, Cambridgeshire – aerial photograph looking east showing ornate residence and garden facing south over a long vista. Bassingbourn was owned by the Tiptoft family c. 1428-87. (Cambridge University Aerial Photographs)

Worcester House, which lay between the arched water gate and Thames Street. The Tiptoft family and its descendents owned property in the parish of St. James Garlickhythe between 1413 and 1551. (Agas map detail)

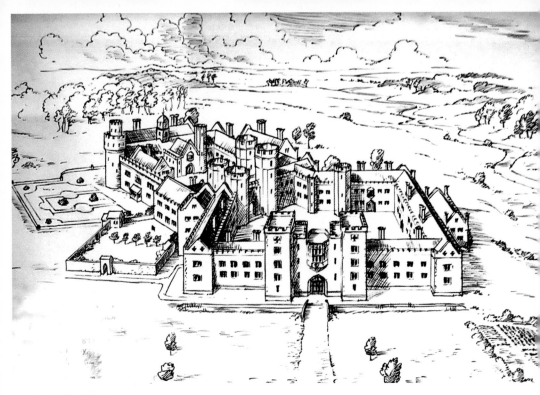

(*Above*) Modern reconstruction of Elsyng Palace in the sixteenth century. The extent of fifteenth century work is not established. The antiquary John Norden said it was 'builded by an Earle of Worcester'. (Enfield Council, Forty Hall)

(*Left*) White vine initial 'G'(rammatica) and wreath enclosing the arms and helm of John Tiptoft, Earl of Worcester, at the beginning of Suetonius's *De grammaticis et rhetoribus*, written by John Free, probably in Padua, for Worcester. (BL, Harley 2639, f. 2. British Library

Could Warwick have ever imagined that he and his blood kin would have to kneel before the haughty Woodville widow upstart, sensing her multitudinous, profiteering relatives looking down and doubtless gloating as they revelled in the reversal in positions since 1460?

Edward was a young man and possibly thought the storm would blow over. He probably had not reckoned with quite how unpopular his arrogant wife and her grasping greedy relatives would prove or quite how furious and unreconciled would be Warwick. Maybe if the Woodvilles had been humble and unobtrusive Warwick might have come to tolerate them. The Woodvilles were anything but. Also, Warwick had two growing daughters, Isabel and Anne, and his siblings had their own offspring who were being pushed back in the eligible marriage queue by Elizabeth's many relatives. It is possible that Warwick was especially angry because he felt he had been strung along negotiating for the hand of Bona, while a good many of the baser members of the royal household gloated, knowing his match-making was all in vain.

The new Queen's father and brother also had ideas about chivalry that conveniently drew attention to the Woodvilles and hence away from the Nevilles. The leaders in chivalric displays were the Burgundians and foreign policy now increasingly favoured Burgundy over France. Warwick would prove unable to learn his lesson after getting his fingers burnt badly over Bona. He was incorrigible in pursuit of French alliances, and perhaps favours from King Louis, for he would seek a marriage for the King's sister Margaret with Philip of Bresse, a brother of Bona. Charles of Burgundy, however, was also interested in Margaret. And the Queen and her siblings—descended through Jacquetta from Peter of Luxembourg, count of Saint-Pol—preferred the Burgundians, with their love of the joust, at which the Woodvilles also excelled.

All this made the situation particularly dangerous for Worcester. He was close to both Edward and Warwick. Eventually, if the latter rebelled, he would have to choose between Plantagenet and Neville, unless he could again, as in 1455 and 1458, get out of the way.

On the 31st of January 1465 a courtier, Thomas St Leger, was sentenced to lose his hand for fighting by the Lord Steward Worcester, whose responsibilities included keeping order in the royal palaces. He was pardoned by the King, 'on account of his good service to his father and himself'.[3] On the face of it the Earl applied the law and the King tempered justice with mercy. There might have been more to the situation. The King's older sister Anne was married to Henry Holland, Duke of Exeter, who had been in exile since Towton. She was enamoured of St Leger— and detaching his hand would not have been popular with the King's sibling. An understanding might have been reached that the law would be followed but the King would be merciful.

The contrasting sad story of one John Davy, dating to 1461, has survived in at least two sources. One recounted: 'One John Davy had his hand stryken of at the Standard in Chepe by Jugement of the lawe, bycause he smote a man byfore the kynges Juges at Westmynster contrary to the lawes ; and the kyng commaunded that he shuld haue the lawe in exsamples.'[4] In 1443 Henry VI had, however, pardoned Thomas Watson for striking Adam Cope with a dagger because he had 'committed the offence in ignorance and he and Adam being now reconciled'.[5] Men without royal lovers or merciful monarchs could be less fortunate than St Leger.

In 1465 the Tower might have been getting rather crowded as the Queen and her many relations joined the royal household. Worcester, as the Tower's Constable and Lord Steward of the Household, would have been in charge of integrating the Woodvilles into the royal palaces. Given the Woodvilles' arrogance this might have tested his diplomatic talents. There is circumstantial evidence that his personal response was again to detach himself. Worcester must have had a complex relationship with the Woodvilles. He knew his own recent paternal line was modest. He may have liked the Queen's brother Anthony Woodville, who had scholarly aspirations and would translate the *Dicts and Sayings of the Philosophers*. The Queen's father Richard Woodville had a good record as a soldier in France and jouster. The Woodvilles were greedy and arrogant but they were also fecund, beautiful and brave. They were probably a lot more fun than the petulant Warwick and harsh Montagu.

The church of All Hallows lies to the west of the Tower. Much rebuilt, it has survived the Fire and the Blitz. It always had a close relationship with the Tower, providing surplus capacity for the chapel of St Peter. In 1465 Edward IV raised the Lady Chapel of All Hallows to the status of 'King Edward's Chantry', governed by a fraternity whose master was Worcester. Under its ordinances two chaplains would celebrate perpetually in the chapel for the welfare of the King, Queen, Queen Mother, the King's brothers and dead father and brother, and Yorkists who had died bringing the King to the throne. The services would follow the Sarum Use, prevalent in the royal religious establishment, and possibly reflecting continuing choral interest by the Earl.[6] Setting up All Hallows as his central place of worship may have enabled Worcester to remove an aspect of his life from the Tower while remaining close to it.

In March the young Henry Percy was taken out of the Tower, possibly to make space for the Woodvilles. He went to the Fleet, which was a civil prison and notably more comfortable, for those who could pay, than nearby Newgate. The Fleet served as a prison for the Court of Common Pleas, Chancery, the Star Chamber and for those held by the Exchequer for debts to the King. Prisoners had considerable freedom of movement outside if they could afford a guard. At this point Percy became the responsibility of Elizabeth Venour who was the Fleet warden. The warden was also keeper of Westminster Palace and she must have known Worcester. Elizabeth Venour was granted 26s. 8d. a week for Percy's expenses and diet. £69 14s. 1d. was paid to Venour from mid-March to early November 1465.[7]

Elizabeth Venour led an adventurous life which included two marriages, abduction and rape, divorce and a celebrated trial over the principle, established by a statute passed in Parliament under Richard II, that should any woman, after being ravished, then consent to marriage, both she and the ravisher should be disinherited, and all inheritances should pass to their next heirs.[8] The colourful Elizabeth might have ensured her noble young prisoner's time was pleasant. Certainly Percy's experiences in the Tower under the charge of Worcester, in the Fleet supervised by Venour, or later as the ward of Herbert, did not turn him against the Yorkists. Percy and John Paston shared each other's company in the autumn of 1465 when the latter was spending one of three stints at the Fleet's pleasure. John Paston wrote to his wife Margaret:

My Lord Persy and all this house
Recomaund them to yow, dogge, catte, and mouse,
And wysshe ye had be here stille,
For the sey ye are a good gille.[9]

Henry amused Margaret and she wrote 'of yowr grett chere that ye made me, and of the coste thate ye dede on me'.[10]

Events which might have seen administratively routine proved very significant for the future. Young Percy, treated well by Edward and Worcester, became a Yorkist. Herbert also had responsibility for the young Henry Tudor, son of Edmund Tudor and Margaret Beaufort. Percy would move from the Fleet to the charge of Herbert, whose daughter Maud he subsequently married. Maud had previously been betrothed to Herbert's ward, Tudor. Percy was returned to the Tower after the execution of Herbert by Warwick on the 27th of July 1469 and was released two months later, after taking an oath of fealty to Edward and giving bonds of £8,000. Percy later transferred his loyalties to the future Henry VII, whom he knew when the two Henrys, Percy and Tudor, were Herbert's wards.

Worcester had to look to himself as the politics in the royal household became more venomous. Ultimately the only escape—from the political breakdown threatened by the Woodvilles and the irreconcilable resentment they caused the Nevilles— was again to leave the country. From 1462 on there had been various plans for the Earl's involvement in Irish affairs which would now afford a way to leave England.

Worcester had been appointed Lord High Chancellor of Ireland in 1462, probably in a *de facto* honorary capacity. In January 1464 Edward IV had been sufficiently concerned about the Irish situation on the 22nd of January to appoint the one man he could always trust in any situation, Worcester, as Chancellor, with the intention he actively took up the role, and on the 26th of January Bishop Sherwood of Meath was made his deputy.[11] Notwithstanding, or unaware of Edward's appointment, on the 25th of January the Deputy Lieutenant, the Earl of Desmond, made the Earl of Kildare Chancellor. Recognising the facts on the ground Edward IV confirmed Kildare's appointment on the 20th of February. In the summer of 1464 Desmond and Bishop Sherwood, between whom a state of near war existed, were summoned before Edward to resolve their differences.[12] Desmond left Ireland in July and returned in September 1464. In August Desmond probably stayed with Edward when he was granted for life an annuity of £40.[13]

In 1465 Worcester became again involved in the Yorkist Irish question when Clarence was reappointed Lord Lieutenant of Ireland and the Earl was made his deputy. He was to have 400 archers who would reside with him. On the 8th of June a commission had been issued to 'Thomas Grene to take certain cannons and habiliments of war and other things pertaining to the King's artillery ... and to deliver them to the King's kinsman John, Earl of Worcester, who is going to Ireland with an armed force for the safe-custody of that land'.[14] Worcester did not go—as perhaps he was still indispensible in England to the King or, as yet, he had no real wish to leave the country.

On the 17th of April 1465 events were set in progress that culminated in the great tournament more than two years later between Anthony, Lord Scales, the King's new brother-in-law, and Antoine, the Great Bastard of Burgundy, the son of Duke Philip. Scales was delightfully ambushed by the fair ladies about the Queen who put a collar of gold on his thigh with a jewel *fleur de souvenance*, or forget-me-not, which he interpreted as the prize for some yet undone act of chivalry. Scales resolved to challenge Antoine, the great jouster. The next day: 'The King's highness commanded the Earl of Worcester, great Constable of England, ... to enact and remember that memorable act ... of the worshipful arms ... to be accomplished in his royal presence, between him and the said noble knight the Bastard of Burgundy ... the Constable said his high commandment should be performed according to the duty of his office'.[15]

On the 22nd of April the Earl duly wrote to the Bastard: 'Greetings from John, Earl of Worcester, Lord Tiptoft and Powys, High Constable of England. By virtue of our office we must make written accounts of notable deeds of arms and see that they are published abroad as examples to all men. We let it be known that ... Sir Anthony Woodville presented himself to the King bearing a flower of souvenance [forget-me-not] and besought the King to command Chester Herald to take the flower to the Bastard of Burgundy. This the King granted.'[16]

It was likely that the challenge was not solely inspired by some pretty maids who felt the charming young Scales needed shaking up with a bit of errantry. Indeed the whole thing sounded as though it was conceived by the Woodvilles and received the support of the King. A tournament between Woodville and Burgundy's champion served several purposes. It could, of course, project the authority of the King and kingdom and impress the Burgundians as to the merits of an English alliance. But it also served to advance Woodville ambitions and provide a stage where they knew they could shine. The Woodvilles might have considered the fate of Edward II's executed favourite, the Gascon Piers Gaveston, who was hated by the English aristocracy for the humiliation he dealt its members while jousting in the lists.

Twenty-five years earlier Anthony's father's reputation as an accomplished knight caused him to be selected to fight the redoubtable Pedro Vasques de Saavedra, chamberlain of the Duke of Burgundy, who came to London in 1440 to 'renne a cours with a sharpe sper*e* for his sou*e*reyn lady sake'.[17] This sounds truly Quixotic. The author of Don Quixote, Miguel de Cervantes (1547–1616), added the name Saavedra in 1590 in imitation of a distant poet and soldier relative Gonzalo de Cervantes Saavedra. Henry VI prematurely halted the event. Remarkably, both Scales' father and Pedro would be present at the 1467 event advising and supporting, respectively, Anthony and Antoine. On the 23rd of May 1465 the Chester Herald returned from Burgundy with his report of the Bastard's willingness to take up the challenge. It would, however, be two years before lances were levelled.

On the 26th of May 1465 Elizabeth Woodville was crowned Queen of England. The Duke of Clarence was appointed Lord Steward of England.[18] This was not the same position as the Lord Steward of the Household and since 1421 appointments were made *pro tempore* to preside at coronations and the trials of lords. Elizabeth's coronation was intended to be a great affair with grand European relatives of the Queen Mother, Jacquetta, invited to polish up Elizabeth's rather modest birth on her father's side. Clarence, as Steward, led the ceremony, on a horse encased completely, from head to the ground, in trappings richly embroidered with garnets and spangles of gold. The Earl of Arundel, as both Constable and Butler, then rode on a horse trapped from head to ground in cloth of gold. The Duke of Norfolk as Marshal, followed in the same fashion.

The surviving detailed description of the coronation nowhere mentions Worcester. It is possible that he was detained elsewhere. He may have been there but deliberately kept a low profile, having played his part in the organisation and remaining discreetly in the wings, letting Clarence take credit. Warwick was absent, perhaps by common understanding, on an embassy. Maybe Worcester did not want to break with Warwick by being prominent in crowning Elizabeth. Worcester had, however, been at court a few days earlier on the 23rd of May 1465 to receive the Chester Herald back from Burgundy where he had issued a challenge to Antoine, the Bastard of Burgundy, on behalf of Anthony Rivers to joust. This perhaps indicated that there was no obvious reason why he could not have been present at the Queen's coronation three days later.

On the 22nd of September 1465 the Chancellor, George Neville, was installed as Archbishop of York at Cawood Castle. Having not been present—at least in an obvious official capacity—at the Queen's coronation, Worcester was very much there at George's installation, a great occasion not, however, attended by the King. The seating plan and the menu survive and it was, depending on the point of view, either a feast of consummate sumptuousness or a shocking display of gluttony, particularly for an ecclesiastical occasion.

In total 28 peers, 59 knights, 10 abbots, 7 bishops, and numerous lawyers, clergy, esquires, and ladies, attended with their retinues numbering in thousands. They consumed 113 oxen, 6 wild bulls, 1,000 sheep, 304 calves, 2000 pigs, over 500 stags, bucks and roes, 4000 pigeons and 4000 crays, 2000 chickens and so on.[19] The Earl of Worcester sat close to the Earl of Oxford at the highest table. The former had been, and the latter was now, married to a Neville sister. But three years earlier Worcester had condemned Oxford's father and brother to death so conversation might have been a little stilted: five years later Oxford would return the harsh compliment to Worcester.

The Yorkist regime's position was strengthened when, in October 1465, Henry VI was captured and brought to London with his legs tied to his stirrups. Thus the man who had done so much to promote Worcester's early career was now his prisoner in the Tower. Previous superfluous kings of England had not fared well in captivity. Both Edward II and Richard II had died conveniently.

Henry was more use alive than dead, for that way his son Edward—who was at liberty and entirely lacking in his father's merciful character—would become the more promising focus of Lancastrian resistance. But while Worcester was in England Henry was decently treated. 'There he was brought to the Tower of London, where he was kept for a long time by two squires and two yeomen of the crown, and their men, and anybody was allowed to come and speak to him.'[20] Indeed, the attendance allowed to him sounded very like those organised by the Tower's Constable, Worcester, for Henry Percy and the two de Vere boys. When Henry was released in 1470 his condition was not reported as being less than his station deserved. It is possible that it deteriorated while Worcester was in Ireland after 1467. But while the Earl lived so did Henry. (When Edward IV recovered the throne in 1471, after Worcester and Henry's son Edward were dead, the hapless Henry VI quickly followed the examples of the murdered kings Edward and Richard.)

On the 6th of November 1465 a commission of oyer and terminer was appointed to consider the question of what to do about Sir Gervase Clifton, who appears frequently in the record, often associated with acts of violence and rebellion.[21] He was a loyal Lancastrian who had married Maud Stanhope, formerly the wife of Thomas Neville, the brother of Richard, John and George, who was killed at the Battle of Wakefield in 1460. The remarriage might not have been popular with the Nevilles for she was not mentioned as appearing at the funeral of her previous husband Thomas and her previous father-in-law the Earl of Salisbury in 1463. Maud was a great heiress as she and her sister had inherited Lord Cromwell's estate. Unfortunately for her, at this time the Woodvilles were in need of more property to support the elevated station to which Elizabeth's marriage was accustoming them.

This was a very high-powered commission whose many members included Warwick, Worcester, the chamberlain William Hastings, and the chief justices Markham and Danby, as well as the Lord Mayor of London. If dirty work was to be done then responsibility was to be spread wide. This seems to be the last time the two earls, both identified as the King's kinsmen, worked together.

Clifton was eventually pardoned but at terrible cost to his wife Maud's estate as she was forced to give sixteen manors, totalling about 400 marks annually, during her life to Anthony Woodville, the King's brother in law.[22] To make sure the property was delivered Clifton had to surrender bonds worth £6,000 to the King on Woodville's behalf. Worcester was to keep the bonds. If the value of the estates proved less than 400 marks in a year then further properties would have to be surrendered.[23] 'These grants to Anthony Wydeville represented 80% of Maud's wealth and property – an enormous price to pay for marrying a man of inconvenient political loyalties.'[24]

On the 11th of February 1466 Elizabeth Woodville gave birth to her first royal child, Elizabeth. This child was eventually to marry Henry VII and reconcile Lancaster and York. It is through her that upstart Woodville blood still runs in the royal family—and indeed that of most royal families of Europe. At the time, however, while there may have been relief that the royal couple could produce a healthy child, there must have been disappointment that the baby was not a son.

Following childbirth, women secluded themselves and would then attend church for a ceremony of purification, or 'churching', followed by a banquet. A much repeated description by Gabriel Tetzel, who was in the retinue of the Lord of Rožmitál, described the occasion (the quote is given at the beginning of the chapter).[25] Who was the mighty noble who sat alone in the King's place? If the translation of '*comes*' as 'earl' is correct then the most obvious candidate might be the Lord Steward of the Household and Constable of the Tower—the widower Earl of Worcester.

The Queen, sitting alone, was attended by the Queen Mother and King's sister who stood—but had to kneel if she spoke to them—until her first dish was served. The feast lasted for three hours in silence. Tetzel wrote that when the dancing began he had never seen such beautiful maidens.[26] Rožmitál attended Mass with the King and Tetzel recorded, 'I think there can be no better singers in all the world.'[27] Earlier, Tetzel reported seeing forty-two of the King's singers in the churching procession, who sang 'very sweetly' (the continentals admired the sweet harmonies of the *contenance angloise*).

Tetzel then recounted, 'Soon afterwards my lord and his companions were invited by two earls to their house. They gave us indescribably splendid dishes to the number of about sixty according to their customs. We saw there exceptionally splendid tapestries.'[28] Was the house the Erber, the home of the Nevilles, determined to demonstrate their power by matching the King's munificence?

Clear rules were now needed for the forthcoming tournament between the two Anthonys. In June 1466 Edward ordered his Constable to draw up ordinances, 'to be observed and kept in all manner of justes and peace royal'.[29] Worcester, a man of exceptional clarity of thought who was prepared to turn his mind to any challenge, must have sought advice. A set of regulations for a tournament survive in a manuscript which was probably made for, and certainly belonged to, Sir John Asteley.[30] He was an experienced jouster, who, like Worcester was also made a Garter knight in 1461. The Earl, however, also drew on his Italian experience and connections. His ordinances probably derived from a similar set used at the court of Francesco Sforza, the Duke of Milan, in 1458. Sforza was the uncle of the Earl's travelling companion to the Holy Land, Roberto da Sanseverino, whom Worcester was known to have met again in Padua in January 1459. The Earl's ordinances concluded gallantly: 'Reserving always to the queenes highness and the ladyes there present, the attributing and gift of the prize after the manner and forme accustomed.'

Edward also wrote to the Chancellor, George Neville, telling him to prepare safe conducts for a year and a half for as many men as the Bastard wanted to bring. It becomes clear why Edward trusted Worcester and increasingly disliked the Nevilles. The former produced ordinances with no fuss, so fit for purpose that they remained in use for more than a century. Neville, however, complained about the potentially unlimited number of men—it is not clear whether this was in the role of prudent Chancellor or upstaged Neville—and the King, doubtless irritated, wrote back saying under a thousand.[31] On the 29th of October a safe conduct was issued to the Bastard, limited for eight months, for a party up to one thousand. By this time, however, it was probably too late in the year for a great tournament.

On the 6th of June 1466 it is recorded in the patent rolls that a ship, named *le Martyn*, was taken to Portsmouth and despoiled of its cargo of wine. No captors were then identified.[32] But in 1475, nearly five years after Worcester's death, reparation was made to one Arnold Trussell for the loss of his ship *le Martyn* in 1466. Piracy was endemic so there was nothing unusual about this act. What is surprising is that it emerged in the later year that 'the ship and merchandise were seized off the coast of England by the masters and mariners of a ship of John, Earl of Worcester, Constable of England'.[33] It seems surprising that the high-minded Worcester would personally be directly involved in piracy. It is more likely that, acting independently, the crew of his ship found *le Martyn* irresistibly tempting. In 1466, however, Worcester's name had been hushed up.[34]

The Earl of Worcester's friend and correspondent, the Canterbury monk Henry Cranebroke, died on the 8th of December 1466, 'and had commital … and a funeral in the choir and mass and the burial by Prior Goldstone and the community; in his thirty-second year a monk'.[35] Their friendship might have gone back to 1443, when they were both at Oxford, and certainly to the early 1450s when they corresponded in rather bad attempted classical Latin – the Earl's being worse.

By 1466 it must have been clear that it would be nigh on impossible to reconcile the Woodvilles and the Nevilles. Worcester appears to have been personally considerate about Neville sensitivities and did nothing to inflame them. But he now, apart from organising the great tournament of 1467, may have been actively seeking to get out of the snakepit of the court to find his own stage on which he could play the leading part unchallenged.

Chapter 17

Soldier – 1466 to 1467

And the Earle of Woster to Walles, to Denbe as it is said.[1]

Plumpton correspondence

In 1466 the Earl of Worcester's career took a new direction as he became a soldier in his own right, first in Wales, then in Ireland, and finally in England. This was a remarkable development as, before this date, despite the frequent fighting of the period, the Earl had never been recorded as being present in an actual battle. By 1466 the man who had no known military record at the beginning of the reign of Edward IV would emerge as the individual most used to repress rebels. This reflected Worcester's remarkable versatility, Edward's absolute trust in him and perhaps his wish to be away from the court.

North Wales was the one mainland area which had not been effectively brought under Edward IV's control. 1466 saw the first serious armed rebellion in Britain for two years. The castle of Harlech, on the coastline of north-west Wales, was near impregnable as long as it could be resupplied from the sea and it provided a focus for Lancastrian resistance.[2] In the autumn of 1466 the Lancastrian Sir Richard Turnstall led the garrison on a raid that reached Wrexham, seventy miles away in north-east Wales, and so alarmed Shrewsbury that it sent out men to establish whether Tunstall and other men of Harlech 'intended to do any evil to this town or not'.[3] The nervous captains of Beaumaris, Caernavon and Montgomery castles had to be assured they would have adequate reinforcements.[4] Turnstall supposedly conspired with the inhabitants of Chester, who may have wanted simply to secure themselves against attack, the crown having failed to do so. The Harlech rebels captured Holt castle, a substantial fortification on the Anglo-Welsh border.

This raid was no insignificant affair. It had traversed the entire width of north Wales, captured a major border castle, made a show of force before Wrexham, and alarmed the English in Shrewsbury and the mighty castles of north Wales. Worcester was the man sent to to try to resolve the problem with the authority to capture Harlech 'by any means he chose'. The bailiffs of Shrewsbury accounted in the year 1466–7 for the financing of soldiers raised on royal command to accompany John Tiptoft to Denbigh and Harlech castles. Worcester failed to take Harlech but was paid £400. He had at least proved he could lead a military expedition without disaster.

By the end of 1466, on the basis of reports from the English in Ireland, which were certainly not unbiased, it was clear that the current Deputy Lieutenant, the Earl of Desmond, was a busted flush and possibly a traitor to boot. An effort earlier that year by Taig O'Brien, Prince of Thomond, to make himself High King was thwarted not by the efforts of Desmond but by the refusal of the Irish to make common cause. Desmond had been forced to buy off O'Brien, who invaded his lands in Munster, and laid himself open to accusations of treason. The men from Offaly in Leinster were ravaging the English county of Meath, having captured the Deputy Lieutenant, who had to be rescued by the citizens of Drogheda he was supposed to be defending. To the south of Dublin, O'Byrne country was out of control and increasingly well armed.

This time there was no question that Worcester would go to Ireland with a sub-stantial force and with the intention of very properly and thoroughly repressing the rebels there. After a series of largely self-inflicted setbacks under the rule of the increasingly compromised and ineffectual Earl of Desmond, only the requirement to organise the great tournament between the two Anthonys delayed Worcester's departure.

By early 1467 the Earl was preparing for what he must have intended to be a long period away from England as Deputy Lieutenant. The holder of the post was, in practice, the chief officer of the English government in Ireland. He did the actual work of the Lord Lieutenant, who was of close royal blood and, with the recent exception of Richard Duke of York, tended to be absent from Ireland. The Deputy Lieutenant commanded the army and, as one part or another of the country was generally in a state of rebellion, he was usually kept busy. He also pre-sided over the King's Court which perambulated the country. Any appeal against his judgement lay with the King.

His considerable administrative authority was tempered by the increasingly limited reach of English power. Ireland was divided into four territorial units: Connacht, Munster, Leinster and Ulster – respectively roughly the north-west, south-west, south-east and north-east quarters. The Irish word for these units is *cúige*, or fifth part, as originally there were five, the extra unit being Meath which had been split between Leinster and Ulster.

By the fifteenth century English occupation was largely restricted to the four counties around the city of Dublin: Meath, Dublin, Kildare and Louth. There were also three earldoms: Kildare (FitzMaurice), largely in Leinster; Ormond (Butler) in Leinster and Munster but currently attainted; and Desmond (FitzGerald) in Munster. The earldoms had extensive territories well outside the regions of effective English authority and the earls were in varying degrees gaelicised, particularly Desmond.

The division of Meath between Leinster and Ulster had important conse-quences when Worcester was in Ireland. The Bishopric of Meath lay within the archbishopric of Armagh in Ulster but politically it was part of the territories controlled by the English from Dublin. Meath thus straddled a fault line—potentially explosive—between Armagh and Dublin. Since 1353 the Archbishop of Armagh was titled Primate of All Ireland. When a man as contumacious and combustible as William Sherwood was Meath's bishop, trouble surely beckoned.

On the 11th of February 1467 the Earl of Worcester divested himself of many offices and thoroughly made ready for a long period in Ireland. Wyrcester's Annals reported, 'this Earl sold all offices and lands that he had, because of the gift of the King in England'.[5] The commissions of 1467 repeatedly referred to 'the Earl of Worcester who is going to Ireland *for the repression of rebels* there'. The preparations were thorough in the expectation that there would be serious fighting and both archers and cannon were made ready. In April there was a commission to the Mayor of Bristol, William Canynges, and Richard Joye, master of *le George*, which belonged to Worcester, to be ready to ship 700 archers going to Ireland with the Earl of Worcester.[6] In May there was a further commission to take wagons, carts, horses and oxen and workmen and labourers.[7]

At the end of July the Earl obtained a general pardon covering any actions before the 1st of February—perhaps fearing his enemies might seek revenge while he was in Ireland.[8] This enumerated his main offices: Constable of England, Constable of the Tower of London, Constable of the Castle of Portchester, Treasurer of England and Steward of the King's Household. The specific reference in the pardon to descent from Edmund, Earl of Kent—both Edward IV and Worcester were descended from this son of Edward I by his second wife, Margaret of France—might have indicated a longer-term plan, as the position of Lord Lieutenant was reserved for the royal family. In July and August Worcester ensured that his sister Philippa, wife of the executed Lord Roos, and his niece Eleanor were provided for with manors and income.[9] On the 5th, 12th and again on the 18th of August there were commissions to John Sutton of Dudley, Knight, and others to take the muster of the Earl of Worcester and 700 archers at Beaumaris.[10] John Sutton was the younger brother of Edmund Sutton, whose first wife was Worcester's late sister Joyce.[11]

This was a well-funded expedition while Worcester was in England and able to supervise preparations (but once he was out of England in Ireland and no longer able to control funding, the supply of money became erratic at best). In the 1467 Easter term £721 16s. 8d. and 250 marks were made over to Worcester. In the Michaelmas term there was a further £2,896 16s. 8d.[12] All he lacked to take with him to Ireland was a wife.

As the Earl tried to tie up his affairs in England it became clear how dependent Edward was on him, not only for his advice and judgement but also for money.

The King owed Worcester £1,600. The Earl generously remitted half the debt. In turn the King awarded his loyal lord £400. As the King did not have the funds to repay Worcester he was granted all the customs receipts from the port of Bristol until the £1,200 had been paid.[13]

By early September Worcester must have said his *adieux* to the King who, for the first time in six years, would have to try to keep order himself. While Edward IV was assisted to the throne by the Nevilles in 1461, the importance of Worcester to his remaining on it between 1461 and 1467 has been underestimated. The Nevilles' support was always conditional on their perception as to whether Edward advanced or threatened their interests. Worcester remained consistently loyal to the King. Indeed it is possible only to marvel at the extraordinary range of the Earl's activities between 1461 and 1467 in support of Edward. As well as his main offices, he had been spymaster, soldier, sailor, commissioner, diplomat and even besieger. He was trusted to act independently in Wales and would again be so in Ireland. There had been no wife and children, and no great old estate or castle to distract him. He had become the royal servant *par excellence*. Now, however, before leaving for a new stage for his protean talents in Ireland, he would take a final great bow in London.

Chapter 18

Tournament master of ceremonies – 1467

The Earl of Worcester held the place of Constable; … and knew well how to perform his office.[1]

Olivier de la Marche (1425–1502), *Memoires*, commenting on the tournament management

The fifteenth-century tournament was a continuation of politics by other means. Until the previous century fighting in battle and in a joust remained broadly similar. Now any resemblance had vanished. In order to avoid the risk of collision a barrier divided the lists. Field and tournament armour became quite distinct. That for real battle became a miracle of flexibility and lightness designed to enhance mobility on foot: jousting armour rendered its wearer almost blind and immobile on horseback. Vision forward through the frog-mouth helm was possible only by lowering the head, which was raised at the point of impact, and lateral vision was impossible. A lance had to be placed in the contestant's hand which was invisible to its owner. The shield, discarded on the field as superfluous, given the quality of plate armour, was carried by the jouster as a *targe* or target. The equipment and the show were so expensive that this was essentially a royal or great ducal sport, engaged in only in the furtherance of some broader political objective.

The tournament also was a surrogate world of pretence where true gentlemen could dress up and affect to be knights errant and impress damsels; and a release for a frustrated nobility whose members knew they could not, in reality, behave on the field of battle like mounted knights of yore without getting slaughtered. There was little chivalry in the War of the Roses battles where foot soldiers, particularly archers, held the upper hand – and even less in the aftermath when ransoms were few and executions common. To compensate there was the tournament, an expensive exercise in nostalgia, useful for the furtherance of special interests. It is perhaps not entirely coincidence that the organiser, the Earl of Worcester, and the English combatant, Anthony Woodville, both had scholarly interests and saw chivalry as the means to an end.

The great tournament of 1467 between Anthony, Lord Scales, the brother of the Queen, and Antoine, the bastard son of Charles Duke of Burgundy, doubly fitted this political pattern. Internationally, this tournament cemented close relations with Burgundy. Domestically, it gave the Woodvilles the opportunity to consolidate their presence: jousting was what the Woodvilles, father and son, did well and they could assert their family's authority by leading in a great show.

Like the pilgrimage in 1458 the tournament of 1467 is extremely well documented in manuscripts which give detailed parallel English and Burgundian descriptions. The English side is found in *Landsdowne MS 285* which must have been written by a herald who was both knowledgeable and well placed.[2] The Burgundian view is given in *Leeds, Royal Armouries Library, Codex RAR.0035(I.35)*, written by a Burgundian with deep heraldic knowledge (for brevity, the former text will be referred to as that of the 'English herald' and the latter as of the 'Burgundian'). There are also sophisticated accounts by the continentals—Olivier de la Marche in his *Memoires* and Jean de Waurin in *Anciennes Croniques d'Engleterre*—while the London chroniclers produced rather cruder reports.

The man at the centre of all phases of the tournament organisation and management was Worcester, which was somewhat ironic as, until that time there was no record of him personally striking a blow either in anger on the battlefield or at play in any tournament. But he was ideally suited to organise a contemporary tournament. He had an exceptionally clear mind, was able to draw up rules which remained in use for more than a century, and was a brilliant master of ceremonies who appeared to relish involvement in grand events without making his presence obtrusive.

The tournament had to reflect the might of England, the merit of the Woodvilles and the advantage to the Burgundians of a match between its Duke and the King's sister. Thus it needed to be an exciting show but it was imperative, for diplomatic reasons, that no-one important was killed, seriously injured, too unceremoniously dumped, or caught cheating. Fatalities and serious injury were rare but could still occur. Lance splintering was a particular danger. As a young man Federico da Montefeltro, Lord of Urbino (1444–82), lost his right eye (he had the bridge of his nose removed to retain peripheral rightwards vision—hence the extraordinary profile in contemporary portraits). In 1559 King Henry II of France died of septicaemia after being wounded in the eye by a lance fragment.

In May 1467 the Bastard of Burgundy finally arrived in England after a voyage itself not devoid of adventure. He came with over 400 people: lords, knights, squires of the households and stables, heralds including the Golden Fleece King of Arms, archers, ushers, sommeliers, a fruitier and a saucier, chaplains, doctor of theology Master Antoine de Terni and his six followers, armourers, saddlers and valets.[3] They were attacked at sea and fought off five carvels of Spanish pirates. One man was killed with a crossbow bolt to the head, another lost overboard, and a third had his leg shot off and subsequently died.[4] These are the only known fatalities of the event.

There is a surprising divergence over dates for reaching Greenwich. The two most detailed sources, the Burgundian and English heralds, gave Saturday the 23rd of May and a week later.[5] The former recorded details of one secret meeting which might have been expunged from the main English record by shifting the dates forward a week.

One man had the stature, title and experience to meet the newcomers. The Burgundian herald, from the seaward side, wrote (his misrecording of the name if anything adding to the authenticity of the report), 'On Saturday the twenty-third day of May ... my lord the Bastard found before Greenwich a noble knight called Sir William of Tiptoph Earl of Dourchestette, Constable of England in a fair fuste, or galliot, with sixty oars, and five barges full of the most notable Londoners with several little ships who all attended my said lord and sailed with him.'[6] The Constable Worcester did reverence to the Great Bastard Antoine and took him to the Bishop of Salisbury's residence in the Strand. The English herald recorded the scene from the landward side, putting the date exactly a week later, reporting there 'came to receive and to meet him the Earl of Worcester, Constable of England, accompanied with many other lords knights squires and many aldermen and rich commoners of the City of London.'[7] The Bastard may have had innovations which he wished to keep from prying eyes, for 'His harness secretly was ordained to the said bishop [of Salisbury's] place at Chelsea.'[8]

On Sunday the 24th of May the Burgundian herald reported the Bastard went to Mass at St Paul's and was seen by many people. In the evening he had supper with the illegitimate son of the Duke of Brittany—affording the opportunity for mutual discussions of ducal bastardy.[9]

Possibly the sending of the harness to Chelsea was a cover to enable covert events. The Burgundian source recorded a meeting of which the English reports appeared unaware. Officially, Edward first welcomed the Bastard on the 3rd of June but they met several days earlier. 'On the twenty-ninth day of May [Friday] the King of England came secretly to the place of Chelsea to visit my lord the Bastard and he only had my lord Hastings Great Chamberlain, the Earl of Essex Grand Master of the Household, John, Lord of Buckingham, Lord Rivers, Sir James Douglas, Sir Thomas Abouron, and Sir Thomas Montgomery in his company.'[10] The King and the Bastard 'took a turn in the garden and the two of them spoke for a good half hour. And, at the end, the King called Lord Rivers and these three spoke for a time.'

The meeting between Edward IV and the Bastard was probably to discuss the marriage of the King's sister Margaret to Charles, the heir to the Duke of Burgundy. Worcester was not present in the King's escort. Given how omnipresent he was otherwise during the tournament the question might be asked why not? Possibly he did not wish to get embroiled in an exercise that would deeply offend the Nevilles. This meeting had important and immediate consequences, for Edward IV felt empowered to mount what was effectively an anti-Neville coup. He may have secured a Burgundian alliance that released him from, indeed totally undermined, Warwick's French plans for his sister.

On Sunday the 30th of May, the Burgundian herald reports that Clarence and Worcester visited the Bastard in Chelsea.[11] This was possibly a courtesy call to check the Bastard was happy with his conditions and to outline the timetable for the week of the fighting. Neither Worcester nor the King's brother, Clarence, appeared associated with Edward IV's and the Woodvilles' shift towards alliance with Burgundy.

Three days later the English and Burgundian heralds' dates converge and both record the coming of Edward from Kingston to London in order to meet the Bastard and to attend Parliament. There, according to the English herald, the King was met by princes, dukes, earls, barons, knights, esquires, the mayor, aldermen, sheriffs and commoners of the City, with the 'sound of clarions, trumpets, shalmes and other'.[12] The escort party was led by the Constable Worcester, 'bearing his baton on the right hand, the Earl Marshal [Sir John Howard] on like wise on the left hand, the Lord Scales bearing the King's sword in the middle between both', and escorted to St Paul's.[13]

The two contestants met on Fleet Street. The English herald wrote, 'the Bastard and his fellowship beheld the King coming. And the Lord Scales perceiving that, turned his horse suddenly and beheld him; the which was the first sight and knowledge personally between them.'[14] The Burgundian herald reported, 'The Bastard went to London to see the entry of the King who entered his city very grandly... And so, carrying the sword before him, was Lord Scales, who brandished and flourished it very proudly, when he passed before my lord looking up at him as he was at a window.'[15]

On the 3rd of June, the English herald reports that the King 'commanded his Sheriffs of London to make the barriers to be made in Smithfield; the which by the advice of the Constable, calling to him the King of Arms, the said barriers were made in length the contained of iv and x yards, and in breadth xxiv yards of size, the field made firm, the stable assigned.'[16] On the same day the King then attended Mass and held Parliament in Westminster Abbey. All dressed as befitted their rank, carefully noted by the Burgundian herald.

[The King] dressed in a cape of crimson velvet with a royal chaperon round his neck furred with letuse [winter weasel fur] with head-gear made from crimson velvet with a big bourrelet covered with letuse having with him the following dukes and earls; that is: the Duke of Clarence, and the Duke of Suffolk, the Earl of Arundel, the Earl of Worcester, the Constable, the Earl of Kent who carried the King's sword before him, Earl Rivers the Queen's father, ... All these Dukes, Earls, and Barons were dressed in royal capes like the King except that they had on the right shoulder from the breast to the back bends of letuse as wide as a palm. The Dukes had four, the Earls three, and the other barons two.[17]

In a foretaste of things to come Parliament was then opened by the Bishop of Lincoln, John Chadworth, not George Neville, the Chancellor and Archbishop of York. Richard Neville, the Earl of Warwick, was absent on an embassy to the French. John Neville, Earl of Northumberland, did not attend.

On the 5th of June Lord Scales came to London and was received with great pomp by Worcester and conveyed to Ely Palace.[18] The leading men accompanying Scales and the Bastard gathered in the Palace of St Pauls at a meeting, chaired by Worcester, to review the articles governing the tournament.[19] Counsel for both sides discussed the interpretation of the articles governing the affair to ensure there were absolutely no misunderstandings at such a politically important and potentially dangerous event. The Earl was unhappy about the clarity of one of the articles and suggested amendments for approval by the counsels of both combatants. The attention to detail recorded by the English herald was remarkable. For example, the Bastard's council 'demanded a question upon the second chapter on the foot arms. Where as it is said in the said chapter "And we shall fight with spear, axe, and dagger; and we shall cast each of us only a spear: and then we shall fight with other weapons unto time than one of us be borne to the ground. Whether the intent was, that the hand, the knee, or the whole body, should be brought unto the ground, or one of them?"'[20] Thus, could one side claim victory when the other had touched the soil with just his hand or only when he was entirely forced over? Now it might seem astonishing that—encased in armour, almost blind, with a cacophony of the sounds of blows, of metal upon metal, and of the roars of the crowd—the combatants could recall any of the rules at all.

While the festivities preceding the tournament were underway, on the 8th of June Worcester was one of the group of councillors who went with the King to Whitehall, London residence of the Archbishop of York, to remove the Great Seal from the Chancellor George Neville who was unwell, doubtless adding to the sense of humiliation. He may have been seen as the Neville spy in the King's council. This now put Worcester clearly in the camp perceived by Warwick to be hostile to the Neville interest.[21]

Warwick would be particularly infuriated by the low type of men involved. 'Warwick was so wrath that he could not contain himself; and he said to the admiral of France, "Have you not seen what traitors are about the King's person?"

But the admiral answered, "My lord, I pray you, wax not hot; for some day you shall be avenged." But the Earl said, "Know that those very traitors were the men who have had my brother displaced from the office of Chancellor, and made the King take the seal from him."'[22] For a second time Warwick was humiliated before the French. It cannot have helped that the Queen's brother—tournament man of the moment Anthony Woodville—was one of the party who stripped his brother George of the great seal.

The fighting on horseback took place on Thursday the 11th of June. It is described in great detail in several sources. Worcester, the master of ceremonies, was every-where and executed his role flawlessly. The Burgundian Olivier de la Marche, who was an expert in such matters and an impartial observer, recorded, 'The Earl of Worcester (Volsestre) held the place of Constable; and he was accompanied by the Marshal of England [Sir John Howard], and knew well how to perform his office.'[23] This was high praise indeed from a representative of the Burgundian court which had perfected as performance art the holding of great tournaments.

Both Burgundian and English sources described in detail the quite staggering opulence of the occasion. The former recorded:

> On the east side [of the lists] there was a high tabernacle made for the King which was grand and spacious hung with silk cloth the colour of azure strewn with gold fleur-de-lys and with scrolls where it was written 'Forever'. In the middle of the tabernacle was a high-backed chair covered with rich cloth of gold and stuffed with cushions of the same. At the base of this tabernacle on two sides of the steps were the seats of the Constable and of the Marshal hung and adorned with tapestries.[24]

The apparel of the Constable, Worcester, and the Marshal, Howard, was equally magnificent.

> The said Constable and Marshal came to the field with a great follow-ing of men-at-arms and archers … The Constable's men all wore the same white apparel some with goldsmiths work and the others without. And the Marshal's men wore vermilion with a little lion on the front and back … The said Constable and Marshal's persons were arrayed in legharness, gorgets, and journades – the Constable's of cloth of gold and the Marshal's of goldsmiths work – and mounted on trappered destriers – the Constable's of crimson cloth of gold and the Marshal's of blue and violet silk strewn with loops of hanging silk.[25]

The English herald described how the Constable and the Marshal escorted Anthony, Lord Scales, to the bar before the King who commanded them to ask Scales the cause for his coming. 'The Lord Scales answered and said, to accomplish and perform the Acts comprised in the Articles by him unto the Bastard of Burgundy sent. The King certified of the same by the Constable and Marshal, commanded him to enter the field.'[26] Then the Bastard entered the field. A further flavour of the occasion's richness might be gleaned from the Burgundian herald's description of the Bastard's appearance as he entered the lists, fetched in by Worcester and Howard.

> My lord the Bastard had led before him a destrier trappered with the arms of Burgundy with the bar, this destrier was led by four knights of his company. And he himself was mounted on a grey with a hanging harness half cloth of gold and half cloth of silver strewn with half-white half-gilt bells and six knights of his company led him by hand. Then he had seven horses trappered very richly. The first with ermine. The second with green cloth of gold. The third with crimson velvet with big silver eyes which were all strewn with teardrops. The fourth with crimson cloth of silver bordered with green velvet. The fifth had a bard covered with fine gold brocade. The sixth with sable marten. The seventh with blue velvet strewn with embroidered barbicans of fine gold. His pages and one palfrey man rode these horses arrayed in green satin pourpoints, cloth of gold berrettas lined with black velvet on their heads, having blue and violet damask journades bordered with yellow silk fringes.[27]

The Bastard told the King he had come to accomplish the acts of arms contained in articles sent to him by the Lord Scales.[28] The proclamation was then read. Edward licenced the two noble lords and knights to perform the deeds of arms, 'for the augmentation of marshal discipline and knightly honour necessary for the tuition of the catholic faith against heretics and miscrants, and to the defence of the right of kings and princes and their public estates'.[29]

The crowd was warned on behalf of the King, Constable and Marshal that no one should approach the lists or 'make any noise, murmour or shout, or any other manner token or sign whereby the said right noble and worshipful lords and knights which this day shall do their arms within these lists, or either of them, shall move, be troubled or comforted; upon Payn of imprimsonment and fine and ransome at the King's will'.[30] Upon which the Constable, 'commanded a herald to cry, "*Laissez aller*".'[31]

The first day was a great anticlimax in terms of fighting but it was not without high drama. The contest on horseback was first, with lances and then with swords.

The course with lances sounds as if it was quite brief, perhaps because it was so potentially accident-prone and, if only for diplomatic reasons, it was crucial that no one be killed, seriously injured or humiliated. Oliver de la Marche recorded, 'so they put the lances into the arrests, and ran that course without reaching or overtaking one another.'[32]

Then they fought with swords. It seems as though the Bastard was getting the better of this for both heralds described a great blow on Scales' helm. The Burgundian wrote, 'It was so strong that afterwards it could be seen on Lord Scales' helm, on the side of the visor that had been split, that it was three inches wide, and a grain of wheat could pass through the gap. By this stroke the sword was fractured in two places.'[33]

Fighting was then suddenly halted by a dreadful wound to the Bastard's horse—causing profound alarm not just because of fear of injuring the body of the Bastard but as it might have been the result of an illegal action by Scales that could potentially ruin his, and more seriously England's, reputation. Perhaps the Burgundian sources were being discreet, for it was the English herald and Fabyan who attempted to explain what happened. This herald wrote, 'And the Bastard horse head having upon him a chamfron [horse head armour] smote against the Lord Scales' saddle.'[34]

The chronicler Fabyan recorded: 'By a pyke of iron standynge upon the fore parte of the sadyll of the lorde Scalys, whervvith the horse beynge blynde [wearing a blinkered chamfron] of the Bastarde, was slryken into the nose thrylles.'[35] The horse died the next day. The Burgundian herald revealed, 'They found a great hole there in the throat as if from Lord Scales's sword. It had had an estoc inside its mouth.'[36] An estoc was a long pointed sword designed specifically for stabbing through the gaps between armour plates, so the wound must have indeed been deep. It seems that the Bastard's horse, which had limited or no vision, had impaled itself on a long object. If this had been a sword then Scales would have lost, as the Tiptoft rules decreed that he who strikes a horse 'shall have no prize'.

De la Marche recorded that 'The King of England … showed himself much enraged against the said Lord Scales, for that he thought that he had committed falseness in the furniture of his horse: yet he had not, but this stroke and this fall happened by mischance.'[37] The English herald said Scales immediately realised his behaviour was suspicious: 'Seeing him down, turned about him, holding up his sword : and then seeing that he could not rise, rode straight and alighted before the King, and made take his trapper [horse cloth covering] showing that his horse had no chamfron or peser [breast armour] of steel.'[38] Meanwhile the Bastard remained astride his fallen horse so he could not be judged unhorsed.

There is a difference in the record over whether the Bastard would continue fighting that day. The Burgundian herald said the King declared the fighting on horse over and, although the Bastard was prepared to continue, ordered the contest on foot be delayed until the next day. 'The King had my said lord questioned asking if he wanted to perform the feats of arms on foot and, when he had answered yes, he did not want to allow it at all.'[39] Thus it was the King who stopped the show. The English herald recorded that the King gave the Bastard the option of continuing. 'And where before the Constable at Paul's [St Paul's bishop's palace] it was agreed that if any horse failed it should be lawful to his master to have another; he was demanded whether he so willed : his answer was, "that it was no season". Then the King commanded him to go to their lodging.'[40]

It is possible that the Bastard, although he realised the necessity of diplomatic behaviour, privately believed he had been unchivalrously treated. De la Marche wrote, 'my said Lord the Bastard returned to his lodging, and said to me at going into his chamber, "Doubt not: he [Scales] has fought a beast to day, and tomorrow he shall fight a man".'[41] The King, clearly alarmed that the exercise was turning sour, sent Worcester to visit the Bastard, doubtless to try and smooth things over: 'And at that hour came the Constable, from the King, to know if he were at all wounded: but Monsieur the Bastard answered that he thanked the King, and that he had no wound, but was ready to do his arms on foot on the morrow, praying that it might please the King to grant him so.'[42]

The 12th of June was the day for fighting on foot. 'The said Constable and Marshal did their duty in the morning to put their men in order.'[43] Olivier de la Marche described how the Bastard was given a choice of three weapons: casting lances, pole-axes or daggers. The King, however, being first shown the weapons, removed the lances, probably because the outcome of their use was too unpredictable and dangerous.[44]

Lord Rivers made the sign of the cross three times over his son, Lord Scales, who then advanced brashly 'changing his axe from hand to hand', according to the English herald.[45] The Burgundian described him holding his axe sometimes at his neck, sometimes on high.[46] Scales' behaviour sounds like one overexcited, whereas the Bastard's advance was measured. The Bastard wore his bascinet visor down whereas Scales' face was uncovered, something called 'jepdous' by the English herald. Perhaps this was why the Burgundian herald recounted that Scales shouted, 'Hey, over here, over here,' presumably implying the Bastard could not see him. To which the Bastard responded, 'These words dismay me not a whit unless you come closer.'[47]

All connoisseurs agreed that the hammering and smashing with the axes was most commendably and chivalrously done. De la Marche recorded, 'I never saw the fight with axes so fiercely.'[48] There was a clear difference of fighting style with the axes noted by the English herald: the Bastard led with the 'small end' while

Scales struck with the head. Neither party, observed de la Marche, used his dagger. It does sound as though the Bastard was getting the better of it. But then Scales hit the Bastard on the side of the visor, and forced the point of his axe into the visor. At this point the King, presumably alarmed that someone would be seriously injured, cried, 'Whoa!'

The English herald reported the King commanded the combatants to be friends. The Burgundian, however, had more to say: 'The Bastard stopped while Scales, despite being held by the guards who endeavoured to part the fighters, dealt him some more strokes.'[49] Whereupon the (doubtless exasperated) Bastard 'was forced to deal him such a powerful stroke with the axe-head to his head, and did so with such force that he was master of them'.[50] De la Marche described how both men then went away with their axes round their necks to show they had not been unweaponed.

There followed further *post pugnam* debate as to the outcome. This was somewhat partisan but still generous. The Burgundian herald and de la Marche observed that Scales' coat of arms was torn and gashed. De la Marche said the Bastard 'showed well that he was a true knight, experienced in arms and in craft'.[51] Fabyan wrote, 'when the Kyng sawe that the Lord Scalys hadd avauntage of the Bastard, as the poynt of his axe in the vysour of his enemyes helmett, and by force thereof was lykly to have born hym ovyr'.[52] He described Scales as having the honour on both days. The antiquarian Stowe, writing later, said that Scales' axe, having become lodged in the Bastard's visor, the Bastard requested that he might be allowed to complete his feat of arms. It was decided that if the combat were to continue it would have to be started with the men in the same positions as when it was stopped, whereupon the Bastard, doubting the outcome, relinquished his challenge. The chronicler Gregory, perhaps unwittingly, made the most perceptive comment as to the victor: 'Ask of them that felt the strokes, they can tell you best.'[53]

Probably to the vast relief of the King and Council—and perhaps to the disappointment of the crowd—no one had been killed (except the poor horse), injured, disqualified or otherwise disgraced. The two days of combat had achieved their objective of sealing the relationship between England and Burgundy, faultlessly managed by the Constable Worcester. But, judged in terms of diplomacy, it had been a close run thing that could easily have been ruined by allegations of cheating or unfair intervention. The Bastard comes out of it all very well—as a man who put aside personal vanity for the greater cause.

The Burgundian herald recorded that later that night the combatants played tennis together: 'And, after the reception, they took part in, and played at *paume*, or tennis, four against four. That is: the King, my lord the Bastard, Lord Scales, and the Marshal against Sir John Woodville my lord Scales's brother, Sir Thomas Abouron, Thomas Vacquant, and my lord of Rabondenghes Bailli of Saint-Omer.

And neither side won.'[54] The Constable was not described as present. He was probably preparing for the next day.

On Monday the 13th of June there was further fighting but not involving Scales or the Bastard. The Constable, Worcester, was not off the hook and still had to supervise events. That day the fight was between a Gascon squire, Louis de Bretelles, and Lord Jehan de Chassa, Lord of Monnet. This was notably more violent and prolonged—perhaps as nothing important diplomatically was at stake. The Burgundian herald noted: 'At the King's pleasure, although they only ought to have run eleven courses, they ran nineteen. During these Louis de Bretelles had several buffets from which the following days he suffered greatly from strong pains in his face.'[55]

The next day a great banquet, attended by the King and Queen, was held at the Grocers' Hall in the City of London. Also noted as present were the Earls of Arundel and Worcester.[56] The following report by the Burgundian herald reads like a modern high society column. 'The supper was long and I would have taken pains to describe all these ladies but had it not been for Lady Scales who promised me (by her grace) [a list] to give me in writing, as she did.'[57]

On Wednesday the 15th of June there was a fight between two esquires – one Burgundian the other Gascon, respectively Philippe Bouton and Thomas de la Lande. Three years later this Thomas would be up before the Constable, Worcester, in his judicial role in less fortuitous circumstances and condemned to be beheaded for his part in the Lincolnshire rebellion. Now there were accusations of unfair play because de la Lande's lance arrest was too advantageous, infuriating the King who wanted no accusations of cheating to mar the event.[58]

The next day there was another banquet held by the King's older sister, the Duchess of Exeter. The Duke, Henry Holland, could not attend as he was detained in exile, leaving the field clear for one whose love was reputed less than courtly, Thomas St Leger. There was no mention of the presence of any male Nevilles. Indeed, given the recent removal of the seal from George, the Neville trio were probably not that happy. Intriguingly, however, Worcester's niece Isabel Neville made a belated appearance according to the Burgundian herald. The Bastard 'went to the Duchess of Exeter's residence where she held a banquet for the King, the Queen, and for my lord the Bastard. All the oft-named princesses were there; and the Countess of Northumberland who had newly arrived. And, if the feast had been joyous on Sunday, it was no less so on Tuesday.'[59]

Isabel may have attended the banquet at the invitation of her uncle, Worcester. But her husband John may have come to London to see his brothers, Richard and George, smarting from their recent humiliations, for a Neville council of war. The trio would have been a disaffected brood, Richard humiliated again over another unwanted French alliance and George stripped of the seals, symbol of his office as Chancellor. Maybe John heard reports that Henry Percy wanted the return of what he saw as the family's title of Earl of Northumberland. As Isabel was 'newly' arrived she cannot have attended the previous events. Her presence alone implies that she possibly had a somewhat detached position from the disaffected Nevilles. She may have wanted to maintain bridges and not miss all the events orchestrated by her uncle.

On Thursday the 18th of June, the Bastard dined with the King and played at tennis, according to the Burgundian herald. 'On Thursday morning my lord the Bastard was invited to dinner by the King. He went there and, after dinner, they played at *paume*. The King, my lord the Bastard, Sir John Woodville brother of my lord Scales, and Sir John Howard against four others. And thus they lost a hundred *saluts*.'[60] Who were the 'four others'? Might one have been the tireless Constable, Worcester, who now had no more fights to supervise?

They also visited the former King Henry. This is rather surprising as the deposed King is generally thought to have been kept in the Tower of London. 'Going to this game of *paume* after dinner, the King led my lord the Bastard to see King Henry in a tower where he was imprisoned at Westminster to whom he had little to say because they scarcely understood each other.'[61]

On the 21st of June the feats of arms, ceremonies and festivities were brought to a sudden close by news of the death of the Bastard's father, Philip the Good, Duke of Burgundy.[62] The welcome that the Bastard had was compared with that received by the Emperor in 1416. 'It was even said by the elders that the Emperor Sigismund, when he had been in England, was not so enthusiastically welcomed, and from the Commons in particular.'[63] The Earl of Worcester's father had been appointed Steward to the Emperor's Household while in England. The son had matched the father.

This had been a fortnight of high drama and near flawless spectacle where the contest could have degenerated into tragedy or farce. The Plantagenet-Woodville party cemented the Burgundian alliance and a coup was mounted against Neville power. Worcester yet again displayed his versatility. He had written the ordinances. His management had been impeccable. He was everywhere without being over-bearing. The sophisticated Burgundians and the English herald noted and appreciated his talents, although they seem to have been lost on the English chroniclers who, astonishingly, appear to have refused even to acknowledge his presence.

Part 4

IRELAND

Chapter 19

Remarriage and arrival – 1467

The Earl ... having a thousand archers at the expense of the King crossed the sea to Ireland. ... On the way he married the widow of Roger Corbet, a knight, at Ludlow, sister and heir of Walter Hopton, an heir of William Lucy, a knight.[1]

William of Wyrcester's chatty Annals which mention the
Earl of Worcester on several occasions

By early September the Earl, on his way to Ireland, had nearly everything in place to repress rebels in Ireland and restore proper authority. He had with him 'many worthy people', 700 archers, many cannon and a retinue.[2] He wanted only for a wife to share his residence in Dublin Castle and produce heirs. And suddenly the apparently confirmed bachelor Worcester got one, perhaps impetuously, after fifteen years—one Elizabeth Corbet *née* Hopton.

The Earl expected to be many years in Ireland. Maybe he was ready, indeed was determined, to make a complete new start. By leaving England he put behind him associations with the quick deaths of his first two wives. The Earl had seen marriage to him as a death sentence for young noble ladies and when he eventually remarried he went for a Marcher knight's widow with a proven ability for surviving childbirth. Elizabeth was, like Worcester, in her early forties and no spring chicken. She came with a respectable property, recently much augmented, for she was a coheir of the Lucy family estate.[3]

Like her namesake Elizabeth Greyndour, Corbet is, however, personally a mystery, existing only through the names of the three men she married and the children she bore. A middle-aged widow of knightly family who apparently dropped all to go to Ireland with a supremely intelligent and cultivated earl—close to the King, with a reputation for severity, whose first two wives died soon after marriage—she must have had considerable spirit. Worcester was not quite Blue Beard but marriage to him, en route to Ireland to repress the rebels there, must have been seen to have had its risks. But it also brought advantages. The Earl was rich and in a position to promote her other children. The eventual heir to Roger and Elizabeth Corbet, Richard, became a ward of Walter Devereux, Lord Ferrers, who was one of Edward IV's closest and longest serving companions. Elizabeth may have elicited a more common touch from the erudite earl. It was notable that while

Worcester was disliked by the merchant and legal class in London, the same type in Ireland would respect and admire him.

Anyway, there is something almost touching about the Earl marrying a similarly aged woman after what may have been a whirlwind wooing, if not quite a romance. After that the pair were fined by the King for the temerity of 'their trespass in intermarrying without licence'.[4] The King cannot have been too angry for the fine was a negligible 10 marks which was then cancelled. When the Earl of Worcester's second cousin Margery Despenser remarried Roger Wentworth without permission this was deemed so far below her that Henry V set the fine at a teeth-gritting £1,000.

The worthies the Earl bought with him included his former brother-in-law Edmund Sutton who had remarried Matilda, daughter of Thomas Lord Clifford, and they would go on to have several children. Edmund's younger brother William Sutton became Lord Chancellor and Keeper of the Great Seal of Ireland from 1469 to 1472. Also William Stanley, the younger brother of Lord Thomas Stanley, lived in Ireland later during Worcester's administration.

Worcester brought with him a substantial part of his library according to George Neville, who would be asked by Oxford University, following Worcester's death, to find his books. If anyone who knew anything of the Earl questioned his commitment to Ireland they would have been convinced by him bringing his books. In *The Declamacion of Noblesse* Flamyneus told Lucresse, 'And first I shal shewe you my lyberary, wel stuffed with fayr bookes of Greke and latyn, wher vnto in euery aduersyte is my chief resorte for counseyll and comforte.' Whether the Marcher knight's widow had much interest in 'Greke and latyn' is not known—although it is doubtful—but the Earl and his new lady had sufficient 'commycacyon and comforte' to produce a son in 1469. Thus a nursery must have been added to the Earl's household.

The precise date of the Earl of Worcester's arrival is not recorded but it was likely in late September or early October. He appears to have hit the ground running, both politically and militarily. He at once summoned a parliament which first met on the 11th of December in Dublin. The Irish Parliament was no occasional and subservient body. Its records show it passed much legislation and it had a remarkable, and growing, independence from Westminster.

The Earl wasted no time going out on campaign. By the 16th of October he was leading the Dublin worthies and people into the country of the troublesome O'Byrnes to the south of the city. 'Memorandum : Business was not transacted in the assembly on fourth Friday after the 19th of September, 1467, as the Mayor, Bailiffs, and Commons of the city were in O'Byrne's country [county Wicklow] with John, Earl of Worcester, Lord Deputy of Ireland.'[5] Rebels there were well-financed by endemic smuggling which had resulted in a recognised improvement in their military equipment. There was no record of fighting so a show of strength with at least some of the 700 archers was sufficient.

The Irish Parliament passed legislation guaranteeing the liberties of Ireland generally and of the Holy Church, and the franchises of Dublin, Waterford, Drogheda and other towns in particular.[6] 'Black rents' (basically protection money) hitherto paid to the King's enemies were now to be redirected to the King's lieutenant.[7] Also, Worcester, 'inflamed with the fervour of devotion and of charity', endowed a chantry in honour of God, the Virgin, St Katherine and St Secundinus, in the church of St Secundinus of Dunshaughlin in the Bishopric of Meath on 11 December 1467.[8] Among those also cited were Thomas FitzMaurice, the Earl of Kildare, Worcester's wife Elizabeth, William Sherwood, Bishop of Meath, Richard, Abbot of St Thomas the Martyr, John Cornell, Chaplain, Walter Delahide, Barnaby Barnewall, John and Walter Chevir and Philip Bermingham.[9] There may have been a genuine desire for reconciliation. Bermingham and the Chevirs had been staunch Lancastrians.

The endowment indicated the Earl expected to be in Ireland for some time and intended to conciliate at least the Kildare and Ormond parties. The absence of the Earl of Desmond was conspicuous and—in the light of events—ominous. Either he was invited and refused to come or he was already *persona non grata*.

Overall, Worcester appears to have made a sound start. Perhaps it was going a bit too smoothly, and some drama was necessary, for now the Earl thoroughly shook everything up.

Chapter 20

Executioner – 1468

He [William Sherwood, the Bishop of Meath] caused the Archbishop [John Bole of Armagh, primate of all Ireland] to be cited before the Earl of Worcester, at Grenoke [Co. Meath]: Tiptoft's threat to tie the Archbishop's feet was insulting to the prelate.[1]

> Report to the Bishop of Meath of the Archbishop's
> objections to his disobedient and injurious behaviour.

The beheading of Desmond, Ireland's premier earl, at the gallows ground in Drogheda stunned contemporaries and has baffled historians ever since. There were also other executions at the same time of youthful Irishmen, recorded very inconsistently, which have blackened the reputation of Worcester. There are no contemporary accounts which clearly elucidate events. There are, however, some overlooked documents (one quoted at the chapter beginning) which throw a new light on what happened.

Parliament was moved from Dublin to Drogheda, where Desmond would be more vulnerable, and opened on the 4th of February under Worcester. A bill was immediately brought forward and passed attainting Thomas FitzGerald, Earl of Desmond, Thomas FitzMaurice, the Earl of Kildare, and Edward Plunket, Seneschal of Meath. The attainder was:

> at the request of the Commons, that for divers causes, horrible treasons, and felonies prepensed and done by [Desmond, Kildare and Plunket] as well in alliance, fosterage, and alterage with the Irish enemies of the King, as in giving to them horses and harness and armour, and support- ing them against the faithful subjects of the King, ... against the laws of the King and the laudable statutes of this land of Ireland. .... And each of them be adjudged and deemed traitors, and attainted of treason, and forfeit all their goods.[2]

In short, Desmond, Kildare and Plunket formed treasonous alliances with Irish enemies and gave them weapons to use against the English. It was then up to Worcester to determine punishment in his role as Deputy Lieutenant. *A Fragment of Irish Annals* provides the most detailed source from an Irish perspective:

A council of the foreigners of Ireland was held in Droichead Átha ...
Despite the wishes of his friends and advisers Tomás ... . the Earl
of Desmond, went to that council to comply with the command of
the English Justiciar, the Earl of Worcester, to promote the welfare of the
foreigners. First of all the Earl went to Nás Laighean [Naas] to meet the
Justiciar and he received from him all that he desired along with pleasant
words; and the Earl and that foreign Justiciar went together to Droichead
Ácha and the council met there. From that council came a terrible and
unlawful loss, that is, the Earl of Desmond was arrested by the Justiciar
through the most loathsome treachery in the [Dominican friary]. Along
with him were arrested there Kildare as well as the choicest of his friends
from among the foreigners [i.e. the English] who had accompanied him.[3]

The fragment, in what may be an interpolation, then adds, 'On that same day he
[Worcester] had beheaded two innocent young children of high rank.'[4] Humiliating
but non-fatal punishment was meted out to the Seneschal of Meath, who had
failed to defend the county: 'He had Edward Plunket, one of the nobles of the
foreign youths of Ireland, flogged through the streets of the town like a villain or
scoundrel.'[5] Maybe it was the least that could be inflicted to placate the English
of Meath who were furious at his failure to defend them against Irish incursions.
Thomas FitzMaurice, Earl of Kildare, was imprisoned.

Desmond was in custody from Friday till Monday. 'Then that splendid, generous, wise and powerful lord was beheaded without just cause.'[6] The Irish annals
are full of the shocked response. For example, 'The learned relate that there was
not ever in Ireland a foreign youth that was better than he. And he was killed in
treachery by a Saxon Earl.'[7] The English expressed no disapproval. Indeed, when
the Irish rebelled, they responded aggressively and enthusiastically in taking up
the opportunity to fight the Irish. The annalist William of Wyrcester reported
that Edward IV was initially displeased.[8] This indicated that Worcester was acting
independently in determining the appropriate punishment following attainder by
parliament. The King, however, does not seem to have remained angry long with
his most loyal servant, as there were no repercussions. So why did one earl execute another? Initially, two reasons put forward for Desmond's death might be
considered.

First, Worcester's execution of Desmond was explained as resulting from the
spiteful character of Queen Elizabeth and her capricious attitude towards the
instruments of state authority. A memorandum of the early 1540s to the council
described how Edward IV had questioned Desmond in England in the summer
of 1464:

What do you hear spoken by [of] me? ... He answered ... nothing but honor and much nobility. ... At last his Majesty ... required him ... to declare *his* own opinion ... the ... Earl said, '... no fault ... saving only that your Grace hath too much abased your princely estate in marrying a lady of so mean a house and parentile ... perchance agreeable to your lusts, yet not so much to the security of your realm and subjects.' ... His majesty ... said that he had spoken most true. Not long after, the said Earl having licence to depart into his country ... the King and the Queen his wife ... fell at words [and] his grace ... said: 'Well I perceive now that true [what] Desmond, told me.' ... Her Grace ... conceiving upon those words a grudge ... against the said Earl, ... devised [letters] under the King's privy seal, and directed to the ... governor of ... Ireland, commanding him ... to send for the said Earl, dissembling some earnest matter ... and at his coming to object to such matter, and to lay such things to his charge, as should cause him to lose his head. ... The said Lord Justice [Worcester] ... willed [Desmond] to make his repair unto him and other of the King's council. ... Where without long delay or sufficient matter brought against him ... the said Lord Justice ... caused him to be beheaded, signifying to the common people for a cloak [cover story], that most heinous treasons were justified against him in England. ... The King ... declaring himself to be utterly ignorant of the said Earl's death ... caused to be put [the Lord Justice] to a very cruel and shameful death.[9]

The Book of Howth, a sixteenth-century manuscript history of Ireland, compiled by an Anglo-Irish lord Christopher St Lawrence, 8th Baron of Howth (c. 1509–1589), explicitly identified Worcester by name as the receiver of the Queen's missive in a second memorandum from the 13th Earl James (1540–58) to the English Council.

King Edward's wife, ... was informed that the Earl of Warvicke and the Earl of Desmound was greatly offended and also was grieved with the marriage of the Queen, and said openly that better it were for the King to follow his friends' counsel, which went about to prepare for him a convenient and a meet marriage, ... rather than to marry a traitor's wife. The Queen ... often did move the King thereof, which little he did regard, considering it was spoken for very love they bare to their assured friend and prince.[10]

The Queen—probably as outraged by her husband's nonchalant indifference to her complaints as by the insult itself—then stole the King's signet seal and forged the letter to Worcester with fatal results to Desmond, 'as sampull of other which rebelliously would talk of the Queen'.[11] Some of this does have some ring of truth. It is quite possible that Warwick and Desmond, as earls of ancient lineage, had disparaged between them the royal marriage, and also that the Queen heard of this and was enraged.

These memoranda were written as a part of a mid-sixteenth century Desmond family campaign in England to recover the Irish manor of Dungarvan lost in the fifteenth century by the Desmonds to the Ormonds. The latter were reported to be outraged when the former were given the privilege of being free not to appear in person before the King's deputy or the council in Ireland—because this had resulted in the execution of the 7th Earl of Desmond—and apparently took revenge by grabbing the former's property. The story of the Queen's subterfuge, with the forged letter, purported to provide an explanation for how Worcester had been induced to execute Desmond. Some generations later, shaky history meant the memoranda's authors were unaware of Henry VI's brief return to the throne, so they assumed Edward IV was the king who executed Worcester. The sixteenth-century authors considered they needed, in making the claim to recover the lost manor, to set out the background to Desmond's beheading—and hence the exemption privilege. But why concoct the elaborate and frankly highly improbable story of the forged letter? Nothing can be clear but it sounds, firstly, like the kind of propaganda that might be used to blacken the Queen's and Worcester's reputation in the run-up to and during the Readeption; and secondly, the sort of rumour that rumbled on for years without being recorded until the memoranda were written. Maybe, also, in order to strengthen the aim of memoranda reclaiming the wrongfully lost manors, it was felt necessary to make the events leading up to their loss sound as nefarious as possible.

There are many reasons why the account in the memoranda might arouse scepticism. The story assumed Desmond's knowledge of the King's marriage in August 1464, when the Irish earl was in England, before the King told the Council in September 1464.[12] Also, there were over three years between the date when Desmond was in England and the arrival of the Earl of Worcester in Ireland and Desmond's death—a long time for the angry Queen to wait for revenge—and another three until Worcester's execution—again a protracted delay until the King summoned him to face justice. The punctilious Earl was an expert in royal documentation, familiar with the King's hand, and a scholar. He was, thus, unlikely to fall for a forgery. Anyway, a letter written under the privy seal from England had little power to compel in Ireland after 1460. Worcester, well versed in legal niceties and conscious of Ireland's increasing independence, would have been aware of the 1460 statute passed by the Irish Parliament which decreed, 'this land of Ireland is … corporate of itself,' free of any English laws except those approved by the Parliament of Ireland.[13] There was anyway considerable reluctance, even in

England, to obey commands under the privy seal.[14] Further, if the letter had been a secret instruction—and Worcester was a discreet man—how could anyone else have known of it at the time and why, then, did its existence only emerge over seven decades after it was written?

A second explanation was that the Earl 'had claims upon the manors of Inchiquin and Youghal, in the vicinage of the Munster Geraldines', which 'may have had something to do with the execution' of the Earl of Desmond.[15] These manors had been in the possession of Bartholomew de Badlesmere, executed in 1322. They then passed to his daughter, Margaret, who married John, 2nd Baron Tiptoft, the father by his first wife of Robert 3rd Baron Tiptoft, and by his second wife, of Payn, Worcester's grandfather. Therefore any claim on the Irish properties would have passed to the three daughters of the first marriage and their lines, as they were coheirs to the bulk of Robert's estate. Also, by the turn of the fourteenth and fifteenth centuries it was government policy to discourage absentee landlords, and control of the manors passed from the three Tiptoft coheir daughters to the Butler Earls of Ormond who then swapped them for other properties with the FitzGerald Earls of Desmond in 1422. Thus the Tiptofts had long ceased to have any interest in the two manors and, even if they did, such an interest would have passed along Robert's line rather than Payn's.

In the sixteenth century two explanations were put forward for Desmond's execution by perceptive commentators. In 1515 coyne and livery was cited as the particular offence in an admirable memorandum to the Council from Sir William Darcy which explained the reasons for the decline of the King's authority in the four provinces of Ireland. Coyne and livery was a charge to billet and supply the chief's professional soldiers, kerns and galloglasses, enforced by those same soldiers.

The rational administrator Darcy recorded: 'Item. The four shires here which should obey the King's laws, called Meath, Louth, Dublin, and Kildare, the foresaid abominable order of coyne and livery was begun in them above 50 years by Thomas Earl of Desmond, ...; and he was then the King's Deputy; for the which order and precedent he was put to execution.'[16] Darcy did not say that the specific charge against Desmond was imposing coyne and livery. It was, however, understood to be the fundamental reason why the Anglo-Irish parliament was determined to punish him. In 1463 Edward had specifically warned Desmond not to impose coyne and livery on the English.

The Jesuit Edmund Campion, who was to spend several years in Ireland, wrote that Desmond's indiscretion regarding Edward's marriage played a part in his death. 'The Earle of Desmond ... had spoken certaine disdainfull words against the late marryage of King Edward with the Lady Elizabeth Grey, the said Lady being now Queene, caused his trade of life, (after the Irish manner, contrary to sundry old statutes enacted in that behalfe) to be sifted & examined by Iohn Earle of Worcester his successour. Of which treasons he was attaint and condemned, and for the same beheaded at Droghedah.'[17] Thus Desmond's criticism of the Queen's marriage made Worcester look into Desmond's broader kinship arrangements, 'contrary to sundry old statutes', which might have been in breach of the 1365 Statutes of Kilkenny that made treasonable intercourse, sexual and other, between the English and Irish.[18]

Darcy's and Campion's explanations for Desmond's execution are different but not incompatible. They give two credible underlying reasons for the execution. The former described the exaction of coyne and livery which genuinely did infuriate the English. The latter wrote that Worcester investigated Desmond's personal affairs after the Irish earl was disparaging about the King's relationships. Indeed, Worcester would have deeply resented the criticism of his King and Queen, not just out of patriotism but because, as the translator of *The Declamacion of Noblesse*, he was not going to take kindly to abuse based upon inadequate lineage as opposed to personal qualities.

The imposition of coyne and livery on the English was exceptionally inflammatory. Contemporary images of Irish soldiers, galloglasses and kerns give them a terrifying outlandish appearance, with bare feet, vast moustaches and partially shaven heads, armed with huge swords and vicious long-shafted axes. The powerful English distaste for such soldiers was reflected in Tudor plays about the medieval period. In Marlowe's *Edward II*, when the Earl of Lancaster described disorder in the realm, he said of Ireland, 'The wild O'Neill, my lords, is up in arms, / With troops of Irish kerns that uncontrolled / Doth plant themselves within the English pale.' In Shakespeare's *Henry VI Part 2* Cardinal Beaufort proposed that the Duke of York go to Ireland where 'The uncivil kerns of Ireland are in arms / And temper clay with blood of Englishmen.' The poet Edmund Spenser, who served in Ireland under Elizabeth I, wrote of kerns and galloglasses: 'These be the most barbarous and loathly of any people, I think, under heathen … They oppress all men; they spoil as well the subject as the enemy; they steal; they are cruel and bloody … licentious, swearers and blasphemers; common ravishers of women and murtherers of children.'[19] The presence of such men not just in the Pale but actually billeted in homes in the four English counties was an abomination.

Desmond's treasonous relationships and imposition of coyne and livery still does not fully explain why Worcester actually executed Desmond once he had been attainted by parliament. He did not, contrary to reputation, execute everyone and in 1468 Kildare and Plunket lived. Therefore other possible factors might also be reviewed, including personalities and the character of the Irish parliament.

Worcester and the Irish were ever likely to prove a volatile combination. Possibly he had unpleasant memories of the Irish earlier in his life. Worcester's father had been plagued in Cambridgeshire, in his last years, by James Butler, Earl of Ormond. Worcester might have encountered the Irish at Oxford who were so unruly they were not allowed their own halls but were split between residences.[20] The Earl's behaviour indicated he wished to make a fresh beginning, seeking to leave his old life behind, with all its unhappy memories, false starts and dead ends. Prior to leaving England for Ireland he obtained a plenary pardon for those sins for which he would have to account to God and a full pardon for his offences on earth. He sold or surrendered all his offices, got a wife after fifteen years as a widower and packed up his beloved library to take with him. Thus he would have wanted to impose order from the start. The Earl's personal life had been torn apart in the early 1450s by family deaths at a time of unrest extending from Cade's revolt to the Dartmouth standoff. After many years he had again married. It might be conjectured the Earl was not going to let unrest disturb his family life again and would act ruthlessly to stop it. Also, the lesson of 1405, 1415 and 1462 in England was that after executing an earl or two the situation quietened down.

It might further be conjectured that Worcester harboured deeper and longer-term ambitions to be Ireland's sole ruler, staying there permanently, and Desmond was his main rival. Not only was the Earl of Desmond executed, but the two other Irish earls, Kildare and Ormond, were, by 1468, both attainted. The Irish Parliament had attained real independent powers. Recognition of Worcester's status as the King's cousin paved the way for his appointment as lord, not deputy lieutenant—to which position he would be raised in 1470.

The Earl of Desmond must have resented his displacement by Worcester and perhaps made his displeasure known by not welcoming his successor, remaining holed up in his Munster fastnesses and neither attending the St Seceundinus foundation nor Parliament. He may not have been a discreet man. It is possible, given Campion's account, that he was indeed heard to be tactless about the King's marriage. He might also have made rude comments about the childless Worcester and his new but mature-in-years wife. Lest it appear that the Earl of Desmond was an innocent, overwhelmed by events, it should be recognised that he was a man of his times, quite capable of abusive behaviour. He was reported by the Cistercian monastery of St Mary, O'Dorney in Munster to the Pope for extorting various dues from it and many other crimes against the abbot and convent.[21]

Worcester and Desmond may have instinctively disliked each other. Desmond was, in his own eyes, the premier Irish earl, the friend and defender of Edward IV. He was also so much that Worcester was not and must have wanted to be. While Worcester was descended from some Norman *miles* from a village south of

Fécamp who accompanied the Conqueror, the Geraldine Earls of Desmond traced themselves back to Girardus of Florence – a place well known to Worcester and of infinitely greater splendour, culture and learning than some village in Normandy. (The Gherardini were one of Florence's great founding families. Indeed the subject of Leonardo's da Vinci's *Mona Lisa* was born a member.) Desmond had fought battles and led the Yorkist army victorious in 1462 at Piltdown. Worcester had no known record of any fights but had killed in cold blood those captured by others. Desmond had many fine sons and Worcester had none. It seems quite possible that secretly, or not so secretly, one earl despised and disdained the other, who in turn envied and felt threatened by the first.

In this drama, however, the full role of one character has tended to be rather overlooked. William Sherwood, Bishop of Meath, the Iago of his era, appeared from nowhere fully formed, a man who refused any authority that did not suit him, contemptuous of the Irish, contumacious to his own archbishop, John Bole of Armagh, and a natural instigator of dissent and discord. He had a passionate hatred for Desmond who had oppressed the English in Ireland and failed to protect them from raiding. 'The Meath gentry showed themselves extremely sensitive to any Irish practices which might seem to undermine traditional English arrangements for defence, and they found a leader in Bishop Sherwood.'[22]

Sherwood is a mystery but such a man must have had some back story. The name Sherwood is perhaps a clue. The humanist bibliophile Bishop of Durham and student, like the Earl of Worcester, at the Great Hall of the University was John Sherwood. William Sherwood, Bishop of Meath, was possibly from a branch of the Sherwood family which provided several prominent citizens of York and was loyal to the House of Plantagenet.

There is circumstantial evidence of Sherwood's major role in encompassing Desmond's death. After his execution the Geraldines ravaged Meath because they blamed the bishop for Desmond's death. An Irish historian wrote: 'Some say that William Sherwood, Bishop of Meath, was an active person in prosecuting this earl; for before this there were great animosities between them.'[23] That Sherwood might have had a specific role in affecting Worcester's judgement may seem conjecture, although soundly based, but for a document in the register of Archbishop Bole, probably dated to the end of 1469, which explicitly described the relationship between Sherwood and Tiptoft. The summary of a report by Richard Rowe, the messenger of Sherwood, of discussions with Archbishop Bole aimed at re-establishing relations between bishop and archbishop—in which the latter objected to the former's 'disobedient and injurious' behaviour towards him—set out eight specific instances. The first six established the bishop as a man totally contemptuous and disobedient towards his superior. The last two of these six recorded:

5. He has slandered the Archbishop by allegations of tyranny and injustice.

6. He has hindered the personnel of the Archbishop and interfered with the exercise of Armagh's jurisdiction.[24]

These demonstrate how violently the bishop could attack the archbishop. The seventh and eighth articles explicitly brought Worcester into the story.

7. He caused the Archbishop to be cited before the Earl of Worcester, at Grenoke (now Greenogue in Co. Meath) [St Nicholas church was closely associated with the ecclesiastical establishment in Dublin]: Tiptoft's *threat to tie the Archbishop's feet* was insulting to the prelate.[25]

This allegation is quite breathtaking. The Bishop of Meath managed to get his own archbishop, no less than the Primate of all Ireland, summoned before the Deputy Lieutenant. The threat to 'tie the Archbishop's feet' might seem rather disrespectful to the office of archbishop but not itself unduly dangerous until it is recalled that traitors' feet were tied to horses en route to execution. When Henry VI was taken to captivity in the Tower his legs were tied into the stirrups. The expression carried more than a hint of real menace. This, if true, did not reflect well on the Earl. It was also out of character. In England, at least, Worcester maintained excellent relationships with the Archbishop of Canterbury.

The eighth allegation is, if anything, even more astonishing.

8. After certain documents relating to a case concerning the archdeaconery of Meath were stolen from the Archbishop's register, the *bishop had them altered and shown to the Earl of Worcester* and to the archdeacon of London (Richard Martyn), to the detriment of the Archbishop.[26]

This related to a case other than Desmond's. But a bishop who could stoop to stealing and forging might do anything to destroy his enemy. Campion later said that Worcester examined Desmond's life, provoked by the Irish earl's disparaging comments about the King's marriage. Could Sherwood have then provided Worcester with doctored evidence of Desmond's 'trade in life contrary to old statutes'?

In 1470, goaded beyond bearing, Bole excommunicated Sherwood. In 1475 it was recorded:

Archbishop John [Bole], before his death, had lawfully declared William [Sherwood], Bishop of Meath, to have incurred the sentences of suspension and excommunication, the guilt of perjury, the penalties of contempt, and the note of irregularity. This sentence, passed five years ago and confirmed by the provincial council, has been ignored by the bishop. *Since ecclesiastical sanctions have failed, the dean and chapter request the King's lieutenant in Ireland, or his deputy, to act as secular arm against the bishop.*[27]

As long as Sherwood had the confidence of the English in Ireland he was invulnerable. He was appointed Deputy Lieutenant in 1475 but was so unpopular that in 1477 he was removed. Yet he was Lord Chancellor of Ireland from 1475 to 1481.

Another overlooked factor might have been the Irish Parliament which was asserting its independence and powers. The English in Ireland may have hated the Irish but they were also keen to establish independence from the Westminster government. It was an act of attainder passed by the Irish Parliament that condemned Desmond. Parliament might also have been playing at score settling. Possibly the Lancastrian Ormonds and others were still smarting from the defeat at Piltdown by Desmond in 1462. John Chevir, a member of the Ormond party who was one of those who joined the confraternity of St Secundinus, was the first known speaker of the Irish Parliament.

At least there is no question that Desmond *was* executed, even if the reasons are uncertain. The only thing sure about the other two people who died, if indeed they did die, was that they were male and young. The reporting of events is anomalous. The deaths were described in Italian and English sources. Remarkably, the Irish sources did not mention the damning executions, except the *Fragment of Irish Annals* which said, 'the Earl of Worcester had beheaded two innocent young children of high rank.'[28] This text survived in England and these deaths might be an interpolation. If Worcester had indeed executed two juveniles it might seem likely the Irish would have added this to his crimes. Usually the *Fragment* is quite precise about names but it does not give them here. Had the juveniles been legitimate sons of the Earl of Desmond it would surely have named names.

Bisticci wrote that the Earl was berated in 1470 by a Dominican friar when being brought to execution, 'because wanting to extinguish certain lords, enemies of the state he made to be killed two most innocent babes'.[29] This sounds as though causing the deaths of the two juveniles was an accusation that was made against the Earl at his trial and this was reported to Bisticci.

It is English sources in Ireland and England who described the boys as sons of Desmond. The Register of the Mayors of Dublin records, '1469 – This yeare the Earle of Desmond and his two sonnes were executed by ye Earle of Worcestre in

Drogheda.'[30] The year is wrong but this is the only contemporary source that says the two juveniles were sons of Desmond.

The sixteenth century *Book of Howth* had a pathetic description of the execution of the two boys at Drogheda.[31] The *Great Chronicle of London* said that Worcester 'put to deth ij sonys of therlys of desmund which were soo tendyr of age'.[32] In *The Mirror for Magistrates*, a sixteenth century poem written as an English continuation of John Lydgate's *The Fall of Princes*, Worcester's ghost acknowledged his greatest crime as the 'death of th'earle of Desmund's noble sonnes'.[33]

It seems unlikely that the two young men were legitimate sons of Desmond. If they were the sons of an earl they would be likely to have had names, as did the five other sons of Desmond—James, Maurice, Thomas, John and Gerald. If two of these five were executed, this would certainly have been recorded. If there were two other sons then, again, surely their names must have been known and Desmond would consequently have been described as having seven, rather than five, sons. Also, no matter how cruel the period, sons were not generally executed because of the sins of their fathers and the consequent rumpus would certainly have been much greater if that is what had taken place. Infamously, Lord Clifford killed the Earl of Rutland in 1460 after the Battle of Wakefield, asserting, 'your father killed my father and now I will kill you'. The point was that the event stood out as egregious and that the names were known. Also, this was not a calculated execution but a killing soon after the heat of battle.

What then was the relationship between Desmond and the two boys? In Ireland kinship was complex and not necessarily based on blood—indeed adopted children could be closer than natural offspring. One possibility might be that Desmond, as Deputy Lord Lieutenant, had taken the boys as part of an agreement deemed treasonable with a native ruler and treated them as foster sons.[34]

Fosterage was the practice whereby a child was sent to be reared and educated in the home and with the family of another member of the tribe, who then became foster-father, and his children the foster-brothers and foster-sisters of the child. The fosterage relationship was regarded as something sacred. The foster-children were often more attached to the foster-parents and foster-brothers than to the members of their own family. After the Anglo-Norman invasion the English of all ranks often fostered their children with the Irish. Fosterage was denounced by those anxious to keep separate the two races, and the government passed laws forbidding such relationships under the penalty of treason. The 1367 Statutes of Kilkenny forbade marriage, concubinage and fosterage as high treason with death as the punishment.

The reported 'tendyr age' of the executed pair may have been based on a misunderstanding of Irish usage. A translation of the passage in the *Fragment of Irish Annals* described the flogged Edward Plunket as a 'youth' which shows that this meant someone born a son of a particular group and not literally a child.[35] Edward Plunket was the Seneschal of Meath and clearly not a boy.

Thus the juveniles might have been high-born hostages, fostered as sons, who had been exchanged as part of an agreement made by Desmond with Irish lords and brought up in his household. Once Desmond was attainted their lives were deemed forfeit on the basis that the alliance was treasonable. Such an analysis fits well with Campion's report that Desmond's criticism of the royal marriage 'Caused his trade of life, (after the Irish manner, contrary to sundry old statutes enacted in that behalfe) to be sifted & examined by Iohn Earle of Worcester his successour'.[36]

In what seems part of the demonisation of Worcester—and, therefore of note in the context of his reputation for cruelty—there were two later lurid accounts of the execution of the sons, the younger of whom asked the executioner to be considerate of the boil on his neck. The *Great Chronicle of London* recounted, 'Thys man as above is said was ffamyd Crwell & mercylees ffor soo much as he put to deth ij sonys of therlys of desmund which were soo tendyr of age, that oon of theym having a Byle or sore In his neck said unto the executioner whan he shuld smyte off/his hede, Gentyll Godffadyr beward of the sore in my neck.'[37] The *Book of Howth* has the same story with even more pitiful speeches.[38] Worcester's killings perhaps reinforced the demonology of the Yorkists as murderers of pairs of young brothers.

Then there is the story of the page Baggott who was executed after Desmond by Worcester, who was infuriated by the youth's loud treasonous lamentations following the execution of his master.[39] This story, which sounds highly implausible, perhaps demonstrates how developed was the process of turning the Earl of Worcester into a pantomime villain. It does, however, contain a passage that might throw some light on events.

> But soone after this, the King, being truely informed of all this vnexpected vpror of almost the whole realme, commanded Tiptoft for England, and examined the matter. Tiptoft then, producing his commission for the Earles death under the Kings privys seale, cleared himselfe of that; but the King, more narrowlye pryeing into the business, and being greiued for the Earle's death, brough Tiptoft vpon the stage for killing the page, which he did without any commission; wherevpon Tiptoft was condemned that his head should be cut off, which was accordingly done.[40]

While discounting the story of the Queen's forged letter it is possible that, while Worcester was able to establish, at his own trial, when many charges were flung at him, that the execution of Desmond was legal—because it followed from the attainder by the Irish Parliament—he may have been less able to do so in the case of juveniles beheaded at the same time. In the popular record the tradition then developed that he was executed for his cruelty to the two young males.

Desmond was executed probably not just because of one but a perfect storm of factors. He had too many enemies among the Anglo-Irish powerful in Parliament. He had imposed coyne and livery on the four English counties. He had failed to defend them against incursions, particularly in Meath. His kinship relationships and transactions with the Irish were possibly technically treasonable under the Statutes of Kilkenny. Worcester might have heard reports of unflattering comments made by Desmond about the royal marriage which—given his close relationship with the King and possibly the Queen—he found particularly offensive. This caused him, as Campion wrote, to analyse Desmond's own relationships and he found they breached the Statutes of Kilkenny.

It is possible that the Commons in Parliament acted on their own initiative in passing the act of attainder on not only Desmond but also Kildare and Plunket. The focus of the demand for revenge was likely Bishop Sherwood of Meath, which county had born the brunt of Irish attacks. Sherwood had a personal vendetta against Desmond and a record of quite mind-boggling misrepresentation.

When Desmond unwisely came to Drogheda to defend himself, almost immediately two juveniles in his retinue may have been executed—possibly as the consequence of breaches the Statutes of Kilkenny which would usually have been passed over. Worcester then had to determine actual punishment for Desmond, Kildare and Plunket after they were attainted. The latter two he spared, although Plunket—the Seneschal of Meath, which county he had manifestly failed in his duty to protect—was flogged. He chose death for Desmond probably because he believed there was a strong case against him and he could not afford to appear weak before the Anglo-Irish whose support he needed. Experience, anyway, in England had shown the effectiveness of executing earls in the reigns of Henry IV, Henry V and Edward IV. Further, on a personal basis, he may have resented insults to the royal marriage—and, being recently remarried himself after fifteen years, he did not want to see another marriage end in tragedy against the backdrop of constant unrest, which he was thus determined to stamp out at once.

These are conjectures but the key point is that Desmond's death almost certainly had not just one but multiple causes. Now, having sowed the storm, Worcester would reap the whirlwind as the Irish rose up in revolt.

Chapter 21

Campaigner – 1468

Wher as Taig O'Connor and others of his fellowship beying with the said Gerot in the felde were lyke and at the poynte to be [surrounded by] your saide depute lieutenant … but halle be it thei were favourrably rescued. the saide Erle of Kildare and tresuourer then being present with the saide Gerot in the felde. … Neverthelasse your saide depute lieutenant folowed with his retenue unto the tyme he putte him to rebuke.[1]

> Letter to Edward IV from the Anglo-Irish
> calling on him to support the embattled Deputy Lieutenant.

The execution of Desmond provoked a bitter but inchoate response as the Geraldines were divided and the Irish, while attacking the English, continued their local feuds with similar enthusiasm. Notwithstanding, for the first time in his life—as far as is known—the Earl of Worcester went campaigning when there was actual fighting. The military operations of 1468 are generally overlooked in the context of wars in Ireland but if the evidence is sifted this was not an insignificant episode. The Earl clearly intended to play an active role in suppressing rebellion and in the process greatly increased his powers and capacity for independent action. The Irish Parliament now made him Seneschal of Meath, where the attainted Edward Plunkett had proved ineffective.[2] The Lieutenant was granted by Parliament the power to charge and discharge the Lords and Commons of Ireland.[3] Later the Deputy Lieutenant was empowered to authorise the Chancellor to adjourn and prorogue Parliament.[4]

After the execution of Desmond, the Treasurer, Sir Roland FitzEustace, Baron Portlester, was arraigned before Worcester by one Sir John Gilbert for having incited Desmond to try to assume the kingship of Ireland. FitzEustace denied the charge and demanded trial by combat. Gilbert was required to provide evidence by Worcester but could not and fled to join the rebellious Taig O'Connor of Offaly. Gilbert was attainted by Parliament which acquitted FitzEustace, whose daughter was married to Kildare. FitzEustace, however, deemed it wise to flee Dublin, having sprung his son-in-law Kildare from prison. They then joined Gerald FitzGerald, the executed Earl of Desmond's rebel brother.[5] Thus Worcester faced two sets of rebels: on one hand Taig with Gilbert; and on the other Gerald FitzGerald with Kildare and Portlester. Taig, joined by Kavanagh, King of Leinster, took the opportunity to raid long-suffering Meath.[6]

Map 7: 1467–70 – Irish campaigns.

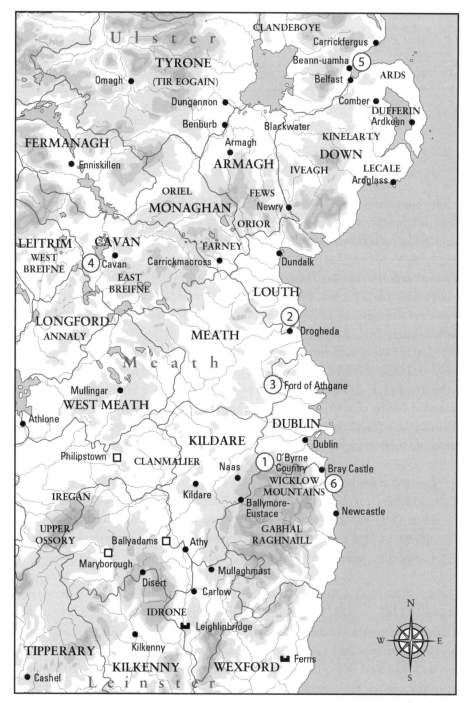

(Continued)

(Continued)

1.	O'Byrne country	1467, October	Worcester leads men of Dublin
2.	Drogheda	1468, February	Desmond attainted and executed
3.	Ford of Athgane, Meath	1468	Worcester puts Gerald FitzGerald, Kildare and FitzEustace to 'rebuke'
4.	Cavan	1468	Worcester invades Offaly and burns Cavan
5.	Beann–uamha	1468, June	Con O'Neil of Ulster defeats and kills the Seneschal of Ulster, James Savage
6.	O'Byrne country	1469	Worcester retakes Bray castle and repels counter-attack

The Geraldine reaction was violent but divided from the onset. The executed Thomas's brother Gerald and oldest son James rose in revolt not just against the English but each other. Gerald wanted the earldom of Desmond for himself and claimed that the late Thomas's sons were bastards.

Meath was the focus of the raids as its bishop, William Sherwood, was considered to have played a key role in causing Desmond's death. The most coherent source for the fighting in 1468 is a long letter from the Anglo-Irish begging for more support from Edward IV for their Deputy Lieutenant, Worcester, whom they clearly held in high regard. 'Gerot [Gerald] of Dessemond accompanyed unto him your Irishe enemyes called Galloglaghes [mercenaries of Norse-Gaelic origin] to the nombre of 2,000 and horsmen to the nombre of 2,400 … came in to your counte of Mithe and ther your owen propre landes beyng in the marche spoyled and rubbed, and diverse of your townes … wasted and destrued.'[7] Worcester wasted no time in giving chase.

> The right mightie and oure full good and gracieux lord John Erie of Worcestre … arredied him with all celerite possible to have mette and resist the saide Gerot. And when he undrestode your saide depute lieutenaunt comyng to your town of Trym, he withdrewe him and his host to a place within your counte of Mithe called the forde of Athgane.[8]

The site of the Ford of Athgane was clearly a strategic point as, in the parliamentary session of 1467 to 1468, a law was passed providing for the 'King to have an acre of land adjoining the Ford of Athgane to build a castle for defence'.[9] Unfortunately there is no other record of this 'rebuke', so it is unclear if it was in the nature of a skirmish, followed by a quick retreat, or a battle. Remarkably, despite all the fighting of the period, this unnamed clash is the only time the Earl of Worcester was recorded by name as present in some show of arms on open ground.

FitzEustace and Kildare then abandoned the Geraldine cause. 'After whos departire [Gerald, following 'rebuke' by the Earl of Worcester] the saide Erie of Kildare and Tresourer [Portlester] offred to submitte them to your saide depute lieutenaunt.'[10] Kildare was later pardoned by Edward IV and the Irish Parliament removed his personal attainder, subject to his bringing Leinster back to peace. Gerald of Desmond, however, remained unreconciled and obdurate, perhaps determined to assert his right of succession to his brother's earldom rather than avenge his death.

Dublin City recorded that Worcester took the fight to Offaly in May 1468. 'Memorandum : Business was not transacted in the assembly on the fourth Friday [15 May] after Easter [19 April, 1468] because the Mayor, Bailiffs and Commons of the City were engaged in a hostile incursion upon O'Connor's country, under the command of John Tiptoft, Earl of Worcester.'[11] Conn O'Connor Faly, Lord of Offaly was captured and imprisoned at Worcester's request by Edmund Butler, 8th Baron of Dunboyne, Seneschal of Tipperary. Thus the capture of the late Earl of Desmond in 1466 was avenged. O'Connor's brother Taig continued to resist, earning himself the epithet 'defender of Offaly'.

Worcester also campaigned in Ulster, and in Cavan both the friary and the nearby O'Reilly castle were burnt. The Irish annalists noted the event, so clearly it had an impact. 'O'Reilly's mansion-seat and the monastery of Cavan were burned by the English and the Saxon by whom the Earl of Desmond had been beheaded.'[12] Burning was not something usually done in England. Cavan was, however, perhaps inured to it in the fifteenth century. In 1429 the friary, along with the town, had been burnt by the English of the Pale. In 1452 the friary was again immolated by an inebriated monk, one *Ua Mothláin*, who took a candle to his bedchamber and burnt the whole monastery down.

Elsewhere in Ulster there was a disaster. Its Seneschal James Savage rode into Con O'Neill's country in the north-east and was slain. The Irish proclaimed that 'a great victory was gained by Con'.[13] English sources denounced duplicity but did not deny disaster. 'The said James and othre your subiectes … were distrussed and slayne by the saide Con, to the uttermost perdicion of your said counte of Ulster.'[14] The battle appears to have taken place near to modern Belfast and close to the Carrickfergus castle.

In an effort to placate James FitzGerald, son of the executed Thomas, he was recognised as successor to his father on the 31st of August, possibly to under-mine Gerald, who may have seemed the more dangerous. In fact, James proved obdurate and refused to reconcile with the English. Gerald was attainted for treason in October. On the 9th of December Worcester issued a general com-mission to James and Edmund Butler to negotiate a peace or truce with Irish enemies, English rebels and outlaws.[15] James's mother Elys was able to acquire sufficient support in Munster for her son against Gerald FitzGerald, and finally James's title as Earl of Desmond was secured at Cork with the consent of laymen and clergy.

Perhaps by executing Desmond Worcester had created for himself a bed of thorns but he dealt with the situation as best he could without help from Edward. The English of Ireland had appealed to Edward IV to support his Deputy Lieutenant.

> Wherfor considering the smalle nombre of your trewe subiectes that rest-
> eth with your saide depute lieutenaunt in comparison to the grete nom-
> bre of your Irish enemyes and Englishe rebelx, ... and the grete labor
> costes and expenses that your saide depute lieutenaunt so outrageouse
> and intolerable withstanding your saide enemiez, to provide and sende
> unto him souldiars and goode withall, with whiche your saide lande may
> be conserved and your subiectes therof defendet. And without that our
> saide goode lorde your depute lieutenaunt be assured therof in all hast
> possible we can not undrestande howe your saide lande may be conserved
> and defendet. [16]

Worcester did not receive the requested support from the King.

There was no more fighting recorded involving Worcester during the remain-der of his governorship except in 1469 when the O'Byrnes—who after Worcester's show of strength in 1467 had been quiet throughout the following year—took Bray Castle, which in turn Worcester besieged and retook, only to find himself having to repel a counter-siege.[17]

Worcester did not just campaign. Various records in the Irish rolls of parliament indicate a systematic effort to improve the state of defences around the four English counties, particularly the much-ravaged Meath. More effective arrangements were agreed for the castles of Cloncorry, Ataghtyn, Coransford, Ballivor and Ballycor, while the building of a tower at the Ford of Athgane was to be undertaken. Kells was authorised in 1468 to finance the strengthening of its walls.[18] In 1467, a statute had provided for the construction by Worcester of a fortress on Lambay Island for protection against the Spaniards, French and Scots who plundered Ireland's coast and sold arms to the O'Byrnes, whose equipment had improved notably in the 1460s. It is not certain that it was actually built.

The Earl of Worcester had to meet much of the cost of imposing order on Ireland out of his own pocket. During the greater part of this period, Ireland was left to itself as far as the English treasury was concerned. Wages were sent for Worcester's men in 1469 but Edward owed the Earl £4,535 by 1470.[19]

At the time the warfare in Ireland was recognised as significant. In commemoration of Drogheda's signal service to the state King Edward gave, on 12 July 1468, to the Corporation of Drogheda a sword, to be carried before the Mayor, 'for their good services *in wars in Ire.* in the company of the K.'s kinsman John, e. Worcester'.[20]

The campaigns of 1468 are generally treated as a postscript to the events surrounding the execution of the Earl of Desmond. They were, however, substantial operations and, through a combination of fighting and diplomacy, the Earl of Worcester survived the 'wars in Ireland' without support from England. The overall scorecard is quite impressive: the Earl had put to rebuke the invasion of Meath led by Gerald FitzGerald, the brother of Desmond; he campaigned in Offaly (Leinster) and captured its ruler Conn O'Conner Faly and burned Cavan (Ulster); he led a show of strength in O'Byrne country in 1467, which was quiet in 1468, and recaptured Bray Castle there in 1469; and he fortified the borders of Meath and possibly the Island of Lambay. He reconciled with Kildare, the Butlers and generally the Lancastrians. North-east Ulster was, however, lost. James FitzGerald, 8th Earl of Desmond, was unreconciled but neutralised by intra-Geraldine fighting. The country proved the graveyard of the military reputations of Richard II and Robert Devereux, 2nd Earl of Essex, in the late fourteenth and sixteenth centuries respectively. The Earl of Worcester had at least managed rather better than these.

With the exception in 1469 of limited campaigning in O'Byrne country there appears to have been peace between the English and Irish between mid-1468 and the end of 1469 when the Earl of Worcester returned to England. Therefore, some perspective should be brought to Worcester's time in Ireland. He was there for more than two years, from October 1467 to at least late 1469. Violence against his regime was largely confined to the three months from March to May 1468. After that, while the Irish fought among themselves, they appear largely to have left the English alone. This was a considerable improvement over the period when Desmond was Deputy Lieutenant.

Chapter 22

Legislator, coinage reformer, departure – 1468–1469/70

Admissions to Dublin franchise: by special grace: John, Earl of Worcester.[1]

Worcester was accorded this honour in 1469

Historians of Worcester's period in Ireland focus on the execution of Desmond and the enigma of the execution of two juvenile males. In fact, these executions and the subsequent rebellion account for only about a tenth of the period the Earl was there. Parliament was in session for much of this time and passed a great deal of legislation and there was also a major coinage reform.

On arrival in September or October 1467 Worcester promptly called the Irish Parliament. This was in session from the 11th of December 1467 to the 15th of November 1468 at Dublin and Drogheda; and after the 27th of January 1469 at Drogheda, Dublin, Bray and then Dublin again. This was a major parliament during which 84 Acts were passed. 'Tiptoft's Drogheda parliament ... anticipated the more famous and lasting one of Poyning's Parliament of Drogheda in 1494–5.'[2] Unusually, there was no specific anti-Irish general legislation.

The Earl of Worcester oversaw the strengthening of the independence of the Irish Parliament, giving the Lieutenant the power to charge and discharge the Lords and Commons and the Deputy to adjourn and prorogue Parliament. This followed legislation of 1460 which stated, 'Henceforth, no person or persons being in the said land of Ireland shall be, by any command given or made under any other seal than the said seal of the said land, compelled to answer to any appeal or any other matter out of the said land.'[3] Thus by 1468 Ireland, developing considerable autonomy from Westminster and Worcester, acting through its Parliament, potentially had real independence.

Worcester was an expert on coinage. Twice already he had been Treasurer in England and sat on a committee in 1455 appointed in the Parliament after the Battle of St Albans to look at the problem of bullion, the shortage of which was a major cause of the mid-fifteenth century Great Slump. Given his financial expertise and subsequent reforms in Ireland, it seems probable that he played a part in the English currency reform associated with Hastings in the 1460s. Maintaining a satisfactory coinage was a chronic problem everywhere.

In Ireland, if the currency had a gold content the same or similar to that in England then coins left the country to the detriment of trade. One solution was to have coins in Ireland of similar size but slightly lower precious metal content than in England – which would, in theory, discourage exporting the coinage to England. This, however, had the adverse consequence of inflation in Ireland, which was also detrimental to trade. In 1465 Edward IV approved Irish coins that were very similar in design to, but with lower precious metal content than, English coins. English merchants petitioned the King to make the Irish coins more distinctive or of metal parity, and Irish merchants were unhappy as coins still left for England.

The Earl of Worcester's solution was to introduce a new coinage which had both a sharply lower precious metal content and a very dramatic design.[4] A profit was intended on the new coinage—as the face value was reduced by less than the precious metal content—that would contribute to the cost of his Irish operations.

The image was intended to be so distinctive that no confusion between English and Irish coinage was possible. The obverse had the head of Edward. The reverse showed a sun with twenty-four rays and a rose at its centre. This was Worcester's tribute to the still young King whose symbol was the sun-in-splendour, following the *parhelion*, or triple sun, seen before the Battle of Mortimer's Cross. The use of earlier coins was made illegal and their owners were obliged to surrender them for reminting. As they faced taking a loss on their old coins, many exported them before the reminting could be enforced on them, thus exacerbating the already inadequate volume of coinage. The new debased but beautiful coinage succeeded in the aim of discouraging export of the new coins; unfortunately, it also,

Figure 9: The Earl of Worcester's beautiful but debased coinage – the double groat.

predictably, was inflationary. This led to futile efforts by Parliament to fix prices and complaints that trade was suffering further.

The order of events is uncertain but Edward IV eventually ordered the Irish coinage to revert to the English standard. The episode shows the Earl of Worcester in a human and fallible light. He attempted a radical and beautiful solution—which also revealed his devotion to the King—that failed.

It is not clear when the Earl of Worcester left Ireland or precisely why. The last known date he was there was the 15th of November 1469 when one Thomas Talbot was released from future service on the basis of the good service he had done in the past.[5] Worcester was possibly recalled to England as a result of, or in order to attend, a Great Council meeting in England in November, which attempted to reconcile King Edward to Clarence, his rebellious brother, and to Warwick. The Council decided on shows of reconciliation at the Christmas and Epiphany feasts when Clarence and Warwick were received back into the King's peace. In his place in Ireland the Earl left his former brother-in-law Sir Edmund Sutton. The Earl must have hoped to return to Ireland for, according to a letter from George Neville to Oxford after his execution, he left much of his valued library in Ireland.

Reviewing his overall record the Earl showed he was capable of learning. He had become a competent independent campaigner. Also—having made himself unpopular in England with the City of London—in Ireland he was respected by Dubliners. The City records twice report how the city folk decamped to follow him on forays against the Irish. The first occasion was in 1467 to O'Byrne country, the second in 1468 to O'Connor's country. The petition sent to Edward IV on 28 June spoke of the Earl in very supportive language. In 1469 the Earl was admitted to the franchise of Dublin. Admission conferred a coveted status, since free citizens enjoyed important trading privileges and the right to vote in municipal elections.

That said, the Earl does not sound a lenient ruler—although, given the general disorder, severity was probably recognised overall as no bad thing. For example, the Rolls of the Irish Parliament record that Prior Keating of the Hospital of St John of Jerusalem, an ally of the Earl of Kildare, was imprisoned in 1468 and had to pay a fine of £40.[6] Richard Verdon of County Louth had held his land exempt from subsidy, 'until now lately in the time of the Earl of Worcester, who by the rigour of his lordship, caused the said Richard to pay the subsidy for his said demesne contrary to the usage of the country'.[7] One Thomas Hammond, when ordered to show Parliament his title and rights to his lands, 'dared not appear for fear of his life from the Earl of Worcester'.[8] The Archbishop of Dublin was later restored to his right in Lambay Island after the Earl of Worcester 'took to farm the said island for the term of 59 years, against the will and consent of the said

Archbishop, paying thereout yearly 40 shillings'.[9] Yet, despite Worcester's butcherly reputation, in Ireland there was no record of the atrocities that often marked English repression there—unless the executions of the Earl of Desmond and the two juveniles are seen in this light.

The Earl left London en route to Ireland in 1467 a bachelor, gained a wife in Shropshire, and in Ireland on the 14th of July 1469 a son.[10] Not surprisingly, the infant was called Edward and the King sent an extremely expensive gold cup as a present. This birth may have caused consternation in the Neville household. Much of the status of John Neville—the younger son who remained loyal throughout 1469 when his brother Richard Earl of Warwick turned traitor—depended on his tenure of the title of Earl of Northumberland taken from the Percys and perhaps the expectation that his wife Isabel would receive from her mother, Joanna *née* Tiptoft, a third of the Earl of Worcester's estate.

Appraisal of Worcester's period in Ireland can be unbalanced by focussing too much on the execution of the Earl of Desmond and the juveniles and the subsequent revolt. He remained in Ireland for well over a year after the revolts and was not recalled from Ireland because he was failing, but because the King was losing control in England. As in 1461, when in Italy, again in late 1469 or early 1470 the Earl was summoned back from an overseas environment, now Ireland, he found more congenial than England by Edward IV to secure his shaky hold on the throne.

Within months of his return Worcester would be the most powerful man in England, on whom the King appeared wholly reliant. The independent command in Ireland unleashed the full force of his personality and power eventually went to his head. His perceptive and generally sympathetic Italian biographer Bisticci wrote, 'None the less there are men of great state who do not know, in acquiring power to govern, how to govern such power without becoming overweaning—thus it happened to this nobleman.'

Part 5

TRIUMPH AND TRAGEDY – 1470

Chapter 23

The Lincolnshire campaign

6 March, Edward IV, Robert Bishop of Bath and Wells, the Chancellor, in a certain small chapel near the inner chamber of the King near the 'Wyndyngsteyre' in Westminster palace, delivered into the King's hands the Great Seal, ..., in presence of ... John Earl of Worcester, William Hastynges ...

7 March, at Abbot's Waltham he had the seal opened in his presence ... and the seal was again enclosed in the bag, and sealed with the privy seal in presence of ... John Earl of Worcester, William Hastynges ...

10 May: on which day the King, in a small chamber next the garden of the palace of the Bishop of Salisbury at New Sarum in presence of John Earl of Worcester [and] William Hastynges.[1]

> The Close Rolls recording those with the
> King at the beginning and the end of the Lincolnshire campaign

The pen is mightier than the sword. In 1470 was fought an unsung yet extraordinary military operation known as the Lincolnshire Campaign. The rebels were defeated without a great defining battle. Instead this was a profoundly intellectual exercise contested at a distance, where the main weapon of the royal party was letters—used to gather an overwhelming force, cut the rebels off from both support and refuge, and spread the word of the King's vast forces, probably exaggerated. This resulted in the rebels being run ragged the length and breadth of the kingdom. The campaign was also marked by the use of terror: executions not only as punishment but also to strike fear. The Close Rolls record only two men as being always with the King at the campaign's beginning and its end, the Constable of England, the Earl of Worcester, and the Chamberlain William Hastings.

England's humanists and scholars showed their mettle. Also described as being with the King during the campaign were the King's secretary, William Atteclyff, and his Treasurer, William Grey, Bishop of Ely. These two and Worcester had been at university in England and Padua and Grey and the Earl had studied under Guarino de Verona. Foreigners had little doubt it was the Earl who was calling the shots in 1470. Later that year the Milan State Papers called him 'the Grand Constable of England [who] had command and control of King Edward's forces'.[2]

The biographer Bisticci wrote that he had 'All the King's treasure in his hands and there were few matters of the Kingdom that did not pass through his hands'.[3] Prior Stone of Canterbury called him '*dominus comes de Worsetyr mariscallus Anglie*', or the Lord Earl of Worcester the Marshal of England.[4]

By 1469, after stirring things up in Ireland, Worcester had largely restored order. In England, however, the King had lost control and several of his in-laws and closest supporters had lost their heads. Warwick—already resentful over Edward's choice of wife—saw ambitions for his daughters, Isabel and Anne, to marry the King's brothers, George Duke of Clarence and Richard Duke of Gloucester, thwarted. Clarence, against royal wishes, married Warwick's daughter Isabel in July 1469. A rising led by one so-called Robin of Redesdale, a Neville proxy, was joined by Warwick and Clarence. The Earl of Pembroke and Edward's forces were defeated at the Battle of Edgecote Moor. Beheadings followed with Pembroke, William Herbert, brother Richard (27–28 July) and Earl Rivers and his second son John (12 August) adding to the Nevilles' wretched record of illegal executions.

The deaths of the Queen's father and brother must have poisoned completely the relationship between the Nevilles and the surviving Woodvilles. Also, Pembroke had had charge of Henry Percy, who was, in both his and much of the north's eyes, the rightful heir to the earldom of Northumberland. He had been well treated by Worcester after his father's death, fighting as a Lancastrian at Towton in 1461. Percy was married to Pembroke's daughter, Maud, and the execution of his father-in-law might have helped fix his loyalty to Edward's Yorkist cause.

Edward, who was not present at Edgecote, suffered the indignity of being captured subsequently by George Neville, Archbishop of York, ostensibly a man of God. But without broad support the Nevilles were unable to hold him, leading to compromise and *faux* ceremonies of reconciliation. The thoughts of Queen Elizabeth *née* Woodville and Maud Percy *née* Herbert, who both saw fathers and other close relations illegally executed, were unlikely to have been forgiving. 1469 had not been Edward's finest hour and late that year or early in 1470 he must, probably egged on by the Queen, have recalled from Ireland the one man he could really trust and whose absence meant he was not compromised by recent failures. Worcester may have left England in 1467 to avoid having to choose between Edward IV and the Nevilles. But, the matter having been determined by his recall, his loyalty to Edward was total.

On the 27th of October 1469 Henry Percy had sworn fealty to Edward IV and was released. He petitioned for the return of his paternal titles and estates. By 1470, as Percy turned 21, the issue of whether to restore him to the earldom of Northumberland had become pressing. Having resolved to remove the title from

John Neville and to give it to Percy, the question became how to do it without alienating the one Neville brother who remained loyal.

It seems likely that a plan was conceived, with the genuine intention of treating John well and softening the blow: first, his son was made a duke betrothed to the King's daughter Elizabeth; second, he was given the property of the Earl of Devon; and third, he was elevated to the title of marquis.[5] Waurin considered John Neville—'*ouquel le roy avoit donné grant terre and seignourie*', or to whom the King had given great lands and lordship—well treated.[6] John's loyalty was perhaps misunderstood: it was not really to the King or his brothers, it was to whoever secured for him the one thing he really cared for, and that was the northern title of Earl of Northumberland.

On the 5th of January 1470 George Neville, John and Isabel's son, was created Duke of Bedford. This was a remarkable elevation. The last Bedford was the warrior brother of Henry V. George was also betrothed to Edward's daughter Elizabeth. Now Worcester's sister Joanna was a duke's grandmother. Paradoxically, the elevation of the child George to a dukedom may have exaggerated John Neville's problem, as it made much more stark the inadequacy of his estate income to sustain the title. The birth of Edward Tiptoft in 1469 meant Worcester's line could survive as long as he or any other Tiptoft heirs did. Now it appeared Worcester's estate would not be divided among his sisters. Isabel Neville, the daughter of Joanna Ingaldisthorpe *née* Tiptoft, stood to lose a third share of a considerable inheritance if the infant Tiptoft came into his father's property.

The New Year of 1470 started with trouble in Lincolnshire. Early in January Lord Welles and his brother-in-law, Sir Thomas de la Lande, raided the manor of Sir Thomas Burgh, Edward's Master of the Horse. Rumours soon circulated of a conspiracy between Warwick and the King's brother, the Duke of Clarence.

This year Edward and his advisers acted much more decisively. On the 8th of February there were issued commissions of array for the eastern and south-eastern counties.[7] On the 2nd of March there was a commission for Yorkshire in which John Neville was the first mentioned.[8] The next day Edward IV announced that he was going to muster an army on the 12th of March at Grantham, in Lincolnshire. He wrote to Coventry, 'telling them to have persones hable and of power wel and defensibly arayd to labour in our servise'.[9] The King proclaimed a general pardon for all offences committed before Christmas. He ordered Lord Welles and his brother-in-law, Sir Thomas Dymoke, to appear before him, which they did and, reaffirming their loyalty, received a royal pardon. In Lincolnshire rioting continued and there were calls for the restoration of Henry VI. By the end of February Warwick had left London, having promised to support Edward IV.

On the 27th of February John Neville was given most of the estates of the Earls of Devon.[10] Three days later Sir Robert Welles, the son of Lord Welles, published a summons in Warwick's name in Lincolnshire churches to muster at Ranby Howe two days later, to resist Edward who would come to destroy them. On the 6th of March Edward heard of Sir Robert Welles' summons to Ranby and was determined to go in person to Lincolnshire. Clarence wrote to Edward to say he was going to join Warwick and help suppress the unrest in Lincolnshire. Edward ordered Lord Welles and Dymoke to join him en route northward.

The next day Edward signed letters, with the secular nobles present being Worcester and William Hastings, at Abbot's Waltham, north of London.[11] These included the commissions sent to Warwick and Clarence.[12] Thus the King demonstrated he was treating them as trustworthy (the previous year they justified their rebellion on the basis of their unworthy treatment).[13] On the 9th of March the royal party was at Huntingdon, where the King told Lord Welles and Dymoke that unless they convinced Welles's son Robert to call off the revolt they would face execution, as their pardons applied only until Christmas.

At Stamford on the 12th of March the King was informed that Sir Robert Welles was unexpectedly at nearby Empingham, five miles west of Stamford, and intending to rescue his father. The unexpected battle there was known as Losecoat Field, following the discarding of weapons and jackets by the enemy.

Before the battle Lord Welles and Dymoke were beheaded between the armies. The deaths seem harsh. Their executions were in advance of the finding of evidence of conspiracy involving Warwick and Clarence on the bodies of the slain. Also, they had obeyed the summons to join Edward. It was acceptable legally to execute leaders captured in the heat of battle or retreat. Here, however, the executed men were voluntarily prisoners before a battle that might or might not happen. Those advising the King thought it wrong that the King should risk his life while those whose treason put him in this dangerous position should live. 'Wherefore his highnesse in the felde undre his banere displaied comaunded the said lorde Welles and sir Thomas Dymmoke to be executed.'[14] Thus under the law of arms, banners being displayed, the King directly ordered their execution.

Whether the beheadings can be added to the charge sheet against Worcester is uncertain—due to the absence of evidence as to his movements since the 7th of March—but it does seem possible he was present, although not yet officially in the role of Constable. The King had not planned to fight that day, as he had not expected Sir Robert to be so close. Therefore, these executions were not premeditated. Rather, they sound like the aggressive but improvised action of men determined to retain the initiative lost last year and to make absolutely clear their ruthless determination.

Robert Welles attacked, goaded by the sight of the beheading of his father, before joining up with Warwick's and Clarence's forces. There was not much of a battle

Map 8: 1470 – Lincolnshire campaign.

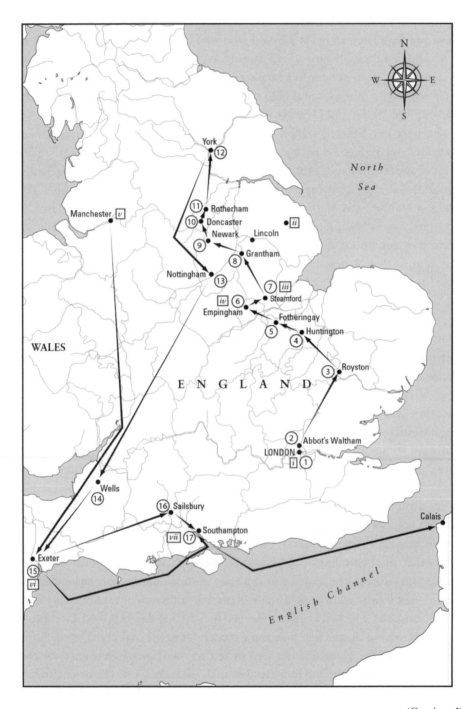

(Continued)

(Continued)

i	*London*	*February, end*	*Warwick leaves London*
ii	*Ranby Hove*	*March, 4*	*Sir Robert Welles publishes rebel summons in Warwick's name to Ranby Hove*
1	London	March, 6	Worcester among witnesses of delivery of the great seal to Edward IV
2	Abbot's Waltham	March, 7	Worcester witnesses Edward IV use great seal
3	Royston	March, 8	Edward receives news rebels are approaching Stamford and letter from Warwick and Clarence saying they are coming to his aid
iii	*Stamford*	*March, 8*	*Rebels approaching the King's position*
4	Huntington	March, 9	Edward tells Lord Welles to order his son Robert Welles to submit
5	Fotheringay	March, 10–11	Edward informed rebels heading to meet Warwick in Coventry
iv, 6	*Empingham*	*March, 12*	*Executes Lord Welles and Thomas Dymoke, defeats Robert Welles who is captured*
7	Stamford	March, 13	Edward writes to Clarence and Warwick informing them of victory
8	Grantham	March, 14–15	Appoints Worcester Constable for life, Robert Welles admits conspiracy with Clarence and Warwick, de la Lande and Neille executed
9.	Newark	March, 16	Further correspondence with Clarence and Warwick
10.	Doncaster	March, 19–20	Welles and Richard Warin executed, Edward musters a great force
11.	Rotherham	March, 21	Edward hears Clarence and Warwick had fled from Chesterfield to Manchester
v,	*Manchester*	*March, 21*	*Clarence and Warwick at Manchester (previous movement not shown)*
12.	York	March, 22–27	Edward appoints the Earl of Worcester Lord Lieutenant of Ireland
13.	Nottingham	March, 29–31	Edward proclaims Clarence and Warwick traitors, writes to men of Salisbury instructing them to prepare to receive a host of 40,000
vi	*Exeter*	*April, 3–10*	*Warwick and Clarence reach Exeter and meet up with wives who arrived earlier*
14.	Wells	April, 11	Edward's forces arrive
15.	Exeter	April, 14–19	Edward's forces find Clarence and Warwick have fled for Calais
16.	Salisbury	May, 5	Worcester among witnesses of use of Great Seal by Edward IV
vii, 17.	*Southampton*	*May*	*Worcester condemns Warwick's men abandoned after his failed attempt en route to Calais to free his ship,* **The Trinity.** *The bodies' degradation causes revulsion*

since the royal guns caused the Lincolnshire men to flee in panic. Reportedly, Welles' men cried out, 'A Warwick! A Clarence!' Some men were found to be wearing Warwick's and Clarence's liveries. Letters were found in the abandoned helmet of a servant of Clarence revealing Welles' cooperation. Whether or not the conspiracy evidence was found or fabricated, it was systematically used to develop a convincing story of treason by Warwick and Clarence.

Robert Welles and Sir Thomas de la Lande, taken prisoner at the battle, gave evidence damning both Warwick and Clarence as instigators of a plot intended to dethrone the King and place the crown on his brother Clarence. The King's party now had hard evidence of the pair's treasonable intent. The rebels, however, were not aware this was known. This gave the King the upper hand and he could string the traitors along while strengthening his force and cutting off their support and their lines of escape.

The next day, the 13th of March, Edward was at Stamford. He wrote to Warwick and Clarence calling on them to disband their forces and come to him. They promised to obey. News came of risings in Yorkshire in support of Warwick and Clarence and the King instructed the still loyal John Neville to deal with the situation. Meanwhile, a revolt in Yorkshire collapsed on hearing of Losecoat Field—perhaps proving the psychological effectiveness of the pre-battle executions.

The next day at Grantham Edward, who 'was learning to cling more and more to the Earl of Worcester', formally reappointed him to the role of Constable of England.[15] Worcester was also made Lord Lieutenant of Ireland in place of Clarence. The last appointment was notable as this was a position that was granted only to those regarded as close royal family. The Earl was now Constable of England, joint Constable of the Tower and Lord Lieutenant of Ireland.[16]

On the 15th of March, 'there was [be]headed Sir Thomas de la Launde, and one John Neille [sic – Neille was not a Neville], a great Captain', doubtless supervised by the newly confirmed Constable of England, Worcester, in order to send brutal messages to those who supported traitors.[17] Sir Thomas had fought in the great tournament of 1467 against Philippe Bouton and had attracted the King's ire when accused of cheating.

While correspondence shuttled back and forth between Edward and the two rebel peers, pre-emptive action was taken to deal with the threat from the West Country. Commissions of array for Devon, Cornwall, Gloucestershire and five other counties were issued. The arrests were ordered of the Beauchamps, de Lisles, and the Courtenays in Devon. On the 19th of March at Doncaster Sir Robert Welles and Richard Warin, Captain of the Lincolnshire footmen, were executed before Edward's army. As news spread to Clarence's and Warwick's forces of the defeat at Losecoat Field, the subsequent executions and the promise that those who abandoned arms would be pardoned, the men abandoned their leaders. Most had followed them expecting to fight *against*, not for, the King's enemies.

At Doncaster the overwhelming strength of the forces gathered about the King was apparent. John Paston observed: 'The King took the field, and mustered his people; and it was said that there never was seen in England so many goodly men, and so well arrayed in a field.'[18] From the 22nd to the 27th of March Edward was in York, where he was joined by his brother Richard and John Neville.

On the 23rd of March the King ordered Edmund Sutton, Deputy Lieutenant, to Worcester—who was now Lord Lieutenant in place of Clarence in Ireland—to arrest Clarence and Warwick if they tried to flee to Ireland. The next day in York Clarence and Warwick were openly proclaimed traitors.[19] On the 25th of March Edward gave to Henry Percy the title of Earl of Northumberland. John Neville was made Marquis of Montagu.[20] Two days later Edward, Gloucester and Worcester left York with a great host in pursuit of the rebels. From Nottingham on the 29th of March Edward wrote to Salisbury instructing it, 'in nowise suffer our said rebels [Clarence and Warwick] and traitors to come or enter into our city of Salisbury. ... And beside this, we charge you ... [to provide for] the number of 40,000 men'.[21] An army of this size was huge by medieval standards and it is more likely that, while his force was substantial, the intention was to spread the belief that the King's force was of crushing magnitude.

Earlier, according to a mysterious entry in the cathedral escheator's accounts for 1469–70, Clarence's pregnant wife Isabel, the daughter of the Earl of Warwick, stopped at Wells, en route to Exeter. The accounts record, '10 shillings of gift of the most illustrious king Edward / 5 shillings of ... Duke Clarence / 5 shillings ... of lady Clarence / 5 shillings ... of Warwick'.[22] Either the escheator clumped together separate royal and noble donations or there was a clandestine meeting, perhaps in a last ditch effort to resolve differences. It was all rather curious.

On the 3rd of April Warwick and Clarence reached Exeter, rejoining the heavily pregnant Isabel. Shipping was organised to take them from Dartmouth to Calais. Warwick appears to have planned further opposition from the continent. He must have written to his followers Sir Geoffrey Gate and Sir Richard Clapham and possibly his brother-in-law, the Earl of Oxford. All would try to join him in France. Warwick wrote to Southampton from Exeter on the 7th of April urging the observance of what purported to be a royal safe-conduct granted to two alien merchants, possibly part of a plan to recover his great ship *The Trinity* which was anchored there.[23] Three days later Warwick set sail for Calais from Dartmouth.

The next day the royal army was in Wells and the *Chronicle of Exeter* recorded, 'The King prepareth all things in readiness to pursue and follow them [Warwick and Clarence] and came to this city the 14th April 1470 with 40,000 men but the birds were flown.'[24] He had with him 'all his nobility', namely, the Bishop of Ely, then Lord Treasurer, the Dukes of Norfolk and Suffolk, the Earls of Arundel, Wiltshire, Worcester, Constable of England, Shrewsbury, Ryvers, the Lords Hastings, Monteroye, Stanebury, Ferrys and Dudleigh.[25] That the size of the army was an astonishing 40,000 men had gained credence as either this was based on fact or the bluff had been successfully sold.

The royal party moved on to Salisbury for Easter week—the 22nd to the 29th of April. There, 'John Twynyho esquire of Somerset, to the King. Bond in 1,000 marks payable… Condition, that if the said John shall wait on the Earl of Worcester, Constable of England.'[26] On the 25th of April Edward issued a Commission to seize all castles and possessions of Clarence and Warwick and over fifty of their supporters. Edward, backed by a huge army, dominated England: the great Kingmaker had fled the country.

The Lincolnshire campaign has not attracted much interest as a military operation in its own right. There was no major land battle and, therefore, no obvious point of focus. Yet it saw possibly the largest army ever assembled on English soil in the Middle Ages—or, even more interesting, a convincing bluff was able to create the impression that such an army had been put together. Paston, as seen, commented not just on the size of the force but on its quality as well.[27] While it is clear that a very impressive force was assembled, given the short notice and the rapidity of movement during the chase it is unlikely that the army can have been 40,000 men. But this only adds lustre to the impressive strategy and organisation behind the campaign: either Edward and his Constable really did put together, on the move, a force that size or they convinced others that they had done so and that resistance was futile. Either feat is remarkable.

Overall, this was a campaign won by planning, letter-writing to cut off support and refuge pre-emptively, executions before armies to spread terror, and probably bluff over the size of the king's forces. At this time one man—the Earl of Worcester—was notable both as a man of letters and an executioner. In mitigation, it might be admitted that remarkably few people died during the campaign, a small number at Losecoat Field, and six leaders were executed, spread out over several days for maximum effect. But some particularly unpleasant executions were to follow.

Chapter 24

The Impaler of Southampton

And after this the Kynge Edwarde came to Southamptone, and commawnd-
ede the Erle of Worcetere to sitt and juge suche menne as were taken in the
schyppes, and so xx. persones of gentylmen and yomenne were hangede,
drawne, and quartered, and hedede; and after that thei hanged uppe by
the leggys, and a stake made scharpe at bothe endes, whereof one ende was
putt in att bottokys, and the other ende ther heddes were putt uppe one; for
whiche the peple of the londe were gretely displesyd; and evere afterwarde
the Erle of Worcestre was gretely behatede emonge the peple, for ther dysor-
dinate dethe that he used, contrarye to the lawe of the londe.[1]

Warkworth's description of the execution of
Warwick's men taken at Southampton

W arkworth's account of events at Southampton has stuck in the record
and done lasting damage to the Earl of Worcester's reputation. While
accepting that something very distasteful occurred the chronicler's
account sounds inherently improbable. Therefore, in order to try to understand what really happened, the sequence of events needs to be disentangled and
reconsidered.

Warwick had conceived of a bold plan to recover *The Trinity* from Southampton.
Warkworth reported: 'The Lorde Scales, the Quenes brother, was sent thedere by
the Kynges commawndement, and other withe hym, and faught with the seide
Duke and Erle, and toke there dyverse schyppes of theres and many of ther men
therein; so that the Duke and the Erle were fayne to flee.'[2] Warwick had set sail
from Dartmouth for Southampton by the 10th of April so his men must have been
captured a few days later. Quite separately, other of Warwick's men were captured
by John Howard more than a week later at Southampton. The *Chronicle of London*
reported: 'And in thester weke Sir Gefferey Gate and one [Richard] Clapham,
seruauntes of the said Erle of Warwyk, wer takyn at Hampton by the lord Howard
and his Company.'[3]

Hearne's *Fragment* reported that it was Worcester and John Howard who
apprehended Warwick's retainers. 'Sir Geoffrey Gate, Knight, with the 'foresaid
Clapham, had prepared at Southampton a company of their 'complices to have
passed into France, to those Lords of Clarence and Warwick; but their purpose

was soon disclosed. For the Earl of Worcester and the Lord Howard prevented them.'[4] According to Leland there was fighting. 'In Southampton Worcester was present at the trial of certain nobles, among whom Clapham, who had wounded in combat there men of the King's majesty.'[5] Another Leland document said, 'they were taken at the 'skirmouch of Southampton'.[6] This appeared an intelligence-led operation. If Warkworth was correct, then Edward IV got wind of the plan to recover *The Trinity* and had Scales challenge Warwick at sea. The purpose of Gate and Clapham, to go later to France with men, was also uncovered. In 1462 use of 'intelligence' had also thwarted the Oxford plot.

On the 1st of May King Edward granted property in Southampton, belonging to the Earl of Warwick by right of his wife, to Worcester in a move possibly calculated to reinforce the divide between the two earls.[7] Now Worcester was financially benefiting from Warwick's discomfort.

In early May there took place events which have done the most to ruin Worcester's reputation. There may indeed have been two separate trials, or two distinct parts to one trial, of Warwick's men, taken in Southampton: one for Clapham and Gate; the other for men captured separately in the sea fight. At the trial of Gate and Clapham, the former had his pardon and afterwards went to sanctuary: Clapham was beheaded.[8] The harsher punishment may have been as he had wounded members of the arresting party but the form of death, by beheading, was relatively merciful. The punishment reserved for those taken in the ships would indeed be singular and unforgettable (as quoted at the beginning of the chapter). Worcester almost certainly had no discretion as to the outcome, death, but maybe some as to its manner, as long as it was memorable.

In Warkworth's description the condemned men were hanged, drawn and quartered. This death could be protracted and very painful but it was respectably English. It was the impaling that followed death which offended decency. But in practice what happened, as described by Warkworth, was impossible. If the bodies had been quartered, they could not have been hung up by the legs and impaled. Since there was general consensus that there was some form of impalement, Warkworth's account must be wrong about the quartering and probably also about the disembowelling.

It is Warkworth who has generally been repeated in modern times. It is similar with Gregory's account of the precedence debacle at the feast of the sergeants of the coif, which was equally improbable. Leland, who was much more favourable to the Earl but still nuanced, said nothing of hanging, drawing and quartering and made clear impalement was *post mortem*. He did not describe the bodies as being suspended upside down, but he wrote, 'There is savagery to the guilty who after death, were thrust through with sharpened stakes upward from the rear, raised up into the winds, as an example of vice but a doleful [sight] and as the common people openly said cruel and unmerited. ... the Earl should ... have had the courage to be merciful ... I know this mark to have been later fatal to him.'[9]

In another document, *Collecteana*, Leland wrote in English that Edward 'Caused the Erle of Wicestre to sit yn Jugement of certen Gentilmen, taken at the Skirmouch of Southampton, wher the Erle causid the Bodyes of certen condemnid Men, after they wer hangid, to thruste thorough the Fundament up to the Hed with Stakes. For the which Cruelte he fel yn Indignation of the Common People.'[10]

Stowe followed Warkworth in describing the bodies as being suspended inverted but said nothing of the drawing (disembowelling) and quartering (he placed drawing before hanging where this meant being dragged behind a horse to the place of execution). Stowe wrote of the condemned that 'After hanged up the legs of a Gallows, ... and then having stakes put in their fundaments, their heads were set on those stakes, (an horrible spectacle).'[11]

The King and his advisers had resolved to make an unforgettable example of Warwick's followers. Was this simply sadism or was there some rational if harsh explanation? During the Wars of the Roses it was usual to execute the leaders but not the led. The attempt to take Warwick's ship *The Trinity*, was, however, egregious for two reasons. The first was that it was an act of piracy: in the period this could be treated very harshly and a whole ship's complement executed (for example, at Hamburg, in 1402, Klaus Storbeker and seventy-three pirates were beheaded and, in 1573, Klein Henszlein and thirty-three pirates were decapitated and the heads prominently impaled on stakes).

The second was that Edward, who was with Warwick in 1459 and 1460, would have been only too clear in his mind that Warwick intended to use Calais again as a pirate base to harass English and other shipping in order to wear down the regime. Hence the determination to send a very clear message to anyone who might think of following Warwick into piracy.

Personal experience may have played a part. Anthony Woodville might have recalled being captured in Sandwich in 1460 by Warwick's men, taken with his father to Calais and there humiliated by the Earls of Salisbury, Warwick and his now brother-in-law, the king, then the Earl of March. Woodville might also have wanted revenge on Warwick for the illegal executions of his father and brother the previous year. Worcester had been chased by pirates in the Mediterranean in 1458—so he too might have had a particular indisposition to piracy.

The idea for the punishment may have come from the Earl's foreign travels, which may have left lodged in his mind some disturbing memories of the treatment of the captured Turks from his time on Rhodes. Here in 1458 William Wey described reports and sights that would also have been familiar to the

242 Sir John Tiptoft

Earl: '18 had stakes placed in the fundament going out through the backs and chests.' Also, many were 'hanged some by the feet some by the neck on both sides of the city in order that it was open [in sight] by all passing.'[12] Figure 8 shows an image of such punishments in Rhodes.

Can anything be said in mitigation of the Earl's role? Which death was preferable in terms of avoidance of pain: partial hanging, disembowelling alive and quartering; or hanging and heading, and after death the body being suspended by the feet upside down and the head spiked on a stake 'putt in att bottokys'. The modern (and rational) answer would be the latter; and Worcester might conceivably—having been ordered by the King to make a memorable example that would strike fear into pirates—have chosen visual impact after death over suffering before it.

Notwithstanding, contemporaries did not see it that way. In the Middle Ages *post mortem* degradation was perceived as part of the punishment. (In Canterbury in 1451 the men executed during *the harvest of heads* had been quartered and then pardoned to be buried entire rather than have their quarters exposed).[13] What Worcester did was seen as monstrous and un-English, a particularly unseemly innovation that caused universal disgust and ruined his reputation.

By mid-1470 unsavoury reports must have been swirling about Worcester. There had been the 1462 Oxford plot executions which stretched to breaking point the proper jurisdiction of the Constable's Court. From Ireland what shocked in England was, possibly, not stories of Desmond's execution but garbled accounts of the deaths of two juveniles. In England reports of sticking stakes in fundaments must have circulated quickly, possibly misreported by Warwick's followers, which caused shock to a people inured to seeing live disembowelling and burning and who were not distressed by gibbeted bodies, nor quartered segments and staked heads. Such degradation was something unpleasantly foreign that the cosmopolitan Earl had brought back from his travels, like the also un-English Laws of Padua.[14]

Throughout their lives the relationship between Warwick and Worcester was close. Even when divided by the Lincolnshire campaign, so far there had been no direct confrontation. Events at Southampton put Worcester and Warwick unambiguously on opposite sides. Edward cannot have been unaware of the close links between the two earls and intended to make the breach open and irreconcilable with the unseemly execution of Warwick's followers after judgement by Worcester.

Chapter 25

The Nevilles fight back

He [Worcester] gave money to one of the shepherds to buy him some bread. Going to a property that was near where he always used to buy he was seen to buy more than usual. And looking for this Duke [Earl] in this time, when the shepherd left, some men-at-arms were ordered to search in this wood to see if he was hiding there. Going there, and finding him, they took him and led him to London, And deprived him of the good sum of money he had.[1]

Bisticci described the capture of the Earl of Worcester in October 1470

The Earl of Warwick's humiliations would get worse, despite having already been flushed out, chased the length and breadth of the country, thwarted in his effort to retrieve *The Trinity*, and his executed men's corpses degraded. Meanwhile, the Earl of Worcester was getting ever closer to King Edward, gathering great offices. But Warwick would engineer a quite extraordinary fight back.

Light is thrown on Edward and Worcester's movements in May in the Chapter Register of Salisbury Cathedral, kept by the clerk of the chapter, Machon, in an exceptionally vivid document. On the 5th of May Bishop Richard Beauchamp summoned the canons, congregants, vicars choral and chaplains to the chapter house and read them the riot act. The King was on his way back to Salisbury from Southampton and it sounded as though, while he was there last during Easter week, behaviour was less than exemplary. The Salisbury Cathedral registers show that for centuries the vicars choral were in a chronic state of insubordination. The Bishop's speech provided welcome light relief coterminous to the dismal events in Southampton.

The Bishop informed the assembled clerics, 'the most illustrious now lord King Edward IV of England was swiftly to return from the Port of Southampton all the way to the same church and City of Salisbury'.[2] He exhorted them, in the name of the lord Christ, that

they will summon great diligence, and ... gravity ... expended in Divine [services], and they ... should celebrate, each of them, the masses serially and singly, so as no interval should come from failure to celebrate mass. All, henceforth in the Choir, at the time of Divine [services], will cause nothing to be done, whatsoever, in making a din in raising or lowering their stall seats, and [will take care] with beats and bars, thus that the ears of any should not be offended, under pain of the statute, etc.[3]

The vicars choral in particular were warned, as clearly there had been misbehaviour in the past:

Likewise, to the vicars, …as the lord Reverend Father, the Bishop, has peremptorily advised in the past—that should it come to pass, henceforth, that any of them, at night or day, should perpetrate and offend, or to do anything against the statute and customs of the Church, through their entry in the City and Town of Salisbury, and are caught by the laity of their church, in temptation to sin, they will be punished by officials of the laity, by authority of same lord Bishop in the agreed manner, as to the nature of the transgression, crime, or offense. As the punishment of the few should create fear among the many.[4]

The Bishop might have warned that after events in Southampton—about which shocked reports were spreading—the King and Worcester, who took singing and ceremony most seriously, were likely to be in no mood for levity.

By the 10th of May the King was back in Salisbury, dealing with administrative issues. There were two meetings that day. Machon's register described one in the chapter house between Edward IV, Richard his brother, Worcester the Constable of England, and Lord Audley.[5] The second, outlined in the Close Rolls, was in the Bishop's Palace. At the start of the Lincolnshire campaign, two months earlier, on the 6th of March, the King, Worcester, Hastings and others had met, 'in a certain small chapel … in Westminster palace'.[6] Four days later, 'the King, in a small chamber … of the Bishop of Salisbury', Worcester, Hastings and others had 'the seal produced, and certain letters directed to John Duke of Norfolk and John Duke of Suffolk were sealed'.[7] These were the men whom the King now relied on most. Only Worcester and the King were present at all meetings.

On the 24th of May Edward was admitted to the confraternity of the Chapter of Salisbury. Machon's account of the ceremonial makes it clear that the King was there in person and not by proxy.

Lord King Edward, upon the cloak of gold cloth in the same Chapter House, with knees bent prostrate to the ground, according to the custom, himself humbly of entreaty, as a brother to be received, and, as is of custom, to be admitted, by offering his right hand within the hands of the said Reverend Father, … under this series of words:

'In the name of God, Amen. We, Richard, by divine permission Bishop
of Salisbury, … receive into the Confraternity of that Church Cathedral
… you, most excellent, most dread, and most christian Prince, Edward,
by the grace of God King of England and France & lord of Ireland, willing and granting that you should be a partaker, both in life and in death,
of all masses, prayers, fastings, abstinences, vigils, and other good works
which by us or our confraternities of this church.'

Machon also noted: 'They have conferred admissions in the Chapter, Lawrence
Bishop of Durham and Edward Bishop of Carlisle, and also John Earl of Worcester
into the Confraternity of the same Church.'[8] Worcester was now a member of
the confraternities of All Hallows Barking, St Secundinus Dunshauglin and
Salisbury—and probably Canterbury, as was his father, since he would be remembered in its necrology.

By May Worcester must have seemed the most powerful man in the country after
the King. He was Constable of England and of the Tower. In Ireland, he was Lord
Lieutenant and his brother-in-law, Edmund Sutton, was Deputy. Soon he would
be Treasurer again. He was everywhere with the King. The campaign against
Clarence and Warwick had been a brilliant success—they could only find refuge
with the duplicitous Louis XI, who was anathema to decent Englishmen, and the
relationship between Louis' two great refugees, Margaret of Anjou and the Earl of
Warwick, was poisonous.

By now, or soon, the great Earl of Warwick must have known his loyal servant
Clapham had been beheaded, his men's corpses degraded with impunity and his
property passed to others including Worcester. In 1467 his brother George Neville
had endured the removal of the great seal by a party that included the King and
Worcester and many men he despised as base. Earlier in 1470 his other brother
John had lost the title of Earl of Northumberland, replaced by the unresonant title
of Marquis of Montagu.

Also, the birth of Worcester's son Edward, after the father had been fifteen years
a widower, had eliminated much of the Tiptoft property Warwick's brother John
had expected to inherit through his wife, Worcester's niece. It is probably realistic
to surmise that by now Warwick fostered feelings towards his quondam brother-
in-law in England not dissimilar to those of Henry II towards Becket.

Warwick had landed in France on the 5th of May at Honfleur after further fighting at sea with Sir John Howard. He would soon be joined on the 13th of May by his
brother-in-law, the Earl of Oxford, whose father and brother Worcester had condemned in 1462. King Louis engineered a grotesquely hypocritical reconciliation
between Warwick and Margaret two days later. Warwick's unhappy temper cannot

have been enhanced by being forced to stay on his knees before Margaret for a quarter of an hour, making an excruciatingly dishonest atonement and promise of loyalty, probably sustainable only through an incandescent desire for revenge on those who had humiliated him in England. On the 22nd of July, at Angers Cathedral, Warwick swore allegiance to the House of Lancaster. Three days later his daughter Anne was betrothed to the bloodthirsty young Edward, son of Henry VI and Margaret of Anjou. Now both Clarence, brother of Edward IV, and Edward, son of Henry VI, were married to Warwick's daughters. Thus, regardless of which of his sons-in-law displaced Edward IV, Warwick could not lose. Clarence, however, had less to rejoice about as Warwick's machinations no longer put him in line for the throne.

On the 2nd of June there was a commission of array for south-western England, 'for defence against George, Duke of Clarence, and Richard, Earl of Warwick, rebels'. Worcester was the lead commissioner in the Forest of Dean and the counties of Devon, Dorset and Cornwall.[9] He was the second commissioner in Gloucester and Southampton and third in Wiltshire. Only for Herefordshire was he not mentioned at all. The ordering was partly a matter of precedence but his participation in matters of defence generally must have been regarded as essential.

The royal party arrived on the 6th of June at Canterbury and stayed for about a week.[10] With the King was, according to Prior Stone's chronicle, *dominus comes de Worsetyr mariscallus Anglie*, thus crediting the Earl with the role of Marshal of England. Edward IV was determined to make both sides of the channel as secure as possible against the risk of reinvasion. His focus, however, was too much to the east. When the invasion did come it was in Devon, for which Worcester had responsibility in the recent commissions of array. On the 13th of June the King and Worcester inspected the preparedness of Dover and Sandwich.

Back in Canterbury, Edward held a Great Council at *Meister Omers* which, according to Stone, was expected to last 'a long time' (there still survives to the east of Canterbury Cathedral the building called *Master Homeri*).[11] The first lord listed as present was the Marquis of Montagu, John Neville, the ex-Earl of Northumberland, the second, the new Earl of Northumberland, Henry Percy, and the Earl of Worcester was third. The first may have harboured feelings of considerable, if repressed, resentment towards the other two: the former had taken from him the Earldom of Northumberland, while the latter's late remarriage had produced a son, so John's wife Isabel lost her co-share of the Tiptoft estate.

According to Stone, when Edward heard 'the news' on the 15th of June—which was possibly of Warwick's negotiations with King Louis and Margaret of Anjou—the council broke up early and the King left for London. There may have been some question of Worcester returning to Ireland, now that his work in England was believed to have been done as, on the 2nd of July, a safe conduct was issued to one Hugh Hunte who was 'going to Ireland … in the company of the King's kins-man John, Earl of Worcester, Lieutenant of Ireland'.[12] It seems probable, however, that the Earl did not go.

Worcester was again made Treasurer in place of William Grey, Bishop of Ely.[13] He had now held this position three times. 'The Earl of Worcester's influence over the King was growing daily, and on 10th July the Treasureship of England was added to the offices the Earl already held.'[14] He was probably reappointed because of his proven record of fundraising for military operations in times of crisis, as in 1453 and 1462. He now had an array of offices possibly unique in British history and appeared to be the only man whom Edward wholly trusted, both for his loyalty and ability, as the threat of invasion grew.

On the 11th of July there was a commission of oyer and terminer, led by Richard Duke of Gloucester, including John Marquis of Montague, Henry Earl of Northumberland, and John Earl of Worcester, in the county and city of Lincoln. This must have been intended to deal with those unpunished for their involvement in the rebellion earlier that year. This is the last record in the Patent Rolls of the Earl while alive. Even at this date it must have been assumed that John Neville was loyal and could work with Henry Percy.

At the end of July Lord FitzHugh, Baron Ravensworth, who was married to another Neville sister, fomented a rising in northern Yorkshire. John Neville requested Edward's approval to raise men to suppress his brother-in-law's revolt but used the opportunity to build his own forces near Pontefract. In August Edward IV moved north to deal with FitzHugh personally. One source, Waurin, implied that Worcester went with the King.

In early September a storm scattered John Howard's fleet in the channel. On the 9th of September, the storm having abated, Warwick, Clarence, Oxford and Jasper Tudor set sail for England and the rebels landed variously between Dartmouth and Plymouth four days later, unopposed. They had aimed for the West Country which was hard to monitor. The King and Worcester had focused on securing Kent which was volatile and close to London. The danger was that the rebels would travel directly from the West Country to their strongholds in the midlands and the north. They declared their support for Henry VI and denounced the 'seditious persons' around the throne without saying the name of Edward IV.

Clearly no-one around the King grasped the extent of John Neville's bitterness and the danger he might pose. It was one thing to expect him to put down rebels who threatened his own authority in the north—and quite another to ask him to fight his own equally bitter brother, were Warwick to come north, after his own preferred regional title had been removed.

Warwick appears not only to have been unopposed but to have rapidly gathered a fighting force. The Milanese ambassadors to the French King reported to Galeazzo Sforza, the Duke of Milan and husband of Bona of Savoy, that 'Immediately the Earl landed in England countless multitudes thronged to him in his favour and they continually pushed King Edward hard. Upon two occasions they had crossed swords with his vanguards, and had always beaten them.'[15]

Perhaps success was due not only to their and Henry VI's popularity but also to the unpopularity of the King and Worcester, the main instrument of his rule. The beheadings on the Lincolnshire campaign and the degradation of the bodies at Southampton alienated popular opinion. Even the generally supportive Leland wrote, 'for the which Cruelte he fel yn Indignation of the Common People'.[16]

Luck was with Warwick and his forces on his return. But the fortunes of war favour the bold and Worcester must at least share the responsibility for failure to stop Warwick and to read Montagu's mind better. Those intellectual qualities that enabled the royal party brilliantly to outwit Warwick and Clarence on the Lincolnshire campaign could not grasp Warwick's refusal to accept defeat and recover from setback nor Montagu's anger despite what rationally might seem ample compensation over the loss of the earldom of Northumberland.

Edward moved to Doncaster to await reinforcements from John Neville, where he was warned by Alexander Carlisle, Chief Minstrel, and Alexander Lee, a priest, that his enemies, in large numbers, led by that same Neville, were only six or seven miles away, and intended to take the King. The chronicler Warkworth noted,

> The Lord Marquis Montague had gathered six thousand men, by King Edward's commission and commandment, to the intent to have resisted the said Duke of Clarence and the Earl of Warwick. Nevertheless the said Marquis Montague hated the King, … ; and when he was within a mile of King Edward, he declared to the people, … he … had first given to him the Earldom of Northumberland, and how he took it from him, and gave it to Harry Percy, … and now, of late time, he had made him Marquis of Montague, and gave a pye's-nest [magpie's nest] to maintain his estate with ; wherefore he gave knowledge to his people, that he would hold with the Earl of Warwick, his brother, and take King Edward if he might, and all those that would hold with him …[17]

John Neville's betrayal utterly blindsided the King and his followers. John had been tactlessly treated. But he might have been 'bounced' into a decision by his brothers Richard and George that he regretted later.

Edward had quite insufficient forces to resist the Nevilles, who had gained an ugly reputation for illegal summary execution in 1464 and 1469 and were not likely to be as moderate towards him as in the previous year when they had captured and then released him. These executions can have left the King's companions in little doubt as to where to make the choice between discretion and valour.

The chronicler Waurin wrote that Edward had in 'Doncaster, with him … lord Hasting, the *comte de Ourxestre* and the Marquis de Montagu, to whom the King had given great lordship and land and there was the Archbishop of York; the Archbishop's and Montagu's people disputed with those of King Edward. … the Archbishop and Montagu had four thousand men in their party, who struck at the King's men.'[18] *Ourxestre* is translated as Worcester. Waurin subsequently, however, described how *Euxcestre,* clearly in the context Worcester, was executed.[19] Foreign contemporaries had remarkable difficulty spelling the Earl's title (see Appendix 3) and it is hard to make a definite judgement whether '*our*' and '*eu*' were completely interchangeable.[20] If they were, then Waurin believed Worcester was with Edward at the time of John Neville's betrayal.

Another continental historian Commynes described how Edward 'had with him a wise knight called Hastings, great chamberlain of England, the greatest in authority with him. He had for wife the sister of the Earl of Warwick.'[21] Commynes did not mention Worcester, who outranked Hastings, a man who was indeed married to a Neville sister and who would have been the 'greatest in authority' if Worcester were not there. Thus Waurin's reference to Worcester being with the King at the time of the decision to flee England may be an error. The reference, however, is intriguing and in 1470 the King seldom moved without Worcester.

Who should take responsibility for the King being forced to flee? The obvious candidate for blame is his chief minister and commander. If Worcester was with the King and his party at Doncaster, as Waurin apparently described, then, in the hurried councils that determined flight, he may have faced recriminations as scapegoats were sought. Worcester was *mariscallus anglie* and in the June commission of array he had had specific responsibility for Devonshire where Warwick had landed.

Edward and his close affinity fled to King's Lynn, arriving at the end of September, and departing for Burgundy, where they arrived at Texel by the 3rd of October. Someone must have been deputed or volunteered to go to London and warn the Queen to get to sanctuary with her daughters—before news of the King's flight was generally known in London and the Nevilles arrived. If Worcester was indeed with the King then he would have made a most extraordinary decision: while the King, and most of his party fled to Burgundy, he returned to what was probably then the most dangerous place on earth for him, the snake pit that was London—perhaps to secure the pregnant Queen's safety and then to try to rejoin the King, having taken as much money from the Treasury and his own resources as he could gather.

Waurin, who appears to have placed Worcester with Edward IV at Doncaster, wrote that the Earl did not flee with Edward. '*Le conte d'Euxestre qui n'alla pas avec le roy*

Edourd, lequel conte amene a Londres,' or, 'the Earl of Worcester did not go with King Edward, this Earl was brought to London.'[22] It is not clear, however, whether '*amene*' refers to Worcester's going to London immediately after Edward fled or his return to London following his capture after he had fled from London. The other report of Worcester's movements was in Bisticci's life, published over twenty years after events. 'King Edward could not bring about a peaceful state but had to flee … This Duke [Earl] wanting to keep faith with his lord, departed from London with a good amount of money to go and find his majesty the king and support him as much as possible.'[23] This might be seen as locating Worcester in London at the time the King took flight. Bisticci emphasised the loyalty of the Earl who sought to help his King.

The first half of October saw an astonishing reversal in the fortunes of the occupants of London's Tower where Worcester was still its titular joint Constable. In early October this had two rather different occupants. One was the heavily pregnant Elizabeth. The other was the once and (briefly) future King Henry VI. On the 1st of October, 'it was noised abroad throughout the city that Edward the Fourth King of England had fled'.[24] Order began to break down in London as the men of Kent, clearly still not repressed by so many earlier commissions, threatened the City and its sheriffs, who had to organise patrols of the streets. The same day, 'the Mayor and Sheriffs every day to wit for 10 days rode about the City with armed men both before nine and after nine.'[25]

There were revolving doors as the Lancastrians came out of sanctuary and Yorkists went in. The Queen, who was close to childbirth in specially prepared rooms in the Tower, took sanctuary in Westminster, and William Grey, the Bishop of Ely, in St Martins.[26] Coming out was the man who escaped execution at Southampton: 'And then Sir Gefferey Gate, and other suche as were Sayntuary men, went to the pryson of the kynges bench, and set owte suche persones as were of their affynyte.'[27] There was a dangerous power vacuum between the coming of the news of Edward's fleeing England on the 1st of October and the arrival of the Archbishop of York, George Neville, four days later. 'Many Duchmen and also some Englisshmen, suche as kept berehowses, were dispoyled and Robbyd.'[28]

On the 3rd of October the Tower was given up by appointment to the City of London civic authorities on condition that named occupants could go to sanctuary, and Henry VI was taken from his place of captivity to the Queen's apartments which had been prepared for her confinement.[29] The civic authorities took custody of the Tower. Also, 'Henry the Sixth who … for many years past had been confined in a certain cell … , was conducted by the said Mayor and Aldermen to a certain chamber adorned with handsome furniture which the said Queen Elizabeth had fitted up and in which, being enceinte, she purposed being brought to bed.'[30] Subsequently, George Neville arrived at the Tower and took over from the City Aldermen and commoners.

The following day Warwick and Clarence entered the City of London.[31] They immediately went—with a large following, including Oxford, Shrewsbury and Lord Stanley—to the Tower and 'took away the lord the King Henry the Sixth and brought him the same day before nightfall to the Bishop of London's palace'.[32] Clarence was probably less than delighted, as he expected Warwick would be attending on him in a royal role and not Henry. Warkworth noted: 'Kynge Herry … whiche was nogt worschipfully arayed as a prince, and nogt so clenly kepte as schuld seme suche a Prynce; thei … brought hyme to the palys of Westmynster, and so he was restorede to the crowne ageyne.'[33] Henry was not taken to Westminster but lodged at the palace of St Paul's with Warwick.[34]

Meanwhile Worcester must have fled London, for 'Vpon Sonday [the 9th of October] at nyght therle of Worceter was taken'.[35] He must have left earlier, on Friday or early Saturday. Bisticci wrote: 'This Duke wanting to keep faith with his lord, departed from London with a good amount of money to go and find his majesty the King and support him as much as possible.'[36] London was a remarkably dangerous place yet the Earl must have avoided capture for several days for he collected much money. The Earl did have experience of dressing down in Oxford and the Holy Land. He had explored Florence alone and attended the lecture of John Argyropoulos *incognito*. Still, he was a man of commanding presence with one of the best-known faces in London. He may eventually have been found out and then fled, for Bisticci wrote that the King's foes pursued him.

Worcester was captured in woods in Huntingdonshire which had been granted to him in 1461 and which he might have seen as a refuge. There was one fifteenth-century source for the story that the Earl was captured hiding up a tree: Bisticci, who was writing in Italy (the quote is at the beginning of the chapter). The Earl had given money to a shepherd to buy bread and the man went to his usual supplier, which person was suspicious because more bread than usual was purchased. He alerted men-at-arms already in the area pursuing the Earl and they found him hiding in a tree. They took him to London, having despoiled him of the large amount of money he was planning to take to Edward.[37] Again, the Earl's loyalty cannot be questioned. The scene must have been a bathetic one: the man who had recently been the greatest in the kingdom after Edward was extracted from up a tree, laden with gold but garbed as a humble shepherd. Hollinshed also later reported the story of the tree: 'This earle of Worcester was taken in the top of an high tree in the forest of Weibridge in Huntingdonshire.'[38]

Bisticci described Worcester's hostile reception in London: 'Arriving in London, as the people are want to do, all shouted that he must die. And the main reason the cause of his death, he had introduced certain new laws that have long been in Italy, against the will of all the people, and for this they condemned him to death.'[39] It does seem rather surprising that the 'people' were so upset by legal niceties—which might seem detached from the stresses and strains of everyday life—but quite ordinary people were often remarkably litigious and legally wise as well as both proud and protective of their native common law, which was an integral part of their English identity.

The Earl was not popular and could expect short shrift. 'Therle of Worceter was taken, wherof moche people reioysed, …; for he was cruel! in doyng Justice, and therfore he was namyd the Bowcher of England.'[40] Another Latin source recounted, '*Captus est ille trux carnifex et hominum decollator horridus, comes de Wiccester, et in Turri London incarcerates,*' or, 'that ruthless butcher and harsh beheader of men, the Earl of Worcester, was captured and incarcerated in the Tower of London.'[41]

It is unclear under what authority another Constable of the Tower could have been appointed so Worcester may have been both joint Constable of, and his own prisoner in, the Tower. Therefore, the Earl would have been in a position to ensure that his own inevitable execution was memorable. He was a great organiser of showpiece events. Bisticci would describe how fine was the 'great scaffold, all decorated and with tapestries and carpets and other ornaments'.[42]

Now his captors had to work out what to do with the new prisoner in the Tower. Paston wrote on Wednesday the 12th of October, 'The Erle of Wyrcester is lyek to die this day or tomorrow at the furthest.'[43] But the Earl lived on—which implies that there was some disagreement as to how to deal with him. Ultimately, summary execution was decided against. Instead the Earl would have a trial and by consent die honourably. As Shakespeare's Brutus put it of Caesar: 'Let's carve him up like a dish fit for the gods, not chop him up like a carcass fit for dogs.' Thus a trial had to be organised for Saturday. As the recrowning of Henry VI took place on Thursday that left only Friday to gather charges and prepare the strategy for conducting the process.

Worcester had to be got from the Tower to Westminster. The trial of Lord Audley in 1497 gave something of the process. He was 'had from The Tower to Westm. the Axe of the Tower borne byfore hym'.[44] The trial could only have one outcome. If it was on a Saturday, then allowing for the sanctity of Sunday, the Earl would have expected he would die on Monday. Before leaving the Tower, he must have started his preparations for death and such farewells as he was allowed to make.

For Worcester there were two distinct lurches in the downward circle of Fortune's wheel. First, from the time he knew of Edward's decision to flee he was aware that the situation was desperate but that he might play a part in retrieving it. But second, from the moment of his capture, he can have held no illusions that all hope was gone. The only question was under what form of judgement and how he was to be rendered dead and buried.

Chapter 26

The Trial

Whether the King may command against the Common Law, or an Act of Parliament, there is never a Judge, or other Man in the Realm, ought to know more by experience, of that the Lawyers have said, than I. ... In a Case of my Lord Typtoft, an Earl he was, and learned in Civil Laws who being Chancellor [Constable], because in execution of the King's Commission he offended the Laws of the Realm, he suffered on Tower Hill.[1]

> Bishop Gardiner's letter of 1547, to the Protector Somerset,
> against the lawfulness of the Injunctions of Edward VI.

Perhaps no other man in English history had held so many powerful positions when the monarch was both adult and able as the Earl of Worcester had by the late summer of 1470. What might he not have done or achieved once the Neville threat was nullified? He could have gone back to Ireland as Lord Lieutenant, where its parliament now had near home-rule powers, and shown how a kingdom should be governed. He might have remained in England and, again its Treasurer and Constable, made it, as Fortescue described, the 'mightieste and most welthe realme of the worlde'. Perhaps he would have turned Edward's court into the finest and most learned in Europe, with marvellous ceremonies and choirs, or endowed a great Oxford college with the best library in Europe. He might even have imitated Malatesta Novello who, in 1452, had founded the *Biblioteca Malatestiana*, the first public library in Europe. His interests would likely have turned as much to his own kin as to the public good and he would have been well-placed to start a dynasty with his son as the first, or even after him the second, duke. For leisure he may have carved out time to build at Bassingbourn a retreat to match the Medici's Fiesole or a d'Este *delizie*, or gone on to translate more texts and investigate the possibilities of the new printing process after the Germans, based in the Steelyard, sent him two bibles printed in Germany. Now the Earl knew all he could do was prepare for death.

Worcester owned a copy of John Lydgate's *Fall of Princes*, 'discryuing the falls of princes, princesses and other nobles'. This was based on Giovanni Boccaccio's *De casibus virorum et feminarum illustrium* or *On the fate of famous men and women*, which related the biographies of famous people at the height of happiness then falling to misfortune when least expected. People of the Middle Ages were brutally aware that the wheel of fortune could turn precipitously—that disaster and death stalked every man and might embrace him at any time. A poem in the *Carmina Burana* bemoans *Fortuna's* wounds:

Fortune rota volvitur:	The wheel of Fortune turns;
descendo minoratus;	I lessened descend;
alter in altum tollitur	another is raised on high

Fortuna eventually upset all human works: its impact could be delayed by the exercise of virtue—the moral force that provided the basis for true nobility and friendship in the Earl's translations—but not stopped. Worcester, Warwick and Montagu had, through their actions of 1470, exhausted their reserves of virtue, the first by his executions, even if commanded by the King, the second and third through their treachery; all would be dead before a year was out.

There must have been an intense debate as to what to do with the captured Earl in the first week of the Readeption. It must be recalled how long and how intimately the fates of Worcester, the Nevilles, and, indeed, Henry VI had been intertwined. The Neville vendetta was with the Woodvilles and Edward IV, not Worcester. Despite events at Southampton, rather than exulting in the capture of the Earl, the Neville party may at best have been split and some members were perhaps mortified.

It is even possible that the Nevilles even considered doing a deal with the Earl, but such was his unswerving loyalty to Edward – still alive and at liberty – that Edward that this might have been viewed, almost certainly rightly, as futile. Even if the Nevilles had any inclination to be merciful, it is unlikely that Clarence did after the death of his child off Calais. Cruel necessity probably demanded the death of the Earl, and all credibility would have been lost by the Nevilles in the eyes of Margaret and her blood-lusting son Edward, had he not died soon. Notwithstanding the disorder of regime change, Worcester was, however, accorded a trial and executed not only without any degradation but with all honour possible. This cannot have been an accident but must have reflected the regard and respect in which he was still held by his captors.

What might feeble Henry VI have made of this? He had possibly played a more than supportive role in the advanced education of the young John Tiptoft, in securing his marriage to the widow Cecily *née* Neville of his friend the Duke of Warwick, in getting him an earldom, and in appointing him at 24 to the position of Treasurer. In turn, although Worcester returned to England in 1461 a Yorkist—after Henry was deposed by Edward and the Nevilles—he had ensured, while he was Constable of the Tower and in England, that Henry was decently treated and remained alive. It was the King's decision what to do with heads post-decollation.

The chroniclers make it clear that Worcester's head was honourably buried with the body, not spiked on London Bridge.

Revenge is a dish best served cold. Worcester had condemned the 12th Earl of Oxford and his oldest son to death in 1462, presiding as the Constable of England over the Court of Chivalry. Thus the 13th Earl of Oxford was appointed Constable in 1470 to condemn Worcester and avenge his family. This is the standard clichéd version and it makes for simple drama but reflection might indicate it to be wrong. A major accusation reported against Worcester was that he had applied the Law of Padua—that is civil or Roman law in place of common law. It was, therefore, most unlikely that his case would be pursued in the Court of Chivalry, as this was the civil law body he was accused of misusing.

These were confused times, with a disordered administrative structure, so to expect anything too regular might be unrealistic. Careful sifting of contemporary and later evidence provides tantalising clues of the real nature of the charges and of the type of trial which took place probably in the Court of the High Steward.

Perhaps the Nevilles wanted someone else's fingerprints on the case; hence the appointment of the justifiably vengeance-seeking Oxford. But Warwick was the controlling force at the time and the trial and execution must have had his approval. The Milan State Papers reported bluntly, 'Recently they captured the Grand Constable of England, who had command and control of King Edward's forces. Warwick had him beheaded forwith.'[2]

The first piece of evidence that Worcester was actually tried by the High Steward's court is a brief record that was included in *Harleian 2194*, which was catalogued as 'A Book ... treating of Lords High Stewards of England ... with the trials of several Criminals who were Tried before them'. The first three records were: 'Of the Trial & Execution of Richard FitzAlan, Earl of Arundel; Of the Trial and Execution of John Lord Tiptoft [date given as 1469]; Of the trial of Edward Plantagenet Earl of Warwick'.[3] This might seem to close the question—as making it manifestly clear that the Earl was tried in the Steward's not the Constable's Court—but it might be added there was a reference to indictment being part of the process. *Harleian 2194* said, 'hee was arraigned at Westminster, and indicted of Treason, and many other crymes'.[4] The Court of the High Steward used common law, which required indictment, whereas the Constable's Court used civil law where this process had no part. Also, by way of circumstantial evidence the trials of Perkin Warbeck and the Earl of Warwick in 1492 were both conducted under Oxford as Lord Steward and these might have followed precedents set by Worcester's trial. Several sources say the trial took place in the now demolished White Hall, where the House of Lords met, which lay to the south of Westminster Hall. The site is now a car park with an equestrian statue of Richard I at its centre.

For example, 'therle of Worcetur Rayned at Westmynster in the Whyte halle.'[5] In the Steward's court the accused's fellow lords acted as triers.

What, then, were the charges? *Harleian 2194* had said treason and many other crimes. Indeed, the obvious charge might seem treason against the rightfully restored King Henry VI and brief contemporary descriptions of the event might be expected to use the term. This charge was, however, unlikely to have been levelled explicitly as the main accusation at Worcester's trial because nearly all his captors, particularly the Nevilles, were if anything in an even more compromised position than the Earl. The Nevilles had fought against Henry VI between 1459 and 1461; Worcester had returned when Edward IV was already on the throne. The strategy adopted at the trial may have been to present a two-pronged attack— of charges based on actions in England and Ireland. In the former the charge was treason for he had displaced common law with civil law, lampooned as the Law of Padua. The latter, more moral than legal, was that he executed juveniles illegally in Ireland. The flavour of these charges—which, in the circumstances, were probably rapidly cobbled together—was best captured by Bisticci. His source was close to events, where he described how, when the Earl went to execution, the populace shouted he should die for applying the Law of Padua. An accompanying Italian friar, possibly Bisticci's source, told Worcester his predicament followed from his cruelty in killing two children.

There follows a more complete version of Bisticci's passages about the Law of Padua, which are generally somewhat abbreviated in published translations, as they are repetitious.

> When they [the Earl and his captors] had reached London, the people, ... all clamoured for him to die, the chief reason being for his death was that he had renewed certain laws, which he had brought back from Italy, against the will of all those people and for this reason he was condemned to death. ...
>
> And when he went to die, the people ... rejoiced greatly, and shouted he must die as ... he had made a law which was against the people ... because he had brought back from Italy the laws which are called the laws of Padua, and this, in passing, everyone shouted that he would die, because he had made the law of Padua, where he was at the university.[6]

A key piece of overlooked evidence which casts light on Bisticci's report is a letter from Archbishop Gardiner in 1547 to Edward Seymour, the Lord Protector Somerset. Gardiner wrote, 'Now whether the King may command against an act of parliament, and what danger they may fall in, that break a law with the King's consent, I dare say no man alive at this day hath more experience, what the judges and lawyers have said, than I.' He raised two related issues: the King's power to issue commands contrary to laws passed by Parliament; and the consequences for those who obeyed such commands which broke the law. 'First I had experience in mine old master the lord Cardinal [Wolsey], who obtained his legacy [papal legateship] by our late sovereign lord's [Henry VIII] request at Rome; ... Yet because it was against the laws of the realm, the judges concluded the offence of the *praemunire*.' *Praemunire* was the offence of undermining royal authority, which Wolsey had committed in obeying the pope instead of King Henry. Gardiner continued, discussing a trial in the 1520s where 'The lawyers, for confirmation of their doings, brought in a case of my lord Typtoft, an earl he was, and learned in Civil Laws, who being Chancellor [Constable], because in execution of the King's commission he had offended the laws of the realm, suffered on Tower-hill.' Thus Worcester had obeyed the King but in doing so had broken England's law and had been executed. As even a king could not himself break the common law, the Earl could not argue obedience to the King in justification.[7]

At the time Gardiner was engaged in an ingenious argument in defence of his rejection of Edward's injunctions of 1547 requiring the destruction of images in churches.[8] Despite being a Catholic he could obey the Act of Supremacy—which made the King the master of the Church of England—as it was passed by proper process through the King and Parliament acting together. But he could not obey the injunctions as they were not legal because they were not ordained by Act of Parliament. Indeed, given the example of the executed Lord Tiptoft, Gardiner might put his very life in danger by obeying King Edward but not the laws passed by Parliament.

Gardiner's letter did not record the specific action by Worcester where he executed the King's commission contrary to the law. Given, however, the hostile criticism about applying the Law of Padua, for which Bisticci said the Earl had to die, the action was probably carrying out such commissions in the Constable's Court when it did not have proper authority. In 1462 Warkworth said Oxford was condemned by Paduan law and it is indeed questionable whether that court then had proper jurisdiction, as there is no evidence of a formal state of war.[9] Given the lack of contemporary English records it is, however, impossible to be certain whether Worcester was executed for misusing the Constable's court or using it at all. That said, given the hurried circumstances, it is questionable how precise were the charges.

Accompanying the charge of abusing common law there may also have been allegations related to the executions of juveniles in Ireland. Bisticci reported the words of the Italian friar who accompanied the Earl to his execution: 'My lord, you are led here today because of your unheard of cruelties you made to be killed two most innocent babes.'[10] This and later accounts—surprisingly, it must be recognised—imply that the garbled tales of the deaths of the two youths in Ireland really did play some part in Worcester's trial and execution.

Worcester may have been accused of illegal beheadings in Ireland. Something of this might be caught in the story of his execution of Desmond's lachrymose page, Baggott, in Ireland in 1468. Here Edward IV, informed of the uproar in Ireland, recalled Worcester. 'Tiptoft then, producing his commission for the Earles death under the Kings privys seale, cleared himselfe of that; but the King, more narrowlye pryeing into the business, ..., brought Tiptoft vpon the stage for killing the page, which he did without any commission; wherevpon Tiptoft was condemned.'[11] While discounting the story of the Queen's forged letter and Edward's involvement, it is possible that the charge of executions in Ireland, like those in England, did come up at Worcester's trial. Whereas the Earl was able to establish that the execution of Desmond after attainder by the Irish Parliament was legal, he may have been less able to justify the beheading of two juveniles at the same time.

This might seem far-fetched, but in *The Mirror for Magistrates* the Earl's ghost admitted his worst crime was the death of Desmond's noble sons. Somehow the reports of the death of the juveniles in Ireland do seem to have become imbedded in recollections of the reasons for Worcester's own execution and cannot be entirely ignored.

The peer, being tried by the Steward's Court, did not have a counsel to present his case or notice of the prosecution case or witnesses. Worcester was probably sharper and more knowledgeable than his fellow peers. It is possible that he defended himself skilfully to the extent that he was allowed. The occasion was probably deeply embarrassing for the lords triers and Oxford. The Earl had ample opportunity to make his captors squirm: Clarence had betrayed his brother; the Nevilles had turned coat and their executions in 1464 and 1469 had been genuinely illegal; Richard Neville, having campaigned to put Clarence on the throne, had now restored Henry VI; the actions of Oxford's father and brother in 1462 were manifestly treasonous and his two young brothers had been well-treated by Worcester. Nearly everyone present had served Edward IV, including Oxford.

No-one was really fooled by the charges against the Earl. He was guilty of loyalty to Edward IV. *Harleian 2194* said he was condemned 'the rather because hee was a favourett of Edward the fowrth'.[12] The antiquarian Leland wrote, 'he endured trial for his head [life] regarding his love towards the departed Edward'.[13] Waurin saw his execution as shameful. '*Le conte de d'Euxestre ... fut incontinent decapitaté*' or the Earl of Worcester was shamefully beheaded.[14]

But there could anyway be only one verdict—death. The sentence, however, was, by the standards of the time, generous. A comparison of the descriptions of the executions of the Earl of Worcester in 1470 and Lord Audley in 1495 makes clear the singular absence of degradation.

And vpon the Satirday folowyng was therle of Worcetur.

Reyned at Westmynster in the Whyte halle, and there Endited of treason. And vpon the Monday folowyng adiuged to go from thens *vpon his fete* vnto The Tower hill, and there to be heded.
And as he was comyng from Westmynster toward his Execucion the people presed so fast abowte hym that thofficers were fayne to turne in to the *fflete* [Fleet Prison] wi hym ;
and ther he *restid* that nyght
and till vpon the Tewesday at after none, which was Seynt Lukys day and the xviij day of October,
he was brought through the Cyte, and so to The Tower hill *vpon his fifete*

and there behedid
vpon whos sowle & all Christen Jhesu haue mercy. Amen ! [15]

[from another source] his *body and his hede was buryede togedyr* at the Blacke Frerys in Londone, with alle the honoure and worschyppe that his frendes coude do. [16]

And the same day was the lord Awdley had from The Tower to Westm'. the Axe of the Tower borne byfore hym.
And there in the White hall a-Reyned and adjudged ; and that after none *drawen* from Westm'

vnto *Newgate*,

and there *Remayned* all nyght.
And vpon Weddensday in the mornyng, about ix of the Clok, *drawen* from the said Gaole of Newgate vnto The Tower hill *w' a cote armour vpon him of papir, all to torne* ;
and there his hede stryken off : vpon whos Soule, and all christen god haue mercy ! amen !
And after his *hede set vpon the Brigge*. [17]

Chapter 27

Death

And in alle other places unto his deth, at which deth every man that was there might lerne to die, and take his deth paciently ; wherein I hope, and doubt not, but that God receyued his soule into his everlasting blysse. For, as I am informed, he right aduysedly ordeyned all his thynges, as well for his last will of worldly goodes, as for his sowle helthe.[1]

Caxton's account of the Earl of Worcester's death.

I n less than a month the Earl of Worcester had gone from being the most powerful man in England and Ireland after the King to facing death. The still young king he had served had fled and been replaced by another who was a nincompoop. The Earl would die without the consolation of seeing his life's work redeemed by Edward's return. Many brave men might at the least have been in a state of utter shock by so absolute a reversal and the destruction of so much effort. Some might have disintegrated. The reports of the death of the Earl are, however, completely consistent, even from those generally unsympathetic, in describing the way he met his end as exemplary. It also revealed special insights into late medieval attitudes to death and possibly the impact of continental, particularly Italian, practice.

Bisticci recounted the Earl, on his final walk to the scaffold, was accompanied by many friars, Italian and English. Had contemporary Italian practice been followed, these would have visited him first on Sunday night, his last before his expected death—in order to support and help prepare him for the ordeal ahead. He may also have been attended by fellow members of his own Confraternity of All Hallows.

The late Middle Ages saw major changes in the attitude towards those facing execution, who could be redeemed by the manner in which they faced death. In Italy the custom was developing of 'comforters', usually friars or confraternity members, coming to the condemned on the night before execution and remaining with them until parted by death. Lorenzo de' Medici was a member of the confraternity of *Santa Maria della Croce al Tempio*, which attended those sentenced to die.[2] Although appropriately punished for their crimes, those facing death could still gain redemption by approaching and enduring it in the correct spiritual state—which involved acceptance, contrition, application of the appropriate sacraments, and the patient endurance of pain.

The comforters tried to ensure the condemned person was spiritually prepared for death and ready for the particular judgement that was faced immediately after it, where his soul would be sent to paradise, purgatory or hell. Few could be confident of immediately going to paradise, consignment to hell was final, and a long stretch in purgatory was the best which most might expect—but its protracted torments, expiating sins, were not a pleasant prospect and mitigation by a good death was understandably sought.

On Monday the Earl was collected by an unidentified commander of the Tower and maybe the executioner whose axe blade now pointed towards the condemned man. Leland provided a detail which indicated that indeed the great Earl had put aside earthly vanities to meet death humbly and patiently. In 1467, when he organised the great tournament as Constable of England, he was arrayed in leg harness, gorget and journade of gold, mounted on a destrier trappered in crimson cloth of gold. Now 'he stripped voluntarily mindful of death, as Westminster was left behind, in sandals, with the commander of the Tower of London'.[3]

The Earl thus divested himself of all finery of rank and humbled himself to meet his fate with humility and acceptance in shirt and open-laced shoes. Indeed, he would turn his death into a fitting final act in the play of life. Caxton made clear that Worcester played his part perfectly: 'Pacyently and holyly, without grudchyng, in charyte to fore … he departed out of this world, which is gladsome and joyous to here. Thene I here recommend his sowle unto your prayers; and also, that we, at our departing, may depart in such wyse, and that it plese our Lord God to receyve us into his evirlastyng blysse.' The journey from Westminster to the City encompassed much of the Earl's world. He had simultaneously been Treasurer in Westminster to the west, and Constable of the Tower of the London to the east, and Lord Steward of the Household in the palaces at both locations.

Contemporary reports made it clear that the Earl went on foot to the Tower. This point might not sound important now—but then it would have been understood that he was not being degraded by being drawn on a hurdle or tied to a nag. Nor was he attired in a paper coat and hat, like Lord Audley in 1497, or festooned with the broken accoutrements of knightly order hung around his person, as Sir Ralph Grey was threatened with in 1464.

As the Earl left Westminster Palace Yard he must have looked towards the precinct of Westminster Abbey knowing that the heavily pregnant Queen Elizabeth had taken sanctuary there. Also, that she must soon give birth to her fourth child, after

Map 9: 1470 – Route from Westminster to Tower Hill taken by the Earl of Worcester on 17–18 October to his execution.

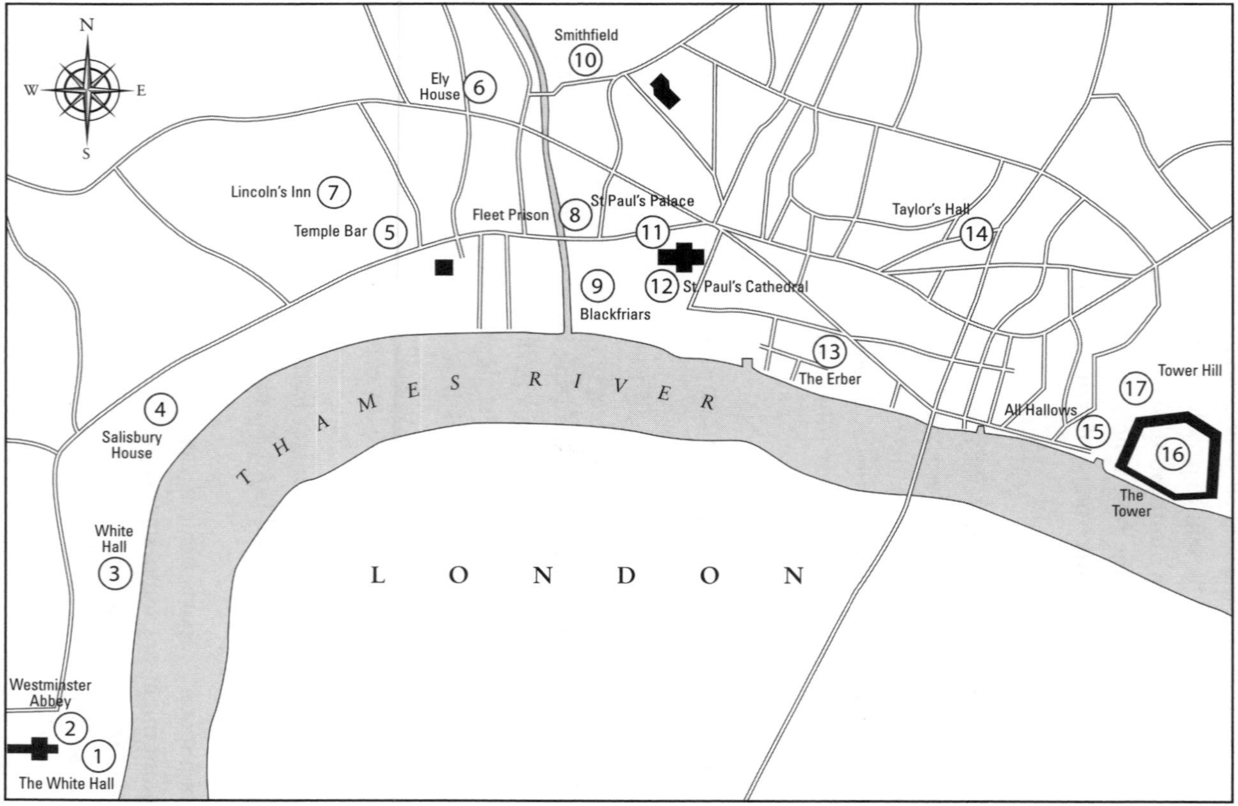

The White Hall

① ②
Westminster Abbey

③ White Hall

④ Salisbury House

⑤ Temple Bar

⑥ Ely House

⑦ Lincoln's Inn

⑧ Fleet Prison

⑨ Blackfriars

⑩ Smithfield

⑪ St Paul's Palace

⑫ St Paul's Cathedral

⑬ The Erber

⑭ Taylor's Hall

⑮ All Hallows

⑯ ⑰ Tower Hill

The Tower

THAMES RIVER

LONDON

N
E
W
S

(Continued)

(Continued)

1.	The White Hall	Worcester condemned here 15 October
2.	Westminster Abbey	Elizabeth Woodville in sanctuary, soon to give birth
3.	Whitehall	Archbishop of York, George Neville's London residence
4.	Salisbury House	escorted the Bastard of Burgundy here in 1467 for great tournament
5.	Temple Bar	Worcester handed over to the sheriffs of the City of London
6.	Ely House	chronicler Gregory says Worcester insulted the Lord Mayor of London here in 1464
7.	Lincoln's Inn	two of Worcester's kinsmen took 'repasts' while in his service
8.	Fleet Prison	held overnight 17–18 October as press too great to continue
9.	Blackfriars	buried in nave after execution 18 October
10.	Smithfield	organised great tournament here in 1467
11.	St Paul's Palace	Henry VI currently resident after release from the Tower
12.	St Paul's Cathedral	escorted Duke of York here with Earl of Warwick after battle of St Albans 1455
13.	Dowgate Street	The Erber, London residence of the Nevilles
14.	Threadneedle Street	Taylor's Hall, Earls of Worcester and Warwick freemen
15.	All Hallows	Worcester was warden, confraternity established in 1465
16.	Tower of London	Worcester Constable since 1461
17.	Tower Hill	the scaffold

three girls, by Edward IV. The Earl may have regretted that he would never know, on this earth at least, the sex of the child or its fate, should the Readeption hold.

The procession shifted along King's Street to the Eleanor Cross at Charing. Then it moved onto the Strand with its great noble and episcopal palaces to the right and still open country to the left. The Earl passed the Bishop of Salisbury's house in the Strand to which he had escorted the Bastard of Burgundy in 1467 during the magnificent tournament.

Mid-afternoon, at the Temple Bar, the Earl was passed over to the City Sheriffs. Word had clearly got around, for a great multitude had come to marvel at him. Later commentators imply murder was their intent but contemporary accounts indicate they wanted to gaze at the final passing of the great man who had been much among them. The route along Fleet Street took the Earl between Lincoln's Inn to the north and the Inner Temple to the south. Bisticci described how the people had cried that he must die for he had introduced the Law of Padua. Maybe common law lawyers came out to mock the Earl.

Lynching lords was almost a popular pursuit in late medieval England and the commons could be remarkably undeferential about murdering or mal-treating members of the nobility if the opportunity arose. Worcester gained an extra night when the mob choked his passage through the City. Thus spoke his remarkably un-self-pitying ghost in the sixteenth century *A Mirror for Magistrates*:

> That whan I should have gone to Blockam feast,
> I could not passe so sore they on me prest.
> And had not bene the officers so strong
> I thinke they would have eaten me aliue, ...
> Thus one days life they malice did me give.[4]

The press had now become so great that the sheriffs decided to conduct Worcester to the Fleet prison to pass one extra night.[5] It is a measure of the Earl's honour-able death that he stayed there. In 1497 Lord Audley would stay in the truly foul nearby Newgate prison.

The Fleet prison was not the abominable jail the image of a medieval gaol might convey. It lay on what was once an islet to the east side of the Fleet River and was now moated and walled. One Robert Worth was warden in 1470, hav-ing replaced Elizabeth Venour who kept Henry Percy after 1465. On entry to the Fleet the prisoner had to pay fees according to his rank. The admission fee ranged from £13 5s. for an archbishop to 19s. for a yeoman. For an earl the charge was £9 4s. 0d. When all the formalities were concluded and other charges added, prisoners stood drinks all round ranging from twenty shillings worth of wine for an Archbishop down to a single pot of ale for a yeoman.

Maybe, like a Roman senator awaiting death, Worcester perambulated around the warden's gardens, conversing with friends and discussing scholarly texts. Like the condemned late-Roman patrician, Boethius, might he have passed his last night taking consolation in communion with my Lady Philosophy? Next day the fee for discharge from the Fleet for superior persons like the Earl was £3 5s.—perhaps it was waived in the circumstances.

Early Tuesday morning the Common Council met to ensure no repetition of the previous day's disturbances. 'Memorandum that, during the feast of saint Luke the Evangelist, John, Earl of Worcester, was beheaded at Tower Hill. And the sheriffs who attended to the preservation of the peace—while the said Earl was led to the place of punishment—had attended upon taking cognisance [a record] of the persons sent to the Guildhall from all Wards of the City, accord-ing to the numbers subscribed.'[6] There followed the numbers of men provided by each ward: Cheap, Cripplegate (30 men each); Bread Street, Farringdon

Without & Farringdon Within, Langbourn (20 men each); Candlewick, Cornhill, Queenhithe, Walbrook (16 men each); Aldersgate (15 men); Billingsgate (14 men); Broad Street, Dowgate, Vintry (12 men each); Castle Baynard, Coleman Street, Portsoken, Tower (10 men each); Lime Street (8 men); Aldgate, Bishopsgate (6 men each); Bassishaw (5 men). Only Cordwainer did not provide anyone.

As the Earl walked back down the lane from the Fleet prison, escorted by the three hundred City men, the central tower of Blackfriar's church would have been visible. Soon, he would be laid to rest to the west of that tower. On reaching Fleet Street he would have turned left towards Ludgate. He must have travelled this route countless times when shifting between the City and Westminster—sometimes in great processions, like the show of strength in December 1450 when Henry VI had been induced to exert his authority after the Cade rebellion. After the 1st Battle of St Albans in May 1455, York led Henry VI in procession to St Paul's. With them was Warwick, who carried the King's lance and Worcester brought the royal sword.[7] More recently, in May 1467, the Earl of Worcester had met the Bastard of Burgundy on the Thames estuary and escorted him through the City to Salisbury House on the Strand.

The route past St Paul's went near its bishop's palace at the north-west corner of the cathedral itself. The Earl's path took him close to the lodgings of the restored Henry VI and Warwick. Having circled the enclosure around St Paul's, the dolorous procession probably headed down Watling Street, then along East Cheap and lastly Tower Street. All along or near were places deeply familiar. The great Neville house, the Erber, lay off Downgate Street to the south. Here the Earl must have been a guest with his first wife Cecily Beauchamp, née Neville, the sister of Warwick. To the northwest in Threadneedle Street was the Taylor's Hall. He and many players in the current deathly drama were freemen. As the procession approached Tower Hill it would have passed the church of All Hallows, where the Earl led the confraternity and was perhaps now accompanied by some of its members. The scaffold was about eight feet high, if similar to that on which Oxford suffered in 1462. It would have afforded an excellent immediate view of the Tower, where the Earl had been Constable, and All Hallows, key locations of his secular and religious life.

Even hostile chroniclers agreed Worcester died commendably. Fabyan, who said that the Earl, 'For his cruelnesse was called the bochier of Engläde', wrote he was 'ladde to The Tower Hylle, where he toke his deth full pacyently'.[8] Bisticci describes how 'They wanted him to die as royals died and so had made a great scaffold, all decorated and with tapestries and carpets and other ornaments'.[9] Seldom was a medieval man put to death with such honour: undegraded, protected, honoured by the beautiful scaffold, and ultimately head and body buried together in his own chapel.

The Earl had made some preparations well in advance, having obtained a plenary indulgence in 1465. 'Indult that the confessor of his choice may grant him, being penitent and having confessed, plenary admission of all his sins, once only, namely in the hour of his death; with the usual clauses against abuse of the present indult.'[10] That hour had come. Worcester reserved his private *coup de théatre* to last. According to Bisticci, 'Now it was time to cut off the head, master John turned to the villain [executioner] and requested he cut off his head in three blows in reverence of the most Holy Trinity, although it could be cut off in one. This was a sign of the greatest faith and spirit.'[11] Most condemned would have hoped for no more than one blow. A previous earl executed on Tower Hill, Richard FitzAlan, Earl of Arundel reportedly told the executioner, 'Torment me not long, strike off my head in one blow.'

In the later Middle Ages death by execution could allow for redemption through contrition and pain. 'The hour of death, when the soul took leave of the body, was a moment of extreme dread ... in which the believer had to give final proof of his or her true contrition and submission to the will of God.'[12] The experience of pain might mitigate the time in purgatory. The request for three blows has been seen as an egregious act of gothic horror confirming Worcester's reputation for the macabre—adding masochism to the charge of sadism. But the act was not unique, and this and the presence of 'comforters' would have placed his execution firmly in a late medieval pattern in which executions were a subtle ritual of expiation and communal participation. The condemned could be transfigured in the eyes of the spectators into a holy vessel whose suffering signalled his reconciliation with the community and offered hope of remission from hell or time in purgatory.[13]

For the thirteenth-century Medieval Christian philosopher Thomas Aquinas, bodily pain could be a source of 'inward joy' in imitation of Christ who, by suffering death when executed on the cross, brought the opportunity of redemption to man. Punitive pain became a conduit for the soul's movement toward health and joy. In a more popular expression of the idea, the illustration of a German municipal code was captioned, 'If you bear your Payn patiently / it shall be useful to you / Therefore give yourself to it willingly.'[14] The reports of the death of Worcester repeatedly use the word patiently.

By dying well the offender not only healed the breach between himself and God, but was also reconciled with the community that participated in his death. By voluntarily increasing the suffering of death, in a manner linked to Christian symbolism, the condemned might magnify penitence and with it the chance of

redemption. Given the sympathetic reports of the Earl's execution, even by chroniclers usually hostile, it would appear the Earl, by the manner of his death, did
indeed achieve a degree of reconciliation with the living.

The Earl was not the only fifteenth-century Englishman to request multiple
blows. In 1405 Richard Scrope, the Archbishop of York, had requested five: 'I for-
give you, but I pray that you give me five wounds on my neck with your sword,

Figure 10: Archbishop Scrope in 1405 requested he be executed with five blows for the
Five Wounds of Christ—two more than the Earl of Worcester in 1470, who asked for three
for the Holy Trinity.

for I long to bear them for the love of my Lord Jesus Christ, who, obedient to his Father even unto death, bore the first five wounds for our sake.'[15] That the death had entered the popular vernacular and not just Latin texts was revealed in an English carol.

> Full hertly here to yowe I pray.
> Here I wyll the commende,
> thou gyff me fyve strokys with thy hende,
> And than my wayes thou latt me wende
> To hevyns blys that lastys ay.[16]

Apart from sparing himself some moments of agony Worcester might have felt it overweening to match an Archbishop in similarly requesting five blows, settling instead for three.

But could there have been another motive? The Earl might also have been paying a subtle tribute to the King, called this *Sun of York*, Edward IV, whom he served unto death. The soldiers of the still teenage Edward, then Earl of March, had been disturbed on the morning of the Battle of Mortimer's Cross in 1461 by the appearance of three suns in a phenomenon called a *parhelion*. The young Edward, precociously resourceful, sagely interpreted this to his frightened soldiers as the sign of the Holy Trinity, signifying God was on their side. As Shakespeare described:

> *Three glorious suns*, each one a perfect sun;
> Not separated with the racking clouds,
> But sever'd in a pale clear-shining sky.
> See, see! they join, embrace, and seem to kiss,
> As if they vow'd some league inviolable:
> Now are they but one lamp, one light, one sun.
> In this the heaven figures some event.

Edward used the *Sun in Splendour* as his emblem. Even as he died, was the great Earl of Worcester subtly subverting his execution and turning it into an acknowledgement of the young Yorkist king? His death may have rent the fault lines between the Nevilles, paving the way to the defeat and deaths of Richard and John at the Battle of Barnet in 1471, and the return to the throne of King Edward.

Thus ended the life of the man who, a month earlier, had been the greatest after the King in England and Ireland. Nor was the Earl simply an administrator and a soldier. The *Canterbury Necrology* recorded the death of 'Lord John, Earl of Worcester, Lord Typtoft, a man most learned … in all the noble and divine arts, as well as versed

Figure 11: *A parhelion*, or triple star, as was seen before the Battle of Mortimer's Cross; and Edward's *Sun in Splendour* on the Earl of Worcester's Irish coinage (note the smaller suns on either side)

in the study of worldly letters'.[17] The seventeenth-century antiquary Fuller noted that the axe 'cut off more learning than was in the heads of all the surviving nobility'.[18]

The chroniclers were explicit that the head was buried with the body and not, as usual, spiked on London Bridge. 'Whenne he was dede, his body and his hede was buryede togedyr at the Blacke Frerys in Londone, with alle the honoure and worschyppe that his frendes coude do.'[19] This unusually generous treatment merited specific recording.

Contemporary and near contemporary reports were again clear about where the Earl was buried—even though most modern books place him in Ely Cathedral, where the tomb is almost certainly that of his father. Fabyan wrote that he was interred 'in a chapel standynge in the body of the churche, which he before tyme had foundyd'.[20] Leland even gave the position: 'the sanctuary of the Dominicans of London, near the River entrance, in which place and he has been buried between two columns toward the south.'[21]

Later the Earl of Worcester's chapel may have been remodelled by his sister Joanna so she could be buried with him. In 1494 she willed, 'My stynkyng and corrupte body to be buryed in the chappell of oure lady ... in the same place where the body of Sir John Tiptoft late Erle of Worcester my brother restif buryed.'[22] Leland provided a description of the tomb: 'Joanna, the sister, lamenting to such an extent the brother's mournful fate ... has placed a torch, and a tomb made of marble, in which place on a tablet this inscription: Joan D. Inguldesthorpe the sister of Earl John has made this chapel, with whom here she rests.'[23] What more could this inscription have said?

Sir John Tiptoft, Earl of Worcester, Lord Tiptoft and Powys, Mariscallus Angliae, Constable of England, Constable of the Tower, thrice Treasurer of

England, Steward of the Household, Lord Lieutenant of Ireland, keeper of the sea, councillor and commissioner, knight of the Orders of the Garter and of the Holy Sepulchre, leader of the confraternity of All Hallows, member of the confraternities of St Secundinus, Dunslaughlin and the chapter of Salisbury Cathedral, pilgrim to the Holy Land, orator to the Pope, student at Oxford, Padua and Ferrara, firm protector of his family and friends, liberal patron of scholars, benefactor of books to the Universities of Oxford and Cambridge, most true to King Edward IV unto death, most noble through service to him and England.

Epilogue

September 1604

Saturday the 18th – A tragedy presented by the English; he [the Dauphin Louis] listened to them with cool intent, gravity and patience until it was necessary to cut the head off of one of the characters.

Wednesday the 29th – He said that he wanted to perform theatre: *Monsieur*, said I [Jean Héroard], *how will you say that?* He replied: *Tiph Toph, Milord*, while raising his voice.[1]

> The Journal of Jean Héroard, appointed in 1601
> physician to the new-born Dauphin, the future Louis XIII.

Did this entry in the diary of Jean Héroard refer to a lost Jacobean tragedy, recorded in French as *Tiph, Toph, Milord, ce qu'il fallut couper la tête* or Lord Tiptoft whose head must be cut off, performed by English actors before the young Dauphin? Certainly the life and death of John Tiptoft, Earl of Worcester, was the stuff of tragedy; that too of Richard Neville, Earl of Warwick, and John Neville, Marquis of Montagu. All died, turned against each other by the divisions caused by Edward IV's marriage to Elizabeth Woodville. The Nevilles's betrayal of Edward IV might have meant they merited their fate but did Worcester deserve his? He had laboured hard between 1451 and 1455 to maintain the throne for Henry VI, a man quite unfitted for the role, and equally so for the much abler but very young Edward IV, after returning to England in 1461 when Henry's deposition was a *fait accompli*. John Tiptoft was a much greater man than most in bad times—and his record and role in history merits a thorough reappraisal. He deserves more than to be recalled by the epithet 'The Butcher of England'.

In Chapter 4 the questions of how the young Earl of Worcester might have been affected by his work as a commissioner of oyer and terminer, dealing out death in the aftermath of the Cade rebellion, and whether he merited the title of Butcher, were set out. The answers were deferred until his record over his life could be considered. The point was then made that nothing known of his actions before he became Constable of England in 1462 indicated his character had been changed by participating in, ordaining, and witnessing executions in the early 1450s. It does, however, seem likely that reports, and probably the sight of the physical remains, of the executions of over 200 Turks, which included impalement and flaying, on Rhodes in 1458 did become lodged in his mind, resulting in the unusual degradation of bodies at Southampton in 1470.

For the Earl of Worcester to be rightly titled the Butcher certain tests are posited. He must: be egregiously cruel by the standards of the day; be seen to have misused the law to facilitate execution for its own sake; have killed in numbers beyond those acceptable even for exemplary justice; have employed not simply cruel but unusually degrading punishments; and taken pleasure in the act of condemning to death and witnessing execution.

The Earl, as he walked to his execution on Tower Hill, was informed bluntly by the Dominican Friar, 'my lord, you are led here because of your unheard of cruelties'.[2] The Earl needs to be judged by contemporary standards to establish if such a charge can be sustained. On Worcester's travels in Europe and on pilgrimage he would have encountered or heard of extreme cruelty. In Italy Pope Pius, in his *Commentaries*, vividly described Italians tyrants. For example, Braccio da Montone, tyrant of Perugia, 'cut a fine figure. He could be pleasant and charming in conversation, but in his heart he was cruel. He would laugh as he ordered men to be tortured and racked by the most excruciating torments, and he took pleasure in hurling his wretched victims off the tops of towers. … When eighteen friars … dared to oppose him, he had their testicles beaten to a pulp on an anvil.'[3] Cruelty by city rulers seemed almost commonplace. Sigismondo Malatesta of Rimini was 'gifted with eloquence …, a profound knowledge of history and more than a passing understanding of philosophy', yet he 'surpassed every barbarian in cruelty'.[4] Galeazzo Sforza, Duke of Milan and the eventual husband of Bona of Savoy, took sadistic pleasure in devising tortures for men who had offended him, and reportedly enjoyed pulling apart the limbs of his enemies with his own hands. In Florence, Ser Maurizio da Milano, Chancellor of the *Otto di Guardia*, was named 'The Butcher', as 'he took such delight in tormenting men that just the sight of him instilled fear'.[5] Outside Italy, Vlad Draculea III, Prince of Wallachia (1431–77), impaled 1,000 captured Turkish cavalry in 1459, reserving the highest stake for Hamza, the Bey of Nicopolis. In 1462 he wrote to Matthias Corvinus, the scholarly King of Hungary, 'I have killed peasants men and women, old and young, who lived at Oblucitza and Novoselo… . We killed 23,884 Turks without counting those whom we burned in homes or the Turks whose heads were cut off by our soldiers.'[6]

Rulers and leaders could be capable of acts of great cruelty. Niccolò III d'Este (1383–1441), Marquis of Ferrara, killed both his young wife Parisina and his illegitimate son Ugo, having discovered their adulterous relationship. In France Gilles de Rais, Marshal of his country, who campaigned with Joan of Arc, was executed for hundreds of child murders in 1432. In England the Neville brothers, Richard and John, have largely escaped opprobrium despite multiple illegal executions. Edward IV had a reputation for tolerance but there were over forty beheadings after Towton in 1461. The Duke of Gloucester's later reputation when Richard III hardly needs rehearsing but after Tewksbury he was Constable and condemned over a dozen men, many dragged out of Tewksbury Abbey. The execution by the 13th Earl of Oxford, who condemned Worcester, of the harmless young Edward Plantagenet, 17th Earl of Warwick, in 1499 was cruel by any measure. The accusation of cruelty against Worcester would possibly have invited derision from continental commentators. Even in England his actions do not seem particularly remarkable.

The Earl of Worcester's cruelties were recognised as carried out in the context of enforcing the law. The *Chronicle of London* said, 'he was cruell in doyng Justice'.[7] As far as can be determined, his trials followed proper process—although there may have been exceptions for particular reasons. The most obvious one was that of the Oxford plotters in 1462 where, if there was no recognised state of war, then civil law did not have jurisdiction. Oxford and his followers were, however, clearly guilty of treason.

There were only two occasions when the Earl was prominently associated with mass executions. The first was when, in his role as Constable, he completed the executions of those captured at the battle of Hexham in 1464. The number of nobles beheaded under his supervision, fourteen, was the most he ever condemned on a single occasion. This action has not, however, been added to the charge sheet—presumably as it was seen as both legal and proper. The second was at Southampton in 1470, where 'xx. persones of gentylmen and yomenne' were executed and their bodies degraded.[8] This was a large number by English standards but less than half that executed after the Battle of Towton in 1461.

The Earl did not inflict death as a matter of course. In 1462 and 1463 John Clopton and William Plumpton were acquitted. In 1468, despite being attainted along with the decapitated Earl of Desmond, neither the Earl of Kildare nor Edward Plunket were executed. Although Richard Clapham was executed in 1470, Sir Geoffrey Gate was not.

It was not the number of executions at Southampton which caused disgust but the manner. Warkworth's description of hanging, drawing, quartering and stakes up anuses is the one that sticks in the memory.[9] This description, however, cannot be accurate, as it is not possible for a disembowelled, quartered body to be hung up by the feet. All other accounts do not include drawing and quartering and make clear degradation took place after death. The English, however, were a conservative and insular nation and while not averse to cruel punishments disliked unusual ones. So traditional hanging drawing and quartering was acceptable but impalings such as these were not.

There is no surviving evidence that the Earl took pleasure in condemning to death and witnessing execution. The one record of a judgement by the Earl, that of Sir Ralph Grey in 1464, showed his tone was measured and in the circumstances not ungenerous, as Grey was spared degradation. He did not sound like an archetype for Judge Jefferies who appears to have relished the butchery dealt out in retribution after the defeat of the Monmouth rebellion in 1685. On the surviving evidence Worcester was not cruel outside the judicial context, and in comparison to many European and even English contemporaries, he hardly seems cruel at all. Moreover, his punishments were for the good of the state and not for personal ends or gratification; executing a few might have spared many more.

Yet in England some line was crossed. The term 'cruel' appears too often for it to be difficult to deny that it represented widely held public opinion. In the Middle Ages those condemned to death merited empathy, not usually because they were to die or their deaths were cruel, indeed this was seen as just, but because they met it patiently, in a spirit of acceptance, thus earning reconciliation with the community and spiritual redemption. Worcester's executions—in the cases of the Oxford plotters in 1462, the two juveniles, Desmond in Ireland in 1468, and Warwick's retainers taken at Southampton in 1470—however, created empathy for those executed themselves. The Oxford plotters were of high rank condemned by the Law of Padua; the two Irish juveniles were reported as very young; the degradation at Southampton, involving impaling, was un-English.

The charge against Worcester can be summarised by the constitutional historian Stubbs: 'Tiptoft, the cultivated disciple of the Renaissance, has an evil pre-eminence as the man who impaled the dead bodies of his victims.'[10] Thus there is the *frisson* evoked by the contradiction between humanism and barbarism. The Earl seems such a convenient example of this unfortunately intriguing paradox that it has perhaps been too easy to overemphasise his cruelties.

The fates of those who destroyed the Earl should be reviewed briefly to see how Fortune's wheel treated them. The Readeption of Henry VI—already fatal to Worcester—proved cursed. Within half a year Richard and John Neville, Henry VI and his son Edward were all dead and Worcester's *Sun in Splendour*, Edward IV, shone forth again from the throne. The tragic widowed Margaret of Anjou was placed in the custody of the indestructible Alice de la Pole—who had looked after her three decades earlier on her arrival in England—before being ransomed back to France in 1475.

The Earl's death may have fatally divided the Neville brothers. His execution must have put an unbearable strain on the Montagu household, where the Earl had made possible the marriage of John and Isabel, and he was the brother of Isabel's mother Joanna. While Richard Earl of Warwick may have remained blinded by his hatred of Edward IV, both John and George appear to have become increasingly unhappy about their betrayal of Edward IV.

John Neville particularly had good reason to be aggrieved. His act of treachery—which perhaps had for him the unintended consequence of Worcester's death—had not even resulted in his regaining the Earldom of Northumberland. Perhaps Henry VI would not approve it. More likely his brother Richard considered it too dangerous, while the Readeption was unsteady, to compel an adult Percy, secure in his northern fastnesses, to surrender the title. All that John Neville achieved was the keeping of the toddler Edward Tiptoft—and that might have been because his wife and mother-in-law were determined to stop Richard despoiling the infant's inheritance.

The Achilles heel of the Readeption would prove to be its hold over the north. When Edward IV returned in 1471 neither John Neville, Marquis of Montagu, still at Pontefract, nor Henry Percy, the incumbent Earl of Northumberland, lifted a finger to stop him landing and building up his forces. Both the wives of Northumberland and Montagu had no reason to love Warwick, who had caused the executions of the former's father, the Earl of Pembroke, in 1469, and the latter's uncle, Worcester, the following year.

At the Battle of Barnet there was little confidence in the loyalty to the Readeption of John Neville—the man who vied with Edward IV as the best battlefield commander of the age—and he was reputedly killed by Warwick's men. Before the battle, John 'had privily agreed with the King [Edward IV], and had gotten on his livery; but one of his brother's (Warwick) men espied this, fell upon him, and killed him'.[11] Edward allowed Richard and John to be interred at Bisham where Worcester had in 1463 played the most prominent role for a non-Neville in the funeral of the Earl of Salisbury. Hall, in his *Chronicle*, observed, 'Edward ... was more sorrowful and dolorous for the death of the Marquis [than for Warwick], whom both he knew, and it appeared to others, to be inwardly his faithful friend, and for whose sake only he caused both their bodies to be solemnly buried.'[12]

The third Neville brother, Archbishop George, acted as Chancellor to Henry VI. On Edward's return he surrendered Henry VI, whose captivity he then shared in the Tower. He was pardoned in April 1471 but rearrested the following year and imprisoned at the Hammes castle near Calais until November 1474, when he returned to England and died the following year. Neither Neville nor Tiptoft bones would rest in peace for long. The tombs at Blackfriars and Bisham Abbey were destroyed in the dissolution of religious houses.

The Earl of Worcester left a son, Edward, who was about a year old. History says almost nothing about him. He died aged about 16, presumably of natural causes. It may again have been in recognition of the cruel necessity of executing Worcester that he was not retrospectively attainted when Parliament met later in 1470. John Neville was granted Edward Tiptoft's lands during the boy's minority but had to pay for them an annual sum to be agreed with the Treasury.[13] John's intentions can only be speculated at. Did he genuinely intend to preserve the Tiptoft estate for the defenceless son, perhaps prodded by his wife Isabel and mother-in-law Joanna? Maybe John and Isabel planned Edward for one of their five daughters?

After the Readeption failed in 1471 Edward Tiptoft's keeping was returned to his mother Elizabeth and her third husband, William Stanley, who had served in Ireland with Worcester and returned with him for the Lincolnshire campaign.[14] Elizabeth had become a desirable prize, given her inheritances and dowers. Despite being in her mid-40s she had another daughter who did not have issue. Her third husband's intervention at the Battle of Bosworth Field was critical to Henry VII's success but he was later executed for his part in the Perkin Warbeck plot in 1495.

Edward Tiptoft died in 1485 and his estate was divided between his three aunts and their, as it turned out, female lines. The line of the Earl of Worcester's aunt, Joanna *née* Cherlton, also died out and its property was added to that going to heirs of the Tiptoft sisters. Thus, eventually, John and Isabel Neville's heirs did benefit richly from the Tiptoft inheritance.[15]

John and Isabel Neville's two sons, George and John, were without issue. There were five daughters of whom the fourth, Lucy, stood out. In the reign of Henry VII she was noted as one who 'loves not the King' and promoted the rival claim of her de la Pole cousins. She was heavily fined in 1507 and then had the sense to live quietly, surviving until 1534.

Lucy's daughter Elizabeth (by her second husband, Sir Anthony Browne of Cowdray) made a marriage that united many of the great competing blood lines of the mid-fifteenth century when she became the second wife of Henry Somerset, 2nd Earl of Worcester. The legitimate male Beaufort line had been wiped out by deaths in battle and on the block by 1471. But Henry Beaufort, beheaded by John Neville in 1464, left an illegitimate son, Charles Somerset, who was legitimised when Henry VII, whose mother Margaret was another Beaufort, came to the throne. In 1514 he was made the 5th creation Earl of Worcester by Henry VIII.

The 4th creation Earl of Worcester, John Tiptoft, left no surviving heirs. Tiptoft blood, however, lives on still through his sisters, particularly Joanna, whose granddaughter Lucy's descendants mixed that of the great non-royal families of the mid-fifteenth century, the Tiptofts, Nevilles, de la Poles, Hollands and Beauforts.

The Earl of Worcester's life ended tragically and prematurely in 1470. He was too intelligent and cosmopolitan a man for the insular English chroniclers and Irish annalists whose writings have damned his posthumous reputation. Some Englishmen of culture and letters—like the scholar John Free, the printer William

Caxton, both of whom spent long periods in Europe, and the slightly later anti-quary John Leland—understood his importance, and the far more sophisticated Italians and Burgundians much better grasped his qualities. But it is the epithet applied by Fabyan of the 'butcher of England', Warkworth's denunciation of the Law of Padua, Gregory's report of arrogance at the city sergeant's feast, and again Warkworth's description of physically impossible executions and impalements of Southampton, that adhere. Thus the importance of Worcester has been overlooked.

England in the fifteenth century was redefining itself. The century was critical in determining what the country was not; and, having decided this, it could decide subsequently what it would be. England was an island nation, having been ejected from the mainland continent. The failure of the Sturmy expedition, intended to establish direct trading with the eastern Mediterranean, meant the focus became opening up the Atlantic. Politically, after a flirtation with absolutism under Richard II, the King was bound by the laws passed by Parliament. Linguistically, English was completing the displacement of French as the language of culture, politics and the law. Common law established its supremacy over Roman civil law.

The country was reshaping itself without the English aristocracy as a landed warrior class. To become relevant again the aristocracy had to change and find a way forward. Under a weak king, like Henry VI, it could indulge in futile and ulti-mately self-defeating internecine warfare. But when the King was strong, as in the case of an Edward IV or a Henry VII, it could survive by finding a way to serve the interests of the early modern state. The Earl of Worcester, through his life, pointed to many of the answers. In many ways he stood on the cusp of the transition of the medieval and the modern.

Traditionally, the boy of knightly and noble class was sent to the household of a greater magnate for training in martial and chivalric arts. The young Tiptoft's education seemed intended not to prepare him to be a fighting knight but a scholar able to absorb the lessons of humanist learning. He went to Oxford at an older age and for longer than any other secular English Medieval noble. His Oxford was demotic and clerical compared to later centuries but was about to become much more aristocratic and secular as more young peers followed him.

A great aristocrat needed to shine with the reflected glory of the fine minds he gathered around him. 'In all England there were at this time only two men who understood the meaning of patronage in the Italian sense, and of these one was William Grey and the other was John Tiptoft.'[16] Even allowing for hyperbole Worcester must have impressed the likes of Ognibene Bonisoli, Francesco Aretino and Ludovico Carbone, who compared him to Virgil, Minerva, Cato and others. Pope Pius II, as reported by John Free, stated that the Earl stood comparison to Alexander and Lucullus. He understood the importance of oratory and sought, by his offering of books to Oxford, to raise English standards to match those of the Italians.

Worcester went on pilgrimage to the Holy Land but he also pioneered the route of the Grand Tour of Italy, visiting Venice, Florence and Rome—and assuredly other places—and returning with a great trove of books. His years in Italy anticipated the passion of generations of English aristocrats to come. In the seventeenth and eighteenth centuries they would replace the Tudor prodigy house with Italianate designs. At his manor of Bassingbourn the Earl may have planned a rural retreat inspired by the villas of the Medici and the *delizie* of the d'Este.[17]

Politically, Worcester served the state, an impersonal entity, rather than the person of his feudal overlord. Indeed, the Earl bluntly informed the Dominican friar so when challenged on the way to the block. 'Lord you are brought here for your unheard of cruelty, and mostly because wanting to extinguish certain lords, enemies of the state ... The Duke said that he had done it for the state.'[18] *The Declamacion of Noblesse* conceived of true nobility not as that inherited through blood but that earned by merit through service. When in office, particularly in the mid-1450s, the Earl's manner of operation was almost modern—with near daily attendance at the Treasury and the Continual Council, combined with management of Parliament when sitting. He was endlessly appointed to commissions to investigate criminal behaviour, tax raising and evasion, military readiness and insurrection.

By chance, the Earl was a widower without children and a man with no great ancestral castle, *terroire* or affinity. His diocese was London and his houses near and in the City. He was thus ideally placed to be constantly about the King and court. The impressive, efficient and economical royal court of Edward IV, with its wonderful music, spectacular tournaments and beautiful maidens, did not spring from nowhere—and for all the abilities of the young king this maybe bespoke a cosmopolitan, cultured mind, familiar with Florence, Ferrara and possibly Mantua and Milan. It was Worcester, with his tightly drawn ordinances, who set the model for tournaments, which had a political, rather than quasi-military, purpose that lasted through the next century. And it was he who restored order to the system of precedence after the proliferation of noble ranks. Knightly orders and chivalry were harnessed to the service of the state. He stage-managed the great tournament of 1467 which cemented Anglo-Burgundian relations.

Worcester may have brought a Machiavellian finesse to both war and intelligence. Someone masterminded the Lincolnshire campaign of 1470, won without the need for a proper battle, the enemy defeated by pre-emptive letter writing, the assembling of overwhelming force which may have involved an element of bluff, and morale-sapping executions. To the beheadings of the Earl of Oxford in 1462 and the Earl of Desmond in 1468 the dictum 'execute earls early and the situation will cool down' might apply.

Worcester's importance transcended his life, which ended in personal failure. The medieval English peerage would have had good reason to fear for its future—to the extent that it was capable of rationally analysing its condition. More likely, the aristocracy simply felt an uncomprehending anxiety, as the old certainties evaporated and the risk of unnatural death was ever present at the hands of the common archer, executioner or lynch mob. The Earl's life offered the English aristocracy a way forward as educated courtiers rather than feudal warriors. In his life and untimely death he anticipated the great royal servants, Sir Thomas Cromwell, Earl of Essex (1485–1540), and Sir Thomas Wentworth, Earl of Strafford (1593–1641)—also setting a precedent that such loyal service was not without risk.

The Earl of Worcester's life was noteworthy not just because it offered a lifeline to the late medieval English aristocracy but also because it raised several timeless issues inherent in the *condition humaine*.

Is it possible to justify doing bad things for the good of the state? The Italian Dominican friar who accompanied Worcester to Tower Hill challenged him over the execution of two juveniles. The Earl justified an action, bad in itself, on the basis of the greater good embodied by the state. 'The friar replied, that for the state one ought to do only [that which is] just and honest and not the opposite; according to the words of St Jerome, no compassionate man ever died a bad death and the opposite happened to the impious and cruel.'[19] Ultimately, this is an ethical question without a right answer, but Worcester may have believed that the greater good could justify a reprehensible action.

What is the answer to the conundrum that disobedience to orders might mean personal extinction, yet obedience required actions judged immoral and could also lead, if the tables turned again, to death? If Worcester obeyed the command of the King, where this was contrary to the common law, then obedience to the King was no defence. Bishop Gardiner wrote, 'Lord Typtoft, ... in execution of the King's Commission he offended the Laws of the Realm, he suffered on Tower Hill.' The Earl's ghost explained in the *Mirror for Magistrates*,

> For I enforst by meane of governaunce,
> Did execute what eur my king did byd.
> From blame herein my selfe I can not ryd,
> But fye vpon the wretched state, that must
> Defame it selfe, to serue the princes' lust.

The spirit asked what his enemies would have done?

> Obey the King, or proper death procure?
> They may wel say their fancy for a face,
> But life is swete.

The ghost's solution was that only those who are willing to disobey their king should take high office.

> Let none such office take,
> Save he that can for right his prince forsake.[20]

But he, or the author of his words, must have known this was no real answer. On this basis there would be very few takers for such work. The sovereign might allow no disobedience. In Shakespeare's *Henry VI* the lieutenant of the Tower, the position held by Worcester, told the briefly liberated king in 1470, 'Subjects may challenge nothing of their sovereigns.'

How is it possible for highly educated, cultured men to kill and torture, apparently dispassionately? Worcester loved learning but willingly condemned to death without compunction. Human nature, unfortunately, has the capacity to both create and appreciate beauty while also inflicting bestial cruelty. A better question is why might sensitive and intelligent men act cruelly if not out of simple sadism? Here an explanation might be found in making politics an art, as in Italy, where music, rhetoric, ceremony and the visual arts were employed to further political objectives. Subtlety was valued over brute force. A few executions, early on in a regime or a military campaign, might put an end to dissent. Machiavelli's dictum that a prince cannot always follow those practices by which men are regarded as good may have worked with the 1462 Oxford plotters, for until the Neville revolt in 1469 there were no more English, court-based conspiracies. It did not succeed, however, with the Irish, after the execution of Desmond in 1468. Worcester doubtless considered the Irish response irrational but there are limits to reason which highly intelligent men often fail to appreciate.

What is true nobility and, if it is seen as earned rather resulting from birth, where might be the problems? Worcester's views might be revealed by his selection for translation of Buonaccorso's *De vera nobilitate* as *The Declamacion of Noblesse*. Gayus Flamyneus declaimed, 'I trowe that noblesse resteth not in the glorye of an other man, or in the flyttynge goodes of fortune, but in a mannes owen vertu and gloyre.' This, to modern ears, might sound only right. Nobility should be earned and not depend on arbitrary inheritance. In practice, the situation is more complex and might depend on how developed the society is overall. In the fifteenth century men of quite modest background, like John Fastolf, might rise high as captains in France. In 1282, however, when Worcester's ancestor Robert Tibetot was selected as Marshal in Wales, the Constable of England, Humphrey de Bohun, Earl of Hereford, protested successfully because of Robert's social inferiority, even though he had an excellent military record and was close to the King. Then earls could not serve paid household knights.

A system based on earned rather than inherited nobility might seem superior but it could be unstable and possibly dangerous. In 1460 Paston reported that the Earl of Warwick berated the future father-in-law of Edward IV, saying, 'His father was but a squire, and brought up with King Henry V, and since made himself by marriage, and also made a lord; and that it was not his part to have language of lords being of the King's blood.'[21] In 1464 Woodville's daughter Elizabeth married Edward IV. Had she known this would lead to the deaths of her father, two brothers and two sons, might she have settled for being his mistress and not so disrupted precedence?

Lastly, there is the endless riddle of managing England's relationship with Europe. Worcester was respected (and liked) by the Italians and Burgundians, Roberto da Sanseverino, the Capodilista cousins, Vespasiano da Bisticci, Ognibene Bonisoli, Francesco Aretino, Ludovico Carbone, Olivier de la Marche and Jean de Waurin. He was instinctively in tune with the trend of European scholarship and sought to bring the most up-to-date developments to England. He could address and work with that para-European body *par excellence*, the papacy. He is the most obvious candidate for the intellect behind Edward IV's efficient court, with its use of ceremony and chivalrous orders and contests to project authority, drawing on continental models. But in England he was hated because 'he had brought back from Italy the laws which are called the laws of Padua, and everyone shouted that he would die'.[22] This was a country heading for a religious Brexit, with the split with Rome under Henry VIII—ironically masterminded by another great Englishman who spent time in Italy, Thomas Cromwell. The cosmopolitan, intellectual Worcester was disliked and damned by the little-Englander chroniclers and the mud thrown by the likes of Warkworth and Gregory has stuck—so the Earl's greatness and importance has remained largely unrecognised.

Appendix 1

Man of letters

The antiquary John Leland compared Henry VIII to his scholarly royal and noble predecessors. No king after Henry I was included. The two most recent were of noble not royal rank.

> The name of your Majeste, whos glorie in lerning is to the worlde so clerely knowen, that though emonge the lyves of other lernid menne I have accurately celebratid the names of Bladudus, Molmutius, Constantinus Magnus, Sigebertus, Alfridus, Alfridus Magnus, Æthelstanus and Henry the firste, Kinges and your progenitors; and also Ethelwarde, secunde sunne to Alfride the Greate, Hunfride Duke of Glocestre, and Tipetote Erle of Worcester; yet conferrid withe yowr Grace they seme as smaule lighttes ... yn respecte of the day-starre.[1]

Leland thought Tiptoft important indeed in the development of English scholarship when he had listed those who brought back learning from Italy. 'Fosterer of the talented, our Britain also has borne Free, Tiptoft, and Flemming; then Grocyn followed these lights of learning, and Celling, Linacre, Widow, and pious Latimer, Tunstall the Phoenix, Stokesley and Colet, Lyly and Pace—a festal crown of men!'[2]

The Earl, however, was so busy with other affairs that there were relatively few mature years for him to devote to scholarship. As he wrote in 1460 to Oxford University, 'I have not been able to show clearly enough my loyalty to you in my life thus far, being obstructed by private then public affairs.'[3] His time as a patron and man of letters appears largely to have been compressed into the years in Italy between 1458 and 1461. Unfortunately his letter book has been lost and, while Caxton said there were other 'virtuous werkys, which I haue herd of', only two translations the printer attributed to the Earl survive. Therefore there is only limited evidence as to why Leland judged him so highly.

Translations – Caxton printed two translations in one of his first books in 1481, *On Friendship* or *De Amicitia* by Cicero, and *The Declamacion of Noblesse*, a translation of Buonaccorso's *De Vera Nobilitate*.

The *De Amicitia* is generally regarded as an early work as it is clumsy and rather literal. *The Declamacion*, however, is both polished and lively. It is likely that the Latin original by the Florentine Buonaccorso was obtained on one of the Earl's visits to Florence between 1459 and 1461.

Despite possibly fifteen centuries separating authorship of *De Amicitia* and *The Declamacion* they have much in common and the choice by the Earl to translate them is revealing. Both translations are from Latin texts, albeit one from the first century BC and the other the fifteenth century AD, and both are in the form of imagined dialogues. They involve the main types of relationship a person can enter where there might be some discretion: the choice of a partner of the opposite sex; and friends of the same sex. Both relationships have, at their basis, virtue. *The Declamacion* posed a choice between nobility of birth and nobility of virtue; and in *De Amicitia* the foundation of proper friendship was virtue.

The Earl's choice of texts reflected ideas that interested him. Worcester, whose grandparents spanned city worthies to top nobles, must have pondered the issues of nobility, friendship and virtue. *The Declamacion* asserted that 'Noblesse resteth not in the glorye of an other man, or in the flyttynge goodes of fortune, but in a mannes owen vertu and gloyre'. Worcester's own friendships with the monk Henry Cranebroke, the scholar John Free and his tutor and companion John Hurley proved durable. In 1458 he left manuscripts with Cranebroke, in 1460 and 1461 he studied with Free, and when Hurley died in 1469 he left a cup and property to the Earl whom he had known for three decades. On the other hand the Earl's close relationship with the Nevilles broke down in the late 1460s. 'Ffor syth that virtue is the verray knotte of friendship it is harde for friendship to a byde, when men departe from virtue.' The Nevilles rebelled against their king while Worcester degraded the bodies of Warwick's retainers. Not only did the friendship break down but all paid with their lives for the loss of virtue.

Letters – Worcester's correspondence can be divided into several groups.

- **Cranebroke correspondence – 1451/2** – A correspondence of three letters survives between the Earl and the Canterbury monk Henry Cranebroke (*BL. MS. Royal 10 B IX, f. 122*).[4] The first addressed to Cranebroke from Tiptoft in a rather bad Ciceronian style, the second in English from Tiptoft to Cranebroke. This is the one document where Tiptoft the man is revealed, despairing following the death of a wife. The last was a letter in Latin addressed by Cranebroke to Tiptoft also attempting, somewhat more accurately, a classical Latin style. The letters have been neatly transcribed onto a single sheet by the monk in his note book of collected texts and must have been part of a much larger exchange of letters. The correspondence demonstrated both men's interest in Cicero, which was shared by the circle around Sir John Fastolf.
- **Oxford University – 1460** – In 1460 Worcester wrote to Oxford offering books (*Bodley MS. 80*).[5] The letter style is polished and he may have used the services of his secretary and client John Free. The University replied comparing Worcester to a second Humphrey.[6]

- *Liber epistolarum Johannis Tiptofti* – **possibly 1460/61** – A great loss is Tiptoft's letter book which the early eighteenth century antiquary Thomas Tanner reported was housed in the library of Lincoln Cathedral. There were twenty-one letters. Tanner identified seven of them.

  The letters from the Earl were to: Laurentius More who R.M. Mitchell thought was the captain of the Venetian galleys, Lorenzo Moro; Wilelmus Atteclyff (William Atteclyff), a Cambridge and Padua alumnus, Henry VI's physician and Edward IV's secretary and ambassador; magister Vincent Clement, the Catalan cleric, Oxford doctor of divinity and proctor at Rome for English clients; and John Free, Oxford, Padua and Ferrara alumnus, Tiptoft's client, secretary and friend.

  To the Earl were letters of: Galeotus Martius, a Paduan alumnus and scholar; Guarino da Verona, the great scholar and teacher from Ferrara; and again John Free.

  Three of the known correspondents were Italian, More, Martius, and Guarino, one, Vincent, a Catalan who lived mostly in England and Italy, and two English men, Free (who was in Italy) and Atteclyff (who had earlier also been a student at Padua).

  The letters from the Earl at least must have been copied (the three Cranebroke letters are not originals but copies by the monk onto a single sheet and possibly the Lincoln letters were similarly made into a single document). The most obvious candidate as the copier was John Free, who died in Italy in 1465. These copies were perhaps brought back to England by John Gunthorpe or Robert Flemming. In 1465 the latter possibly donated a collection of texts to Lincoln College, Oxford. Somehow the Tiptoft collection ended up in Lincoln Cathedral. The diocese of Lincoln then included Oxford.

  This correspondence can be linked to Italy or to the time when Worcester was there. The presence on the list of Vincent Clement and William Atteclyff is of note as this indicates communication with Yorkist supporters in the period when the Earl was in Italy. In November 1460, when the Yorkists were in control, Clement was appointed the King's proctor in the papal court. In February 1461 Atteclyff fled England and was captured by the French; he was ransomed by Edward IV and became his secretary and ambassador. These letters provide circumstantial evidence of the Earl's relationship with the Yorkists during his time in Italy.

- **1465 challenge to the Bastard of Burgundy** – There survives a long formal letter from the Earl of Worcester, in his role of Constable of England, to Antoine the Bastard of Burgundy conveying the challenge from Anthony Woodville (*Lansdowne, MS. 285, f. 2*).

Library – There is good evidence that the Earl of Worcester assembled a remarkable library. His Italian biographer Bisticci wrote of the Earl: 'He departed from Padua, came to Florence, and he wanted to go to Rome, having the greatest numbers of copies of books.'[7] In the eulogy to Guarino, Ludovico Carbone declaimed against the Earl, 'being exceedingly fond of books, has plundered our Italian libraries to enrich England'. At least thirty-five of the Earl of Worcester's books have been identified (for a continually expanding list see bonaelitterae.wordpress.com). The surviving books are remarkable for several reasons. The texts selected were at the cutting edge of contemporary scholarship. They included such recently discovered authors as Lucretius, Manilius and Silius Italicus. Some of the manuscripts commissioned in Padua had beautiful illuminations, including the arms and helm of the Earl of Worcester at the beginning of the *De Grammaticus et Rhetoribus* of Suetonius (see Plates). A number of texts were annotated by the Earl alone (revealing he learned to write the humanist italic script), by John Free, and in some cases by both. Some were marked by the Earl's distinctive *manicula* or drawn pointing hand, indicating a key piece of text. Many English noblemen and women collected books, largely bibles, books of hours, English and French verse and prose; Worcester's surviving books however reveal a serious scholar who had personally collected and studied in Italy.

After the Earl's execution in October 1470 the University of Oxford wrote to Archbishop George Neville desperately asking him to find the books promised to them by Tiptoft. Neville replied saying he had secured some of the books but the rest were in Ireland. The accounts for Cambridge for 1470–71 show an emissary was sent to Neville regarding books promised to the University.[8] Worcester's property remaining in Ireland was granted to the Earl of Kildare.[9] Curiously, the Kildare Book of Hours records that on the 14th of July, '*Isto die natus erat Edwardus fil: Johannis comitis Wigornie circa horam terciam post meridian 1469*,' or 'This day was born the son Edward: of John Earl of Worcester around the third hour after midday 1469.'[10] The Kildare library was scattered in a rebellion of 1642 but the Book of Hours had already left the collection.

Despite the early date in the history of printing the Earl of Worcester had at least two printed books. At some time, between 1466 and 1468, Worcester arranged with the Hansa merchants at the London Steelyard to bring him two printed Bibles. Gerhard von Wesel of Cologne mentioned in his accounts that he had received the Bibles on behalf of 'my lord Worchester'.

Ordinances – The Earl of Worcester devised two important sets of ordinances. These were functional works and testament to the Earl of Worcester's clarity of mind.

- **Tournament** – Orders and statutes for joust and triumphs by J. Tiptoft (*Cotton Tiber. MS. E. viiii. 35*). These were devised for the great tournament of 1467. The rules were so clear and precise that they remained in use throughout the next century.

- **Precedence** – Orders made by John Tiptoft, Earl of Worcester and Constable of England, in the sixth year of Edward IV for the placing of nobility in all proceedings (*Cotton Tiber. MS. E. viiii. 35*). The rules for precedence had been reasonably straightforward when there were earls and barons only. The addition since the reign of Richard II of dukes, viscounts and marquises, as well as the depredations of war and attainder, had greatly complicated the situation. Whereas dukedoms were meant to be restricted to the closest royal family, the conflict of York and Lancaster meant several families, no longer immediately close to the king, counted dukes among their number, all with competing elevated ideas as to their status.

  To Worcester was attributed a solution to the problem of how to rank the eldest sons of peers. 'What was known among the old heralds as *Tiptoft's Rule*, because it was of his devising, provided that the eldest son of every one of a created degree is *tanquam* the next degree under him, but is to take the place after the next created degree.' Thus, a Duke's eldest son was placed after the marquises.[11]

Orations – The Earl of Worcester understood the importance of oratory. He offered in 1460 to send books to Oxford University so that the English could match the Italians, the masters of eloquence. So brilliant was the Earl's own oratory that in the following year he brought tears to the eyes of the Pope, Pius II. Tanner recorded an *Orationem at Patavienses*. In England he appears to have been selected to speak on behalf of delegations. In 1453 the Earl addressed Convocation, 'in his crystal-clear vernacular, the threatening dangers of the commonwealth of this once very famous and flourishing realm, in a solemn and elegant speech devised and delivered with great sharpness of mind'.

Dedications and addresses – The Earl of Worcester merited several dedications and other addresses:

- Circa 1451 John Manyngham, register of Oxford University, dedicated a selection of texts now titled the Manyngham 'miscellany' (*Trinity College MS. 438*). Worcester was then around 24 years of age and had held as yet no great position. He was clearly, however, identified as a man to cultivate and seen as seriously interested in classical texts.

- In 1461 John Free dedicated his translation from Greek to Latin of Synesius's *Encomium Calvitii* or *In Praise of Baldness* (*Bodley MS. 80*).
- Leland wrote that Free also dedicated lost poems to the Earl 'in which Bacchus remonstrates with the goat gnawing the vine'.
- Probably in 1460 or 1461 Ognibene Bonisoli dedicated a translation of Xenophon's *De Venatione* (*Beinecke, MS. 149*).
- In 1461 Francesco Aretino (also known as Francesco Griffolini of Arrezo) dedicated a translation from Greek to Latin of Lucian's *De Calumnia* (*Arundel MS. 277, f. 107b*).
- Ludovico Carbone wrote a charming elegy to the Earl sadly declining his offer of work in England as he could not leave Borso d'Este's service (*Vatican Library, MS. Ottob. lat. 1153, f. 207r–v*).
- William Caxton's epilogues to the late Earl of Worcester's translations of *De Amicitia* and *The Declamacion of Noblesse* were extraordinary paeans to his merits.
- But when Leonardo Bruni dedicated a copy of Aristotle's *Politics* to the Earl of Worcester he was dissatisfied with the reception and gave it to Pope Eugenius IV instead.

Tiptoft's Chronicle – There was a chronicle titled *Chronica Regum Anglicae de diversis historiographis per dominum Johannem Wigornii comitem sparsim collectae*. The attribution was by the antiquary Sheldwych but there is a question whether it is the work of the father or the son. It took material from the Brut history of Britain published in 1437, meaning it cannot have been completed before that year. The last ten pages display first-hand knowledge of history of the reigns of Henrys IV and V so the father must have been involved in the writing of the text even if he was not the main author.

Appendix 2

Estate and houses

The Earl of Worcester's inheritance

The Earl of Worcester inherited a very substantial estate from his father who had only received two manors from his father, Sir Payn Tiptoft. This estate was composed of five basic elements.

Inheritance through the Earl of Worcester's father

1. **Paternal grandfather – Payn Tibetot –** The Tiptoft family itself was the smallest source of property as the great bulk of the Tibetot estate was divided between Payn's three older half-nieces, Margaret, Millicent and Elizabeth. Two manors were placed *in tail mail* (that is, they could be passed on only through the male line) by his father, John de Tibetot, to ensure Payn inherited something.

2. **Paternal grandmother – Agnes Wrothe –** Quite unexpectedly the male Wrothe line failed and Agnes, after her death, inherited the substantial Wrothe estate which included manors in Middlesex and Hampshire. This also brought Elsyng house near Enfield in Middlesex, which became the main family residence near to but not in the City of London. There was also a house in the parish of St James Garlickhythe which may have been that owned by the Earls of Worcester, including the Earl Tiptoft, up to 1551.

3. **Properties bought or granted to his father – Sir John, Lord Tiptoft and Powys –** For nearly four decades John Tiptoft served the King as a soldier, administrator, parliamentarian, and councillor. For this he was well paid and the money was reinvested in property. His first marriage to Philippa Gournay *née* Talbot brought him very substantial property. Her earlier second marriage to Matthew Gournay left her great estates in Somerset and Dorset and in Gascony. Tiptoft sold the reversion of the English Gournay estates to Henry V in 1417 for £4,000. This proved a good deal as John lived for another twenty-six years. He also used the reversion proceeds to buy further properties. When Tiptoft ceased to be the Seneschal of Aquitaine in 1423 he was owed £11,100 by the crown. As this could not be repaid he was granted further extensive estates in Gascony. On his death in 1443 the Gournay properties in England returned to the crown. Those in France should have been passed onto

the younger John Tiptoft but already effective control over them had been lost and was never recovered.

Inheritance through Worcester's father, Joyce Cherlton

4. **Maternal grandfather – Edward Cherlton** – Lord Cherlton was an important Marcher lord with substantial properties on the Welsh borders. These were divided between the lines of his daughters Joanna and Joyce. When, in turn Joanna's line died out, the property she had inherited was divided among the Earl of Worcester's coheirs.

5. **Maternal grandmother – Eleanor Holland** – Eleanor's father, Thomas Holland, 2nd Earl of Kent, had three sons and seven daughters. Only four of the daughters had children and his estate was divided into quarters. In turn Eleanor ultimately had three coheirs: Richard Plantagenet, her grandson by her first marriage to Roger Mortimer, 4th Earl of March, Henry Grey, her grandson by her second marriage to Edward Cherlton; and Joyce Tiptoft her younger daughter by the same marriage. Joyce received a twelfth of the Holland estate.

The Earl of Worcester's father created a vast estate from almost nothing, through his own ability in royal service, and had been an exceptional manager of it. Also he solved the problem of settling property on his two older daughters by purchasing the wardship and marriage of two major landowners, Thomas Roos and Edmund Ingaldisthorp, to whom he married respectively his first and second daughters Philippa and Joanna. He worked hard to ensure his wife received her due share of the complex Holland inheritance.

The Earl of Worcester's estate – The Earl of Worcester made substantial additions to the estate largely through his marriages although most of these additions proved temporary as no heir survived.

1. **Cecily Neville** – Cecily, whose first husband was Henry Beauchamp, Duke of Warwick, brought a substantial dower. The marriage, however, only lasted from 1448 to 1450. Cecily's daughter, Anne Beauchamp, was the ward of William de la Pole, Duke of Suffolk. She died in 1449 leaving as coheirs to a great estate Anne Neville née Beauchamp, the wife of Richard, Earl of Warwick, and George Neville, the son of Edward Neville, Lord Bergavenny and Elizabeth Despenser. On the 10th of June 1449 the Earl of Worcester was granted wardship of Bergavenny's lands, which might have been seen as a sign of royal favour. On the 22nd of May 1450 Worcester surrendered the wardship and the King granted it to the Earl of Warwick who had already commenced a protracted action to dispossess George of much of his inheritance.

2. **Elizabeth Greyndour** – The deaths of Cecily and Anne and the surrender of the Bergavenny wardship reduced the Earl's household's potential income and his second wife, although of knightly class, was a single child with substantial landholdings in Gloucestershire. Elizabeth was even more attractive because she was awarded a third of the properties of her first husband, Lord de la Warre, in dower to hold for her life. The marriage lasted only from 1451 to 1452, when wife and newborn son died on the same day, but the Earl retained her properties for the remainder of his life by claiming tenancy by 'the courtesy of England' (this was the practice of English law which gave a husband the holding, in his lifetime, of his wife's lands from the moment when a child capable of inheriting the land was 'born and heard to cry within the four walls'). Elizabeth's estate passed to her heirs after the Earl of Worcester's death in 1470.

3. **Elizabeth Corbet, *née* Hopton** – The Earl married for a third time in 1467 to Elizbeth Corbet. The Hoptons and Corbets were prominent West Midlands knights and gentry. She was a coheir to the estate of William de Lucy who died in 1461. His estate passed to his widow Margaret and on her death in 1467 it was divided between William's niece Elizabeth and nephew William Vaux. Elizabeth already had two sons and several daughters by her first marriage. She had another son, Edward, by the Earl of Worcester who died in 1485.

Other income – Unlike his father, Worcester does not appear to have striven to expand greatly his estate and his marriages ultimately left no addition to his property. Certainly by the time that he went to the Holy Land he appears to have established his estate so that it could run efficiently without his constant attendance—as it did when he was abroad in Italy and Ireland. His income was considerably augmented by the many great offices he held. He also owned several ships and was involved in trading with Gascony and in wool.

The Tiptoft estate after the Earl of Worcester's death – The Earl of Worcester was not attainted at the time of his execution and he had a live male heir who was a minor. This Edward, however, died without issue and the great Tiptoft estate passed to his coheirs who were his two living sisters, Philippa and Joanna, and the heirs of his deceased sister Joyce. Their inheritance was augmented as the line of the Earl's aunt Joanna *née* Cherlton also died out and its property was added to that which went to the heirs of the three Tiptoft sisters.

Houses

At no date is it possible to say with certainty where the Earl of Worcester actually lived and none of the houses he might have occupied has survived.

Great Eversden Manor – The Earl was born on the 8th of May 1427 at Great Eversden. The building, which must have been a fairly modest affair, was replaced in the seventeenth century by a farmhouse. There was a drawbridge and an oratory in the fourteenth century.[1]

The church of Great Eversden has two misericords which predate a fire caused by a lightning strike in 1464 that resulted in the total reconstruction of the church. They must have been retrieved from the wreckage and reused. One has the Beauchamp shield at centre flanked by a rose and a lion's head that also resembles a sun. Worcester's first wife was a Neville but her daughter was a Beauchamp. The Earl might have built some lost memorial for the souls of his stepdaughter and wives.

Figure 12: Mid-fifteenth century misericord which predates the 1460s rebuilding of Great Eversden church showing the Beauchamp arms – the Earl of Worcester's stepdaughter by his first marriage was Anne Beauchamp.

Elsyng Palace – It seems likely that the Earl's mother's preferred home was Elsyng in Enfield as she was buried in St Andrews church Enfield—and that seems a good candidate for the family home of his childhood, given that it was outside but near to London. The house was inherited with the Wrothe estate. Up until the eighteenth century Elsyng was regarded as built by Worcester. The antiquary John Norden (c.1547–1625) noted it was 'builded by an Earle of Worcester'.[2] Thomas Pennant (1726–98) wrote, 'On the north side of Fourtree-hill, stood Worcester House [now known as Elsyng Palace], built by the accomplished John Tibetot, or Tiptoft, Earl of Worcester ... The manor, which still retains his title, descended to him from his father, Sir John Tiptoft. The house was rebuilt on higher ground, by Sir Nicholas Raynton, knight, lord mayor of London in 1640.'[3]

292 Sir John Tiptoft

On the Earl's death this passed to his sister Philippa's son Edmund, Lord Roos, and then to Roos's sister Isabel and her husband Sir Thomas Lovell, who had custody of the Roos estates after 1492 when Edmund was declared insane. Isabel and Sir Thomas died childless and in 1524 Elsyng was settled on Thomas Manners, also descended from Philippa, later Earl of Rutland. In 1539 Rutland exchanged Elsyng with the King for another property. Elsyng had an important history in the Tudor era as a royal palace but was demolished in the seventeenth century. It was much rebuilt in the fifteenth century and sixteenth century but the Earl of Worcester's part in this is unknown. The building was partly of brick and arranged around two courtyards. In the later sixteenth century it was recorded as having a library, a hall and a chapel. It would be pleasant to think the Earl kept some of his books here.

Worcester House – In the City of London the Earl might have used the house in the parish of St James Garlickhythe, inherited from the Wrothes, whose estates included a house in that London parish.[4] The significance of this was that a large house between Thames Street and the river in the Garlickhythe parish was owned by the Earls of Worcester, although there is no record actually connecting the Tiptofts to this specific property.

A building in Lower Thames Street, which was in Garlickhythe parish, was called Worcester House. The antiquarian John Stowe (c. 1525 – 5 April 1605) wrote, 'In this part of Thames Street … was formerly a large house called Worcester House, as belonging to the Earls of Worcester.'[5] When the Earl of Worcester's property was divided among his sister coheirs and their lines, Worcester House might have gone to the Earl's sister Joanna's granddaughter Lucy Neville, who married Sir Anthony Browne. Their daughter Elizabeth married Charles Somerset, Earl of Worcester. The only documentary evidence relating this house to an Earl of Worcester was in the sixteenth century when, on the 6th of May 1551, the lease of Worcester House was granted by William Somerset, 3rd Earl of Worcester, to one Thomas Parrys.

This house overlooked the Thames as in 1563: 'In sant James in Garlyke heyff, in the plase that w[as the] yerle of Wosetur['s] plase [a woman] was delevered with a chyld, and after caste yt owt of a wyndow in-to Temes.'[6] A house located by the river would have been useful to the fifteenth-century Earl of Worcester who could have taken a boat to either the Tower or Westminster. This house, with an arched water-gate, may be shown in Agas's Map of London in 1561, to the west of Three Cranes, but it does not appear in Hollar's Map of 1647.

All that can be said with much certainty in terms of location is that Worcester was essentially a Londoner. A papal indult of 1459 called him 'John Earl of Worcester, of the diocese of London'.[7] On his return to England in 1461 his general locations are known from an entry in the Lincoln's Inn Black Book: 'Michaelmas Term. Richard Walwyn was admitted to repasts as long as he should remain on the business of John, Earl of Worcester, at London, or at the Tower of London, or near London.'[8] The first and third locations might be Worcester House and Elsyng. Between 1461 and 1470 the Earl was Constable of the Tower and between 1463 and 1467 Lord Steward of the Household. In the early part of his reign Edward IV's main London residence was the Tower and the Earl possibly had rooms there.

Bassingbourn – The manor of Bassingbourn was purchased in the 1420s by Lord Tiptoft and Powys. 'A quite remarkable garden and perhaps associated ornamental landscape seems to have been created in Bassingbourn between 1420 and 1488 the period when the land was held by the Tiptoft family.'[9] This might have been the site of a retreat built by the Earl, inspired by his time in Italy, 'where crucial developments in landscaping were taking place of which Tiptoft could hardly have been unaware'.[10] Leon Battista Alberti (1404–72) advised hillside sites with long views helped by platforms. The site at Bassingbourn matches this specification. The Earl probably stayed with the Medici at their villas of Careggi and Fiesole near Florence and must at least have been aware of the d'Este *delizie* built around Ferrara.

The site was planted with Balkan hazels or *Corylus maxima*. 'Until the 1950s, … there survived on a Cambridgeshire moat a row of gigantic cultivar hazels, probably relics of the orchard of Sir John Tiptoft, celebrated humanist and judicial murderer, dating from c.1465.' Also, 'The hazels of Bassingbourn are fascinating. The most fascinating is the Balkan Nut, *Corylus maxima*, which grew all round the area of the Medieval Castle Manor and was probably brought there by Lord Tiptoft about 500 years ago.'[11] Were it true that the Earl brought back seeds from his pilgrimage, which included stops on the Adriatic Balkan coast, then 'botanist' might be added to his protean talents.

Nothing remains above ground of the houses in Eversden, Enfield, the City or Bassingbourn. This might seem disappointing but it is also revealing. The Earl of Worcester did not have a great ancestral castle in which he might take up residence for part of the year. He was a close and powerful servant of the crown and lived near to the King. Also, his personal interest appears to have been more in books than buildings. Had he lived longer he might have built more but it is probable this would have been a great library. He may have remodelled Elsyng or Worcester House, as befitting his status as a great earl, but no evidence survives.

Appendix 3

Spellings of the Earl of Worcester's name

In fifteenth-century England spelling had yet to be formalised. The difficulty Europeans consequently had with recording the Earl of Worcester's name is almost comical. The following reflects many—but far from all—of the variants found researching this book. It is included for the consolation of English schoolchildren and all those who have struggled with spelling.

English (named source) – *erle of Worcestre, therle of Wurcestre* (Caxton), *my lord Worchester* (von Wesel, agent of the London Hanse in Cologne), *Tipetote Erle of Worcester, erle of Wicestre* (Leland), *Yerle of Worsetur* (Machyn), *Lord Iohn Tiptoft Earle of Wurcester* (Mirror for Magistrates), *Erle of Wyrcestyr* (Paston), *Earle of Woster* (Plumpton), *Sir John Triptoste, Earle of Worcester* (Stowe), *Erle of Worscetre, Erle of Worcetre* (Warkworth).

English (anonymous source) – *Erle of Worcestre, Erle of Worcesture* (description of the burial of Salisbury), *Therl of Worcestre* (Exchequer payments), *therle of Worceter, therle of Worcetur* (*Chronicles of London*), *John, erle of Worceter* (Greyndour Chapel foundation), *Erle of Worcetre* (Register of Stanbury), *John, Earl of Worchester* (Irish statutes), *erl Wysertyr* (Brief Notes).

Latin (English source) – *comes de Wiccester* (Brief Latin Chronicle), *Comes de Wyceter* (Brief Notes), *Dominus Johannes Tiptoth, Comes Wygorniæ* (Wheathamstead), *comitis de Wyrceter* (Ingaldisthorpe tomb), *dominus Iohannes Tupthoff comes Wyngorie* (Wey), *Johannem Tiptoft, Wigornensem comitem* (Rous), *Johannis comitis Wigornie domini Tiptot* (MS Harleian 103).

Latin (Italian source) – *Ioanni Uuocestre comiti Uicorniensi* (Bonisoli), *Johanne De Tiptoft Vigornae Comite Vigornae* (Aretino), *Joanni Anglico Virgorniae Comiti Virgorniae* (Carbone), *Johannes uigorniae comes uigorniae* (in *de judiciis astrologiae*, Haly Abenragel, Escurial)).

Italian – *Conte Giouanni de esseter* (Sansaverino), *Iuhanne de Hosseter* (Capodilista), *Duca di Worcestri* (Bisticci), *Giovanni conte de Vorcestre* (di Taverna).

French – *Le conte de Volsestre* (de la Marche), *messier Guillaume de Tiptoph Conte Dourchestette, Contes darondel et dourcestre* (Leeds Codex RAR, 0035(1.35)), *Le conte de Ourxestre, Le conte de D'Euxestre* (Waurin).

Irish – *le Seon Tipto .i iarla ho Bhusetra* (Torna Ó Maoil (Chronaire's tract on the Geraldines)), *.i. Irla Uorsester* (*Fragment of Irish Annals*).

Endnotes

Preface

1. Bisticci, p. 420.
2. CSPM, p. 143.
3. Bisticci, p. 418.
4. Fuller's *Worthies of England*, vol. 1, p. 234.
5. R. Fabyan, 1811, p. 659.
6. *Three Fifteenth Century Chronicles*, (A Brief Latin Chronicle), ed. J. Gairdner, London (for the Cam. Soc.), 1880, p. 183.
7. W. Caxton, Various epilogues to translations of *The Declamacion of Noblesse* (Tiptoft), *De Amicitia* (Tiptoft), *De Senectute* (anon.), London, 1481

PART 1 – HOUSE OF LANCASTER
Chapter 1 – Family – 1427 to 1440

1. Leland, p. 477.
2. *The Victoria County History, A History of the Country of Cambridge and the Isle of Ely*: Volume 5, Oxford, 1973.
3. J.H. Bayley, *The History and Antiquities of the Tower of London*, App. to Part III, T. Cadell, 1825. A list of the French who served under John, Duke of Bedford, included *Thomas Tybetot, dominus de Tybetot, miles, de Normannia natus* in, *Letters and Papers Illustrative of the Wars of the English in France*, ed. J. Stevenson, London, 1861, p 532.
4. '*Au moment de la terreur, la famille de Thiboutot émigre, le nom de Thiboutot qui, depuis 7 siècles s'était distingué aux armées du Roi de France, disparait.*'(www.maniquerville. com/index.php?page=famille-thiboutot-d-amerique).
5. http://planetipswich.webs.com/ipsmisc.htm
6. Duchess of Cleveland, *Battle Abbey Roll. With Some Account of The Norman Lineages. Duchess of Cleveland. In Three Volumes*, Vol. III, London, 1889.
7. *Lanercost Chronicle*, ed. H. Maxwell, BiblioBazaar, 2013.
8. *Collectanea Topographica et Genealogica*, Volume 4, ed. F. Madden, B. Bandinel, J. Nichols, London, 1834, p. 389.
9. Elizabeth, *née* Tiptoft, who married Philip le Despenser, was an ancestor of Diana, *née* Spencer, the first wife of the current Prince Charles.
10. Sir N.H. Nicholas, *Testamenta Vetusta*, London, 1868, p. 122.
11. Possibly the illegitimate Tiptoft is the same as one William Tiptoft who was committed to the Marshalsea in 1438. This prison was then used to contain those who

offended within the royal household—so, if this was the half-brother of John Tiptoft, then perhaps William had been found work by his successful relatives. S. Jenks, Bills of Custody in the reign of Henry VI, *The Journal of Legal History*, 23:3, pp. 197–222.

12. Usually the effigy is attributed to the Earl of Worcester, but he was buried in Blackfriars. See M. Ward, The tomb of 'The Butcher'? The Tiptoft monument in the presbytery of Ely cathedral, *Church Monuments, Journal of the Church Monument Society*, vol. XXVII, pp. 22–37

13. The life of Sir John Tiptoft, Lord Tiptoft and Powys, is extremely well documented in: *The History of Parliament: the House of Commons 1386–1421*, ed. J.S. Roskell, L. Clark, C. Rawcliffe., Boydell and Brewer, 1993; J.S. Roskell, *Parliament and Politics in Late Medieval England*, The Hambleton Press, 1983, vol. III, pp. 107–150; www.historyofparliamentonline.org/volume/1386–1421/member/tiptoft-sir-john-1443.

14. *Ibid.*

15. J. Weever, *Ancient funerall monuments within the vnited monarchie of Great Britaine, Ireland, and the islands adiacent with the dissolued monasteries therein contained: their founders, and what eminent persons haue beene in the same interred*. ... Composed by the studie and travels of Iohn Weever, John Harper, 1631, p. 209–10.

16. Roskell, *op. cit.*, p. 125.

17. G. Harris, G.L. Harriss, *Shaping the Nation: England 1360–1461*, Oxford University Press, p. 46.

18. A Baron de Powys was charged with campaigning in France in 1449 but this was probably Henry Grey, Earl of Tankerville and Lord Powys, the son of Joanna Cherlton. John Tiptoft's baronial title, like his father, was Lord Tiptoft and Powys.

19. There is evidence that the family was conscious of this royal descent, for the church of Wickambreaux had at its east end a coat of arms of Sir Anthony Browne who married Lucy Neville, Lord Tiptoft and Powys' great granddaughter, which included the arms of the Earl of Kent and the Earl of Worcester (the glass was recorded in 1758 and presumably removed when an Art Nouveau stained glass east window of the Annunciation dating from 1896 was installed).

20. Adam of Usk, *Chronicon Adae de Usk, A.D. 1377–1421*, ed. trans. by Sir E.M. Thompson KCB, London Henry Frowde, 1904, p. 227.

21. W. Stubbs, *The Constitutional History of England*, Oxford, 1896, p. 289.

22. *Transactions of the London and Middlesex Archaeological Society*, vol. 1, London, 1860, p. 100.

23. Sir J. Fortescue, *De Laudibus Legum Anglie*, ed. and trans. by S.B. Chrimes, Cambridge University Press, 2011, p. 25.

24. A. Gibbon, *Early Lincoln Wills*, 1280–1547, Lincoln, 1888, p. 159.

25. A.B. Emden, *A biographical register of the University of Oxford to AD 1500*, 3 vols. Clarendon Press, 1989. vol. 2, p. 988.

26. POPC vol. 3, p. 170.

27. Fortescue, J., *De Laudibus Legum Angliæ*, R. de Hengham, T. Evans, 1775, p. 157.

28. POPC vol. 4, p. xliiii.

Chapter 2 – Oxford – 1440 to 1443

1. J. Tait, Letters of John Tiptoft, Earl of Worcester, and Archbishop Neville to the University of Oxford', *English Historical Review*, xxxv, 1920, pp. 570–4, 1920. This is the source of the original Latin letter which has been translated and abbreviated.

2. J. Rous, *Historia Regum Angliae*, ed. T. Hearne, Oxford, 1745, p. 5.

3. Leland, p. 477.

4. Emden, op. cit, p. 989.

5. The names raise some interesting questions. In the first year who was 'Dominus Joh Typtot' and why is there no mention of a tutor and attendant? Might this be a reference to the father in retirement spending time as a pensioner? Also, in the first term of the 1443–4 academic year the young lord, who was 16, may have been allowed to live as a student without the attendance of the personal tutor 'Hurle'.

6. One possible reason for the selection of University College was that the grandson of the senior Lord Tiptoft's fellow councillor, Lord Hungerford, was resident at University College for three terms in 1437. The 1st Baron, Walter Hungerford, was a fellow councillor with Lord Tiptoft and Powys; his grandson, the future 3rd Baron, Robert Hungerford, was briefly resident at University in 1437–8, aged 9 or 10. Men joined in positions of authority often share experiences of elite education and Hungerford might have recommended the Great Hall.

7. Sir John Fortescue, *Governance of England*, ed. C. Plummer, Oxford, 1885, p. 348.

8. F. Caspari, *Humanism*, 1954, p. 1

9. J. Hughes, Stephen Scrope and the Circle of Sir John Fastolf: Moral and Intellectual Outlook, *Medieval Knighthood IV: Papers from the Fifth Strawberry Hill Conference 1990*, Ed. C. Harper-Bill, R. Harvey, pp. 109–146, Woodbridge: Boydell Press, 1992

10. *The Boke of Knyghthode, Translated from the French of Christine de Pisan, with a dedication to Sir John Fastolf, K.G. by S. Scrope*, ed. G.F. Warner, London, 1904.

11. The *Annales rerum Anglicarum* have been attributed to the pseudo-William Worcester, possibly Wyrcester's son who must have used notes gathered by his father. The *Annales* mention John Tiptoft, the Earl of Worcester, on several occasions, providing often rather wry and deprecating snippets that appear contemporary and were probably at least recorded by William, possibly following discussions with the Earl of Worcester.

12. J. Hughes, Educating the aristocracy in late Medieval England, *History Today*, Feb 1999.

13. L. Martinez, *Power and Imagination: City-States in Renaissance Italy*, Taylor and Frances, 1988, p. 194.
14. Fortescue, *op. cit.*, p. 119
15. R. Kirkpatrick, *English and Italian Literature from Dante to Shakespeare*, Routledge, 2014, p. 91.
16. *Munimenta academica*, or documents illustrative of academical life and studies at Oxford, ed. H. Anstey, vol. I, p. 60.
17. A. Cobban, *English university life in the Middle-Ages*, UCL Press, 1999, p. 202.
18. E. Hahn, *Fractured Emerald: Ireland*, History, 2014, p. 87.
19. Oxford, *Epistolae Academicae Oxon.*, ed. Anstey, H., Oxford, 1901, p. 355.
20. Cobban, *op. cit.*, p. 6
21. *ibid*, p. 55.
22. *ibid*, p. 33.
23. *ibid*.
24. *ibid*.

Chapter 3 – Wardship to earldom – 1443 to 1450

1. *Committee on the Dignity of a Peer of the Realm*, 5th report, Appendix 5, Great Britain, Parliament, House of Lords. 1829 (Rot. Cart. 27 and 39 (anno 27) Hen. VI. n. 43. in Turr. Lond.)
2. When an English tenant-in-chief, a tenant whose direct feudal overlord was the King, died an *inquisition post mortem* was held in each county where he held land and his or her land temporarily reverted to the crown until the heir sued livery, paid a sum of money, and was then able to take possession. Men came of age at 21 and women at 14. Where the heir was underage he or she would be subject to wardship where their lands and marriage passed to the King until they came of age. The wardship and marriage was generally sold but could be bought by the next of kin.
3. Philippa was about 20 and Tiptoft may have decided that his oldest child would marry the ward, who was of baronial rank, when he reached about 16—hence the first daughter being married after the second.
4. Roskell, *op. cit.*, p. 148.
5. 'Houses of Augustinian canons: Priory of Spinney', *A History of the County of Cambridge and the Isle of Ely*, ed. L.F. Salzman, Vol. 2, London, 1948, pp. 249–54.
6. CPR 1441–6, p. 182.
7. *ibid.*, p. 171.
8. *ibid.*, 1441–6, p. 176.
9. Tait, *op. cit.*
10. CPR 1441–6, p. 358.
11. GRP, C61/132 95.
12. GRP, C61/132 83.

13. GRP, C61/133 39.

14. GRP, C61/133 40.

15. E. Brayley, J.N. Brewer, J. Nightingale, *London and Middlesex*, Vol. 4, London, 1816. p. 747.

16. Nicholas, *Testamenta Vetusta*, *op. cit.* p. 254.

17. CPR 1446–52, p. 86.

18. *ibid.*

19. In the autumn of 1449 an army raised to support the remaining possessions in France was placed under the command of Lord Powys, almost certainly Tiptoft's cousin, Henry Grey and the experienced Sir Thomas Kyriell. Grey, Lord Powys, died in January 1450 before the expedition to Normandy left England. John Tiptoft's baronial rank was Lord Tiptoft and Powys but he was advanced to the Earldom of Worcester in July 1449.

20. R.L. Friedrichs, 'The Remarriage of Elite Widows in the Later Middle-Ages', *Florilegium*, vol. 23.1, pp. 69–83, 2006.

21. *Declamacion* (the reference was to Boethius' *Consolation of Philosophy* where Philosophy, in the form of a fair woman, consoled the condemned Roman patrician).

22. *Committee on the Dignity of a Peer of the Realm*, *op. cit.*

23. *ibid.* The next part of the charter, conferring the title, is given at the beginning of the chapter.

24. W.H. Dunham, Notes from the Parliament at Winchester, 1449, *Speculum*, XVII, pp. 402–4, 1942 (contains Harleian MS. 6849, fol, 77a); A.R. Myers, *A Parliamentary Debate of the mid-fifteenth century*, Crown, Household and Parliament in Fifteenth Century England, A&C Black, pp. 388–404, 1985.

25. PRME 1447–60, p. 105–6.

26. *Paston*, vol. 1, p. 124–5.

Chapter 4 – Commissioner – 1450 to 1452

1. R. Virgoe, Some ancient indictments in the King's bench referring to Kent, 1450–1452, Documents Illustrative of Medieval Kentish Society, *Kent Records*, vol. 18, 1964, p. 245.

2. R.J. Mitchell, *John Tiptoft (1427–1470)*, Longmans, London, 1938, p. 21.

3. *ibid.*

4. Augustine suggested in *The City of God* that there are two cities, one earthly and one heavenly: 'Their members live alongside one another in this world but hold different values, expectations and priorities.' He therefore encouraged Christians to see themselves as pilgrims travelling through the world, using its resources but not ensnared by them.

5. *John Benet's Chronicle for the years 1400 to 1462*, ed. G.L. Harriss, M.A. Harris, *Camden Fourth Series*, Vol. 9, Royal Historical Society, 1972, p. 203.

6. *Gregory's Chronicle: 1435–1450, The Historical Collections of a Citizen of London in the fifteenth century*, ed. J. Gairdner, London (for the Cam. Soc.), 1876, p. 97.

7. CPR 1446–52, p. 437.

8. CPR 1446–52, p. 442.

9. This section draws on an extremely useful unpublished thesis: Avrutick, J.B., *Commissions of Oyer and Terminer in Fifteenth-Century England*, M.Litt. thesis, London, 1957.

10. *ibid.* p. 15.

11. *ibid*, p. 81.

12. CPR 1452–61 p. 83 (Wynawey was later pardoned by the King).

13. Avrutick, op.cit., p. 95.

14. I.M.W. Harvey, *Popular revolt* , 1988. p. 205.

15. CPR 1446–52, p. 442.

16. A Short English Chronicle: London under Henry VI (1422–71), *Three Fifteenth-Century Chronicles with Historical Memoranda by John Stowe*, ed. James Gairdner, London, 1880, p. 68.

17. Gregory's Chronicle, *op. cit.* pp. 196–7.

18. *ibid.*

19. CPR 1446–52, p. 453

20. Gregory's Chronicle, *op. cit.* p. 197.

21. CPR 1446–52, p. 444–5.

22. *Political Poems and Songs Relating to English History, Composed During the Period from the Accession of Edw. Iii. to that of Ric. Iii.*, ed. Thomas Wright, London: Longman, 1861, p. 223.

23. CPR 1446–52, p. 475.

24. Paston, vol. 3, p. 124–5; R. Virgoe, *Some Ancient Indictments…*, p. 248.

25. The Earl of Shrewsbury's will revealed that he had a part interest in *The Nicholas of the Tower*. Foss, *op. cit.*, vol. iii, p. 350.

26. CPR 1446–52, p. 532.

27. CPR 1446–52, p. 477.

28. Harvey, *op. cit.* p. 213.

29. Virgoe, *op. cit.*, p. 254–5.

30. *ibid.*

31. CPR 1446–52 p. 508.

32. C. Fletcher, *The Black Prince of Florence*, Random House, 2016. p. 85.

33. British Library, *Chroniques de France*, Royal 20, E 111, f. 28.

34. Reginald West married first Margaret Thorley and had two sons and five daughters. In later life he was a surprisingly vigorous traveller to the Holy Land. The marriage between Reginald and Elizabeth, perhaps due in part to his long absences, was childless.

35. H.B. Wilson, *The History of the Merchant-Taylors School, from its foundation to the present time*, vol. II, London, 1814, p. xxvi.

36. In 1503 the Taylors Company became the Merchant Taylors recognising that its members were actually largely merchants.

37. *ibid*, p. xxvi.

38. Brit. Mus. MS. Royal 10 B IX, f. 122.

39. Mitchell, *op. cit.* p. 21.

40. Gillespie, A., Daniel Wakelin, 2011, p. 221.

41. R.M. Thomson, The reception of the Italian Renaissance in Fifteenth-Century Oxford: The Evidence of Books and Book-Lists, *Italia medioevale e umanistica* 47 (2007), pp 59–75, 2007.

42. The date of compilation may be between 16 July 1449, when John Tiptoft was made an earl, and when Manyngham ended being registrar during 1451. On 6 April 1451, Manyngham was allowed an undergraduate to copy texts. If this manuscript was a result it is datable to April–December 1451. See D. Rundle, *Dublin: Trinity College, MS.438 – Notice humanist miscellany compiled by John Manyngham*, 2009, bonaelitterae.files.wordpress.com/2009/07/dgrms7.pdf

43. Brit. Mus. MS. Royal 10 B IX, f. 122

44. CPR 1446–52, p. 513.

Chapter 5 – Treasurer and councillor – 1452 to 1453

1. D.B. Foss, *The Canterbury Archipiscopates of John Stafford (1443–52) and John Kemp (1452–54) with Editions of their Registers*, Vol. iii, pp. 1–471, unpublished thesis, King's College, London, 1986, p. 55, f. 221.

2. CPR, 1446–52, p. 543.

3. Bertoni, G., *Guarino da Verona fra letterati e cortigiani a Ferrara (1429–1460)*, Ginevra, 1921 (Carbone's eulogy in Appendix).

4. S. Steel, *The Receipt of the Exchequer 1377–1485*, Cambridge, 1954.

5. GRP, C61/138 71.

6. GRP, C61/138 72.

7. W. of Wyrcester, *Annales rerum Anglicarum*, Letters and Papers illustrative of the English in France. J. Stevenson, Rolls Series II, pt ii, 756–92, 1864, p. 770.

8. E404/68/103. Also, apart from the challenges of restoring order to royal finances, the position was not without personal danger. The previous Treasurer but one, James Fiennes, 1st Baron Saye and Sele, had been murdered during the Cade revolt. During the Peasant's Revolt in 1381 the Treasurer, Sir Robert Hales, was killed.

9. Foss, *op. cit.*

10. W.A. Pantin, Canterbury College Oxford, Vol. III, Oxford, 1950, p. 104.

11. Based on image titled 'Court of the Exchequer at Westminster, from a law treatise of Henry VI's reign. The court is presided over by the Lord High Treasurer *probably John Tiptoft, Earl of Worcester*, and four other judges.' In H.T. Evans, 1915, reprinted by Sutton Publishing 1995, p. 21.

12. A.L. Brown, 'The King's Councillors' 1969, p. 115.

13. R. Virgoe, The Composition of the King's Council, 1437–61, *Bulletin of the Institution of Historical Research* 43 (1970), pp. 155–60.

14. C.L. Kingsford, *English historical literature in the fifteenth century*, Oxford, 1913, (B.L. Cotton Roll ii, 23), p. 368 (Benet's Chronicle).

15. CPR 1446–52, p. 580

16. CPR 1446–52, p. 585

17. CCR 1468–76, p. 295

18. *Register of John Stanbury*, Bishop of Hereford, Canterbury and York Society, vol. xxv., 1919, p. 105.

19. In 1461 the Earl appears to have employed Elizabeth's heir after Joanna Greyndour while he was at Lincoln's Inn. In 1465 the Earl was identified by name by Joanna Greyndour as she included the quick as well as the dead in the chantry record (but there was again no mention of the dead baby John). In June 1470 a commission of array for the Forest of Dean called on John, Earl of Worcester, John Barre, knight, Thomas Baynham and William Walweyn, all linked through his second wife Elizabeth's family.

20. Foss, *op. cit.*, vol. iii, p. 350.

21. *Ibid.*, p. 56.

22. *John Stone's Chronicle: Christ Church Priory, Canterbury, 1417–1472*, ed. M. Connor, Medieval Institute Publications, Western Michigan University, 2010, p. 92–3.

23. Foss, *op. cit.*, vol. iii, p. 55.

24. A.R. Myers, *Crown, Household and Parliament in Fifteenth Century England*, A.C. Black, 1985, p. 217.

25. This resilient lady, who received Margaret of Anjou on her first arrival in England, would prove a friend to her in the desperate years after the final defeat of the Henry VI cause at the Battle of Tewkesbury in 1471.

26. J. Gairdner, Original Documents, Ralph Lord Cromwell, *Archaeological Journal*, Vol. 30, Issue 1, 1873, pp. 75–89

27. D.B. Foss. *op. cit.* vol. iii, p. 55.

28. *ibid.*

29. Steele, *op. cit.*, p. 273.

30. R.A. Griffiths, *The Reign of King Henry VI: The Exercise of Royal Authority, 1422–1461*, University of California Press, 1981, p. 393.

31. CPR 1452–61, p. 54.

32. CPR 1452–61, p. 60.

33. PRME 1447–60, p. 213.

34. POPC vol. vi, p. 221.

35. PRME 1447–60, p. 215.

36. Steel, *op. cit.* p. 272–6.

37. Griffiths, *op. cit.*, p. 394.

38. POPC vol. vi, p. 129.

39. POPC vol. vi, p. 136.

40. In 1415 Henry Inglose challenged Lord Tiptoft and Powys to a duel to be fought before the Duke of Bedford, Constable of England, over non-payment for services. There is no record of it taking place.

41. P.A. Johnson, *Duke Richard of York 1411–1460*, Clarendon Press, 1988, p. 123.

42. POPC vol. vi, p. 143–4.

43. POPC vol. vi, p. 151–2,

44. Johnson, *op. cit.*, p. 123, fn. 114,

45. J. Watts, *Henry VI*, 1999, p. 287.

Chapter 6 – 'Triumvir' and sea keeper – 1453 to 1455

1. R.A. Griffiths, The King's Council and the First Protectorate of the Duke of York, 1453–1454, *The English Historical Review*, Vol. 99, No. 390 (Jan 1984), Oxford University Press, 1984, p. 79–82.

2. POPC p. 163–4 (Johnson, p. 124).

3. CPR 1452–61, p. 143–4.

4. Griffiths, *op. cit.* p. 67–82.

5. *ibid*, p. 77–8.

6. *ibid*, p. 79.

7. Paston, vol. 1, p. 265.

8. CPR 1452–61, p. 140.

9. PRME, p. 221.

10. J.F. Baldwin, *The King's Council in England during the Middle-Ages*, Oxford University Press, 1913, p. 197.

11. *ibid* p. 197.

12. *ibid*, p. 355.

13. *ibid.*

14. *ibid.*

15. *ibid.*

16. CPR 1452–61, p. 171–2.

17. POPC vi, p. 174.

18. E28/84/7 to E28/84/37 (based on inspection at the National Archive).

19. POPC vi, p. 220–33.

20. Virgoe, *op. cit.*, op. 159.

21. G. Howard, Greek Visitors to England in 1455–1456, *Haskins Anniversary Essays in Medieval History*, ed. Charles H. Taylor, pp. 81–116, Boston: Houghton Mifflin Company, 1929.

22. Griffiths, *The Reign of Henry VI, op. cit.* p. 732.

23. *ibid*, p.733.

24. Griffiths, *op. cit.*, p. 733, fn 107.

25. *Letters and papers illustrative of the Wars of the English in France during the reign of Henry the sixth, King of England*, ed. A.R. Myers, vol. II, p. 494.

26. Paston, vol. i, p. 293.

27. CFrR, p. 401.

28. *ibid.*

29. *ibid.*

30. CCR, 1447–61, p. 46–62.

31. CPR 1452–61, p. 179.

32. *ibid*, p. 179.

33. Bertoni, op. cit.

34. GRP, C61 141.

35. CFrR, *op. cit.*, p. 402.

36. Stone, *op. cit.*, p. 97.

37. Johnson, *op. cit.*, p. 152.

38. *Ibid.*, p. 152, Foedera, part 2, p. 61.

39. Foedera, part 2, p. 61.

40. Issue Roll 33, Henry VI, Easter, m. 3 (PRO, E403/801)

41. Foedera, part 2, p. 61 (*De Ballio praefati Ducis exonerando*).

42. Steele, *op. cit.* p. 272–6.

43. *Ibid.*, p. 273

44. CPR 1452–61, p. 204.

45. CFrR, p. 416.

Chapter 7 – War and retreat – 1455

1. Benet, p. 215.

2. Paston, vol. 1, p. 416.

3. *Incerti Scriptoris Chronicon Angliae de Regnis Trium Regum Lancastrensium Henrici IV*, Henrici V et Henrici VI, ed. J.A. Giles, London, 1848. p. 214.

4. *ibid.*

5. POPC p. 245–6.

6. *Wingfield College and Its Patrons: Piety and Patronage in Medieval Suffolk*, P. Bloore, E. Martin, Boydel Press, 2015. p. 196.

7. There was a similar attempt to reform the currency in England associated with William Hastings in the 1460s but given that the Earl had again been Treasurer

under Edward IV in 1462 and 1463, it seems at least possible he was involved in the English reforms.

8. Virgoe, *Composition of the King's Council 1437–61, op. cit.*, p. 153.

9. J. Rous, *op. cit.*, p. 5.

10. Weiss, *op. cit.*, pp. 101.

11. J. Leland, trans. from Latin text in Leland, J., *Commentarii de Scriptoribus Britannicis*, ed. A. Hall, vol. 2. Oxford, 1709, pp. 475–81.

12. Fuller, *The History of the Worthies of England*, Vol. 1, p. 234.

13. Bale. J., *Illustrium majoris Britanniae scriptorum, hoc est, Angliae, Cambriae, ac Scotiae Summarium.*

14. *ibid*, p. 307.

15. *ibid*, p. 348.

16. F. Blomefield, C. Parkin, *An essay towards a topographical history of the county of Norfolk*, London, 1769, vol. III, p. 813.

17. The childless Worcester might have taken a genuine interest in Isabel and her welfare. She may have shared her uncle's interest in learning and was perhaps attached to him. Some remarkable and very unusual stained glass survives in the Norfolk church of St Mary Magdalen Wiggenhall which passed to Isabel from the Ingaldisthorpes. The saintly iconography is highly unusual and cerebral. The choices have been related to the Old Sarum rite, which the Earl of Worcester specified for confraternity of All Hallows Barking in 1465, and to saints who the Earl would have encountered commemorated on his travels in Italy.

18. Blomefield, *op. cit.*, p. 813.

19. M. Hemmant, ed., *Select Cases in the Exchequer Chamber*, Selden Society, li (1933), pp. 132–43.

20. CCR 1454–61, p. 300–1.

21. Paston, vol. 1, p. 416.

22. Pollard, *op. cit.*, p. 89.

23. A.J. Pollard, *Warwick the Kingmaker, Politics, Power and Fame*, Continuum Books, 2007, p. 34, p. 205, Hicks, *op. cit.*, p. 130.

24. Johnson, *op. cit.*, p. 213, fn. 97; C76/141 m. 19; CFrR, p. 425.

25. History of Parliament Trust, unpublished article on Robert Ingleton, J. Tuff, Historical, Topographical and Statistical Notices of Enfield, J.H. Myers, 1858, p. 130.

26. CXX. A Letter from the Queen to Sir Edmond Ingaldisthorpe, Knight, touching Henry Chevele a servant of his, *Royal Historical Society Camden Fifth Series Title History, Camden Old Series*, vol. 86, December 1863, p. 150–1.

27. Foedera, part 2, p. 77.

28. P.D. Clarke, P.N.R. Zutshi, *Supplications from England and Wales in the Registers of the Apostolic Penitentiary, 1410–1503*, vol. I: 1410–1464, Boydell Press, 2012, p. 108.

PART 2 – PILGRIM AND SCHOLAR
Chapter 8 – Venice to Jerusalem – 1458

1. W. Wey, *The Itineraries of William Wey* (*Itinerarium Peregrinacionis*), G. Williams, Roxburge Club, 1857, p. 71.
2. S. Jenks, *Robert Sturmy's Commercial Expedition to the Mediterranean (1457/8)*, The Bristol Record Society, 2006.
3. *ibid.*, p. 4–5.
4. CPR 1453–61, p. 517.
5. Mitchell, *op. cit.*, p. 31–2. Among the lost letters of the Earl of Worcester, that were in Lincoln Cathedral library, was one to Laurentius More who has been identified as Lorenzo Moro, the captain of the Venetian Galleys. In his role as Treasurer the Earl would have been familiar with these galleys—for every year they came to London to trade. The galleys brought eight butts of malmsey annually: four of these were intended for the King, two for the Chancellor, and two for the Treasurer (the future King Edward may have found the containers of his gifts unexpectedly useful in dealing with his perfidious brother, George, Duke of Clarence, who was reputedly drowned in a malmsey wine butt).
6. Mitchell, *op. cit.*, p. 198, fn. 12 (Archivio di Stato di Venezia, Senato Mar, vi. Fo. 68).
7. R. da Sanseverino, *Viaggio in Terra Santa*, ed. G. Maruffi, Bologna, 1888. Available as Nabu Public Domain Reprint. The sea voyage section is partly translated in T. Vidoni, The Journal of Roberto da Sanseverino (1417–87), *A study on navigation and seafaring in the fifteenth century*, The University of British Columbia, 1993.
8. *ibid*, p. 105.
9. Sanseverino, p. 59.
10. Jenks, *op. cit.*, p. 71–2.
11. Mitchell, *op. cit.*, p. 32.
12. P. Casola, *Canon Pietro Casola's Pilgrimage to Jerusalem in the Year 1494*, M.M. Newett, Manchester University Press, 1907. p. 155–61.
13. Sanseverino, *op. cit.* p. 40, Vidoni, *op. cit.*, p. 335.
14. R.J. Mitchell, *The Spring Voyage, The Jerusalem Pilgrimage in 1458*, John Murray, 1965. p. 70.
15. Jenks, *op. cit.*, p. 50 (bill presented by John Heytone and other merchants of Bristol against the Genoese before the lords of the council). But the English merchant's petition made no mention of the plague soon to be encountered by the pilgrims. Thus there was the somewhat surprising situation that in late May four English ships were harboured at Candia without report of plague but by the 7th of June plague was raging so severely that the pilgrims were discouraged from disembarking.
16. *ibid*, p. 51.

17. Sanseverino, *op. cit.,* p. 53; Vidoni, *op. cit.,* p. 344.

18. *ibid.*

19. Jenks, p. 71–2 (deposition of William Denys).

20. There may have been a connection between the Hospitallers and Worcester. The first husband of the Earl's second wife Elizabeth *née* Greyndour was Reginald de la Warre, Lord West, who had in 1447 involved himself in local affairs while on Rhodes. The Hospitallers would have wanted to cultivate a great earl who was an ex-Treasurer, close to the King, who had appointed him the previous year to lead a delegation to the pope. In the 1450s the eccentric scholarly Carmelite, Thomas Scrope, was papal legal to Rhodes. His memorial would include Tiptoft arms, indicating he had Tiptoft blood, but it is uncertain how.

21. Sanseverino, *op. cit.,* p. 57–8

22. *ibid,* p. 57.

23. *ibid,* p. 58.

24. *ibid,* p. 58.

25. *ibid,* p. 58.

26. *ibid,* p. 58–9.

27. *ibid,* p, 61.

28. *ibid,* p. 65; Vidoni, *ibid,* p. 349–50.

29. *ibid,* p. 66; Vidoni, p. 350.

30. *ibid.*

31. M. Kempe, *The Book of Margery Kempe 1436,* Jonathan Cape, London, 1936, p. 115.

32. *ibid,* p. 116.

33. Wey, *op. cit.,* p.72.

34. Sanseverino, *op. cit.,* p. 76.

35. Wey, *op. cit.* p. 84.

36. *ibid.,* p. 89.

37. R. Bowers, *Choral institutions within the English church: their constitution and development, c.1340–1500,* D.Phil. thesis, University of East Anglia, 1975, ref. 5058.

38. Wey, *ibid,* p. 73.

39. Wey, *ibid,* p. 74.

40. Capodilista, *op. cit.,* p. 211.

41. *ibid,* p. 211.

42. Sanseverino, *op. cit.* p. 105–106.

43. Wey, *op. cit.,* p. 75.

44. *ibid,* p. 77.

45. *ibid,* p. 78.

46. Drawing based on a painting in Guillaume Caoursin's *Gestorum Rhodie obsidionis commentarii,* Bibliothèque Nationale de France, Lat.6066, f. 8r.

47. Jenks, *op. cit.*, p. 72.
48. *ibid*, p. 23–4.
49. *ibid*, p. 71–2 (Deposition).
50. *ibid*, p. 62 (Memorandum).
51. *ibid*, p. 71–2.

Chapter 9 – Italy I – scholarship, 1458 to 1461

1. G. Bertoni, *Guarino da Verona fra letterati e cortigiani a Ferrara (1429–1460)*, Ginevra, 1921 (Ludovico Carbone's eulogy for Guarino is in the Appendix); dante. di.unipi.it/ricerca/html/Elogio-Carbone.html.
2. *ibid*.
3. Bisticci, p. 417–8.
4. Leland, p. 476.
5. R.J. Mitchell, English Students at Padua, 1460–75, *Transactions of the Royal Historical Society*, Fourth Series, Vol. 19 (1936), pp. 101–16, pp. 105–6.
6. Mitchell, *op. cit.*, p. 65.
7. R.M. Thomson, The reception of the Italian Renaissance in Fifteenth-Century Oxford: The Evidence of Books and Book-Lists, *Italia medioevale e umanistica*, 47, 2007, p 70.
8. Sanseverino, p. 316.
9. Leland, p. 476.
10. BL, Arundel 277, fol. 107 (Aretino dedication to the Earl of Worcester).
11. BL, Arundel 154, fol. 41 (Aretino letter to Francesco Pellato).
12. Beinecke MS 149 (Yale University) (Ognibene Bonisoli's dedication to the Earl of Worcester).
13. Tait, *op. cit.*, pp. 571–2.
14. A.D. Scaglione, Knights at Court: Courtliness, Chivalry, & Courtesy, *Ottonian Germany to the Italian Renaissance*, University of California Press, 1991, p. 221.
15. H. Anstey, *Epistolae Academicae Oxon.*, 2 vols, Oxford Historical Society, xxxv & xxxvi, Oxford, 1898, ii, pp. 354–5.
16. Thomson, *op. cit.*, p. 67. Perhaps Worcester had wanted to learn Greek as well as Latin and his desires were thwarted by diplomatic demands in 1461 and the recall to England. He appears to have understood the importance of Greek as several of the books he commissioned or bought were recent translations from Greek to Latin. John Free dedicated to him a Greek to Latin translation of Synesius's *On Baldness* (maybe the Earl was prematurely losing his hair).
17. R. Strohm, *The rise of European music, 1380—1500*, Cambridge University Press, 2005, p. 392.
18. S. Oosthuizen and C. Taylor, 'John O'Gaunt's House', pp. 61–76.
19. Mitchell, *op. cit.*, p. 65. R.M. Mitchell says this was the only work that passed through Tiptoft's hands known to have been produced in Vespasiano's workshop.

The style of illustration is completely different from Tiptoft's other MSS and supports the theory it was written in Florence not in Padua.

20. In April 1461 he was studying law at Padua, where he was elected rector. By June 1462 he had left Padua and was back in England, where he entered the service of King Edward IV, and was sent by the King to offer the Duke of Milan the Order of the Garter. In November 1463 he acted as the King's proctor in the papal curia.

21. Bertoni, *op. cit.* (App.).

22. Florence, Archivio di Stato, M. a. Pr., F. VI, Doc. 531.

'To the generous and shining man lord Giovanni de' Medicis Florence / Esteemed and honoured Sir / I have to send your Excellency these songs on behalf of the illustrious Lord Giovanni Count of Worcester, on whose behalf I have to send you infinite greetings and thanks for the kind welcome and good company which you gave him, and he begs you to excuse him for sending few light songs [*canzone*] owing to his being short of time, offering to supply in future more foreign songs, and if he can do anything else for your noble self you have only to let him know and you will have it promptly and with pleasure. I send you the said songs in a waxed may it please you to let me know the safe arrival of those songs, so that I can assure his Excellency the said Earl of having given a good opinion of the things I have sent and posted. / Your lordships to command, and may God bless you / From Venice, 17 December 1460 / Ambrosio di Taverni with recommendation'

23. Mitchell, *op. cit.* p. 65.

24. *ibid.*

25. *ibid.*

26. *ibid.*

27. *ibid.*

28. In 1455 payments initiated when Worcester was Treasurer were made by the Exchequer to four Greek scholars including Argyropoulos.

29. Bisticci, *op. cit.*, p. 418.

30. Free, *op. cit.*

31. Caxton, *op. cit.*

32. Leland, *op. cit.*

33. *ibid.*

34. Bertoni, *op. cit.* (App.).

35. R. Weiss, John Tiptoft, Earl of Worcester, and Ludovico Carbone, *Rinascimento*, 8, pp. 209–12, 1957.

36. *ibid.*

37. Bodleian MS 80, *op. cit.*

38. H. Hoyt Hudson, John Leland's List of Early English Humanists, *Huntington Library Quarterly*, Vol. 2, No. 3 (Apr 1939), pp. 301–4.

Chapter 10 – Italy II – politics, 1458 to 1461

1. Bodleian MSS. 80. In R. Weiss, The library of John Tiptoft, Earl of Worcester, *Bodleian Quarterly Record*, 8 (1935–7), pp. 157–64, Oxford. 1935, pp. 102–3.
2. CFrR, p. 434.
3. CPR 1452–61, p. 487.
4. J. Whethamstede, *Registrum*, p. 336.
5. CPaR, vol. 11, p. 539.
6. *ibid*, p. 538.
7. POPC p. 302.
8. Jenks, *op. cit.*, p. 19.
9. CSPM p. 20–1.
10. *Pius II, Commentaries,* ed. M. Meserve, M. Simonetta, vol. II, Harvard University Press, 2007, p. 177.
11. CPaR, p. 596.
12. Johnson, *op. cit.* p. 213–4.
13. *ibid.*
14. CPaR, p. 580.
15. CPR 1452–61, p. 644.
16. CPaR, p. 682–3.
17. *Archivio di Stato, Firenze, M. a. Pr., F. VI, Doc. 531.* Mitchell, *op. cit.*, pp. 65–6.
18. C. Head, Pius II and the Wars of the Roses, *Archivum Historiae Pontificiae,* Vol. 8 (1970), pp. 139–178, 1970, p. 157. Incidentally, might this friar be the same as da Bisticci's source about the execution of the Earl of Worcester.
19. CSPM, p. 44.
20. CSPM, p. 53.
21. CSPM, p. 86.
22. Bisticci, p. 418.
23. Commynes, P. de., *Mémoires*, ed. J. Calmette. 3 vols. Paris, 1924, vol. ii, p. 140.
24. Bisticci, *op. cit.*, p. 418.
25. *Literae Cantuarienses*, ed. J.B. Sheppard, vol. iii. 1043, pp. 215–7 (the letter has a 1454 date but it must be from 1461 because it refers to the Earl being resident in Padua after he had been to Rome).
26. Ognibene da Lonigo, Bodley 80 (printed by Professor Sabbadini in *Antologia Veneta*, vol. I, (1900)).
27. Harris, *op. cit.*, p. 46.
28. CSPM, *op. cit.*, p. 107.
29. Free, *op. cit.*
30. Ognibene Bonisoli, Beinecki MS 149.
31. Aretino, BL, Arundel, 277, fol. 10.

32. Carbone, *op. cit.*

33. Fuller, *op. cit.*, p. 234.

PART 3 – HOUSE OF YORK

Chapter 11 – Constable of the Tower – 1461 to 1464

1. Bisticci, p. 418.

2. W.H. Dunham, *The Fane fragment of the 1461 Journal of the House of Lords*, Yale University Press, 1935.

3. *The Coventry leet book; or Mayor's register*, ed. M.D. Harris, Kegan Paul, 1907, p. 330.

4. *Stone's Chronicle*, ed. Searle, *op. cit.*, p. 84.

5. CPR 1461–67, p. 118.

6. CPR 1461–67, p. 66.

7. *Lincoln's Inn, The Black Books*, Vol I, Lincoln's Inn, 1897, p. 35.

8. C.L. Scofield, *Edward IV*, vol. I, London, 1923, p. 217.

9. C. Ross, *Edward IV*, Yale University Press, 1997 (1974), pp. 308–30.

10. CPR 1461–67, p. 62.

11. CPR 1461–67, p 58.

12. *ibid.*, p. 61. The Constable's entitlements included: 6/8*d.* annually from each boat fishing between The Tower and the sea; 1s. a year from all ships carrying herring to London; a portion of the cargo from every ship mooring at Tower Wharf; all herbage growing on Tower Hill; any horses, oxen, pigs or sheep that fell off London Bridge; any cart that fell into the Tower moat; and all swans swimming under London Bridge.

13. The Garter awards in the early part of Edward's reign were in 1461: George Plantagenet, Duke of Clarence (185); Sir William Chamberlaine, knight (186); John Tiptoft, Earl of Worcester (187); William Hastings, lord Hastings (186); John Nevill, lord Montagu (189); William Herbert, lord Herbert (190); Sir John Astley, knight (191). 1462–3: Ferdinand I, King of Naples (192); Galeard de Durefort, seigneur de Duras (193); John le Scrope, lord Scrope de Bolton (194); Francis Sforza, Duke of Milan (195); James Douglas, Earl of Douglas (196); Sir Robert Harcourt, knight (197). 1465–6: Richard Plantagenet, Duke of Gloucester 198); Anthony Wydville, lord Scales (199); Inigo d'Avalos, count de Monte Odorisio (200). 1468: Charles the Bold, Duke of Burgundy (201).

14. Fane Fragment, *op. cit.*, p. 93.

15. CPR 1461–67, p. 87.

16. CPR 1461–67, p. 93.

17. J. de Waurin, *Recueil des Chroniques (1447–71)*, ed. W. Hardy, vol. 5, Rolls series, 1864, p. 353.

Chapter 12 – Constable of England – 1462

1. *Three Chronicles of the Reign of Edward IV, (A Chronicle of the first thirteen years of the reign (Warkworth), Chronicle of the Rebellion in Lincolnshire 1470, Historie of the*

Arrivall of Edward IV in England), intro. by K. Dockray, Alan Sutton Publishing, 1988. p.5.

2. CPR 1461–71, p. 74. The Constable was originally the commander of the royal armies and the Master of the Horse. He was also president of the Court of Chivalry. The position of Constable had been unfilled since the Battle of Northampton in July 1460 when Humphrey Stafford Duke of Buckingham had been killed.

3. CSPM, p. 106–8.

4. A Brief Latin Chronicle, in *Three Fifteenth-Century Chronicles with Historical Memoranda by John Stowe*, ed. James Gairdner, pp. 164–185, London, 1880, p. 177.

5. CSPM, p. 107.

6. 'Brief notes of occurrences under Henry VI and Edward IV', in *Three Fifteenth-Century Chronicles*, pp. 148–163, London, 1880, p. 162.

7. CSPM, p. 107.

8. Benet, *op. cit.*, p. 232.

9. *ibid.*

10. Wyrcester, *Annals, op. cit.*, p. 779.

11. Benet, *op. cit.*, p. 232.

12. Warkworth, *op. cit.* p. 5.

13. *Chronicles of London*, ed. C.L. Kingsford, Oxford, 1905, p. 177.

14. Brief Notes, *op. cit.*, p. 162. '*Eodem tempore circa festum Sancti Valentini [14 February] dominus Ambry (Aubrey) filius comitis Oxonie erat suspensus et tractus London*' and '*Circa festum Cathedre Sancti Petri [22 February] decapitatus erat comes Oxonie, Will' Terell*' (the date of the 14th of February is improbable, being only two days after the arrests). *Hearne's Fragment* recorded: 'the xxth day of the same moneth bothe the fadir and the son were brougt unto the toure hill, where they suffrid deth bothe on one day; how be it the cronicques late made affermith that therle shuld be executid vi dayes after : for it was a pitivous sigt to see theime bothe fadir and son is such distresse' (Hearne's Fragment, The Chronicles of the White Rose of York, pp. 5–30, 1845, p. 11). The *Brief Notes* come from Ely and the dates and reports seem unreliable but it appears to confirm different dates for the executions of Aubrey and his father. Only the *Brief Notes* said Tyrell was executed on the same day as the Earl of Oxford—an assertion made by no other source.

15. J. de Waurin, *Recueil des Chroniques* (1447- 71), ed. W. Hardy, vol. 5, Rolls series, 1864, p. 353.

'He was raised onto a scaffold in order that all could see him; then he was placed on a chair, then before a great fire, he was bound and tied brutally, and before all the people his stomach was cut open and his entrails pulled from his body, then his genitals were cut off, and all were thrown in the fire; and after his skin [cuyr jus] was scraped from his back and delivered to two friars minor who wrapped it in a towel, and took it and buried it in a chapel: then his body was quartered and the parts hung on the gates of London, and the others had their heads cut off and the bodies were hung on a gibbet.'

16. *ibid*, lxix, fn. 7 (Plumpton Coucher Book, no. 560).

17. Foedera, part 2, p. 146–7. *Lèse-majesté* is the crime of violating majesty, an offence against the dignity of a reigning sovereign or against a state. According to civil laws, the right to levy open war was the preserve of a sovereign prince, who was *empereur en son roialme*, and for a subject or any other without advoual to infringe this right constituted the crime of *lèse-majesté*, because it was an accroachment on royal power (see M.H. Keen, Treason Trials under the Law of Arms: The Alexander Prize Essay, *Transactions of the Royal Historical Society*, Vol. 12 (1962), pp. 85–103).

18. W. Stubbs, *The Constitutional History of England*, Oxford, 1896, p. 289.

19. M. Keen, Nobles, *Knights and Men-at-Arms in the Middle-Ages*, Bloomsbury Academic, 1996, p. 136.

20. N. Machiavelli, *Portable Machiavelli*, Penguin, 1979 (in *The Prince*, Cha. 18, How a prince should keep his word).

Chapter 13 – Treasurer and captain 'by water' – 1462 to 1463

1. *Gregory's Chronicle, op. cit.*, p. 221.

2. CPR 1461–69, p. 115.

3. CSPM, p 107.

4. Paston, vol. 2, p. 96–7 (letter from John Russe to John Paston where the former asked the latter to intercede with Worcester to get the position of controller of Jernemuth (Yarmouth)).

5. CPR 1461–69, p. 182.

6. Paston, vol. 2., p. 102–4 (earlier on the 29th May 1462 a commission had been granted to Sir John Howard and Sir Thomas Walgrave to arrest the ships *Mary Talbot* and *Mary Thomson*, and other vessels in Norfolk, Suffolk, and Essex, for a fleet which the King was fitting out).

7. *ibid*.

8. The following Paston letters also mention Worcester and the bombastic young Debenham, underlining the local impact of the Treasurer's fundraising.

9. Stone, *op. cit.*, fols 70v-71, p. 86–7.

10. Scofield, *op. cit.*, p. 225.

11. *ibid*, p. 256.

12. *London Journal 7*, fo. 8 (see R.R. Sharp, *London & Kingdom*, vol. 1, London, 1894, p. 308).

13. *ibid.*, fo. 15 (Sharp, *op. cit.*, p. 308).

14. Paston, vol. 2, p. 117–9 (no letter date).

15. *Registrum Thome Bourgchier, Cantuariensis Archiepiscopi*, A.D. 1454–1486, ed. F.R.H. du Boulay, University Press, 1957, p. 107.

16. *Brief Notes, op. cit.*, p. 157.

17. *ibid*.

18. Paston, *op. cit.*, vol. 2, p. 121.

19. Wyrcester, *op. cit.*, p. 780–1.
20. CPR 1461–71, p. 282.
21. *ibid.*, p. 286.
22. J.S. Roskell, *Parliament and Politics in Late Medieval England*, vol. III, pp. 107–150, 1983, p. 164.
23. CPR 1461–71, p. 283.
24. Scofield, *op. cit.*, p. 292.
25. Bourgchier, *op. cit.*, p. 98.
26. *ibid*, p. 98.
27. *A Brief Latin Chronicle*, *op. cit.* p. 177.
28. Steel, *op. cit.*, p. 287.
29. CPR 1461–67, p. 301–2.
30. Foedera, part 2, p. 116.
31. A. Crawford, *Yorkist Lord, John Howard, Duke of Norfolk*, c. 1425–1485, continuum, p. 239.
32. Mitchell *op. cit.* p. 93.
33. Gregory, op cit., p. 221.
34. *A Brief Latin Chronicle*, *op. cit.*, p. 177.
35. Scofield, p. 302, fn. 4.

Chapter 14 – Lord Steward of the Household – 1463

1. *Lincoln's Inn Black Book*, *op. cit.*, p. 37.
2. CPR, p. 217.
3. J. Ross, The treatment of traitor's children and Edward IV's clemency in the 1460s, *Essays presented to Michael Hick, The fifteenth century XIV*, ed. L. Clark, pp. 131–41, Boydell & Brewer, 2015.
4. The Earl of Oxford had five sons, the oldest, Aubrey, who was also executed in 1462, and John, George, Thomas and youngest Richard. The chronicler Benet (p. 232) recorded that Oxford was arrested with three sons, one of whom was Aubrey who was executed. Richard was almost certainly too junior to have been brought into the plot. Thomas was the fourth son. The two remaining sons were the second and third sons John and George. It seems probable John was not arrested as he became under the charge of the Nevilles who married him to their sister Margaret. Thus, Thomas and George, whose name was illegible, were probably the responsibility of Worcester.
5. Plumpton et al., *Plumpton Correspondence*, ed. T. Stapleton, London (for the Cam. Soc.), 1839, p. 6–7. Searches have not revealed what was the alluded to relationship. Beckwith was, however, indeed escheator for Yorkshire.
6. See A.J. Pollard, *Warwick the Kingmaker, Politics, Power and Fame*, Continuum Books, 2007, p. 117, and J. Kirby, *The Plumpton Letters and Papers*, Cambridge University Press, 1996, p. 7.

7. Kirby, *op. cit.*, note 33.

8. Stapleton, *op. cit.*, lxix.

9. *ibid*, lxix, fn. 7. Plumpton Coucher Book, no. 560.

10. *ibid*, lxx–lxxi.

11. Kirkby, *op. cit.*, p. 32.

12. *ibid*. 36, 21 June, circa 1465, Plumpton correspondence.

13. The Berynge of an Erle, *The Antiquarian Repertory*, pp. 314–17, London, 1807.

14. Pollard, *op. cit.* p. 86; Roskell, *Parliament and Politics*, vol. II, 1983, p. 298.

Chapter 15 – Keeper of the King's peace – 1464

1. *The Coventry Leet Book*, *op. cit.*, pp. 323–8.

2. Justice Under the Yorkist Kings, J.G. Bellamy, *The American Journal of Legal History*, Vol. 9, No. 2, Apr 1965, pp. 135–55.

3. *ibid.*

4. *op. cit.*, p. 136.

5. *ibid.*

6. CPR 1461–67, p. 303.

7. Scofield, *op. cit.*, p. 318.

8. *ibid.*, p. 318.

9. C.L. Kingsford, *English historical literature in the fifteenth century*, Oxford, 1913, p. 356 (Gloucestershire Annals).

10. *ibid.*, p. 356.

11. CPR 1461- 67, p. 303.

12. *English Historical Documents*, Volume IV, 1327–1485, ed. A.R. Myers, Routledge, 1995, p. 288.

13. *ibid.* p. 289.

14. Avrutick, *op. cit.*, p. 66; Bellamy, op. cit, pp. 136–7.

15. *ibid.*, p. 66–67; Thornley, *England under the Yorkists*, 1921, pp. 160–2.

16. CPR 1461–67, p. 346; Bellamy, *op. cit.*, p. 137.

17. Gregory, *op. cit.*, p. 222.

18. *A chronicle of London*, *op. cit.*, p. 143.

19. J. Stow, *A Survey of London*, Whittaker and Company, London, 1842, p. 143.

20. R. Holinshed, *Holinshed's Chronicles of England, Scotland, and Ireland ...*: England, Vol. III, J. Johnson, 1808, p. 283.

21. CPR 1461–67, p. 348–9, 8 July.

22. Scofield, op cit., p. 349.

23. CPR 1461–67, p. 450. In 1465 Louis provoked such general hostility that a *Ligue du Bien Public* formed to resist him which was joined by François. The *ligueurs* camped around Paris and forced concessions out of Louis at the Treaties of Conflans (5th of October 1465) and of Saint Maur (30th of October 1465). Supporting Brittany

may have temporarily curbed the disruptive powers of Louis, who meanwhile was enticing the increasingly disgruntled Warwick.

24. Trial of Sir Ralph Grey, *MS in the College of Arms, The Chronicle of William de Rishanger, of the Baron's Wars; The Miracles of Simon de Montfort; ed. from Manuscripts in the Cottonian Library*, Camden Society, 1840, pp. 36–9.

25. J. Peele, *An Historical Account of the Order of the Bath, etc*, p. 14.

26. *Coventry Leet Book, op. cit.*, pp. 328–32.

Chapter 16 – Integrating the Woodvilles – 1464 to 1465

1. G. Tetzel, *The Travels of Lev von Rožmitál, 1465–6*, Littell's Living Age, Vol. 4, 1845, p. 34.

2. Paston, vol. 1, p. 505- 6.

3. CPR 1461–67, p. 380.

4. *Chronicles of London, op. cit.*, p. 176.

5. CPR 1441–46, p. 167.

6. CPR 1461–67, p. 428.

7. Ross, Essays presented to Michael Hicks, *op. cit.*, p. 132.

8. Stat. Realm, 6 Ric II, c. 6. d. After the death of her husband William Venour, a Robert Worth, at Edmonton on 5 October 1462, feloniously seized Elizabeth Venour and afterwards, namely on the following Tuesday (12th October 1462), at Westminster, he 'carnally knew' Elizabeth Venour with her consent, by which she hence consented voluntarily to the seizure thereby according to the legal action disinheriting herself (for details of the underlying case behind this, involving a dispute between Babyngton and Venour over the wardenship of the Fleet, see, C.H. Williams, 'A fifteenth-century Lawsuit', *Law Quarterly review*, 1924, pp. 354–64).

9. Paston, *op. cit.*, p. 237–8.

10. *ibid*, p. 239.

11. A. Cosgrove, *op. cit.*, p. 19.

12. S.G. Ellis, *Defending English Ground: War and Peace in Meath and Northumberland, 1460–1542*, Oxford University Press, 2015, p. 6.

13. A. Cosgrove, *op. cit.*, p. 20. CPR 1461–67, p. 340.

14. CPR 1461–67, p. 488.

15. S. Bentley, Tournament between Lord Scales and the Bastard of Burgundy, *Excerpta Historica*, London, pp. 171–222, 1831, p. 189.

16. G.A. Lester, *Sir John Paston's Grete Boke: A Descriptive Index, with an Introduction, of British Library MS Lansdowne 285*, D.Phil. thesis, University of Sheffield, Department of English Language, 1981, p. 299.

17. Paston, vol.2, p. 41.

18. G. Smith, *Account of the Coronation of Elizabeth Wydville*, London: Ellis, 1935.

19. C. Hibbert, *The English. A Social History, 1066–1945*, Harper Collins, 1987, pp. 10–11. The list continued: 204 cranes, 104 peacocks, 100 dozen quails, 400 swans and 400 herons, 608 pikes and bream, 12 porpoises and seals, 1000 capons, 400 plovers, 200 dozen ruffs, 4000 mallard and teals, 204 kids and 204 bitterns, 200 pheasants, 500 partridges, 400 woodcocks, 100 curlews, 1000 egrets, 4000 cold and 1500 hot venison pies, 4000 dishes of jelly, 4000 baked tarts, 2000 hot custards with bread sugared delicacies and cakes, and 300 tuns of ale and 100 tuns of wine.

20. Warkworth, p. 5.

21. CPR 1461–67, p. 490.

22. Friedrichs, *op. cit.*, p. 79–81.

23. CCR, 1461–68, pp. 327–30.

24. L. Friedrichs, Rich Old Ladies Made Poor, *Medieval Prosopography 21*, 2000, p. 221.

25. Tetzel, *op. cit.*, p. 34.

26. *ibid*, p. 34.

27. Tetzel, G., *The Travels of Lev von Rožmitál, 1465–6,* ed. M. Letts, Hakluyt Series II, p.108, Cambridge, 1957, p. 1189.

28. *Ibid*, p.1189.

29. Warrants under the Signet, file 1379, 6th and 7th June 1466.

30. R. Barber, Malory's le Morte d'Arthur and Court Culture, *Arthurian Literature XII*, ed. J.P. Carley, F. Riddy, pp. 133–56, Boydell & Brewer, 1993, p. 147.

31. Scofield, p. 407.

32. CPR 1461–67, p. 553.

33. CPR 1467–77, 1475, p. 559.

34. The context may have been the loss of Gascony which had disrupted the Anglo-Gascon wine trade after 1453. An increasingly uncontrolled illicit trade in wine developed and by the mid-1460s there were serious attempts to stop it. In 1465 a commission was sent to the mayors of Poole and Weymouth, instructing them to seize a Gascon ship in the former and a ship from Rouen in the latter, both laden with Gascon wine and to keep them in safe custody. Such royal edicts had the unfortunate effect of encouraging the seizure of ships and wines of allies. In the same year a Breton ship with a cargo of 92 tuns of wine was taken by English pirates. Also, a Spanish ship which was stranded near the Isle of Wight was despoiled of its wine despite letters of safe conduct. The full resumption of trade with England was encouraged by the Anglo-Castilian peace treaty of 1466 which allowed Castilians to trade on the same terms as the English. On 18 July Worcester had been commissioned to inquire into smuggling on the south coast and seize merchandise. CPR 1461- 67, p. 530.

35. Stone, ed. Searle, p. 15.

Chapter 17 – Soldier – 1466 to 1467

1. Stapleton, *op. cit.*, p. 17.
2. H.T. Evans, *Wales and the Wars of the Roses*, Cambridge University Press, 1915, p. 98.
3. A. Goodman, *The Wars of the Roses, Military Activity and English Society*, 1452-97, Routledge, 1981, Cha. 4. Scofield, op. cit, 1, 423; H.T. Evans, *Wales and the Wars of the Roses*, Sutton Publishing, 1995 (1915).
4. Ross, *Edward IV, op. cit.*, p. 120.
5. Wyrcester, *op. cit.*, p. 788.
6. CPR 1467–77, p. 29.
7. *ibid.*, p. 28.
8. *ibid.*, 1467–77, p. 23.
9. *ibid.*, 1467- 77, p. 17; p. 47; p. 90.
10. *ibid.*, 1467- 77, p. 54; p. 55.
11. *ibid.*, 1467–77, p. 55.
12. A.J. Otway-Ruthven, *A History of Medieval Ireland*, Palgrave Macmillan, 1980, p. 391.
13. *ibid.*, 1467–77, p. 43.

Chapter 18 – Tournament master of ceremonies – 1467

1. Marche, O. de la, *Memoires*, J.A.C. Buchon, *Choix de chroniques et mémoires sur l'histoire de France: avec notices biographiques*, Société du Panthéon litteraire, 1842, p. 523.
2. *Excerptica, op. cit.*, p. 175. The description of the tournament is transcribed on pp. 176–222. There is an analysis in, G.A. Lester, *Sir John Paston's Grete Boke: A Descriptive Index, with an Introduction, of British Library MS Lansdowne 285*, D. Phil. thesis, University of Sheffield, December Department of English Language, 1981.
3. R.D. Moffat, *The Medieval Tournament: Chivalry, Heraldry and Reality, An Edition and Analysis of the Three Fifteenth-Century Tournament Manuscripts*, D. Phil. Thesis, 2 Vols., The University of Leeds, 2000. This contains, *Leeds, Royal Armouries Library, Codex RAR.0035(I.35)*, including, MS 3, *Jousts of my Lord Antoine Bastard of Burgundy done in England* (fols 44r-121v). This manuscript is presumably the same as *Utrecht University Library MS 1177, Section 2, ff. 186r-215v*, which is an eyewitness account of the combat between Anthony Woodville and the Bastard of Burgundy in Smithfield in 1467.
4. *ibid*, p. 314.
5. *ibid* p. 315, *Excerptica*, p. 198.
6. *ibid* p. 315.
7. *Excerptica*, p. 198.
8. *ibid*, p. 198.

9. *Leeds*, p. 315.

10. *ibid*, p. 315.

11. *ibid*, p. 316.

12. *Excerptica*, p. 199.

13. *ibid*, p. 199.

14. *ibid*, p. 199.

15. *Leeds*, p. 316.

16. *Excerptica*, p. 199.

17. *Leeds*, p. 317.

18. *Leeds*, p. 200.

19. Palace of Bishop of London by the north-west corner of old St Pauls.

20. *Excerptica*, p. 200–1.

21. CCR, 1461–68, pp. 456–7.

22. Waurin, *op. cit.*, p. 545.

23. Marche, *op. cit.*, p. 523.

24. *Leeds*, p. 317.

25. *Leeds*, p. 318.

26. *Excerptica*, p. 205.

27. *Leeds*, p. 321, *Excerptica*, pp. 206–7.

28. *Excerptica*, p. 207.

29. *ibid.*, p. 208.

30. *ibid.*, p. 208.

31. *ibid.*, p. 208. *Leeds*, p. 321.

32. de la Marche, in *Excerptica*, p. 209, fn 4.

33. *Leeds*, p. 321.

34. *Excerptica*, p. 209.

35. Fabyan, in Excertica, p. 209, fn 3.

36. *Excerptica*, p. 322.

37. de la Marche, in *Excerptica*, p. 209, fn 4.

38. *Excerptica*, p. 209.

39. *Leeds*, p. 322.

40. *Excerptica*, p. 209.

41. De la Marche, in *Excerptica*, p. 209, fn 4.

42. *ibid*.

43. *Leeds*, p. 322.

44. De la Marche, in *Excerptica*, p. 212, fn 1 [Olivier de la Marche], p. 492–3.

45. *Excerptica*, p. 211.

46. *ibid*.

47. *Leeds*, p. 324.

48. De la Marche, in *Excerptica*, p. 212, fn 1.

49. Leeds, p. 324.

50. *ibid.*

51. De la Marche, in *Excerptica*, p. 212, fn 1.

52. *ibid.*

53. Gregory, *op. cit.*, p. 236.

54. *Leeds*, p. 324.

55. *ibid.*, p.339 (here follow the Feats of Arms of my Lord of Monnet).

56. *ibid.*, p. 325–6.

57. *Excerptica*, p. 214.

58. *Leeds*, p. 324–5; *Excerptica*, p. 214.

59. *Leeds*, p. 328.

60. *ibid.*, p. 329.

61. *ibid.*

62. *ibid.*, p. 330

63. *ibid.*, p. 329

PART 4 – IRELAND

Chapter 19 – Remarriage and arrival – 1467

1. Wyrcester, *op. cit.*, p. 788.

2. *A Brief Latin Chronicle*, *op. cit.*, p. 182.

3. William de Lucy died in 1461 and his estate passed to his widow Margaret. On her death in 1467 it was divided between William's niece Elizabeth and nephew William Vaux who was killed at the Battle of Tewkesbury in 1471.

4. CPR 1467–77, p. 113; CCR 1468–76, p. 7.

5. *Calendar of Ancient Records of Dublin, in the Possession of the Municipal Corporation of That City*, ed. J.T. Gilbert, Vol. 1, Dublin, 1889, p. 328.

6. SRPI, p. 431.

7. ibid, p. 435–6.

8. *A Calendar of Irish Chancery Letters c. 1244–1509*, chancery.tcd.ie. SRPI, pp. 454–60. The choice of St Secundinus was of note—given the Earl's travels and scholarly interests—as he may have been an Italian not a Romano-Briton. In 439, bishops Secundinus, Auxilius and Iserninus came to the aid of St Palladius in Ireland. Tradition appeared to suggest that Secundinus and Auxilius were of Italian origin. In 441 Palladius left Secundinus in charge of the Church in Ireland and he became known as the first Christian bishop to die on Irish soil. Worcester may have enjoyed the Italian connection. Secundinus might have appealed to the Earl not just because he was considered to have been a man of letters. An early Latin hymn in honour of St Patrick was ascribed to Secundinus, though it is uncertain it was actually composed by him.

9. Philip Bermingham (c.1420–1490) was an Irish judge who held the office of Lord Chief Justice of Ireland. He was regarded as 'the most learned Irish lawyer of his

time', which might have appealed to the Earl of Worcester. He was an adviser to James Butler, Earl of Wiltshire, who was executed after Towton and was himself condemned to death as a traitor in 1462 but soon received a royal pardon. He was also a member of the Ormonde (Butler) party and was one of the first known speakers of the Irish Parliament. In 1468 he was appointed joint Lord Chief Justice with Sir Thomas Fitz-Christopher Plunket.

Chapter 20 – Executioner – 1468

1. A. Lynch, The Calendar of the Reassembled Register of John Bole, Archbishop of Armagh, 1457–71, *Seanchas Ardmhacha: Journal of the Armagh Diocesan Historical Society*, Vol. 15, No. 1 (1992), p 164.
2. *Calendar of Carew Manuscripts, Book of Howth, Miscellaneous*, ed. J.S. Brewer and W. Bullen, London, 1871, p. 483.
3. *A Fragment of Irish Annals*, ed. B.Ó. Cuiv, *Celtica*, vol. XIV, Institúid Ard-Léinn Bhaile Átha Cliath, 1981, p. 96.
4. *ibid.*
5. *ibid.*
6. *ibid.*
7. *The Annals of Ulster*, 1853, vol. III, ed. mac Carthy, Dublin, p. 219–21.
8. Wyrcester, *op. cit.*, p. 513.
9. *Calendar of Carew Papers*, 1575–8, ed. J.S. Brewer & W. Bullen, London, 1868, pp. cv-cvii.
   This passage is in an appendix to the introduction to the *Calendar*. At the start of the appendix is the following statement:
   'It has been stated in a note at p. xxxvii of this Preface that coyne and livery were begun by Thomas Earl of Desmond, about 1465, for which he was beheaded. It is, however, just to state that a different cause has been assigned for his execution in a *memorandum written by his grandson*, written in the Irish tongue, and translated into English by his representative, then in the English Court, and addressed to the Lords of the Privy Council.'
10. *Calendar of the Carew Manuscripts at Lambeth*, vol. 5, *The Book of Howth*, pp. 186–7.
11. *ibid.*
12. On 25 August the King granted Desmond an annuity when at Woodstock.
13. J. Lydon, Ireland Corporate of Itself – The Parliament of 1460, *History Ireland*, Vol. III, No. II, 1995, pp. 9–12.
14. For example, in April 1465 there is an interesting letter from Edward regarding disobeyed a safe conduct for a Spanish Kervel. Its relevance lies in its demonstration of the reluctance to obey instructions under the authority of the privy seal. 'The King is very much surprised that a safe conduct has not been made for the

Kervel of Spain lying at Southampton, and for the master and mariners of the same, according to the verbal instructions given by him to the clerk of the rolls, and the privy seal delivered to him by the Earl of Worcester.' In, J.S. Forsyth, *The antiquary's portfolio: or cabinet selection of historical & literary curiosities*, p. 279.

15. *Unpublished Geraldine Documents*, ed. S. Hayman and J. Graves, University Press, by M.H. Gill, 1870, p. 80.

16. *Calendar of the Carew Manuscripts*, ed. J.S. Brewer & W. Bullen, Vol. 1, London, 1867, 1515–74, p. 6–8.

17. E. Campion, *A historie of Ireland, written in the yeare 1571, Ancient Irish histories: the works of Spencer, Campion, Hanmer and Marleburrough*, 2 vols, Dublin, 1809; first printed, ed. J. Ware, Dublin, 1633, Dublin, p. 150.

18. The English chronicler Hollinshed followed Campion almost verbatim: 'but when he had spoken certeine disdainefull words against the late marriage of king Edward with the ladie Elizabeth Greie, the said ladie being now queene, caused his trade of life after the Irish maner, contrarie to sundrie old statutes inacted in that behalfe, to be sifted and examined by Iohn erle of Worcester his successor; so that he was atteinted of treason, condemned, and for the same beheaded at Droghedagh.' R. Holinshed, Holinshed's *Chronicles of England, Scotland, and Ireland*, London, 1807, p. 78.

19. E. Spenser, *A View of the Present State of Ireland*, c.1596, p. 525.

20. E. Hahn, *Fractured Emerald: Ireland, History*, 2010. p. 87.

21. A. Cosgrove, The Execution of the Earl of Desmond 1468, *Journal of the Kerry Archaeological Society*, viii, 1975, p. 26.

22. Ellis, *op. cit.*, p. 66.

23. C. Smith, *The Antient and Present State of the County and City of Cork: in Four Books*, London, 1774, p. 28.

24. Lynch, *op. cit.*, p. 164.

25. *ibid.*, p. 164.

26. *ibid.*, p. 164. Richard Martyn was possibly the Earl's chaplain. In 1461 the prior of Canterbury wrote to one Richard in Italy to thank the Earl for his labours obtaining an indulgence for the St Thomas. In 1462 a Richard Martyn was presented to the church of Micheldean, where the Earl held the advowson through his life tenure of the Greyndour estate. Richard Martyn held a succession of archdeaconships including London. In 1471 he joined Edward's council. In 1477 he was appointed Chancellor of Ireland for life but did not perform any duties. He was succeeded by the contumacious Bishop Sherwood. In 1482 he became Bishop of St Davids.

27. *Ibid.*, p. 164.

28. *Fragment of Irish Annals, op. cit.*, p. 96.

29. Bisticci, p 420.

30. Mitchell, *op. cit.*, p. 120, in *Register of the Mayors of Dublin*, BL, Add. MS. 4791, fo. 139.

31. *Calender of the Carew Manuscripts at Lambeth*, vol. 5, *The Book of Howth*, pp. 186–7. 'Immediately after the Earl of Worcester went to Drogheda, where as was two of the Earl of Desmond his sons at learning. The eldest, scarce at the age of 13 years, was there beheaded. The youngest brother, being like case to be executed, having a bill [boil] of fellone upon his neck, said to the persecutor these words: "Mine own gentle and beloved fellow, whatsoever else ye do with me, hurt not nor grieve not this sore that is upon my kneck, for it troubleth me and grieveth me much; therefore take keep thereof." And with that this innocent's head was smitten off, for which cause those that stood by did much lament.'

32. *The Great Chronicle of London*, Guildhall Library MS. 3313. 500 copies printed by Sign of the Dolphin, London, 1938, p. 213. See, A.M. Campbell, The Great Chronicle of the City of London, *The Journal of the Rutgers University Library*, Vol 3, No 1 (1939), pp. 7–12, p. 213.

33. The Infamovs end of the Lord Tiptoft Earle of Worcester, for cruelly executing his Prince's butcherly commaundementes, An. 1470, *Mirror for Magistrates*, ed. J. Haslewood, Lackington, Allen, and Company, 1815, Volume 2, Part 1, p. 203.

34. The Earls of Desmond had a reputation for long and strictly illegal familial links with the Irish nobility. There were traditions that the Earl of Desmond had foster-age relationships with Taig O'Connor of Offaly which might explain his relatively easy liberation from captivity in 1466. In the previous century the Desmonds had also become linked to the O'Briens of Thomond through fosterage. In 1466 the Earl of Desmond was forced to come to an accommodation with Taig O'Brien that was alleged to be treasonous. The Statutes of Kilkenny, 1366, provided that 'marriage, fosterage, or gossipred with the Irish, or submission to the Irish law, should be considered and punished as high treason.'

35. *Fragment of Irish Annals, op. cit.*, p. 96.

36. Campion. *op cit*.

37. *The Great Chronicle of London, op cit*.

38. *Calender of the Carew Manuscripts at Lambeth, op. cit.*, pp. 186–7.

39. *Unpublished Geraldine Documents, op. cit.*, vol. 1, p. 69.

'Then the Earle's page, by name, Baggott, so to the Baggott of the county of Limerick, who was a very comely youth, … this youth, I say, being then disturbed in mind, and not able to take any rest that night, Roose vp to the chamber window where his Lord and master lay; and, seeing that sight of men and armes, cried out to his Lord, and sayed, O my Lord! O my dear Lord! here are all the men in Ireland marching vp the street in armes; therefore, my Lord, rouse vp your spirits, and bless yourselfe, for my mind tells me they are for noe good intent; whereat the Earle made answer, Alass, my boy, I wish there were but half the men of Munster only. Suddenly these men forced into the Earles lodging, and barbarously handled and apprehended him; and, without any farther deliberation, in the morning chopt off his head. It would (as mine author sayeth) move the hardest heart to pitty haue compassion, to see the dolefull lamentations and behaviour of this youth Baggott, seeing the innocent bloud of hi Lord and master soe suddenly and inhumanely spilt before his face, to whome, as he said, all Ireland within eight days after would gladly bowe and submitt itselfe.'

40. *ibid.*

Chapter 21 – Campaigner – 1468

1. I.D. Thornley, *England under the Yorkists, 1460–1485; Illustrated from Contemporary Sources*, Longmans, Green, 1921, pp. 257–9

    (letter from the Lords of Ireland to Edward IV, 28 June 1468. P.R.O. "Ancient Correspondence", LVIII, no. 50; the last paragraph is not included in Thornley and has been transcribed from the original PRO document which is extremely difficult to read at this point).

2. SRPI, p. 467.

3. *ibid*, p. 489.

4. *ibid*, p. 575.

5. Thornley, *op. cit.*, p 257. Fragment of Irish Annales, *op. cit.*, p. 97.

6. *ibid.*

7. Thornley, *op. cit.* 256–7 – *A Fragment of Irish Annals* supported this account. 'A hosting by Gearóid … into Trian Meadhónach [Middle Trim] on which he burned Fiodhard [Fethard, Tipperary]. Another hosting by Gearóid against the foreigners of Midhe to avenge on them the death of the Earl' (*Fragment of Irish Annales, op. cit.*, p. 97).

8. Thornley, *op. cit.*, p. 257.

9. SRPI., p. 627.

10. Thornley, *op. cit.*, p. 257.

11. *Calendar of Ancient Records of Dublin, in the Possession of the Municipal Corporation of That City*, ed. J.T. Gilbert, Vol. 1, Dublin, 1889, p. 328.

12. *Annals of the Four Masters*, M1468.25, www.ucc.ie/celt/online/T100005D/text010.html. *The Annals of Ireland by the four masters translated into English*, ed. M. O'Cleary, Irish Roots Café, 2003.

13. *ibid.*, M1466.17.

14. Thornley, *op. cit.*, p. 258.

15. *ibid.*, 9 Dec 1468, Drogheda, chancery.tcd.ie/document/patent/8-edward-iv/8.

16. *ibid.*, p. 258.

17. P.J. Burns, N.C. Burns, D. Byrne-Rothwell, *The Byrnes and the O'Byrnes*, Colonsay Books, 2010, p. 77.

18. Ellis, *op. cit.*, pp. 68–9 (source, H. Berry, p. 627).

19. G.E. Steven, *Ireland in the Age of the Tudors*, 1447–1603, Routledge, 2014, p. 68.

20. 12 July 1468, Drogheda, chancery.tcd.ie/roll/8-Edward-IV/patent

Chapter 22 – Legislator, coinage reformer, departure – 1468–1469/70

1. Calendar of Ancient Records of Dublin, *op. cit.*, p 332.

2. E. Curtiss, *A History of Medieval Ireland (Routledge Revivals): From 1086 to 1513*, p. 332, fn. 1.

3. Lydon, *op. cit.* p. 9.

4. S.G. Ellis, The Struggle for Control of the Irish Mint, 1460-c. 1506, *Proceedings of the Royal Irish Academy*, Vol. 78, pp. 17–36, 1978. The Earl of Worcester drastically revalued the coinage so that an Irish groat was only 22½ grains (compared with 41 grains in the 1465 issue). However he introduced a 'groat sized' coin weighing 45 grains, which he valued at 8 pence and called a double groat.

5. chancery.tcd.ie/document/patent/9-edward-iv/2.

6. *SRPI*, p. 723.

7. *ibid.*, p. 797.

8. *ibid*, p. 677–8.

9. *ibid*, p. 699–701.

10. The Kildare Book of Hours has on fo. vii a note in the calendar under 14 July: '*Isto die natus erat Edwardus fil: Johannis comitis Wigornie circa horam terciam post meridian 1469.*' Mitchell, *op. cit.*, p. 207.

PART 5 – TRIUMPH AND TRAGEDY – 1470

Chapter 23 – The Lincolnshire Campaign

1. CCR, 1468–76, pp. 129–30.

2. CSPM, p. 143.

3. Bisticci, p. 418.

4. J. Stone, *Chronicle of John Stone, Monk of Christ Church 1415–1471*, ed. W.G. Searle, Cambridge (Camb. Antiqu. Soc.), 1902, p. 114.

5. M. Hicks, *The War of the Roses*, Michael Hicks, Yale University Press, 2012, p. 166.

6. Waurin, *op. cit.*, vol. V, p. 611

7. CPR,1467–77, pp.199–200.

8. *ibid.*

9. *Chronicle of the Rebellion in Lincolnshire, 1470,* ed. J.C. Nichols, Camden Society, 1847. p. 25, fn. 19.

10. Ross, *op. cit.*, p. 137.

11. CCR, 1468–76, p. 129.

12. CPR 1467–77 p. 218.

13. Ross, *op. cit.*, p. 137.

14. *Chronicles of the rebellion in Lincolnshire, op. cit.*, p. 10

15. CPR 1467–77, p. 205. Scofield, *op. cit.*, p. 517.

16. *ibid.* In 1469 John Sutton, Lord Dudley, had been made joint Constable with Worcester who could not attend his duties then being in Ireland.

17. Paston, vol. 2, p. 395.

18. *ibid.*

19. CCR,1468–76, pp.137–8.

20. CPR 1467–77, p. 206.

21. W.H. Hatcher, *Hatcher's History of Salisbury*, 1843, p. 174–5.

22. C.M. Church, II. Visit of Edward IV to Wells in 1470, pp. 163–171. Historical Traditions at Wells, 1464, 1470, 1497. *The Archaeological Journal*: vol. 61, 1904, p. 167. 'It does not seem possible to explain this record otherwise than in the plain meaning of the words—that on April 11, according to the Patent Roll, Edward IV was at Wells on his way to Exeter, that the company of his brother George Duke of Clarence, of the Lady Isabel his wife, and of the Earl of Warwick her father, were with the King at Wells, and that each left certain gifts of money for some object as offerings in the church which were entered among the receipts in the Escheator's account for the year 1469–1470, and were passed over to the common fund among other receipts during the year.'

23. P. Holland, The Lincolnshire Rebellion of March 1470, *English Historical Review*, Vol. 103 no 409, 1988, p. 861.

24. *The Exeter Chronicle, 1205–1722*, intro. by T. Gray, The Mint Press, 2005, p. 52.

25. *ibid.*, Lord Ferrars had charge of the Earl of Worcester's stepson.

26. CCR 1469–70, p. 139.

27. Paston, p. 395.

Chapter 24 – The Impaler of Southampton – 1470

1. Three Chronicles of the Reign of Edward IV, *op. cit.*, p. 9.

2. *ibid.*, p. 9.

3. *Chronicles of London, op. cit.*, p. 181.

4. *Hearne's Fragment, op. cit.*, p. 29.

5. Leland, p. 479.

6. Leland, *Collectanea, op. cit.*, Vol. 2, p. 502.

7. CPR 1467–77, pp. 206–7.

8. *Hearne's Fragment, op. cit.*, p. 29.

9. Leland, p. 479.

10. Leland, *Collectanea, op. cit.*, Vol. 2, p. 502.

11. J. Stowe, *Annales, Or a General Chronicle of England*, 1631, p. 422.http://books.google.co.uk/books/about/Annales_Or_a_General_Chronicle_of_England.html?id=PSxDAAAAcAAJ

12. Wey, *op. cit.*, p. 90.

13. *Gregory's Chronicle*, op. cit., p. 90.
14. The use of stakes to kill or to expose was not as un–English as contemporaries might have supposed. In 1326 Simon Redding was executed with Hugh Despenser. He may have had impalement added to his pains, as 'the point of the spear pierced the intestines of the said Simon'. It bespeaks much of the Medieval mind that the chronicler expressed surprise that Redding did not show himself duly repentant: 'and it was said that he did not endure the punishment as a penitent before the people.' In 1403 after death at the Battle of Shrewsbury, Sir Henry Percy was initially buried in Shropshire, but rumours soon spread that he was not really dead. Henry IV had him disinterred and his body was salted and set up in Shrewsbury in the marketplace pillory, impaled on a spear between two millstones.

Chapter 25 – The Neville fight back

1. Bisticci, p. 419.
2. *Machon's Register*, Salisbury Chapter Act Book, 5th May 1470.
3. *ibid.*
4. *ibid.*
5. *Machon's Register, op. cit.*, 10th May 1470
6. CCR, 1468–76, p. 130.
7. CPR 1467–77, p. 220.
8. *Machon's Register, op. cit.*, 24th May 1470. '...there is a record that on May 24th, King Edward with the Bishop Durham and Carlisle and the Earl of Worcester were admitted to the Brotherhood of the Chapter, and there is an account of the ceremonial which makes it certain that the King was admitted in person and not by proxy.'
9. CPR 1467–77, p. 220. In the Forest of Dean the commissioners of array were John, Earl of Worcester, John Barre, knight, Thomas Baynham and William Walweyn. The last three were connected by blood or marriage to the Earl's second wife Elizabeth *née* Greyndour. This showed the continuing relationship with the family of Elizabeth who died eighteen years earlier.
10. Stone, *op. cit.*, fols 88–88v. Searle, *op. cit.*, p. 111.
11. There still survives to the east of Canterbury Cathedral the building called was *Master Homeri*.
12. CPR 1467–77, p. 214.
13. *ibid.*, p. 258.
14. Scofield, *op.cit.*, p. 534.
15. CSPM, p. 143.
16. Leland, *Collectanea, op. cit.*, vol. 2, p. 502.
17. Warkworth, *op. cit.*, p. 10–11.
18. Waurin, *op. cit.*, vol. v, p. 611.

19. Waurin, *op. cit.*, p. 612.
20. See Appendix 3. Earlier in Waurin's text, when describing those in highest authority about the King early in his reign, the chronicler calls Worcester *Euxcestre* in a context where there is no room for ambiguity. Waurin, *op. cit.*, p. 353.
21. Commynes, Calmette, vol. 1, p. 207.
22. Waurin, *op. cit.*, p. 612.
23. Bisticci, p. 418- 19.
24. *London Journal* 7, fos. 223b-224, p. 385, R.R. Sharpe, London and the Kingdom, vol. III, Longman, 1895, p. 385.
25. *ibid.*, fo. 222b, p. 387.
26. Chronicle of London, *op. cit.*, p. 182.
27. *ibid.*
28. *ibid.*
29. R.R. Sharpe, *op. cit.*, p. 386.
30. *ibid.*, p. 387
31. *ibid.*, p. 387.
32. *ibid.*, p. 387
33. Warkworth, *op. cit.*, p. 11.
34. R.R. Sharp, *London and the Kingdom*, London, 1894, vol. III, p. 387.
35. *Chronicles of London*, *op. cit.*, p. 182.
36. Bisticci, p. 419.
37. *ibid.*
38. E. Hall, *Chronicle*, ed. H. Ellis, London, 1809. vol.III, p. 70. 'This earle of Worcester was taken in the top of a high tree in the forest of Weibridge in Huntingtonshire, brought to London, ata parlement arrested and condemned to death, by sir Iohn Vere earle of Oxford.'
39. Bisticci, p. 419.
40. *Chronicles of London*, *op. cit.* p. 182.
41. *A Brief Latin Chronicle*, *op. cit.*, p. 117.
42. Bisticci, op, cit., p. 419.
43. Paston, vol. 2, p. 411.
44. *Chronicles of London*, *op. cit.* p. 216.

Chapter 26 – The Trial

1. G. Burnet, *The History of the Reformation of the Church of England*, Vol. 4, Appleton, 1842, p. 262.
2. CSPM, p. 143. A traditional source, without any attribution, simply said Warwick commanded it. 'The Earl of Worcester was executed by the secret orders of the Earl of Warwick, conveyed to the Earl of Oxford, by whom he was judged.' In *The Chronicles of the White Rose of York*, *op. cit.*, pp. 192–3.

3. *Catalogue of the Harleian Collection of Manuscripts*, 1759.

4. BL, Harleian 2194, fo., 11.

5. Fabyan, *op. cit.*, p. 659.

6. Bisticci, *op. cit.*, p. 419.

7. Stephen Gardiner, on another occasion, asserted: 'with the Emperor's Ambassador Chapinius when he was here, and in the Emperor's Court also … that the King's Majesty was not above his Laws.' Burnett, *op. cit.*, vol. 2, p. 138.

8. S. Alford, *Kingship and Politics in the Reign of Edward VI*, Cambridge University Press, 2002, p. 57.

9. It should be noted that the chronicler Warkworth, who wrote in 1462 that the Earl of Oxford had been tried by Paduan law, reported, 'so the Erle of Worcetre was juged be suche lawe *as he dyde to other menne*' (Warkworth, p. 13). The comment could be taken to indicate that Warkworth did believe that the Earl had been tried by the Earl of Oxford acting as Constable in the Court of Chivalry. Equally, it might simply indicate that just as the Earl's trial of the Oxford conspirators in 1462 was of dubious process, so in time understandably was that same Earl's own trial in 1470.

10. Bisticci, p. 420.

11. *Unpublished Geraldine Documents*, *op. cit.* vol. 1, p. 69.

12. Harleian Manuscripts No. 2194, fo. 11.

13. Leland, p. 479.

14. Waurin, *op. cit.* 612.

15. *Chronicle of London*, *op. cit.*, pp. 183–4, p. 217.

16. Warkworth, p. 13.

17. *Chronicle of London*, *op. cit.* 217.

Chapter 27 – Death

1. Caxton, *op. cit.*

2. T. Dean, K.J.P. Lowe, *Crime, Society and the Law in Renaissance Italy*, Cambridge University Press, 1994, p. 57.

3. Leland, p. 480.

4. *A Mirror for Magistrates*, *op. cit.*

5. M. Bassett, The Fleet Prison in the Middle-Ages, *The University of Toronto Law Journal*, Vol. 5, No. 2 (1944), pp. 383–402, University of Toronto Press.

6. *London Journal*, minutes of the proceedings of the Commmon Council in Journal 7, folio 225.

7. *John Benet's Chronicle*, *op. cit.*, p, 215.

8. *Fabyan's Chronicle*, *op. cit.*, p. 659.

9. Bisticci, p. 419.

10. CPaR, p. 521.

11. *Ibid.*, p. 420.

12. M. Aston, *Death, Fifteenth-Century Attitudes, Perceptions of society in late Medieval England*. ed. R. Horrox, Cambridge University Press, 1994, p. 207.

13. T. Olson, The Medieval Blood Sanction and the Divine Beneficence of Pain, 1100–1450, *Journal of Law and Religion*, Vol. 22, No. 1 (2006/7), pp. 63–129, Cambridge University Press.

14. Olson, *op. cit.*, p. 40

15. C. Maidstone, *The Martyrdom of Archbishop Richard Scrope*, trans. S.K. Wright, english.cua.edu/faculty/wright/maidston.cfm

16. The Death of Archbishop Scrope: English Carol, english.cua.edu/faculty/wright/carol.cfm, Cambridge, Trinity College MS. 652, fol. 171 r.

17. Mitchell, *op. cit.* p. 136.

18. Fuller, *op. cit.*, p. 234.

19. Warkworth, *op. cit.* p. 13.

20. Fabyan, *op. cit.*, p. 659.

21. Leland, *op. cit.*, p. 481. There was a further indication of the tomb's position in the later 1505 will of Robert Castell. 'If convenient, above ('*desuper*') the chapel erected and founded, in honour of the B. V. [Blessed Virgin] Mary, by Joan, late Lady de Ingaldisthorpe, and sister of John, Earl of Worcester, and the west wall of the church' (G. Crabbe, *The Antiquary* (Volume 24), p. 14). If *desuper* is interpreted as *beyond* Joanna's chapel, in the sense of moving west from the crossing passage under the Tower, then Castell's tomb was to be placed in the nave between Joanna's chapel and the west end wall. *The Chronicle of London* confirmed the Earl was buried in his own chapel when describing the later burial in 1497 of lord Audley. 'And the Trunke of the lord Awdley was buryed … fast by the Chapell of the Erle of Worcetir' (p. 217). This again was confirmed by the antiquary Stowe: 'sir Iohn Tiptofte Earle of Worcester beheaded, 1470. and by him in his Chapple, Iames Tutchet, Lord Audley, beheaded 1497' (*Stowe's survey of London*, p. 341).

22. M. Ward, The Tomb of the Butcher, *Journal of the Church Monuments Society*, vol. XXVII, 2012, p. 23. Joanna wanted to be buried with her brother, John Tiptoft, and not with her husband, Edmund Ingaldisthorpe or daughter Isabel Neville. Care was taken for the long-term upkeep of the chapel by Joanna. When the Tiptoft estates were partitioned among coheirs, she received Eversden where Worcester was born. She gave the manor in 1491 to Queen's College, Cambridge, to endow a fellowship and to secure the 'yearly payment of £13 6s. 8d. to the London house of Blackfriars, where she and her brother were buried'.

23. Leland, p. 481.

Epilogue

1. Héroard, J., *Journal de Jean Héroard sur l'enfance et la jeunesse de Louis XIII* (1601–1628), Firmin Didot frères, fils et Cie, 1868, p. 86.
2. Bisticci, *op. cit.*, p. 420.
3. Pope Pius, *Commentaries*, p 273.
4. *ibid*, p. 327.
5. Fletcher, *op. cit.* p. 85.
6. J. Waterson, *Dracula's Wars: Vlad the Impaler and his Rivals*, The History Press, 4 Jul 2016.
7. *Chronicles of London, op. cit.*, p 182.
8. Three Chronicles of the Reign of Edward IV, *op. cit.*, p. 9.
9. *ibid*.
10. Stubbs, *op. cit.*, p. 288.
11. Stowe, *op.cit.*, p. 423.
12. Hall, *op. cit.*, p. 297.
13. CPR. 1467–77, p. 289.
14. *ibid.*, 297.
15. *ibid.*, p. 297.
16. Mitchell, *op. cit.*, p. 100.
17. S. Oosthuizen and C. Taylor, *'John O'Gaunt's House', Bassingbourn. Cambridgeshire: a fifteenth-century landscape.* p. 61–76.
18. Bisticci, p. 420.
19. Bisticci, *op. cit.*, p. 420.
20. *ibid*.
21. Paston, vol. 1, p. 505–6.
22. Bisticci, *op. cit.*, p. 419.

Appendix 1 – Man of letters

1. J. Leylande, *Englandes Antiquitees, Geven of him as a Newe Yeares Gyfte to King Henry the viii, in the xxxvii Yeare of his raygne. c. 1536.* In J. Leland, *The itinerary of John Leland*, publ. by T. Hearne, Vol. 1, Hearne, 1768. p. xxi.
2. H.H. Hudson, John Leland's List of Early English Humanists, *Huntington Library Quarterly*, Vol. 2, No. 3 (Apr 1939), pp. 301–4.
3. J. Tait, 'Letters of John Tiptoft, Earl of Worcester, and Archbishop Neville to the University of Oxford', *English Historical Review*, xxxv, 1920, pp. 571–2.
4. W.A. Pantin, *Canterbury College Oxford*, Vol. III, Oxford, 1950.
5. Tait, *op. cit.*
6. Corpus Christi College, MS. 423.
7. Bisticci, p. 418.

8. J.C.T. Oates, *Cambridge University Library: A History from the Beginnings to the Copyright*, Cambridge University Press, 1986, p. 30.
9. SRPI, p. 663–4.
10. Mitchell, *op. cit.*, p. 207.
11. State Papers: Domestic Series, James I. vol. lxvii., art. 119.

Appendix 2 – Estate and houses

1. Victoria County History, *A History of the Country of Cambridge and the Isle of Ely*: Volume 5, 1973.
2. F. Grose, T. Astle, *The Antiquarian Repertory: a Miscellany, Intended to Preserve and Illustrate Several Valuable Remains of Old Times*, Vol. 2, 1779, p. 826.
3. T. Pennant, *The Journey from Chester to London*, London, 1782, pp. 414–15.
4. CCR, 1402–5, p. 510, www.historyofparliamentonline.org/volume/1386–1421/member/Wrothe-sir-john-1366–1407. PCC 15 Marche; Parochial Church Council (PCC). Corporation of London RO [Record Office], hr 123/48. The house in the parish of St James Garlickhythe may have been left by John Wrothe and inherited by his daughter Agnes who was the Earl of Worcester's grandmother.
5. J. Stowe, *A survey of the cities of London and Westminster, borough of Southwark, and parts adjacent*, T. Read, 1735, p. 775.
6. H. Machyn, *A London Provisioner's Chronicle, 1550–1563*, ed. J.G. Nichols, Camden Society, 1848, p. 301. quod.lib.umich.edu/m/machyn/5076866.0001.001/1:8.14/--london-provisioners-chronicle-1550–1563?rgn=div2;view=fulltext
7. CPaR, p. 1459. 3 Kal. June (30 May) Mantua (f. 332).
8. Lincoln's Inn, *The Black Books*, Vol I, Lincoln's Inn, 1897, *op. cit.*, p. 37.
9. S. Oosthuizen and C. Taylor, *op. cit.*
10. *ibid.*
11. www.natureincambridgeshire.org.uk/volumes/nature-in-cambs-vol-48–2006.pdf.

Abbreviations

CCR	Calendar of the Close Rolls
CFR	Calendar of the French Rolls
CPaR	Calendar of Papal Registers Relating to Great Britain and Ireland
CPR	Calendar of the Patent Rolls
CSPM	Calendar of State Papers, Milan (Guides and calendars) 1385 to 1618
Foedera	Rymer's Foedera, vol. 5, John Neaulme, 1741
FRHVI	French Rolls of Henry VI, Appendix to the 48th report of the Deputy Keeper of the Public Records
GRP	Gascon Rolls Project, www.gasconrolls.org/en
POPC	Proceedings of the Privy Council
PRO	Parliament Rolls
PRME	Parliament Rolls of Medieval England
SRPI	Statute Rolls of the Parliament of Ireland
Bisticci	V. da Bisticci, Vita di Meser Giovanni duca d'Ulsestri, Inghilese, *Vite di Uomini illustri del secolo XV*
Capodilista	G. Capodilista, *Viaggio in Terrasanta di Santo Brasca 1480 con l'Itinerario di Gabriele Capodilista 1458*
Caxton	W. Caxton, *The Declamacion of Noblesse* (da Montermagno, trans. Tiptoft), *De Amicitia* (Cicero, trans., Tiptoft). *De Senectute* (Cicero, trans. not attrib.), Caxton's epilogues to translations, dedicated to Edward IV, London, 1481 *Declamacion* in above *de Amicitia* in above
Leland	J. Leland, *Commentarii de scriptoribus Britannicis*
Paston	*The Paston Letters*, ed. J. Gairdner
Sanseverino	R. da Sanseverino, *Viaggio in Terra Santa*
Excerptica	S. Bentley, *Excerptica Historica*, London, 1831
Leeds	*Leeds, Royal Armouries Library, Codex RAR.0035(I.35)*

Bibliography

Sir John Tiptoft, Earl of Worcester
Translations:
– Tiptoft, J., *The Declamacion of Noblesse,* trans. from the *Controuersia de Nobilitate* of Buonaccorso de Montemagno. (Transcribed in Mitchell, R.J., *John Tiptoft (1427–1470),* Longmans, London, 1938, pp. 215–41)
– Tiptoft, J, *De Amicitia,* trans. from *De Amicitia* of Cicero. (Text available in British Library in original book and microfilm form.)
Both in three translations printed by Caxton in 1481

Letters:
– *BL Royal 10 B IX, f. 122.* Pantin, W.A., *Canterbury College Oxford,* Vol. III, Oxford, 1950. (Worcester to Cranebroke)
– Bentley, S., *Excerptica Historica,* London, 1831 (Worcester to Antoine, Bastard of Burgundy)
– Tait, J., Letters of John Tiptoft, Earl of Worcester, and Archbishop Neville to the University of Oxford, *English Historical Review,* xxxv, pp. 570–74 at pp. 571–2, 1920

Biography – near contemporary
Italian:
– Bisticci, V. da, *Vita di Meser Giovanni duca d'Ulsestri, Inghilese, Vite di Uomini illustri del secolo XV,* ed. L. Frati, pp. 418–20, Bologna, 1892

trans.:
– Bisticci, V. da, *A Renaissance nobleman: John Tiptoft, Earl of Worcester (d. 1470),* English historical documents. 4. (Late medieval). 1327–1485, ed. A.L. Myers, pp. 1149–52, Psychology Press, 1996. *Duca di Worcestri (1427–1470),* The Vespasiano memoirs: lives of illustrious men of the XVth century, V. da Bisticci, trans. W.G. and E. Waters, pp. 335–8, University of Toronto Press, 1997

English (Latin):
– Leland, J., *Commentarii de Scriptoribus Britannicis,* ed. A. Hall, vol. 2. pp. 475–81, Oxford, 1709

Biography – 16th to 18th century

English (in Latin):

- Bale, J., *Illustrium majoris Britanniae scriptorum, hoc est, Angliae, Cambriae, ac Scotiae Summarium*, Ipswich, 1548. *Scriptorum illustriam maioribus Bryt. catalogues*, Basel, 1559. *Index Brit. Script.*, ed. R. Lane Poole. Oxford, 1902
- Pitts, J., *De Illustribus Angliæ Scriptoribus*, Paris, 1619
- Tanner, T., *Bibliotheca Britannica-Hibernica*, London, 1748. (Based largely on Leland)

English:

- Baldwin, attrib., *The Infamovs end of the Lord Tiptoft Earle of Worcester, for cruelly executing his Prince's butcherly commaundementes, An. 1470*, Mirror for Magistrates, ed. J. Haslewood, Volume 2, Part 1, pp. 201–7, Lackington, Allen, and Company, 1815
- Fuller, T., *Worthies of England*, London, 1662. *Dr Fuller's worthies of England, in three volumes* (Cambridgeshire), vol. 1., Nuttall and Hodgson, London, 1840
- Walpole, H. (Lord Ordford), *Royal and Noble Authors*, ed. Park, London, 1806

Texts with biographical material

English (in Latin):

- Leland, J., *Joannis Lelandi Antiquarii de rebus britannicus collectanea, vol 2*, ed. T. Hearne, London, 1770
- Wey, W., *The Itineraries of William Wey*, ed. G. Williams, Roxburghe Club, 1857

trans.:

- Wey, W., *The Itineraries of William Wey*, trans. and ed. F. Davey, University of Oxford, 2010

English:

- Caxton, W., *Epilogue to translations of The Declamacion of Noblesse (Tiptoft), De Amicitia (Tiptoft), De Senectute (anon.)*, London, 1481
- Leland, J., *The Itinerary of John Leland*, ed. T. Hearne, vol. 1, Hearne, 1768

Italian:

- Capodilista, G., *Viaggio in Terrasanta di Santo Brasca 1480 con l'Itinerario di Gabriele Capodilista 1458*, ed. A.L. M. Lepschy Longanesi & C., no date
- Sanseverino, R. da., *Viaggio in Terra Santa*, ed. G. Maruffi. Bologna, 1888

trans.:

- Vidoni, T., *The Journal of Roberto da Sanseverino (1417–1487), A study on navigation and seafaring in the fifteenth century*, The University of British Columbia, 1993 (Translates some material).

Italian (Latin):
- Carbone, L., *Eulogy for Guarino,* dante.di.unipi.it/ricerca/html/Elogio-Carbone

French (Burgundian):
- Commynes, P. de, *Mémoires,* ed. J. Calmette., 3 vols., Paris, 1924
- Marche, O. de la, *Mémoires ,* J.A.C. Buchon, Société du Panthéon litteraire, 1842
- Waurin, J. de, *Chroniques,* ed. Dupont. Paris, 1858–63. *Recueil des Chroniques (1447–71),* ed. W. Hardy, vol. 5, Rolls series, 1864

Bohemian (trans.):
- Tetzel, G., *The Travels of Lev von Rožmitál, 1465–6,* ed. E. Littell, R.S. Littell, *Littell's Living Age,* Volume 4, T.H. Carter & Company, 1845. Also, ed. M. Letts, Hakluyt Series II, p.108, Cambridge, 1957

Chronicle/Annals
Anon.:
- *Brief Latin Chronicle,*
- *Brief Notes of Occurrences under Henry VI and Edward IV,*
- *Short English Chronicle: London under Henry VI (1422–71),* in *Three Fifteenth-Century Chronicles with Historical Memoranda,* J. Stowe, ed, J. Gairdner, London, 1880
- *Chronicle of Lanercost, 1272–1346,* ed. H. Maxwell, BiblioBazaar, 2013
- *Chronicles of London,* ed. C.L. Kingsford Oxford, 1905
- *Chronicle of the Rebellion in Lincolnshire, 1470,* ed. J.C. Nichols, Camden Society, 1847 (also, in *Three Chronicles of the Reign of Edward IV,* intro. K. Dockray, Alan Sutton Publishing, 1988)
- *Exeter Chronicle, 1205–1722,* intro. by T. Gray, The Mint Press, 2005
- *Giles Chronicle,* in *Incerti Scriptoris Chronicon Angliae de Regnis Trium Regum Lancastrensium Henrici IV, Henrici V et Henrici VI,* ed. J.A. Giles, London, 1848
- *Hearne's Fragment,* in *The Chronicles of the White Rose of York,* 1845
- *Great Chronicle of the City of London,* Guildhall Library, MS. 3313
- *Thomæ Sprotti Chronica,* ed. T. Hearne, T. Smith, T. Cantalupus, Oxford, 1719 (no longer attributed to Sprott, also contains *Hearne's Fragment,* see below)

Named:
- *Chronicon Adae de Usk A.D. 1377–1421,* ed. trans. by Sir E.M. Thompson, London Henry Frowde, 1904
- *John Benet's Chronicle for the years 1400 to 1462,* ed. G.L. Harriss, M.A. Harris, Camden Fourth Series Volume 9, Royal Historical Society, 1972
- Fabyan, R., *The New Chronicles of England & France,* London, 1570 (also, ed. H. Ellis, London, 1811)
- Gregory, W., 'Gregory's Chronicle: 1435–1450', *The Historical Collections of a Citizen of London in the fifteenth century,* ed. J. Gairdner, London (for the Cam. Soc.) 1876

- Kempe, M., *The Book of Margery Kempe 1436*, Jonathan Cape, London, 1936
- Rous, J., *Historia Regum Angliae*, ed. T. Hearne Oxford, 1745
- *Chronicle of John Stone, Monk of Christ Church 1415–1471*, ed. W.G. Searle, Camb. Antiqu. Soc., 1902 (partly trans. in *John Stone's Chronicle: Christ Church Priory, Canterbury, 1417–1472*, ed. M. Connor, Medieval Institute Publications, Western Michigan University, 2010)
- Warkworth, J., *A Chronicle of the first thirteen years of the reign*, ed. J.O. Halliwell London (for the Cam. Soc.), 1839 (also, in *Three Chronicles of the Reign of Edward IV*, intro. by K. Dockray, Alan Sutton Publishing, 1988)
- Wyrcester, W. of, *Annales Rerum Anglicarum*, in *Letters and Papers illustrative of the English in France*, ed. J. Stevenson, Rolls Series II, pt ii, 756–92, London, 1864

Non-English:
- *Pius II, Commentaries*, ed. M. Meserve, M. Simonetta, 2 vols., Harvard University Press, 2003 (Latin and English)

Later:
- Casola P., *Canon Pietro Casola's Pilgrimage to Jerusalem in the Year 1494*, M.M. Newett, Manchester University Press, 1907.
- Hall, E., *Chronicle*, ed. H. Ellis, London, 1809.
- Héroard, J., *Journal de Jean Héroard sur l'enfance et la jeunesse de Louix XIII (1601–1628)*, Firmin Didot frères, fils et Cie, 1868
- Holinshed, R., *Holinshed's Chronicles of England, Scotland, and Ireland ...: England* Vol. III, J. Johnson, 1808
- Machyn, H., *The Diary of Henry Machyn Citizen and Merchant-Taylor of London (1550–1563)*
- Rastell, J., *The Pastyme of People: Or, The Chronicles of Divers Realms*, ed. T.F. Dibdin. London, 1811.
- Stow, J., *Annales*, ed. E. Howes. London, 1631
- Stow, J., *A survey of the cities of London and Westminster, borough of Southwark, and parts adjacent*, T. Read, 1735
- Stow, J., *A Survey of London*, Whittaker and Company, London, 1842. *Survey of London. Reprinted from the Text of 1603*, ed. C.L. Kingsford, Oxford, 1908

Chronicle/Annals – Ireland
- *The Annals of Ireland of the Four Masters*, trans. O. Connellan, Dublin, 1836. *The Annals of Ireland by the four masters translated into English*, ed. M. O'Cleary, Irish Roots Cafe, 2003
- *Annals of the Kingdom of Ireland*, J. O'Donovan Hodges, Smith and Company, 1856
- *The Annals of Ulster*, www.ucc.ie/celt/online/T100001A, 1853
- *A Fragment of Irish Annals*, ed. B.Ó. Cuiv, Celtica, vol. XIV, Institúid Ard-Léinn Bhaile Átha Cliath, 1981

Named later:

- Campion, E., *A historie of Ireland*, in Ancient Irish histories: the works of Spencer, Campion, Hanmer and Marleburrough, 2 vols, Dublin, 1809; first printed, ed. J. Ware, Dublin, 1633
- St. Lawrence, C. (7th Baron of Howth), *The Book of Howth*, ed. J.S. Brewer and W. Bullen, Calendar of Carew Papers, 1575–8, Appendix, p. cv. London, 1871

Calendar/rolls
English and French:

- *The Calendar of the Patent Rolls 1441–46, 1446–52, 1452–61, 1461–67, 1467–77, 1477–85*, London, 1910, etc.
- *The Calendar of Close Rolls 1454–61, 1461–68, 1468–76*, HMSO, London, 1947, etc.
- *Calendar of French Rolls of Henry VI* (in 48th Report of the Deputy Keeper of the Public Records) 1887
- *Gascon Rolls Project*, www.gasconrolls.org/en

Irish:

- *Calendar of Carew Manuscripts. The conquest of Ireland*, ed. J.S. Brewer and W. Bullen, London, 1871
- *Calendar of the Carew Manuscripts*, ed. J.S. Brewer & W. Bullen, Vol. 1, London, 1867
- *Calendar of Irish Chancery Letters c. 1244 – 1509*, chancery.tcd.ie

Milan:

- *Calendar of State Papers, Milan, 1385 to 1618.*, ed. A.B. Hinds, vol. I, London, 1912

Papal:

- *Calendar of Papal Letters (1455–1464)*, ed. J.A. Twemlow, vol. xi, London, 1921, (1458–1471), ed. J.A. Twemlow, vol. xii, London, 1933
- *Supplications from England and Wales in the Registers of the Apostolic Penitentiary, 1410–1503*, Clarke P.D., P.N.R. Zutshi, vol. I: 1410–1464, Boydell Press, 2012. vol. II: 1464–1484, Boydell Press, 2014

Parliament/council – rolls/proceedings
England:

- *Rotuli Parliamentorum, 1439–1468*, ed. J. Strachey et al., vol. v. Records Commissioners, 1767–1832, 1832
- *The Parliament Rolls of Medieval England*, ed. A. Curry, R. Horrox, vol. xii, Henry VI, 1447–1460, Boydell Press, 2005. ed. A. Curry, vol. xiii, Edward, 1460–1470 Boydell Press, 2005

Also:

- Dunham, W.H., Notes from the Parliament at Winchester, 1449, *Speculum*, XVII, pp. 402–4, 1942

- Dunham, W.H, *The Fane fragment of the 1461 Journal of the House of Lords*, Yale University Press, 1935
- Myers, A.R., A Parliamentary Debate of the mid-fifteenth century, *Crown, Household and Parliament in Fifteenth Century England*, A&C Black, 1985
- *The History of Parliament: the House of Commons 1386–1421*, ed. J.S. Roskell, L. Clark, C. Rawcliffe., Boydell and Brewer, 1993

Ireland:

- *Statute Rolls of the Parliament of Ireland: Reign of King Henry the Sixth*, ed. H. Fitz-Patrick Berry, Vol. II, Irish Record Office Series of Early Statutes, HM Stationery Office, 1910
- *Statute Rolls of the Parliament of Ireland: Reign of King Edward the Fourth*, ed. H. Fitz-Patrick Berry, Vol. III, Irish Record Office Series of Early Statutes, HM Stationery Office, 1910

Privy council:

- *Proceedings and Ordinances of the Privy Council of England*, ed. N.H. Nicholas, vols. iii—vvi, London, 1837

Register/calendar

Bishop/abbot:

- Bole, J. by A. Lynch, *The Calendar of the Reassembled Register of John Bole, Archbishop of Armagh, 1457–71* Seanchas Ardmhacha: Journal of the Armagh Diocesan Historical Society, Vol. 15, No. 1 (1992), pp. 113–185, Cumann Seanchais Ard Mhacha/Armagh Diocesan Historical Society, 1992
- Bougchier, T., *Registrum Thome Bourgchier, Cantuariensis Archiepiscopi, A.D. 1454–1486*, ed. F.R.H. du Boulay, University Press, 1957
- Kemp, J., *Register of Kemp* (in D. B. Foss, *The Canterbury Archipiscopates of John Stafford (1443–52) and John Kemp (1452–54) with Editions of their Registers, Volume iii (pp. 1–471): The Register of John Kemp*, kclpure.kcl.ac.uk/portal, King's College London., 1986)
- Stanbury, J., *Register of John Stanbury*, Bishop of Hereford, Canterbury and York Society, vol. xxv., 1919.
- Whethamstede, J., *Registrum Quorundum Abbatum Monasterii S. Albani*, Nabu Public Domain Reprints [no date]

Chapter:

- *Machon's register, (Salisbury Chapter Act Book)*, Salisbury (untranscribed manuscript)

University:

- Emden, A.B., *A biographical register of the University of Oxford to AD 1503*, Clarendon Press, 1989
- Salter, H.E., *Registrum Cancellarii Oxon II*, Clarendon Press, 1932

City:
- *The Coventry leet book; or mayor's register,* ed. M.D. Harris, Kegan Paul, 1907
- *The Register of ye mayors of Dublin, with other memorable observations, 1406–1574,* BL Add. MSS, 4791, fo. 139
- *Calendar of Ancient Records of Dublin, in the Possession of the Municipal Corporation of That City,* ed. J.T. Gilbert, Vol. 1, Dublin, 1889
- *Hist: MSS. Commission,* Report xv. Part 10, (Municipal records of Shrewsbury) London, 1887

Inns of Court:
- *Lincoln's Inn, The Black Books,* Vol. I, Lincoln's Inn, 1897

Manuscripts
British Library:
- *Arundel 154, f. 41* – Aretino letter to Pellato
- *Arundel 277, f. 10* – Aretino dedication to Worcester
- *Cotton Tiber. E. viiii. 3* – Tiptoft's ordinances for justs and triumphs
- *Cotton Tiber. E. viiii. 35* – Tiptoft's ordinances for placing the nobility
- *Harleian 2194 f. 11* – Trials in the court of the High Steward
- *Landsdowne, 285. f. 21,* Letter from Worcester to Antoine, the Bastard of Burgundy
- *Royal 10 B IX, f. 122,* Cranebroke letters to/from Worcester

Bodleian Library:
- *Beinecke 149* – Yale University, Ognibene Bonisoli dedication of *de Venatione* to Worcester
- *Bodley 30* – Account of the Coronation of Elizabeth Wydville
- *Bodley 80* – Worcester letter to Oxford, Free dedication to Worcester, Bonisoli letter to John Free

Other:
- *Corpus Christi College, 423,* Oxford University letter to Worcester
- *Firenze Archivio di Stato, Medici Avanti principati, filza 10, n. 7* – Letter from Alessandro Martelli to Giovanni di Cosimo de' Medici
- *Firenze, Archivio di Stato, M. a. Pr., F. VI, Doc. 531* – Letter from Ambrosio di Taverni to Giovanni de' Medici conveying songs from Worcester
- *London Journal* – Guildhall Library, London (microfilm available)
- *Machon's register* – Salisbury Chapter Act Book, Salisbury Cathedral
- *Plumpton Correspondence and Coucher Book* – West Yorkshire Archive (Leeds)
- *Trinity College, 438* – Manyngham 'Miscellany'
- *Vatican Library, Ottob. lat. 1153, f. 207r-v* – Ludovico Carbone's elegy to Worcester

Letters
Places:

Christ Church priory (letter book), *Literae Cantaurarienses*, ed. J.B. Sheppard, 3 vols., Rolls Ser., 1887–99

Oxford, *Epistolae Academicae Oxon.*, ed. Anstey, H., 2. vols., Oxford, 1901

People:

– Paston et al. *Paston Letters*, ed. J. Gairdner, 6 vols., London, 1904
– Plumpton et al. *Plumpton Correspondence*, ed. T. Stapleton, London (for the Cam. Soc.), 1839, *The Plumpton correspondence*, intro. K. Dockray, ed. Stapleton, Sutton Publishing, 1990, *The Plumpton Letters and Papers*, intro. and ed. J. Kirby, Cambridge University Press, 1996

Book/study – contemporary
– *Libelle of Englyshe Polyce*, ed. Sir G.F. Warner, Oxford, 1926
– Fortescue, Sir J., *Governance of England*, ed. C. Plummer Oxford, 1885
– Fortescue, Sir J., *De laudibus Legum Angliae*, ed. R. de Hengham T. Evans, 1775; Fortescue, Sir J. *De Laudibus Legum Anglie*, ed. and trans. by S.B. Chrimes, Cambridge University Press, 2011
– Pisan, C. de (trans. Scrope), *The Boke Of Knyghthode, Translated from the French of Christine de Pisan, With a Dedication to Sir John Fastolf, KG*, ed. G.F. Warner, London, 1904

Anthology/collection
England:

– Bentley, S., *Excerptica Historica*, London, 1831
– Giles, J.A., *The Chronicles of the White Rose of York*, 1845
– Godwin., F., *De Praesulibus Angliae*, ed. Richardson Cambridge, 1743
– Forsyth, J.S., *The antiquary's portfolio: or cabinet selection of historical & literary curiosities*, 2 vol. London, 1825
– Harrington, Sir J., *Nugae Antiquae*, ed. Park, vol. i., London, 1804
– Nicholas, N.H., *Testamenta Vetusta*, London, 1868
– Pantin, W.A., *Canterbury College Oxford*, Vol. III, Oxford, 1950
– Thornley, I.D., *England under the Yorkists, 1460–1485; Illustrated from Contemporary Sources*, Longmans, Green, 1921 *(contains Letter from the Lords of Ireland to Edward IV, 28 June 1468, PRO "Ancient Correspondence" LVIII, no. 50)*

Also:

– The Berynge of an Erle, *The Antiquarian Repertory*, pp. 314–17, London, 1807 (burial of Salisbury, summarised in *The Gentleman's Magazine*, vol. 163, pp. 31–2)
– *The Chronicle of William de Rishanger, of the Baron's Wars; The Miracles of Simon de Montfort*, ed. from Manuscripts in the Cottonian Library, pp. 36–9, Camden Society1840 (trial of Sir Ralph Grey)

- *The antiquary's portfolio: or cabinet selection of historical & literary ...]* *P.279*, J.S. Forsyth, 2 vol., London, 1825
- *Collectanea Topographica et Geneologica*, ed. F. Madden, B. Bandinel, J.G. Nichols, Vol. 4
- *English Historical Documents, Volume IV, 1327–1485*, ed., A.R. Myers, Routledge, 1995
- *Letters and Papers Illustrative of the Wars of the English in France during the reign of Henry the sixth, king of England*, ed. J. Stevenson, 2 vols, London, 1861
- *Memorials of Oxford*, ed. Ingram J., volume 1, 1837
- *Political Poems and Songs Relating to English History, Composed During the Period From The Accession Of Edw. Iii. to that of Ric. Iii.* ed. Thomas Wright, London, Longman, 1861.
- *Royal Historical Society*, Camden Fifth Series Title history, Camden Old Series, vol. 86, December 1863
- *Rymer's Foedera*, Volume II, 1377–1654, London, 1873
- *Select Cases in the Exchequer Chamber*, M. Hemmant, ed., Selden Society, li, 1933
- *State Papers*, Domestic Series, James I, vol. lxvii, art. 119

Ireland:
- *Unpublished Geraldine Documents*, ed. S. Hayman and J. Graves, University Press, 1870

County/Parish history
Cambridgeshire:
- *Houses of Augustinian canons: Priory of Spinney*, A History of the County of Cambridge and the Isle of Ely, ed. L.F. Salzman, Vol. 2, pp. 249–54., London, 1948
- *The Victoria County History*, A History of the Country of Cambridge and the Isle of Ely, ed. C.P.J. Roach, Volume 5, 1973, Oxford, 1973

Middlesex:
- Brayley, J., E.N. Brewer, J. Nightingale, *London and Middlesex: or, An historical, commercial, & descriptive survey of the metropolis of Great Britain: including sketches of its environs, and a topographical account of the most remarkable places in the above county*, Vol. 4, London, 1816
- Tuff, J., *Historical, Topographical and Statistical Notices of Enfield*, J.H. Myers, 1858

Also:
- *Transactions of the London and Middlesex Archaeological Society*, vol. 1, London, 1860

Unpublished theses
- Avrutick, J.B., *Commissions of Oyer and Terminer in Fifteenth-Century England*, M.Litt. thesis, London, 1957
- Bowers, R., *Choral institutions within the English church: their constitution and development, c.1340–1500.* D.Phil. thesis, University of East Anglia, 1975

- Foss, D.B., *The Canterbury Archipiscopates of John Stafford (1443–52) and John Kemp (1452–54) with Editions of their Registers, Volume iii (pp. 1–471): The Register of John Kemp,* King's College London, 1986
- Gue, E., *The Education and Literary Interests of the English Lay Nobility, c.1150 – c.1450,* D.Phil., Thesis Somerville College, Oxford, 1983
- Harvey, I.M.W., *Popular revolt and unrest in England during the second half of the reign of Henry VI,* unpublished thesis, University of Wales1988
- Lester, G.A., *Sir John Paston's Grete Boke: A Descriptive Index, with an Introduction, of British Library MS Lansdowne 285,* D.Phil. thesis, University of Sheffield Department of English Language, 1981
- Moffat, R.D., The Medieval Tournament: Chivalry, Heraldry and Reality, An Edition and Analysis of the Three Fifteenth-Century Tournament Manuscripts, 2 Volumes, D. Phil. Thesis, 2 Vols., The University of Leeds, Institute of Medieval Studies, August 2010
- Richmond, C.F., *Royal Administration and the Keeping of the Seas, 1422–85,* D.Phil. thesis, University of Oxford, 1963
- Vidoni, T., *The Journal of Roberto da Sanseverino (1417–1487), A study on navigation and seafaring in the fifteenth century,* The University of British Columbia, 1993

Internet

Historical documents:

- Maidstone, C., *The Martyrdom of Archbishop Richard Scrope,* trans. S. K. Wright, The Catholic University of America, 1997, http//:english.cua.edu/faculty/wright/maidston.cfm
- Rundle, D., *Dublin: Trinity College, MS.438 – Notice humanist miscellany compiled by John Manyngham,* bonaelitterae.files.wordpress.com/2009/07/dgrms7.pdf
- Virgoe, R., *Some ancient indictments in the King's bench referring to Kent, 1450–1452,* Documents Illustrative of Medieval Kentish Society, Kent Records, Vol. 18, 1964, www.kentarchaeology.org.uk/Research/Pub/KRV/18/5/215.htm

Places:

- *Nature in Cambridgeshire, The hazels of Bassingbourn are fascinating … ,* www.natureincambridgeshire.org.uk/.../nature-in-cambs-vol-48-2006.pd
- Maniquerville commune, www.maniquerville.com/

Other:

- Gascon Rolls, www.gasconrolls.org/en/edition/calendars
- Calendar of Irish Chancery Letters c. 1244–1509, chancery.tcd.ie
- Ipswich Man, BBC Documentary, http://planetipswich.webs.com/ipsmisc.htm
- Papal Registers, www.british-history.ac.uk/cal-papal-registers/brit-ie
- Parliament Rolls of Medieval England, ed. C. Given-Wilson, etc., Woodbridge, 2005, www.british-history.ac.uk/no-series/parliament-rolls-medieval

Valuable sites:
- Higginbotham, S., *A Neville Feast,* nevillfeast.wordpress.com,
- Rundle, D., *bonæ litteræ: occasional writing from David Rundle, Renaissance scholar,* bonaelitterae.wordpress.com

Biography
Tiptoft:
- Mitchell, R.J., *John Tiptoft (1427–1470)*, Longmans, London, 1938

Plantagenet:
- Johnson, P.A., *Duke Richard of York 1411–1460*, Clarendon Press, 1988
- Clive, M., *This Sun of York*, Cardinal, 1975
- Ross, C., *Edward IV*, Yale University Press, 1997 (1974)
- Santiuste, D., *Edward IV and the Wars of the Roses*, Pen & Sword, 2010
- Scofield, C.L., *Edward IV, 2 vols.*, London, 1923
- Carson, A., *Richard Duke of Gloucester as Lord Protector and High Constable of England*, Imprimis Imprimatur, 2013

Neville:
- Hicks, M., *Warwick the Kingmaker*, Blackwell, 1998
- Pollard, A.J., *Warwick the Kingmaker, Politics, Power and Fame*, Continuum Books, 2007
- Baldwin, D., *The Kingmaker's Sisters*, The History Press, 2009

Woodville:
- Baldwin, D., *Elizabeth Woodville, Mother of the Princes in The Tower*, Sutton Publishing, 2002
- MacGibbon, D., *Elizabeth Woodville, A Life*, Amberley, 2013 (1938)
- Higginbotham, S.H., *The Woodvilles, The Wars of the Roses and England's Most Infamous Family*, The History Press, 2013

Henry VI:
- Griffiths, R.A., *The Reign of King Henry VI: The Exercise of Royal Authority, 1422–1461*, University of California Press, 1981
- Watts, J., *Henry VI and the politics of Kingshi*, Cambridge University Press, 1999
- Wolfe, B.P, *Henry VI*, London, 1981
- Maurer, H.E., *Margaret of Anjou, Queenship and Power in Late Medieval England*, The Boydell Press, 2003

Other:
- Arrowood, C.F., *Sir John Fortescue and the education of rulers*, Mediaeval Academy on America, 1935

- Bertoni, G. *Guarino da Verona fra letterati e cortigiani a Ferrara (1429–1460)*, Ginevra, 1921
- Breverton, T., *Owain Glyndŵr: The Story of the Last Prince of Wales*, Amberley, 2009
- Crawford, A., *Yorkist Lord, John Howard, Duke of Norfolk, c. 1425–1485*, continuum
- Gutkind, C.S., *Cosimo de' Medici*, Oxford, 1938
- Wroe, A., *Perkin, a Story of Deception*, Jonathan Cape, 2003

Books
- Alford, S., *Kingship and Politics in the Reign of Edward VI*, Cambridge University Press, 2002
- Allmand, C., *The New Cambridge Medieval History: Volume 7, C.1415-c.1500*, Cambridge University Press, 1995
- Baldwin, J.F., *The King's Council in England during the Middle Ages*, Clarendon Press, 1913
- Bartlett, K.R., *The Courtyer of Count Baldassar Castilio: Italian Manners and the English Court in the Sixteenth Century*
- Bayley, J.W., *The History and Antiquities of the Tower of London*, Appendix to Part III, T. Cadell, 1825
- Beck, S., *Florence, the Medici and Machiavelli*, www.san.beck.org/8–1b–Florence.html
- Bellamy, J.G., *The Criminal Trial in Later Medieval England, Felony before the Courts from Edward I to the sixteenth century*, University of Toronto Press, 1998
- Bellamy, J.G., *The Law of Treason in England in the Late Middle Ages*, Cambridge University Press, 1970
- Blomefield, C. Parkin, F., *An essay towards a topographical history of the county of Norfolk*, London, 1807
- Brown, A.L., *The Governance of Late Medieval England 1272–1461*, Edward Arnold, 1989
- Burnet, G., *The History of the Reformation of the Church of England*, Vol. 4, Appleton, 1842
- Burns, P.J. Nicholas C. Burns, D. Byrne-Rothwell, *The Byrnes and the O'Byrnes*, Colonsay Books, 2010
- Campenhausen, H. von, *Ecclesiastical Authority and Spiritual Power: The Church of the First Three Centuries*, trans. J.A. Baker Stanford University Press, 1969
- Carpenter, C., *The Wars of the Roses, Politics and the constitution in England, c. 1437–1509*, Cambridge University Press, 1997
- Caspari, F., *Humanism and the social order in Tudor England*, Chicago: University of Chicago Press, 1954
- Cast, D., *The Calumny of Apelles*, London, 1981
- Chaplais, P., *English Diplomatic Practice in the Middle Ages* , A&C Black, 2003
- Charlton, K., *Education in Renaissance England*, Boydell & Brewer, 1990, Routledge, 2013

- Cleveland, Duchess of, *Battle Abbey Roll. With Some Account of the Norman Lineages. Duchess of Cleveland. In Three Volumes*, Vol. III, London, 1889
- Cobban, A., *English university life in the Middle Ages*, UCL Press, 1999
- Cohn, S.K., *The Labouring Classes in Renaissance*, Elsevier, 2013
- Coltman Clepham, R., *The Medieval Tournament*, Dover Publications, 1995 (1919)
- Cosgrave, A., *A New History of Ireland, Volume II: Medieval Ireland*, OUP Oxford, 2008
- Curtis, E., *A History of medieval Ireland from 1086 to 1513* , Routledge Revivals, 2013
- Dean, K.J.P. Lowe, T., *Crime, Society and the Law in Renaissance Italy*, Cambridge University Press, 1994
- Editors, by the, *The History of Ireland, from the earliest authentic accounts. By the Editors of the Modern Universal History*, Dublin, 1784
- Ellis, S.G., *Defending English Ground: War and Peace in Meath and Northumberland, 1460–1542*, Oxford University Press, 2015
- Evans, H.T., *Wales and the Wars of the Roses*, Sutton Publishing, 1995 (1915)
- Fletcher, C., *The Black Prince of Florence: The Spectacular Life and Treacherous World of Alessandro de' Medici*, Random House, 2016
- Foreville, R., *Le Jubilé de saint Thomas Becket du XIIIe au XVe siècle (1220–1470).*, S.E.V.P.E.N., 1958
- Fowler, E., *English Sea Power in the Early Tudor Period, 1485–1558*, MIT Press, 1965
- Frulovisi [see intro.] *Travel Abroad: Frulovisi's Peregrinatio*, ed. trans., G. Smith Arizone Center for Medieval and – Renaissance Studies, Tempe, Arizona, 2003
- Gasquet, F.A., *The Eve of the Reformation*, London, 1900
- Gibbons, A., *Early Lincoln Wills, 1280–1547*, Lincoln1888
- Gilbert, J.T., *History of the Viceroys of Ireland*, Dublin, 1863
- Gillespie, A., D. Wakelin, *The Production of Books in England 1350–1500*, Cambridge University Press, 2011
- Given-Wilson, C., *The English Nobility in the Late Middle Ages*, Routledge, 1987
- Goodman, A., *The Wars of the Roses, Military Activity and English Society, 1452–97*, Routledge, 1981
- Griffiths, R., *King and Country: England and Wales in the Fifteenth Century*, A&C Black, 1964
- Grose, T. Astle, F., *The Antiquarian Repertory: a Miscellany, Intended to Preserve and Illustrate Several Valuable Remains of Old Times*, Vol. 2, 1779.
- Hahn, E., *Fractured Emerald: Ireland*, History, 2010
- Hariss, G.L., *Shaping the Nation: England 1360–146*, OUP Oxford, 2006
- Harper, J., *Ancient funerall monuments within the vnited monarchie of Great Britaine, Ireland, and the islands adiacent with the dissolued monasteries therein contained: their founders, and what eminent persons haue beene in the same interred*, John Harper, 1631
- Harris, G., G.L. Harriss, *Shaping the Nation: England 1360–1461*, Oxford University Press, 2006

- Harvey, M.M., *England, Rome, and the papacy, 1417–1464*, Manchester University Press, 1993
- Hatcher, W.H., *Hatcher's History of Salisbury (Hoare's Modern Wiltshire)*, fol. 1 1843
- Hemnant, M., *Select Cases in The Exchequer Chamber* B. Quaritch, 1933
- Hibbert, C., *Hibbert, The English. A Social History, 1066–1945*, Harper Collins, 1987
- Hicks, M., *The Wars of the Roses*, Yale University Press, 2012
- Jaspert, N., *The Hospitallers, the Mediterranean and Europe: Festschrift for Anthony Luttrell*, Routledge, 2016
- Jefferson, L., *The Medieval Account Books of the Mercers of London: An Edition and Translation*, Ashgate Publishing, 2009
- Jenks, S., *Robert Sturmy's Commercial Expedition to the Mediterranean (1457/8)*, The Bristol Record Society, 2006
- Jones, E.R & A. Walsham, *Syon Abbey and Its Books: Reading, Writing and Religion, C.1400–1700*, Boydell & Brewer, 2010
- Keen, M., *Nobles, Knights and Men-at-Arms in the Middle Ages*, Bloomsbury Academic, 1996
- Kennedy, B., *Knighthood in the Morte Darthur*, Boydell & Brewer, 1992
- Kilpatrick, R., *English and Italian Literature from Dante to Shakespeare: A Study of Source*, Routledge, 2014
- Kingsford, C.L., *English historical literature in the fifteenth century*, Oxford, 1913
- Lander, J.R., *Crown and Nobility, 1450–1509* , Edward Arnold, 1976
- Leland, T., *The History of Ireland from the invasion of Henry II with a Preliminary Discourse on the Ancient State of that Land*, Dublin, 1814
- Lydon, J., *The Making of Ireland: From Ancient Times to the Present*, Routledge, 2012
- Machiavelli, N., *Portable Machiavelli*, Penguin, 1979
- Martinez, L., *Power and Imagination: City-States in Renaissance Italy*, Taylor and Frances, 1988
- Meyerson, D. Thiery, O. Falk, MD, *A Great Effusion of Blood?: Interpreting Medieval Violence*, University of Toronto Press, 2004
- Mitchell, R.J., *The Spring Voyage, The Jerusalem Pilgrimage in 1458*, John Murray, 1965
- Mitchell, R.M., *The Medieval Tournament*, Longmans, 1958
- Myers, A.R., *The household of Edward IV*, Manchester University Press, 1959
- Myers, A.R., *Crown, Household and Parliament in Fifteenth Century England*, Continnuum-3PL, 1985
- Napier, H.A., *Historical Notices of the Parishes of Swycombe and Ewelme in the County of Oxford*, Author, 1858
- Nauert, C.G., *Humanism and the Culture of Renaissance Europe*, Cambridge University Press, 2006
- Nicholas, N.H., *History of the orders of knighthood of the British Empire*, Pickering, Rodwell, 1842

- O'Carroll, G., *The Earls of Desmond, The Rise and Fall of a Munster Lordship*, Sprint-print, 2013
- Oates, J.C.T., *Cambridge University Library: A history from the Beginnings to the Copyright Act of Queen Anne*, Cambridge University Press, 1986
- Orme, N., *From Childhood to Chivalry: The Education of the English Kings*, Taylor & Francis, 1984
- Otway-Ruthven, A.J., *A History of medieval Ireland*, Palgrave Macmillan, 1980
- Pantim, W.A., *Canterbury College Oxford*, vol. III, Oxford, 1940
- Peele, J., *An Historical Account of the Order of the Bath, etc.*, 1725
- Pennant, T. *The Journey from Chester to London*, London, 1782
- Pennington, K., *The Prince and the Law, 1200–1600: Sovereignty and Rights in the Western Legal Tradition*, University of California Press, 1993
- Perrens, F.T., *The history of Florence under the domination of Cosimo, Piero, Lorenzo de' Médicis: 1434–149*, London, 1892
- Phillips, S., *The Prior of the Knights Hospitaller in Late Medieval England*, Boydell Press, 2009
- Prescott, H.F.M., *Jerusalem Journey Pilgrimage to the Holy Land in the Fifteenth Century*, Eyre & Spottiswoode, London, 1954
- Rackman, O., *Woodlands*, Collins, 2012
- Richmond, C., *The Paston Family in the Fifteenth Century: Endings, Colin Richmond*, Manchester University Press, 2000.
- Richmond, C., *The Penket Papers*, Alan Sutton, 1986
- Rogers, N.A.M., *The Safeguard of the Sea, A Naval History of Britain*, Penguin, 1997
- Roskell, J.S., *Parliament and Politics in Late Medieval England*, vol. II & III, pp. 107–150, The Hambleton Press, 1983
- Rubin, P.L., Images and Identity in Fifteenth-century Florence, Yale University Press, 2007
- Sadler, J., *The Red Rose and the White: The Wars of the Roses*, Routledge, 2014
- Saul, N., *For Honour and Fame: Chivalry in England, 1066–1500*, Random House, 2011
- Scaglione, A.D., *Knights at Court: Courtliness, Chivalry, & Courtesy from Ottonian Germany to the Italian Renaissance*, University of California Press, 1991
- Schirmer, W.F., *Der Englishche Frühhumansismus*, Leipzig, 1931
- Sharp, R.R., *London and the Kingdom*, Vol. 3, Hall London, 1894
- Smith, C., *C. Smith, The Antient and Present State of the County and City of Cork: in Four Books* London, 1774
- Smith, G., *Account of the Coronation of Elizabeth Wydville*, 1935
- Spenser, E., *A View of the Present State of Ireland*, c.1596
- Squibb, G.D., *The High Court of Chivalry*, Oxford, 1959
- Steel, S., *The Receipt of the Exchequer 1377–1485*, Cambridge, 1954
- Stephen, L. Davies, S.J. Gunn, C., *Authority and Consent in Tudor England*, Ashgate, 2002
- Steven, G.E., *Ireland in the Age of the Tudors, 1447–1603*, Routledge, 2014
- Strohm, R., *The rise of European music, 1380–1500, (Commis. Ct. of Lond., 314 Wilde)*, Cambridge University Press, 2005

- Strype, J., *Memorials of the Most Reverend Father in God Thomas Cranmer*, The Clarendon Press, 1840
- Stubbs, W., *The Constitutional History of England*, Oxford, 1896
- Thornley, I.D., *England under the Yorkists*, London, 1920
- Vallance, E., *A Radical History of Britain: Visionaries, Rebels and Revolutionaries*, Hachette Digital
- van Rhee, C.H., *The Law's Delay: Essays on Undue Delay in Civil Litigation*, Intersentia nv, 2004
- Ware, J., *The Whole Works of Sir James Ware Concerning Ireland Revised and Improved*, Vol. 2, Jones, 1745
- Waterson, J., *Dracula's Wars: Vlad the Impaler and his Rivals*, The History Press, 2016.
- Weir, A., *Lancaster and York, the Wars of the Roses*, Vintage Books, 2009
- Weiss, R., *Humanism in England During the Fifteenth Century*, Oxford: Basil Blackwell, 1941
- Wilson, H.B., *The History of the Merchant-Taylors School, from its foundation to the present time*, vol. II, London, 1814

Essay collection

- Aston, M., *Death in Fifteenth-Century Attitudes, Perceptions of society in late medieval England*, ed. R. Horrox, Cambridge University Press, 1994
- Bartlett, K.R., The English in Italy, 1525–1558: a study in culture and politics, *(The Courtyer of Count Baldassar Castilio: Italian Manners and the English Court in the Sixteenth Century)* Centro interuniversitario di ricerche sul "Viaggio in Italio", 1991
- Bleach, L., *Battle and Bloodshed: The Medieval World at War*, ed. K. Borrill, Cambridge Scholars Publishing, 2013
- Bloore, P. (ed.), Wingfield College and Its Patrons: Piety and Patronage in Medieval Suffolk, ed. P. Bloore, E. Martin, Boydel Press, 2015
- Catto, J., The Triumph of the Hall in Fifteenth Century Oxford, *Lordship and Learning: Studies in Memory of Trevor Aston*, T.H. Aston, T.A. Ralph Evans, Boydell Press, 2004
- Curry, E. (ed.), Concepts and Patterns of Service in the Later Middle Ages, ed. A. Curry, E. Matthew, Boydell & Brewer, 2000
- McFarlane, K.B., The education of Nobility in Later Medieval England, *The Ford Lectures for 1953*, Clarendon Press, 1973

Essays dedicated to individuals

- (Haskins) Howard G., Greek Visitors to England in 1455–1456, *Haskins Anniversary Essays in Medieval History* ed. Charles H. Taylor, pp. 81–116, Boston: Houghton Mifflin Company, 1929
- (Hicks) Ross, J., The treatment of traitors' children and Edward IV's clemency in the 1460s, *Essays presented to Michael Hicks The fifteenth century XIV, CHECK*, ed. L. Clark, pp. 131–41, Boydell & Brewer, 2015

– (Trapp) English and the Continental Renaisssance, *Essays in Honour of J.B. Trapp*, ed. E. Chaney, P Mack, The Boydell Press, 1990

Journal/transactions

– Anglo, S., 'Anglo-Burgundian Feats of Arms: Smithfield, June 1467', *Guildhall Miscellany II (1965)*, pp. 271–83, 1965
– Armstrong, C.A.J., Politics and the Battle of St. Albans, 1455, *Bulletin of the Institute of Historical Research*, May 1960, vol. xxxiii, no. 87, 1960
– Ashdown-Hill, A. Carson, J., The Execution of the Earl of Desmond, *The Ricardian*, 2005
– Baker, N.S., For Reasons of State: Political Executions, Republicanism, and the Medici in Florence, 1480–1560, *Renaissance Quarterly* 62 (2009), pp. 444–73, 2009
– Barber, R., Malory's Le Morte Darthur and Court Culture under Edward IV, *Arthurian Literature* 12, 1993
– Barber, R., Malory's le Morte d'Arthur and Court Culture, *Arthurian Literature XII*, ed. J.P. Carley, F. Riddy, pp. 133–156, Boydell & Brewer, 1993
– Bassett, M., The Fleet Prison in the Middle Ages, *The University of Toronto Law Journal*, Vol. 5, No. 2 (1944), pp. 383–402, *University of Toronto Press*, 1944
– Bellamy, J.G., Justice under the Yorkist Kings, *American Journal of Legal History*, ix (1965), 1965
– Brown, A.L., The King's Councillors in Fifteenth–Century England, *Transactions of the Royal Historical Society*, (Fifth Series), Vol. 19, December 1969, pp. 95–118, 1969
– Campbell, A.M., The Great Chronicle of the City of London, *The Journal of the Rutgers University Library*, Vol 3, No. 1 (1939), pp 7–12, 1939
– Church, C.M., II. Visit of Edward IV. to Wells in 1470, pp. 163–71, *Historical Traditions at Wells, 1464, 1470, 1497*, The Archaeological Journal, vol. 61, 1904
– Cosgrove, A., The Execution of the Earl of Desmond 1468, *Journal of the Kerry Archaeological Society*viii (1975), pp. 11–27, 1975
– Crabbe, G., *The Antiquary*, Vol. 24
– Ellis, S.G., The Struggle for Control of the Irish Mint, 1460-c. 1506, Proceedings of the Royal Irish Academy, Vol. 78 (1978), pp. 17–36, Royal Irish Academy, 1978
– Freidrichs, R.L., The Remarriage of Elite Widows in the Later Middle Ages, *Florilegium*, vol. 23.1 (2006), pp. 69–83, 2006
– Freidrichs, R.L., L. Friedrichs, Rich Old Ladies Made Poor, *Medieval Prosopography 21*, pp. 222–9, 2000
– Gaidner, J., Original Documents, Ralph Lord Cromwell, *Archaeological Journal*, Vol. 30, 1873, Issue 1, pp. 75–89, 1873
– Griffiths, R.A., The King's Council and the First Protectorate of the Duke of York, 1453–1454, *The English Historical Review*, Vol. 99, No. 390 (Jan 1984), pp. 67–82, Oxford University Press, 1984
– Hardy, S.H., The Medieval Tournament: A Functional Sport of the Upper Class, *Journal of Sport History*, 1, 2 (Fall 1974), pp. 91–105, 1974

- Head, C., Pius II and the Wars of the Roses, *Archivum Historiae Pontificiae*, Vol. 8 (1970), pp. 139–78, 1970
- Holland, P., The Lincolnshire Rebellion of March 1470, *English Historical Review*, Vol. 103, no. 409, pp. 849–69, 1988
- Hudson, H.H., John Leland's List of Early English Humanists, *Huntington Library Quarterly*, Vol. 2, No. 3 (April 1939), pp. 301–4, 1939
- Hughes, J., Educating the artistocracy in late medieval England, *History Today*, Feb 1999
- Hughes, J., Stephen Scrope and the Circle of Sir John Fastolf: Moral and Intellectual Outlook, *Medieval Knighthood IV: Papers from the Fifth Strawberry Hill Conference 1990*, ed. C. Harper-Bill, R. Harvey, pp. 109–146, Woodbridge: Boydell Press, 1992
- Jankovsky, K.P., Public executions in England in the late Middle Ages: the indignity and dignity of death, *Omega (Westport)*, February 1980, vol. 10, no. 1, pp. 43–57, 1980
- Jenks, S., Bills of Custody in the reign of Henry VI, *The Journal of Legal History*, 23:3, pp. 197–222, DOI: 2002
- Keen, M., Treason trials under the law of arms, *Transactions of the Royal Historical Society*, 5th series (12), pp. 85–103, 1962
- Lander, J.R., Henry VI and the duke of York's second protectorate, 1455 to 1456, *Bulletin of the John Rylands Library*. 1960; 43(1), pp. 46–69, 1960
- Lathrop, H.B., The Translations of John Tiptoft, *Modern Language Notes*, Vol. 41, No. 8 (Dec 1926), pp. 496–501, Johns Hopkins University Press, 1926
- Lewis, M.E., A traitor's death? The identity of a drawn, hanged and quartered man from Hulton Abbey, Staffordshire, *Antiquity*, Volume 82/Issue 315/March 2008, pp. 113–24, 2008
- Lydon, J., Ireland Corporate of Itself—The Parliament of 1460, *History Ireland*, Vol. III, No. II, pp. 9–12, 1995
- Lynch, A., The Administration of John Bole, Archbishop of Armagh, 1457–71, *Seanchas Ardmhacha: Journal of the Armagh Diocesan Historical Society*, Vol. 14, No. 2 (1991), pp. 39–108, Cumann Seanchais Ard Mhacha/Armagh Diocesan Historical Society, 1991
- Mitchell , R.J., English Students at Padua, 1460 – 1475, *Transactions of the Royal Historical Society*, 19, pp. 101–18, 1936
- Mitchell, R. J., The Translations of John Tiptoft, *Modern Language Notes*, 61, pp. 15–25, 1926
- Mitchell, R.J., A Renaissance library: the collection of John Tiptoft, Earl of Worcester, *The Library*, 4th ser. 18, pp. 67–83, 1937
- Mitchell, R.J., English Students at Padua, 1460–75, *Transactions of the Royal Historical Society*, Fourth Series, Vol. 19, 1936
- Myers, A.R., The Jewels of Queen Margaret of Anjou, *Bull. John Rylands Library*, xlii, 1959
- Olson, T., The Medieval Blood Sanction and the Divine Beneficence of Pain, 1100–1450, *Journal of Law and Religion* Vol. 22, No. 1 (2006/2007), pp. 63–129, Cambridge University Press, 2006–7

- Oosthuizen, S. and Taylor, C., 'John O'Gaunt's House', Bassingbourn, Cambridgeshire: a fifteenth-century landscape, *Landscape History*, vol. 22, pp. 61–76, The Society for Landscape Studies, 2000
- Parkes, P., Fosterage, Kinship, and Legend: When Milk Was Thicker than Blood? University of Kent, *Comparative Studies in Society and History*, Vol. 46, No. 3 (2004), pp. 587–615, 2004
- Pennington, K., Two Essays on Court Procedure (Introduction of the Courts), *The Jurisprudence of Procedure* 185, pp. 205–6, (unpublished manuscript)
- Plucknett, T.F.T., The Place of the Council in the Fifteenth Century, *Transactions of the Royal Historical Society* (Fourth Series)/Volume 1/December 1918, pp. 157–89, 1918
- Richmond, C.F., "English Naval Power in the Fifteenth Century", *History*, vol. 52, London: The Historical Association, 1967
- Rosenthal, J.T., The Universities and the Medieval English Nobility, *History of Education Quarterly*, Vol. 9, No. 4 (Winter 1969), pp. 415–37, 1969
- Rühl, J.K., Regulations for the Joust in Fifteenth-Century Europe: Francesco Sforza Visconti (1465) and John Tiptoft (1466), *The International Journal of the History of Sport*, Vol. 18, No. 2 (June 2001), pp. 193–208., Frank Cass, London, 2001
- Tait, J., Letters of John Tiptoft, Earl of Worcester, and Archbishop Neville to the University of Oxford, *English Historical Review*, xxxv, pp. 570–74 at pp. 571–2, 1920
- Thomson, R.M., The reception of the Italian Renaissance in Fifteenth-Century Oxford: The Evidence of Books and Book-Lists, *Italia medioevale e umanistica* 47 (2007), pp. 59–75, 2007
- Virgoe, R., *The Composition of the King's Council, 1437–61*, Bulletin of the Institution of Historical Research 43 (1970), pp. 155–60, 1970, *GSR C61 141*
- Ward, M., The tomb of 'The Butcher'? The Tiptoft monument in the presbytery of Ely cathedral, *Church Monuments, Journal of the Church Monument Society*, vol. XXVII, pp. 22–37, The Church Monuments Society, 2012
- Weiss, R., The library of John Tiptoft, Earl of Worcester, *Bodleian Quarterly Record*, 8, (1935–7), pp. 157–64, Oxford, 1935
- Weiss, R., A letter-preface of John Phreas to John Tiptoft, Earl of Worcester, *Bodleian Quarterly Record*, viii, Oxford, 1935
- Weiss, R., John Tiptoft, Earl of Worcester, and Ludovico Carbone, *Rinascimento*, 8, pp. 209–12, 1957
- Williams, C.H., 'A fifteenth-century Lawsuit', *Law Quarterly review* (1924), pp. 354–64, 1924

Index